CliffsNotes®

GED® TEST CRAM PLAN™

2nd Edition

CliffsNotes®

GED® TEST CRAM PLAN™

2nd Edition

Murray Shukyn, Achim K. Krull, and Dale E. Shuttleworth, Ph.D.

Houghton Mifflin Harcourt
Boston • New York

Editorial

Executive Editor: Greg Tubach

Senior Developmental Editor: Christina Stambaugh

Copy Editor: Donna Wright

Technical Editors: Tom Page, Scott Ryan, Barbara Swovelin, Mary Jane Sterling, and Andrew Beames

Proofreader: Lynn Northrup

CliffsNotes® GED® TEST Cram Plan™, 2nd Edition

Library of Congress Control Number: 2014942792
ISBN: 978-0-544-23444-4 (pbk)

Printed in the United States of America
DOC 10 9 8 7 6 5 4 3
4500523933
For information about permission to reproduce selections from this book, write to Permissions, Houghton Mifflin Harcourt Publishing Company,
215 Park Avenue South, New York, New York 10003.

www.hmhco.com

About the Authors

Murray Shukyn is Associate Director of the Training Renewal Foundation. He has been a teacher, author, program designer, curriculum designer, and implementer at the elementary, secondary, and university levels. His involvement with the GED® test stretches over a dozen years, and he has tutored, mentored, and assisted students in reaching their goal of passing the GED® test.

Achim K. Krull is a teacher and author of textbooks, teachers' guides, learning activity kits, as well as commercial articles and books. He has taught high school and outdoor and adult education. He was Chair of the Alternatives Advisory Council of the Toronto District School Board and coauthor of several proposals for new alternative schools. He is currently an instructor for academic upgrading seminars for adult students entering into apprenticeships.

Dale E. Shuttleworth, Ph.D., is Executive Director of the Training Renewal Foundation. His career as a community educator has included experience as a teacher, school-community worker, consultant, principal, program coordinator, school superintendent, and university course director. An author of 10 books and 200 articles in journals and periodicals, he has served as an expert consultant for the Organization for Economic Cooperation and Development (OECD) in Paris and is the recipient of the prestigious Dag Hammerskjold Gold Medal for Excellence in Education.

Acknowledgments

We wish to express our appreciation to the Training Renewal Foundation for the opportunity to work in the world of the GED® test, and the late Peter Kilburn, former Canadian GED® Administrator, for his inspiration, friendship, and encouragement in introducing us to the potential of the GED® test to be a source of fulfillment and liberation in the lives and careers of so many adult learners who have dropped out of traditional schooling accreditation systems.

Table of Contents

Introduction

The GED® test is an opportunity for people who haven't finished high school to obtain a certificate from a recognized authority (the American Council on Education), showing that they have the equivalent of a high school diploma. The newest version of the test, introduced in 2014, allows students to obtain an equivalent high school diploma that is more closely matched to entry-level employment opportunities and post-secondary school admission requirements. This updated test gives you the opportunity to make important upgrades to your life. The GED® test is the only high school equivalency certificate recognized all around the world. A GED® certificate is a passport to the world of advancement on the job and an entry into the wonderful world of post-secondary education.

If you're interested in this book, you must have already thought of the advantages of earning a high school equivalency certificate. If you bought this book, you're on your way to taking the test. The next step is to determine how long you have to prepare for the GED® test. In many areas of the country, the test is given regularly and you can decide for yourself when you want to take the test. While smaller testing centers will offer the new computer-based test more frequently, availability of test-taking opportunities may define your scheduling. Whether you have one week, one month, or two months to prepare, this book can help you do your best on the GED® test.

About the GED® Test

The GED® test challenges your abilities in four main areas: Reasoning through Language Arts, Mathematical Reasoning, Science, and Social Studies. The entire test will take about 7½ hours to complete. For the remainder of this book, we'll refer to these four content areas as "tests."

The Reasoning through Language Arts (RLA) Test is 150 minutes long, including a 10-minute break: 35 minutes for Section 1 (question-and-answer items), 45 minutes for Section 2 (the extended response item, also known as the essay), a 10-minute break, and then 60 minutes for Section 3 (more question-and-answer items). The Social Studies Test is a total of 90 minutes: 65 minutes for Section 1 (question-and-answer items) and 25 minutes for Section 2 (the extended response item). There is no break between Section 1 and Section 2 of the Social Studies Test. *Important to remember:* Leftover time from one section of the RLA or Social Studies Test cannot be transferred to the other sections. Each section is timed independently. The Mathematical Reasoning Test is 115 minutes, and the Science Test is 90 minutes. All four tests are administered on a computer, which requires some keyboarding skills and a basic knowledge of how a computer works. For a list of questions and answers about the test, go to www.gedtestingservice.com/educators/2014-faqs. Please note that this site is designed for use by educators, but the information on it is relevant to anyone considering taking the GED® test. While you are there, check out the section for test-takers for even more information. GED Testing Service® is not affiliated with, and does not endorse, *CliffsNotes GED® TEST Cram Plan,* 2nd Edition.

There is not a set number of questions for each of the GED® tests. The tests are set up by selecting random items from a pool of potential items. Each item has a predetermined level of difficulty and each test will have the same potential score. Your job is to complete every item to the best of your ability and not worry if you end up with a couple more items than your friend who also took the test.

For additional information about what to expect, visit ged.com. At the bottom of the webpage, you'll find links to the four subject tests, where you will see more details on the content.

GED® Test Overview		
Subject Test	**Time Limit**	**Content Notes**
Reasoning through Language Arts, Section 1	35 minutes	extended response item
Reasoning through Language Arts, Section 2	45 minutes	
Break	10 minutes	
Reasoning through Language Arts, Section 3	60 minutes	
Mathematical Reasoning	115 minutes	the first 5 items do not allow use of a calculator
Science	90 minutes	2 short answer items; allow roughly 10 minutes each to answer
Social Studies, Section 1	65 minutes	extended response item
Social Studies, Section 2	25 minutes	

IMPORTANT NOTE: For ease of study, in this book we divided the RLA content into two sections instead of three, combining the Section 3 question-and-answer items with Section 1.

The type of items included in the testing for each content area are indicated below. For more information on the item types, see Chapter I, "The 2014 GED® Test."

Subject Test				
Item Type	**Reasoning through Language Arts**	**Mathematical Reasoning**	**Science**	**Social Studies**
Multiple choice	✓	✓	✓	✓
Fill-in-the-blank	✓	✓	✓	✓
Drop-down	✓	✓	✓	✓
Drag-and-drop	✓	✓	✓	✓
Hot spot		✓	✓	✓
Short answer			✓	
Extended response	✓ (45 min.)			✓ (25 min.)

You can find more information on each of these content areas and see sample items at www.gedtestingservice.com/freepractice/. (*Reminder:* This site is designed for use by educators, and GED Testing Service® is not affiliated with, and does not endorse, *CliffsNotes GED® TEST Cram Plan,* 2nd Edition.) Click on each of the four sections to see sample questions. This set of mini-practice tests is designed to show you the types of questions you will face. The correct answer is given, along with a brief answer explanation.

Keep in mind the following tips:

- **You're expected to create an extended response, an essay, for the Reasoning through Language Arts Test, Section 2, in 45 minutes. On the Social Studies Test, you have to write a shorter extended response in 25 minutes.** Extended response items require some keyboarding skills. If you do not have a reasonable level of typing skills, consider working on improving your skills before arranging to take the test. The only way to prepare for the essay portions of the RLA Test and the Social Studies Test is to begin writing short essays on various topics within the allotted time. You'll probably never guess the topic on the test, so what you're doing is developing the writing and keyboarding skills necessary to produce a short essay in the required time. We will show you the format of the extended response items to help you prepare. One good first step is to look at newspaper headlines and write about them. Find articles or blogs that have opposite opinions on a topic and analyze the arguments. Listen for snippets of conversation and use these as essay topics. In essay writing, presenting material logically and coherently is what matters—not what you write about.

- **The GED® Science Test assumes that you have an understanding of scientific terms.** Read as much as you can about science and look up any words you don't understand. Go to www.gedtestingservice.com/testers/sciencelink for an overview of the topics on the Science Test. You can also do a search using your favorite search engine using the words "key terms" and then the subject area you are researching. For example, you could search for "key terms science" or "key terms earth science."

  Remember that the GED® test is for students at the end of high school, not graduate students at a university or college. Stick to appropriate articles and you'll develop enough of a scientific vocabulary to read any question on the test.

- **The GED® Mathematical Reasoning Test allows you to use a calculator for all but the first five questions.** To access the on-screen calculator, click on the "Calculator" button at the top of the test screen. *Note:* The calculator button will only appear on screen for questions where you are allowed to use a calculator. It is the Texas Instruments TI-30XS Multiview scientific calculator. You can find a manual for this calculator online (www.atomiclearning.com/ti30xs). You should become familiar with this specific calculator before you take the test; learning how to use it while taking a timed test is not the best idea. Besides, you will not be allowed to bring your own calculator to the tests. A calculator, however, can only make calculations easier—it won't solve problems for you. Learn to use the calculator as a tool, but go through the material in this book to learn how to solve the problems.

- **The on-screen calculator is also available for use on some Social Studies and Science items.** On the Social Studies and Science tests, there is an expectation that you can apply mathematical reasoning to the subject matter. In these two tests, the on-screen calculator is provided on certain items where it would be useful to test-takers in answering those items.

- **Some of the question-and-answer items require an answer in a different format.** Since the GED® test is now done on a computer, there are items in all four test areas that will take advantage of the flexibility a computer-based test offers. These alternate format items are not difficult to answer, but they do require some understanding and familiarity. (For more on these items, see Chapter I.) The site www.gedtestingservice.com/testers/mathlink shows you in more detail what to expect on the Mathematical Reasoning Test.

■ **Familiarize yourself with the seven item types.** Chapter I looks specifically at the seven different item types, how they work, and how best to answer them. Be sure to go through that section of Chapter I carefully before you do our Diagnostic Test or any of our practice tests. The 2014 GED® test format is not particularly complicated or more difficult, but it is different. Familiarizing yourself with the item types beforehand is just good preparation.

Where to Take the GED® Test

The GED® test is offered on a regular schedule at various test sites. For a list of the test sites in your area, go to ged.com and click on "Locate a test center" under "Take Action" at the bottom of the webpage. You can call the test center and get information on when the tests are given and, more important, how far in advance you have to apply to take the GED® test. Write down this information. You can also opt to book your test date online or call the test center to schedule. The test is offered at small centers in various locations, rather than at one big test center. As a computer-based test, the test starts when you are ready, and finishes as per the timing built into the test program. This means you have some flexibility in scheduling your test. Advance booking also lets you find out the cost for the test. Individual states set their own prices, so this will vary from area to area. If you find the cost out of your range, ask about subsidies, scholarships, or other financial assistance that might help you pay the fee.

If you need further information, you can call 877-392-6433, or email help@ GEDtestingservice.com, or contact your local GED® Testing Administrator by going to www.gedtestingservice.com/testers/ged-testing-administrator.

If you have special needs, consult www.gedtestingservice.com/testers/computer-accommodations or email accommodations@GEDtestingservice.com. For information about taking the GED® test in Spanish or French or for information on special editions of the test (i.e., large print, braille, audiocassette), go to www.gedtestingservice.com/testers/special-test-editions. Be prepared that you will in all likelihood have to provide medical or other appropriate certification to support your special-needs accommodation request.

Inquire with your local GED® Testing Administrator about what you may or may not take into the test site. For the GED® Mathematical Reasoning Test, an on-screen calculator will be supplied for you, as will an erasable noteboard for rough work. You will probably not be allowed to take water or coffee into the exam room. Keyboards and liquids do not get along. For security reasons, electronics, including tablets, laptops, cell phones, and music players, are not allowed. Leave them at home. And since everything is timed, go to the restroom before starting the test. Finally, double-check with the administrator to make sure that you don't forget something you need or bring something you don't need.

When to Take the GED® Test

Now, you have to figure out *when* to take the test. Instead of setting a random deadline and trying to fit your studying into that time frame, start by taking the Diagnostic Test in

Chapter II. The Diagnostic Test evaluates you in the skill areas that appear on the real GED® test. Take the Diagnostic Test seriously. Stick to the time limits as closely as your watch or clock will let you, never look at an answer until after you've finished the test, and, finally, score your test based on the answers you've written (not what you meant to write). After scoring the Diagnostic Test, review the answers and explanations. Even if you got the question right, make sure that you followed a logical process to get there. If you got the question wrong or guessed at the answer, mark the explanation with an X. This will give you a list of content areas that you need to review and spend more time on.

If you got at least 75 percent of the questions correct, you can decide when you want to take the test and follow the appropriate cram plan (see Chapters III–VI). If you scored between 50 percent and 75 percent, leave yourself more time for preparation. If you scored less than 50 percent, consider doing more extensive preparation (for example, taking a GED® preparation course) before deciding on a test date.

You can take each GED® test separately. You do not need to take all four tests at once. Better yet, any section you pass is complete forever, regardless of what you do on the other sections. If our Diagnostic Test tells you that you did well on one section, consider arranging for that test. Once it is done, you can concentrate on preparing for the other tests of the GED® test.

We also suggest not writing in this book, so that you can redo any of the tests if you feel you need extra review. The test items evaluate not just your knowledge of facts, but also your ability to read and comprehend and to interpret and reason. More practice means you improve in all of those areas. Later in this book, we will give you lots of additional study tips and help.

Regardless of how you do on the Diagnostic Test, don't take this as a failure. We all learn and remember differently, and some of us just need more preparation than others. The important thing to tell yourself is that you're smart enough to recognize that you need to prepare.

The cram plans in Chapters III through VI will guide your studying. Base your planning on your results on each of the four Diagnostic Test subjects, and remember that the real test is being done on a computer, not with pencil and paper. Allow for this in your planning. While the on-screen questions may look different, they are still mainly multiple-choice items. If you feel you need more time to accomplish the objectives in a particular area, consider adjusting your goals and going to a longer cram plan. If you're comfortable with your progress, continue on the schedule you've set.

GED® Test Scoring

The GED® test is broken into four subject tests: Reasoning through Language Arts, Mathematical Reasoning, Science, and Social Studies. To earn your GED® diploma, you need to pass all four of these tests. You can do the complete GED® test in one session, if your local testing center permits. That would take nearly 7½ hours. Most of us would consider that cruel and inhumane treatment, so don't rush into that. You can take each subject test individually. That reduces the time to between 90 and 150 minutes, a somewhat better option. If you do not pass any one of these tests, you need to retake only that subject test, not all four. Once a subject test is complete, it is complete forever, regardless of how you do on the other subject tests.

Scoring of the 2014 GED® test is far more complex than it was on earlier versions of the test. Scores will be compared to those of other test-takers. According to the GED Testing Service®, each person who takes the test will receive feedback indicating their strengths and weaknesses. This means that you can demonstrate how you compare with people who have completed the test and gone on to further their education. One nice feature of doing this test on a computer: You receive your scores and feedback on how you did within 24 hours of completing the test.

TIP: Visit www.gedtestingservice.com/educators/2014-faqs#report for answers to frequently asked questions about GED® scoring.

Most of the test items are a variation of multiple-choice questions. The various question items earn between 1 and 3 points each if answered correctly. No points are deducted for skipping a question or for answering a question incorrectly. Since there are no points deducted for errors, make sure you answer all questions, even if you have to guess. There is always a chance you will be correct, and that is better than nothing. If you want to learn about the intricacies of the scoring, visit the teachers' area of the GED Testing Service® website, www.gedtestingservice.com/educators/assessment-guide-for-educators, where the information is posted.

When visiting the GED Testing Service® site, check the times allocated for each test. Since we started this book, those times have been revised, and may be again. It is never a bad idea to confirm such information.

About This Book

CliffsNotes GED® TEST Cram Plan, 2nd Edition, is your guide to preparing for the GED® test, whether you have one week, one month, or two months to prepare. Chapter I introduces you to the seven item types on the 2014 GED® test and provides reading comprehension strategies. Reading comprehension questions can be found on three of the four GED® subject tests: Social Studies, Science, and Reasoning through Language Arts, so it is worth your time to review these strategies. The Diagnostic Test in Chapter II gives you a sense of where you're starting from—and it helps you figure out how much time you need to prepare. The Diagnostic Test doesn't tell you what your score on the GED® test might be—instead, it gives you a sense of your strengths and weaknesses so you know where to concentrate your studying.

The cram plans in Chapters III through VI give you specific guidance on what to study when; follow these plans, and you won't run the risk of not studying enough. Chapters VII through X, the subject chapters, give you the information you need to brush up on each GED® test subject. And the Practice Tests in Chapters XI through XIV help you assess your progress and determine the focus of your further studies.

This book provides diagnosis, remediation, practice, explanation, and a chance to practice with test questions. It gives you everything except the motivation—only *you* can bring that to the table. With this combination, you can prepare to take the GED® test and look forward to a positive outcome.

I. The 2014 GED® Test

The 2014 GED® test is different from and yet similar to the 2002 test. The 2002 GED® test was basically a test of reading comprehension. The 2014 test is more sophisticated in that it is intended to give you an indication of your potential for future education and employment. Because it is administered on a computer, the test has much more flexibility in the types of items it can use. The various testing items now include not just standard multiple-choice questions, but also drop-down menus (lists) for answer choices, fill-in-the-blank items, and various technologically enhanced formats. You will see details of all seven item types in this chapter. One of the minor changes is in vocabulary. Each test is composed of "items" and not questions. The GED Testing Service® has pointed out that some of the items are in the form of statements to be completed, while others are in the form of questions to be answered. In all cases, each item will consist of two parts: a stimulus and a response. The stimulus may be a text passage, a graphic (map, chart, or table), or some other manner of presenting information or data. The response might be in the form of a multiple-choice question with four answer choices presented to you or a fill-in-the-blank or short answer response or some other format where you have to provide the best answer from your "reading" of the stimulus.

All of this brings you back to the most important skill needed to be successful on the GED® test: reading comprehension. To help you with your reading comprehension skills, we've included a "Reading Comprehension Strategies" section later in this chapter, complete with example questions. But let's not get ahead of ourselves. First, let's talk a bit more about the computer aspect of the 2014 GED® test.

> TIP: For a list of frequently asked questions about the GED® test, visit www.gedtestingservice.com/educators/2014-faqs. The list of questions is long (and thorough), but it is worth your time to look at the questions that interest or affect you.

A. Computer-based Testing

It is worth repeating over and over again that the 2014 GED® test is NOT a paper-and-pencil test. The test is given on a computer, and that has its advantages and disadvantages. If you are unfamiliar with working on a computer, you may have some initial problems working with this test format. If your keyboarding skills are of the "seek and ye shall find" variety, you will find the time limits constraining to say the least. If you fall into either of these categories, some advance preparation is necessary. You can become more familiar with the computer by using one for simple tasks. Arrange with a friend to exchange e-mails; that usually helps you with basics. Do some research on the Internet to learn a bit more about how computers work. If all else fails, consider taking a class in computers at your local school, library, or community center. Many libraries also offer visitors free access to computers. Check for availability and any rules or restrictions that may apply. Any steps you take to become more familiar with computers will help you.

Keyboarding is another story. It is a skill, and as with most skills, it is learned through repeated practice and that takes time. If your keyboarding skills are weak or nonexistent, plan ways to improve them. There are typing tutors available online. Some cost money, some are free, and others offer a free trial and then cost money to use further. It is worth checking out these tutoring programs to see if they would be beneficial to you.

With a desktop computer, there are only two main methods of entering data: One is the keyboard and the other is the mouse. The keyboard allows you to enter data using numbers, words, and phrases. The mouse allows you to select a point on the screen and by clicking the appropriate mouse button, indicate that this is the point you want. You can then manipulate whatever is at that point, dragging it, copying it, and more. This book lacks both a keyboard and a mouse. You have to enter your answers in the old-fashioned way—with a pen or a pencil. In other words, you write your answers on a separate sheet of paper. We provide you with the correct answer and an answer explanation for each item so you can keep track of how you're doing.

If you have difficulty using the mouse in an efficient way, look for a free solitaire game on the computer. Solitaire games require extensive use of the mouse and are good practice (as long as you don't waste time playing them instead of preparing for the GED® test).

B. The Item Types

Because the test is administered on a computer, your test items will be presented in different formats. This section details the seven item types on the GED® test and describes how they will be presented on the computer and in this book.

The 2014 GED® test contains the following seven item types. Note that more than 50 percent of the items on each subject test will be multiple choice.

1. Multiple choice
2. Fill-in-the-blank
3. Drop-down
4. Drag-and-drop
5. Hot spot
6. Short answer
7. Extended response

The following table shows the item types by subject test.

Item Type	Subject Test			
	Reasoning through Language Arts	Mathematical Reasoning	Science	Social Studies
Multiple choice	✓	✓	✓	✓
Fill-in-the-blank	✓	✓	✓	✓
Drop-down	✓	✓	✓	✓
Drag-and-drop	✓	✓	✓	✓
Hot spot		✓	✓	✓
Short answer			✓	
Extended response	✓ (45 min.)			✓ (25 min.)

For the Diagnostic Test and the four subject Practice Tests, we will indicate the item type if it is not multiple choice. If you find the test format hard to understand or intimidating, you will need extra time to get accustomed to answering questions on the computer.

Each of the seven item types is described in detail below.

1. Multiple Choice

Mathematical Reasoning	Question 7 of 50

Calculator Formula Sheet

Herbert was trying to figure out how much carpeting he would need to cover the floor of the square living room in his small apartment. He estimated that he would need 156 square feet of carpet to cover the floor. If his room was 12.5 feet long, how many square feet would Herbert have needed if he had calculated the amount using exact measurements?

- A. 15.625
- B. 156.25
- C. 1,562.50
- D. 15,625

← Previous | Next →

Multiple-choice items comprise a large number of questions in each of the four subject tests. If you have taken or prepared for the GED® test previously, the major difference you will notice is that there are only four possible answers presented. Previously, there were five. You'll use the mouse to select your answer.

2. Fill-in-the-blank

Mathematical Reasoning	Question 26 of 50

Calculator Formula Sheet

What is the decimal equivalent of $\frac{1}{8}$? Enter your answer in the box below; do not round your answer.

← Previous | Next →

Fill-in-the-blank items test your command of the English language since you must provide the correct answer in your own words. On the Science Test, these items will require knowledge of science vocabulary (see the vocabulary sections in Chapter IX). In Mathematical Reasoning, the answer may be a number, a word or phrase, or an equation. On the actual GED® test, you will enter your answer using the keyboard. Remember that synonyms are correct, although they are not listed in the Answer Keys in this book.

3. Drop-down

Reasoning through Language Arts	Question 41 of 57

The paragraphs below are incomplete. For each blank marked "Select...," choose the answer choice that best completes the sentence.

Select... ▼ for your invitation to submit an initial letter of inquiry. The Training Renewal Foundation (TRF) is a nonprofit charitable organization located in the City of Vaughan. Select... ▼ mandate has been to serve disadvantaged youth and other displaced workers seeking skills, qualifications, and employment opportunities.

During 2006, TRF has joined with the Region of York Social Services & Housing Department to create the Employment Assistance and Retention Network Select... ▼ pilot project.

← Previous   Next →

In drop-down items, answer choices are imbedded within the text of an item. You'll use the mouse to see the drop-down list of answer choices and to select your answer. Once you have selected an answer choice with your mouse, it will be incorporated into the text. In this book, the position of the drop-down menu (list) will be indicated by a blank line and the answer choices will appear after the passage in a multiple-choice format.

4. Drag-and-drop

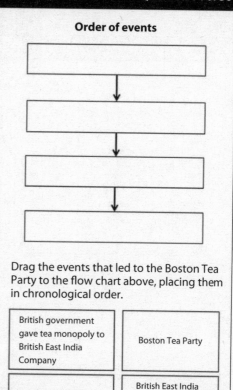

Social Studies   Question 14 of 50

Excerpt from U.S. History For Dummies, 2nd Edition, by Steve Wiegand, copyright 2009 by Wiley Publishing, Inc. Reprinted with permission of John Wiley & Sons, Inc.

Despite the widespread publicity surrounding the tragedy in Boston, cooler heads prevailed for the next year or two. Moderates on both sides of the Atlantic argued that compromises could still be reached.

Then the powerful but poorly run British East India Company found it had 17 million pounds of surplus tea on its hands. So the British government gave the company a monopoly on the American tea business. With a monopoly, the company could lower its prices enough to undercut the smuggled tea the colonists drank instead of paying the British tax. But even with lower prices, the colonists still didn't like the arrangement. It was the principle of the tax itself, not the cost of the tea. Shipments of English tea were destroyed or prevented from being unloaded or sold.

On December 16, 1773, colonists poorly disguised as Native Americans boarded three ships in Boston Harbor, smashed in 342 chests of tea, and dumped the whole mess into the harbor, where, according to one eyewitness, "it piled up in the low tide

Order of events

Drag the events that led to the Boston Tea Party to the flow chart above, placing them in chronological order.

| British government gave tea monopoly to British East India Company | Boston Tea Party |
| Americans smuggle tea to avoid taxes | British East India Company has 17 million pounds of surplus tea |

← Previous | Next →

In the drag-and-drop item type, you will use the mouse to move small images, words, or short phrases to specified locations on the computer screen to answer the question. Drag-and-drop items can test a variety of skills, such as reordering sentences or paragraphs, developing timelines, completing Venn diagrams, forming equations or inequalities, organizing data, or indicating statements as true or false. In this book, you will be presented with a series of options that represent the drag-and-drop content on the computer screen.

5. Hot Spot

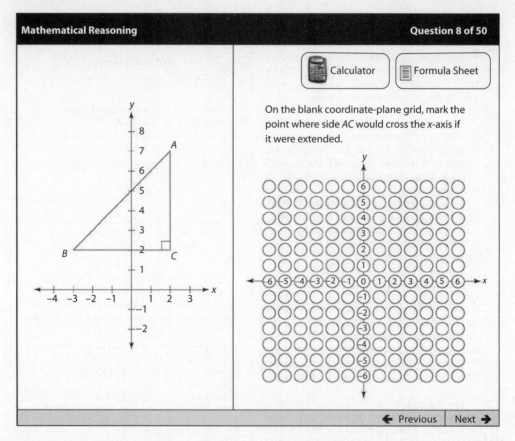

On the computer, hot spot items will be a graphic containing hot spots (virtual sensors) within the image. You will use the mouse to click on a part or parts of this image to answer the question. For example, in Mathematical Reasoning hot spot items, you may be asked to plot points on a number line or grid; while in Science hot spots, you may be asked to identify specified organs in the human body.

6. Short Answer

Stimulus

It should be emphasized that the hydrogen capacity values given in this paper for the aluminum-water reactions are for the materials only. There are, in addition, a number of on-board system requirements that would add more weight and volume. Some examples are containers for the fresh materials and the reaction products, a mechanism for unloading spent materials and loading fresh materials, a reactor that would allow controlled quantities of materials to react, devices for transporting solid and/or liquid materials between the different components, water recovery sub-systems (if used), heat exchangers, pressure control valves, etc. Some of these system components may prove to be very difficult to design and fabricate for reliability and longevity. The highly transient behavior of the fuel requirements for vehicles would be particularly difficult to accommodate with

PROMPT

There was some hope in the scientific community that vehicles could be powered by a reaction between aluminum and water. The results of the experiment seem to indicate otherwise. Explain why this reaction does not appear to be a solution to the environmental problems created by petrochemical-powered vehicles.

Type your response in the box below. This short answer item may take you about 10 minutes to complete.

✂ Cut | 📋 Copy | 📋 Paste | ↺ Undo | ↻ Redo

← Previous | Next →

The short answer item type appears only in the Science Test and requires you to use the keyboard to type in your response. You will be presented with a passage and asked to write a short response to answer the prompt. You may be asked to provide a short summary, a valid conclusion, or a hypothesis. Short answer items should take about 10 minutes each and are scored on a 3-point scale. There is no mention about responses being grammatically correct, but watch your spelling and grammar anyway.

7. Extended Response

Article 1:
Cyberbullying Should Be a Criminal Offense

There is a great deal of evidence that cyberbullying is a serious issue. Studies show nearly a quarter of all teens have been bullied online. That has led to depression, failure at school, and feelings of helplessness and social isolation. In some infamous incidents, it has led to suicide. Current laws seem incapable of dealing with the issue, so the only solution is clearer and stronger laws specifically crafted to deal with this issue.

Cyberbullying is a subset of bullying. It uses communications technology to spread malicious rumors, demean, degrade, and harass victims in every way possible. Instead of physical attacks, these are emotional attacks based on some perception of blemish in an individual. The attacks eventually escalate from insults and harassment to threats of physical violence. Essentially, the victims are isolated and excluded from the community of their peers.

The two articles present arguments for and against laws regarding cyberbullying. One favors the approach of turning cyberbullying into a criminal offense, while the other argues such a step is not necessary.

Analyze both positions, explaining which argument is better supported. Be sure to use specific evidence from the two articles, and from your own life experience and knowledge, to support your response.

Type your response in the box below. You have 45 minutes to write your response.

✂ Cut	🗐 Copy	🗐 Paste	↺ Undo	↻ Redo

← Previous | Next →

Extended response items are essentially essays, which you will write using your keyboard. This item type appears in only two subtests of the GED® test: Reading through Language Arts (RLA) and Social Studies. RLA extended responses will be scored in three areas. The first area is analysis, and here you will have to analyze arguments presented in the item passages. The second area is organization and development, and the third is grammar. Two passages will be presented and you will be expected to write an extended response analyzing the material presented in an organized fashion using correct grammar in a coherent fashion. You will have 45 minutes to write your response for the RLA. The Social Studies extended response item requires the writing of an analytical essay in response to two passages. You will have 25 minutes to write your response. In the Social Studies extended response, you may draw most of your information from the stimulus texts, but should also be able to use your own knowledge of American history and current events to expand upon whatever topic is presented. The focus will be on "Enduring Issues" in American history, such as civil rights, free speech, social issues, and the like. If you are studying for the GED® test in a group setting, it is helpful to read each other's responses and offer constructive feedback.

C. Reading Comprehension Strategies

The most common form of item on the GED® test is multiple choice, and this is the format we have chosen to use for examples in this section. Please note that the example questions in this section are designed to present the different reading comprehension strategies and are not necessarily representative of every item on the GED® test.

Reading comprehension questions can be found on three of the four GED® subject tests: Social Studies, Science, and Reasoning through Language Arts. You'll be asked to read text passages and then answer questions about what you've read. This section outlines some strategies to help you prepare for this prevalent question type.

1. Determining the Reliability of Information Presented in the Questions

Your first task when presented with a question based on a statement that is *supposedly* factual is to determine if that question's statement is accurate. In real life, you can go to other sources and verify the facts and ensure that the material you're using is accurate. On a test or exam, you don't have this luxury. If a statement is made, you have no way of verifying it except from your basic knowledge and outside reading.

For example, if you were presented with a question asking if Christopher Columbus made his voyages during President Lincoln's term of office, your experience and background knowledge would tell you that this is inaccurate because Columbus's exploration took place before there was a country where Lincoln could be elected president. In other words, don't automatically assume that such a statement is true. Use common sense and the knowledge that you bring with you to the test.

2. Using Data to Answer Questions

In this modern age of computers, applications are programs that enable you to perform a task with a computer. For the purposes of the GED® test, *application* means how a particular theory might be used. For example, to create a map, you have to begin with a survey to measure the distances between objects or defined locations. In this case, the measurements are the data, and the map is the application of the data. On the GED® test, you may be asked to use data presented in the reading passage to answer a question. Note that a question might also be based on data that is *not* presented in the reading passage but in a table or a graph.

EXAMPLE:

Christopher Columbus was born in Genoa, Italy, in 1451, to a poor but proud family of five children. He had a limited education but began his seagoing adventures when he was 16. In 1467, Columbus traveled to Iceland and continued his seafaring days as a privateer, plundering ships belonging to the Moors. In one of these battles, off the coast of Portugal, his ship was sunk, but he survived by swimming to shore.

One year later, Columbus began working with his brother, Bartholomew, a cartographer. He married into a wealthy Portuguese family and inherited his father-in-law's maps of the Portuguese possessions in the Atlantic. In 1484, with his maps and experience, Columbus approached the king of Portugal for money to find a fast trade route to the Indies but was turned down.

> Why was Columbus turned down in his appeal for money to find a fast route to the Indies?
>
> **(A)** He had been a pirate.
> **(B)** He had little education.
> **(C)** He married into a wealthy Portuguese family.
> **(D)** Insufficient data

The correct answer is **(D)**. All the answer choices are present in the passage, but none is connected to the king's refusal. Although a lot of information is presented, in order to apply the information to the question, the information must be relevant and related. As you answer the questions on the GED® test, make sure that you use the information in a way that answers the question.

3. Breaking Down Information into Understandable Chunks

Sometimes, information in a question is presented in a large bundle, but in order to answer the questions based on the information, you have to divide it into small parcels.

EXAMPLE:

> Earth is not a still, unmoving object. It may feel that way when you stand on it, but there is a lot going on under your feet. Earth is divided into layers, one of which is the lithosphere, which exists as separate tectonic plates. These plates, or surfaces, sit on a visco-elastic solid layer called the asthenosphere, which allows them to move very slowly. Although you can't feel Earth move, it is moving—just very slowly.

> What causes Earth to move?
>
> **(A)** Movement of the atmosphere
> **(B)** Loose sand under the surface
> **(C)** Movement of the lithosphere
> **(D)** Plane tectonics

The correct answer is **(C)**. This is the best answer, although it's not a complete one. To answer this question, you have to break down the information given. The actual name for this movement is plate tectonics (D), but that is not mentioned in the passage. Instead, there is information about the lithosphere (C) and how it is composed of plates, which can move on a visco-elastic solid layer (the asthenosphere).

4. Determining the Meaning of a Word

Comprehension questions test your ability to understand the material presented. This can depend on the material or the words used in presenting the passage and the questions. You often can figure out the meaning of a word you don't understand by the sentence it appears in.

EXAMPLE:

> There are casualties in every war. The ideal situation is to be able to treat the injuries before they claim the lives of the injured. During the Korean War, a new concept in field emergency care was developed. The United Nations forces developed mobile army surgical hospitals with 150 to 200 beds to treat those requiring surgical care. These hospitals were initially developed to treat casualties requiring surgical services, but

the hospital staff quickly saw the need for treating medical as well as surgical patients. With the limited number of beds in each MASH unit and the constant flow of the wounded, it became necessary to develop a plan of airborne evacuation to take the wounded, once stabilized, to more remote hospitals.

During the Korean War, a MASH unit was

(A) A military assistants survival hospital
(B) A minor accident survival hospital
(C) A mobile army surgical hospital
(D) A movable accident support hospital

The correct answer is **(C)**. There is a lot of information in this passage, but the best answer to the meaning of the acronym *MASH* is mobile army surgical hospital. The other answer choices would fit the initials, but the actual words are spelled out in the passage in the fourth sentence. In addition, the passage mentions that these were surgical units that later began to treat medical emergencies.

5. Recognizing Biases, Inferences, and Effects

Biases, inferences, and effects all have an influence on the passages that you read.

a. Biases

If the passage contains only primary information, all you'll read is raw information. If the information has been analyzed or interpreted, then you should look for the bias of the author. If the author believes that the needs of a large corporation should take precedence over the wants and needs of the people around the plant, then a passage on industrial pollution by the manager of the plant may greatly differ from what an environmentalist would write. The bias of the author is important in understanding the passage in sufficient detail to answer questions about it.

EXAMPLE:

INTERVIEWER: Welcome, Mr. Georges, to "Green Earth," the program that concerns itself with the environment.
MR. GEORGES: Thank you for having me.
INTERVIEWER: Let's start with an item that's been in the news lately.
MR. GEORGES: Fine. What's that?
INTERVIEWER: Your company has been criticized for the amount of particulates you release into the air from your new plant.
MR. GEORGES: Did I mention how many new jobs were created in that new plant?
INTERVIEWER: Since the plant opened, there has been a steady rise in lung ailments and a steady decline in air quality.
MR. GEORGES: We have brought a million dollars into the local economy since we opened. That's pretty significant.
INTERVIEWER: But we have complaints about the constant illness facing many families living near the plant.
MR. GEORGES: Which is worse—starving because there are no jobs or a little hacking cough?

> How do you know from this passage that Mr. Georges is willing to accept pollution and illness for the sake of his factory?
>
> **(A)** He says that he has brought a great deal of money into the local economy.
> **(B)** He is proud of creating new jobs.
> **(C)** He is proud of the look of his new building.
> **(D)** He says that a hacking cough is better than unemployment.

The correct answer is **(D)**. The final sentence in the passage sums up the way that Mr. Georges feels about pollution and the trade-offs he is willing to make. Choices (A) and (B) are mentioned in the passage but have little to do with pollution or Mr. George's bias. Choice (C) is just irrelevant information.

b. Inferences

If you can draw a conclusion that is not exactly stated by the words in the passage, then you're inferring that conclusion. You might be asked to answer a question that is based not on what is said in the passage but on what is inferred—implied—in the passage.

EXAMPLE:

> VQZ Enterprises, Ltd., is pleased to announce the appointment of Hachim Oliveston as our new CEO. Mr. Oliveston is leaving a very prestigious appointment as financial advisor to the president of the United States. During his term as financial advisor, he was able to propose three reductions in corporate income tax and an easing of the rules for off-shore deposits of capital. We know that with Mr. Oliveston at the helm of VQZ Enterprises, Ltd., we will benefit from his vast experience in financial matters. Welcome aboard, Hachim.

> What is the major implication of this appointment?
>
> **(A)** The new CEO can influence the president.
> **(B)** The new CEO can balance the books at VQZ Enterprises, Ltd.
> **(C)** The new CEO can captain a large ship.
> **(D)** The new CEO will understand the Income Tax Act.

The correct answer is **(A)**. From the passage, the implication is made that, because he was a senior advisor to the president, Oliveston would still be able to influence him. Nowhere does the passage explicitly state this, but the implication is there. The other answer choices do not indicate how this appointment could help the company.

c. Effects

An effect is a result of something else and may have to be deduced or inferred from the passage presented. Read passages carefully, remembering to look for a cause if an effect is asked for and vice versa.

EXAMPLE:

Fellow citizens, we are facing a crisis of epic proportions. We are running out of money, and you have indicated to me on many occasions that you do not want a tax hike. My staff and I have gone over the city's budget with a fine-tooth comb. Social services cannot be touched; they are mandated by higher levels of government. We can hope and pray for a mild winter, but it would be a huge error to reduce the street clearing budget to zero. If we did that and it snowed or the leaves fell from the trees, the roads would remain untouched, and you all know what an uproar that would cause. That only leaves one option, and I only hope that you can learn to live with potholes.

Based on this speech, what item must be left out of the budget?

(A) School maintenance
(B) Refreshments at meetings
(C) Street cleaning
(D) Road repair

The correct answer is **(D).** The cause is the lack of money and the fact that certain city services cannot be dropped because they are mandated or would cause a political backlash. The only area that is seen to be possible to not fund is road repair. This is based on the speaker's comment about potholes.

6. Interpreting Questions Based on Opinion, not Fact

A fact has actually happened or is something based on irrefutable proof. An opinion is what someone thinks about it. For example, consider this question: If no one was in the forest when a tree fell, would it make a noise? We are sure that if a tree fell, there would be a noise, but if no one were there to witness the event, could we ever be sure that this was not an exception? This question would be a basis for speculation and opinion but difficult to answer based on fact.

EXAMPLE:

As your representative from the inner core of this great city, I truly believe that the only answer to moving large numbers of people efficiently is the subway. We all understand that transportation is a vital necessity in a crowded city, but buses only add to that congestion. We have to keep the public people-movers underground to leave our streets free and clear for cars and bicycles.

According to the passage, the only solution to moving large numbers of people efficiently is the

(A) Car
(B) Subway
(C) Bus
(D) Bicycle

The correct answer is **(B).** The opinion of the speaker is that subways are best for this purpose. He or she has not presented any facts to back up this opinion. The other choices are mentioned but not as a solution to the problem.

7. Answering Questions Based on Generalizations

If you're presented with a series of facts, statements, or opinions and asked to summarize the facts, statements, or opinions without altering the main meaning or implication of all the information given, then you are generalizing.

EXAMPLE:

> SALESPERSON: Look at this car. It's all electric. That means it uses no gas at all.
> CUSTOMER: Sounds great.
> SALESPERSON: Think about how much money you could save!
> CUSTOMER: But how far can I go before I have to fill up?
> SALESPERSON: Since the Electro Special runs on electricity, you never have to fill up.
> CUSTOMER: How far can I go before I have to do something like plug it in?
> SALESPERSON: Well, if you drive carefully, you could go about 70 miles before you have to plug it in.
> CUSTOMER: But I work 53 miles from the house and still have to get home.
> SALESPERSON: Do you think you could find a job closer to home?

What was the salesperson's goal in this conversation?

(A) To protect the environment
(B) To give the customer a good deal on the car
(C) To sell the car
(D) To satisfy the customer's transportation needs

The correct answer is **(C).** The salesperson is obviously only interested in selling the car. When an objection is raised about the distance to and from work, the salesperson's only comment is a suggestion for the customer to get a job closer to home. The other answer choices are interesting but do not answer the question. We're generalizing from the conversation that the salesperson is interested only in selling a car and not saving the planet from pollution (A), making a good deal for the customer (B), or figuring out the customer's actual transportation needs (D). The main objective of the salesperson is to sell the car. Because this is not specifically stated in the conversation, we're generalizing.

8. Recognizing Types of Information

Information can be divided into three main categories:

- **Primary:** Information that is original and has not been analyzed, interpreted, or explained, such as a journal or statistics
- **Secondary:** Information that is developed from primary information and that interprets it, such as a textbook or an article in a newspaper or magazine
- **Tertiary:** Information about another source of information, such as a database or dictionary

Primary information is usually regarded as accurate, but secondary information may be biased, or even incorrect, depending on the degree of interpretation and the bias of the interpreter.

EXAMPLE:

> Alice's editor assigns her to do a story about Senator George Geores. To do this, she interviews the senator, talks to his friends, researches him in the library, looks him up on the Internet, and speculates about his motives in proposing a bill to limit the manufacturing of gas-powered trucks.
>
> Of all her efforts, which would be classified as a primary source?
>
> **(A)** Her speculation about his motives
> **(B)** Her interview with the senator
> **(C)** Her conversations with the senator's friends
> **(D)** Her library research

The correct answer is **(B).** An interview is regarded as a primary source of information. Choices (A), (C), and (D) are secondary sources of information.

9. Recognizing Value-and-Belief Questions

In order to understand the material on the GED® test, you need to be able to recognize values and beliefs. A belief is a conviction that people believe to be true without supporting proof or evidence. A value is a concept that we believe to be important to our lives and how we live them. Values and beliefs color the writings of many people because they are an important part of the person. When you read a passage, try to understand the value and belief system that underlies the words.

EXAMPLE:

> The Smithington family is concerned about their impact on the environment and has decided to do something about it. At a family conference, they decide the following:
>
> - They will sell their family car.
> - They will ride bicycles as a mode of transportation.
> - They will only buy food grown within a hundred miles of their city.
> - They will investigate solar power panels for their roof.
> - They will replace all their light bulbs with LEDs.
> - They will only do laundry after midnight.
> - They will investigate the savings from reinsulating their home.

> Which word or words indicate a possible action that may or may not take place to reduce the Smithington family's impact on the environment?
>
> **(A)** Sell
> **(B)** Buy
> **(C)** Replace
> **(D)** Investigate

The correct answer is **(D).** Although the family obviously has a strong belief that they can do something to reduce their impact on the environment, there seem to be some actions they are willing to take now, and some they are prepared to consider before making a final decision. The word *investigate* implies an action that will be considered before it is taken.

10. Understanding Relational, Compare-and-Contrast Questions

If you're asked to compare and contrast two sets of information, you have to look for similarities and differences in the information.

If you're asked to discuss the relationship between two sets of information, you have to look at the two sets and see how they compare with each other. They may have a direct relationship in that one set supports the other. They may have an inverse or negative relationship in that they may be opposite opinions. The relationship may be causal, implying that one set of information causes the second set to happen. There may be a dependent relationship in that one set of information may be dependent on the other. In reading passages, it is important to recognize what type of relationship exists and use that to answer the questions.

EXAMPLE:

> Regifting has a bad reputation. Each holiday season we are faced with a dilemma. What do we buy for each person on our list? Often we have a whole collection of gifts that were given to us sitting in a cupboard waiting to be forgotten or fade away. Yet some of these would be perfect for some of the people on our lists. All we have to do is clean them up, wrap them, and they are ready for a new life as wanted and appreciated gifts.
>
> On the other hand, there are dangers of regifting. If you don't have an excellent memory or a good cataloging system, you might give a gift back to the person who gave it to you. That would be embarrassing. With all the new gadgets coming on the market each season, a regifted item could easily be last year's hot item. You have to know your friends and family well and take your chances. There is nothing as lonely as a gift hidden away on a shelf, gathering dust, as it sits and waits for someone to appreciate it.

> In this passage, what is the strongest argument for NOT regifting?
>
> **(A)** Some gifts might have become damaged over time.
> **(B)** A gift might be returned to the original giver.
> **(C)** Older gifts get dusty.
> **(D)** Some gifts get lonely.

The correct answer is **(B).** The passage states that giving a gift back to the person who gave it to you could prove embarrassing. This passage is a good example of compare and contrast in that it presents both sides of an argument and asks a question about one side. A second question might ask about the advantages of regifting or how regifting might be environmentally friendly. With this type of passage, you have to read carefully to see which side of the argument you are being questioned about.

11. Interpreting Strategy Questions

When someone develops a plan of action to reach a particular goal, he is said to have developed a strategy. In some questions' reading passages, especially those about military operations, the strategy developed is an important part of understanding the text.

EXAMPLE:

The Battle of the Little Big Horn was fought between the combined forces of four native tribes and the 7th Calvary Regiment of the United States Army. The fighting took place near the Little Bighorn River in Montana. The Calvary Regiment was led by George Armstrong Custer, who entered battle assuming that the native army was small and, thus, could be easily defeated. This information was provided by the Indian agents in the territory who based their information on false assumptions.

Custer based his plans on his wish to contain the native soldiers rather than fight and possibly kill them. The battle was to begin early in the morning, because Custer believed that all the natives would still be asleep. Looking over the village preparing for the day, Custer assumed that when he began firing the rifles, any nearby units would come to their aid. He was wrong, and the battle was disastrous for the American Calvary, resulting in 268 casualties and 55 soldiers being wounded. One of the casualties was George Armstrong Custer.

What assumptions did Custer make in preparing for battle?

(A) That the native army was small
(B) That the native army would be asleep early in the morning
(C) That Custer could contain the native army because of his superior numbers
(D) All of the above

The correct answer is **(D).** Reading the passage, you can see that choices (A), (B), and (C) were part of Custer's plan or strategy for this battle. His complete strategy may have been more complex, but you can only answer the question with the best answer based on the passage.

As a final comment—read, read, and read some more. Decide what kind of information you are reading. Write short summaries of what you have read. Look up and keep track of any words you cannot define correctly. Read in the different subject areas tested by the GED® test. All of this will help you do well on the GED® test and that is the goal of all this effort.

II. Diagnostic Test

This practice test is not related to the GED Ready™ – The Official Practice Test, produced and distributed by GED Testing Service LLC. GED Testing Service® has not approved, authorized, endorsed, been involved in the development of, or licensed the substantive content of this practice test.

The Diagnostic Test consists of half-length subject tests. There are two exceptions: You'll have the full 45 minutes to write your essay for the Reasoning through Language Arts extended response item and the full 25 minutes to write your essay for the Social Studies extended response item.

Taking the Diagnostic Test can give you a good idea of where to spend the most time in your preparation. The areas covered in this Diagnostic Test are as follows: Reasoning through Language Arts, Mathematical Reasoning, Science, and Social Studies. The total time for the Diagnostic Test is 4 hours and 15 minutes.

Reminder: For this Diagnostic Test, we combined Sections 1 and 3 of the Reasoning through Language Arts Test into one section: Section 1.

Diagnostic Test		
Subject Test	**Number of Questions***	**Number of Minutes**
Reasoning through Language Arts, Section 1	30	45
Reasoning through Language Arts, Section 2	1 extended response (essay)	45
Mathematical Reasoning	25	55
Science	25	45
Social Studies, Section 1	30	40
Social Studies, Section 2	1 extended response (essay)	25

*Note: The actual number of items on the real GED® tests may vary, but the timing remains constant. Check www.gedtestingservice.com for updates, since the times have changed and may change again.

There is not a set number of questions for each of the GED® tests. The tests are set up by selecting random items from a pool of potential items. Each item has a predetermined level of difficulty and each test will have the same potential score. Your job is to complete every item to the best of your ability and not worry if you end up with a couple more items than your friend who also took the test.

Each question is numbered. For multiple-choice questions, you have to choose the best answer out of the four choices given, writing your answer on a separate piece of paper. For the two extended response items and the Mathematical Reasoning portion, you will need additional paper to write your essay responses and to work through some of the math. Other item types, such as fill-in-the-blank, will require that you write in your answer on a separate sheet of paper. On the actual GED® test, you will have access to an on-screen calculator for most questions, except the first five, on the Mathematical Reasoning Test, but the Mathematical Reasoning portion of this Diagnostic Test can be completed without the use of a calculator.

Although you will enter your answers and write your extended responses and short answer responses on the computer during the actual GED® test, you will need to use your own paper to record your answers and responses for this Diagnostic Test.

Try to make your behavior on this Diagnostic Test as close as possible to the actual test conditions. Observe the time constraints. Each subject test on the Diagnostic Test is a separate entity. During your practice, if you finish a subject test before time is up, take the time to review your answers or even to relax. Do not add the extra time you have to the next subject test.

Answer all the questions. There is no deduction for wrong answers, and you get points for each right one. Some questions are worth more than 1 point, but that information might not be readily available to you while taking the test. The important thing is to get as many correct answers as you can. Guess if you have to. Unanswered items do nothing to improve your score. The more wrong answer choices you can eliminate, the better your chances of guessing the correct answer. In multiple-choice items, if you can eliminate three choices, you will have a 100 percent chance of being correct! Unfortunately, for each choice you cannot eliminate, the odds go down.

After you complete the Diagnostic Test, score it and review the answer explanations (especially for any questions you got wrong). For the two extended response items, compare your responses to the sample essays.

Reasoning through Language Arts

Section 1

Time: 45 Minutes—30 Questions

This test consists of excerpts from fiction and nonfiction. Each excerpt is followed by questions about the reading material. Read each excerpt first and then answer the questions following it.

Directions: Choose the best answer to each question. Use a separate piece of paper as your answer sheet and write your answers there for each question.

Questions 1–8 are based on the following text, an extract from a speech by President Obama after a bilateral meeting in the Netherlands, March 24, 2014.

Source: www.whitehouse.gov/the-press-office/2014/03/24/remarks-president-obama-and-prime-minister-rutte-netherlands-after-bilat

… As you know, the Netherlands is one of our closest allies, and our cooperation underscores a larger point—our NATO allies are our closest partners on the world stage. Europe is the cornerstone of America's engagement with the world. And today we focused on several priorities—in Europe and beyond.

First, we obviously spent a considerable amount of time on the situation in Ukraine. Europe and America are united in our support of the Ukrainian government and the Ukrainian people. We're united in imposing a cost on Russia for its actions so far. Prime Minister Rutte rightly pointed out yesterday the growing sanctions would bring significant consequences to the Russian economy. And I'll be meeting with my fellow G7 leaders later today, and we'll continue to coordinate closely with the Netherlands and our European partners as we go forward.

Second, I thanked the Prime Minister for the Netherlands' strong commitment and contributions to NATO. Dutch forces have served with distinction in Afghanistan and joined us in confronting piracy off the Horn of Africa. Through NATO, the Netherlands contributed to the deployment of Patriot air batteries in Turkey and are making important investments in NATO defense capabilities. Dutch forces are also making critical contributions to the international stabilization mission in Mali. So, across the board, the Dutch are making their presence felt in a very positive way, and we're very grateful for that.

Third, we discussed how we can keep expanding the trade that creates jobs for our people. We're already among each other's largest trade and investment partners, but we can always do more. And so I appreciated the Netherlands' strong support for the Transatlantic Trade and Investment Partnership, or T-TIP, which can fuel growth both in the United States and in Europe, especially for our small and medium-sized companies.

Fourth, we discussed a range of global challenges. And as the United States and the P5-plus-1 partners continue negotiations with Iran, we have the basis for a practical solution that resolves concerns over Iran's nuclear program. But at the same time, I think it's important that everyone remember during these negotiations we'll continue to enforce the overall sanctions architecture that helped bring Iran to the table in the first place.

I also wanted to commend the Netherlands for its leadership in the international effort to destroy Syria's chemical weapons, and that includes your role as the host of the Organization for the Prohibition of Chemical Weapons. And more broadly, our two countries are going to keep working together to deliver humanitarian assistance to the Syrian people.

And, finally, we reaffirmed our shared determination to confront climate change and its effects, including rising sea levels, which obviously is something that the Netherlands is concerned about, given your experience with seas and tides. We're pleased that the Netherlands has joined our initiative that will virtually end all public financing for coal-fired plants abroad. It's concrete action like this that can keep making progress on reducing emissions while we develop new global agreements on climate change.

So, a final note. When John Adams was negotiating the treaty that we saw earlier, he wrote that the Dutch have—and I'm quoting here—have always "distinguished themselves by an inviolable attachment to freedom and the rights of nations." That was true then; it remains true today.

So, Mark, I want to thank you and the Dutch for your hospitality, for your organization, for your partnership and for your leadership on the world stage. And I want to thank you for sharing these extraordinary paintings with me this morning. ...

1. What are the Netherlands and the United States united on in terms of dealing with the Ukraine crisis?

    (A) Imposing sanctions
    (B) Military action
    (C) Antipiracy legislation
    (D) All of the above

2. Why does Obama want to commend the Netherlands?

    (A) Leadership in efforts to destroy Syria's chemical weapons
    (B) Host of the Organization for the Prohibition of Chemical Weapons
    (C) Strong support for the Transatlantic Trade and Investment Partnership
    (D) All of the above

Fill-in-the-blank

3. Who is the prime minister of the Netherlands? Enter your answer in the box below.

4. In which of these areas have the Dutch forces been active?

    (A) In Operation Desert Storm, in Iraq
    (B) Fighting pirates off Mali
    (C) Helping with the NATO campaign to place Patriot Missiles in Turkey
    (D) All of the above

5. What does President Obama say about sanctions against Iran?

   (A) Sanctions will continue during negotiations over Iran's nuclear program.
   (B) Sanctions will be discontinued.
   (C) Sanctions will be negotiated with the Netherlands.
   (D) They will consult the other G7 leaders.

6. Why are the Netherlands concerned about climate change?

   (A) They prefer cool weather.
   (B) Rising sea levels
   (C) The risk of tropical disease is spreading northward.
   (D) Increased risk of storms

7. The Netherlands are contributing to NATO by

   (A) Sending troops to support the Ukraine
   (B) Fighting climate change
   (C) Working with G7 countries
   (D) Serving in Afghanistan

8. T-TIP is an organization that

   (A) Expands trade between North America and Europe
   (B) Creates a joint defense force for Europe
   (C) Helps fight climate change
   (D) Destroys chemical weapons

Questions 9 and 10 refer to the following excerpt from the play Easy A? *by Murray Shukyn (2007).*

Lewis's office at City College; books everywhere; desk heaped with papers and behind it sits Lewis, completely absorbed in his reading. A knock on the door, but Lewis doesn't hear or maybe doesn't pay attention. The door slowly opens, and a female student, Connie, enters the office and stands at the desk.

   Connie: I need an A in your course!
   Connie, a mediocre student in Lewis's sociology and education course, seems agitated. Her usually well-groomed auburn hair is windblown. Her usually impeccably applied makeup is missing. Her clothing is, as always, immaculate and fashionable as befits the daughter of one of the largest benefactors of City College.
   Lewis: I beg your pardon.
   Connie: *(with a bit more confidence)* I need an A in your course. Without it, my grade point average falls below scholarship level, and I can't go on to graduate school. Daddy took care of everything else. It's just your course that I need to fix.
   Lewis: *(confused)* I don't understand.
   Connie: *(fully confident)* Dr. Stephson, I need to go to graduate school. All my brothers did, and in appreciation for their achievement, my parents gave each of them a Porsche, an apartment, and an allowance. I need that car. It's just so cool to arrive at a party in a Porsche. What do I have to do to get an A?

Lewis: It's kind of late in the year to advise you to study harder for the tests or to spend more time on your assignments. I don't have my grade book with me, but I do believe that your average so far is a B–.

Connie: *(becoming agitated)* I don't care about tests, studying, or assignments. This is my life I'm talking about. What do I have to do to get you to give me an A?

Lewis: If you're average in my class, you're probably average in the others. How can you expect to finish with an A average?

Connie: Dr. Stephson, you can't be this naïve. With the money my father pumps into this college, I get special consideration by the staff. I do get A's. My father seems to have forgotten to reach out to you and that means I have to do it. What do you want for me to get an A? What do you need in return? Money? Favors? A promotion? Tell me and it can be arranged. You know who my father is and how generous he can be. What do I have to do to get an A?

9. What effect does Connie expect her father's donations to have on her grades?

   (A) Connie expects to be given high grades.
   (B) Connie expects that a building will be named after her father.
   (C) Connie expects the college to give her father an honorary degree.
   (D) Connie expects her father to be introduced as a celebrity at the football games.

10. What effect would a B– in this course have on Connie?

   (A) She would be embarrassed in front of her friends.
   (B) She might have to retake this course in summer school.
   (C) Her self-confidence would decrease.
   (D) Connie would not be able to get into graduate school and, thus, would not get rewarded by her family.

Questions 11 through 16 refer to the following excerpt from the short story "Rip Van Winkle" by Washington Irving (1819).

In that same village, and in one of these very houses (which, to tell the precise truth, was sadly time-worn and weather-beaten), there lived many years since, while the country was yet a province of Great Britain, a simple good-natured fellow, of the name of Rip Van Winkle. He was a descendant of the Van Winkles who figured so gallantly in the chivalrous days of Peter Stuyvesant, and accompanied him to the siege of Fort Christina. He inherited, however, but little of the martial character of his ancestors. I have observed that he was a simple, good-natured man; he was, moreover, a kind neighbor, and an obedient, henpecked husband. Indeed, to the latter circumstance might be owing that meekness of spirit which gained him such universal popularity; for those men are most apt to be obsequious and conciliating abroad who are under the discipline of shrews at home. Their tempers, doubtless, are rendered pliant and malleable in the fiery furnace of domestic tribulation, and a curtain lecture is worth all the sermons in the world for teaching the virtues of patience and long-suffering. A termagant wife may, therefore, in some respects, be considered a tolerable blessing; and if so, Rip Van Winkle was thrice blessed.

Certain it is that he was a great favorite among all the good wives of the village, who, as usual with the amiable sex, took his part in all family squabbles, and never failed, whenever they talked those matters over in their evening gossipings, to lay all the blame on Dame Van Winkle. The children of the village, too, would shout with joy whenever he approached. He assisted at their sports, made their playthings, taught them to fly kites and shoot marbles, and told them long stories of ghosts, witches, and Indians. Whenever he went dodging about the village, he was surrounded by a troop of them, hanging on his skirts, clambering on his back, and playing a thousand tricks on him with impunity; and not a dog would bark at him throughout the neighborhood.

11. According to the passage, where was the village located?

 (A) At Fort Christina
 (B) In a province of Great Britain
 (C) In the Thirteen Colonies
 (D) In New Amsterdam

Drag-and-drop

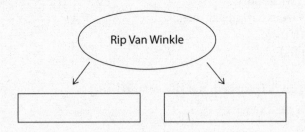

12. Drag the phrases that best describe Van Winkle's personality into the boxes surrounding his name.

 (To answer, write the letter of all answer choices that apply on your answer sheet.)

 (A) Descended from the Van Winkles
 (B) Gallant and chivalrous
 (C) A kind neighbor
 (D) Simple and good-natured

13. Which statement best describes why Rip Van Winkle was universally popular?

 (A) He was henpecked.
 (B) He had inherited the martial character of his ancestors.
 (C) He had a meekness of spirit.
 (D) He often took part in gossiping.

14. What phrase does the author use to describe the Van Winkle marriage?

 (A) Tolerable blessing
 (B) Domestic tribulation
 (C) Great favorite
 (D) Happy and loving

Drag-and-drop

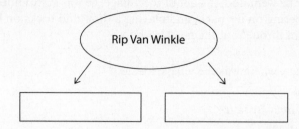

15. Drag the activities that made Van Winkle popular with the children to the boxes around his name.

    (To answer, write the letter of all answer choices that apply on your answer sheet.)

    (A) He assisted them with sports.
    (B) He stopped dogs from barking at them.
    (C) He flew kites with them.
    (D) He trained them to fight.

16. Rip Van Winkle's biggest defenders in the village were

    (A) The other men in the village
    (B) The village wives
    (C) The children
    (D) The local Indians

Questions 17 through 20 refer to the following business document.

Beginning in 1980, Ontario Travel formed an exclusive partnership with Can-Learn International (a division of Can-Learn Limited) to develop, plan, market, and implement educational travel programs with a variety of different constituencies, including school boards, schools, colleges, universities, artistic and cultural interests, trade associations, alumni and senior citizens' organizations, commercial enterprises, professional development groups, and other such affinity groups.

Can-Learn International works with organizational personnel and influences leaders to research and plan custom-designed programs that meet the specific needs and objectives of each program. Can-Learn International assists in marketing such programs and also provides an escort service as required.

Partnering with Can-Learn International, Ontario Travel, as a leading professional travel agency, is responsible for all logistics including accommodations, air, sea, and land arrangements. Ontario Travel also participates with Can-Learn International in the planning, implementation, and marketing of all such programs. Ontario Travel shares any income realized from each of the above programs with Can-Learn International based on a predetermined rate of commission per passenger.

17. To what programs does the partnership agreement refer?

    (A) Professional development
    (B) Citizens' organizations
    (C) Trade associations
    (D) Educational travel

18. What service is NOT mentioned in the partnership agreement?

   (A) Planning
   (B) Retailing
   (C) Marketing
   (D) Developing

19. Which of the following constituencies does the partnership serve?

   (A) Alumni organizations
   (B) Universities
   (C) Commercial enterprises
   (D) All of the above

20. How is income to be shared by the partners?

   (A) Equally
   (B) On a sliding scale
   (C) At a predetermined commission rate per passenger
   (D) 75 percent to Ontario Travel, 25 percent to Can-Learn International

Drop-down

21. The paragraph below is incomplete. For each blank, choose the answer choices that best complete the sentences.

   This has been a busy year, during which our outdoor ranges underwent major upgrades. We now have a rebuilt 50m outdoor rifle and handgun range, as well as an expanded trap range. On the last inspection, (i) _____ all requirements for safety and noise limits. Currently and through the winter, the target shooters are competing in a series of small-bore rifle (ii) _____ available in a few months

Blank (i)	Blank (ii)
(A) the range meets and exceeds	(A) competitions the results will be
(B) the range met and exceeded	(B) competitions, the results will be
(C) the range met and exceeds	(C) competitions. The results will be
(D) the range will meet and exceed	(D) competiton, the results will be

Drop-down

22. The paragraph below is incomplete. For each blank, choose the answer choices that best complete the sentences.

   The aboriginal people had a sophisticated system of tribal government. One example: The "Great Law of Peace" of the Iroquois Confederacy (i) _____ confederation of tribes from Florida to the Canadian Shield. The law created a Council where all tribes could resolve disputes by consensus, avoiding war. This Great Law of Peace (ii) _____ the creation of the American Constitution.

Blank (i)	Blank (ii)
(A) which were a	(A) could also influence
(B) that was a	(B) that later influenced
(C) . This was a	(C) which could later influence
(D) ; it should be a	(D) later influenced

Questions 23 and 24 refer to the following business letter.

THE TRAINING RENEWAL FOUNDATION
750 Millway Ave., Unit 6
Concord, MA 12345

Ted Tingle
Executive Director
Specialty Coffee Association of America
One World Trade Centre, Suite 1200
Long Beach, CA 96831

March 15, 2014

Dear Mr. Tingle:

(1) With reference to our exchange of e-mail, I wish to confirm the following agreement regarding the representation of the Specialty Coffee Association of America (SCAA) by the Training Renewal Foundation (TRF).

(2) SCAA grants TRF an exclusive right for distribution of SCAA's training programs for the period from April 1, 2014, to March 31, 2015. This agreement shall be renewable if both parties determine that they wish to continue.

(3) TRF will handle the entire registration process including receipt of the fees for all training conducted.

(4) TRF will set the basis fee structure and retain the majority of the fees, while SCAA will receive a sum to offset training manual, promotional, and administrative costs.

(5) SCAA will provide master copies of the course description and promotional material.

(6) Handouts will consist of SCAA's Class in a Box training manual, which SCAA will provide.

(7) The training programs will be targeted to all coffee retailers and foodservice operators interested in espresso programs.

(8) SCAA, as well as Coffee Association of America (CAA) members, will be included.

(9) TRF will provide equipment and consumables and arrange accommodation and transportation for the training programs.

(10) Training program fees will be set by TRF to recover these costs.

(11) TRF will be responsible for selecting and compensating the trainers.

(12) TRF will liaise with the print media, while SCAA will liaise with the electronic media.

(13) TRF will follow the SCAA curriculum and use SCAA training materials for this program.

(14) There will be a joint SCAA/TRF promotion of the program to the retail trade, including non-members of both SCAA and CAA.

(15) We will jointly explore the possibility of introducing TRF's Café Equipment Technician training program (possibly in conjunction with the El Camino College program).

(16) As an SCAA program, we will encourage a joint SCAA/TRF Certificate of Completion.

Looking forward to working together.

Yours sincerely,

Dale E. Shuttleworth, Ph.D.
Executive Director

23. Sentence 3: TRF will handle the entire registration process including receipt of the fees for all training conducted.

    Which improvement should be made to Sentence 3?

    (A) Insert a colon after *including*.
    (B) Change *receipt* to *reciept*.
    (C) Insert a comma after *process* and after *fees*.
    (D) Change *will* to *should*.

24. Sentence 4: TRF will set the basis fee structure and retain the majority of the fees, while SCAA will receive a sum to offset training manual, promotional, and administrative costs.

    How should Sentence 4 be corrected?

    (A) Change *basis* to *basic*.
    (B) Change *will* to *should*.
    (C) Change *manual* to *manuel*.
    (D) Change *offset* to *off-set*.

Questions 25 through 30 refer to the following passage.

Executive Summary

(1) BETA is a food equipment reconditioning enterprise being organised to meet a growing need in the restaurant and café industry. (2) By year two, BETA would recondition an average of 500 units per year, generating over $1,000,000 in annual revenue and returning almost half a million dollars in salaries to the local economy through the creation of 13 jobs. (3) This should create additional economic benefits as the employees spend in their community. (4) These are conservative estimates based on the best possible information presently available.

(5) **Objectives** are as follows:
- (6) to centralize the reconditioning of tired transportable restaurant equipment;
- (7) to develop a new industry in the reconditioning and sale of used transportable restaurant equipment,
- (8) to provide employment and training to a popularity with the ability but not the opportunity.

(9) **Advantages** are as follows:
- (10) BETA creates a new industry in a field ready to expand;
- (11) BETA diverts biodegradable equipment from the waste stream;
- (12) BETA allowed a new group of entrepreneurs to enter the café business by providing reliable equipment at a lower price point.

25. Sentence 1: BETA is a food equipment reconditioning enterprise being organised to meet a growing need in the restaurant and café industry.

    Which correction should be made to Sentence 1?

    (A) Change *enterprise* to *enterprize*.
    (B) Change *organised* to *organized*.
    (C) Insert a *colon* after *meet*.
    (D) Change *is* to *was*.

26. Sentence 2: By year two, BETA would recondition an average of 500 units per year, generating over $1,000,000 in annual revenue and returning almost half a million dollars in salaries to the local economy through the creation of 13 jobs.

    How can Sentence 2 be improved?

    (A) Remove the comma after *two*.
    (B) Change *$1,000,000* to *$1000000*.
    (C) Insert a period after *revenue*, and begin the new sentence with *Through the creation of 13 jobs, BETA would return . . .*
    (D) Insert a semicolon after *year*.

27. Sentence 6: to centralize the reconditioning of tired transportable restaurant equipment;

    What changes should be made to Sentence 6?

    (A) Change *centralize* to *centralise*.
    (B) Change *transportable* to *transported*.
    (C) Change *reconditioning* to *conditioning*.
    (D) No change required.

28. Sentence 7: to develop a new industry in the reconditioning and sale of used transportable restaurant equipment,

    Which corrections are required for Sentence 7?

    (A) Change *transportable* to *transported*.
    (B) Change the comma after *equipment* to a semicolon.
    (C) Change *reconditioning* to *reconditioned*.
    (D) No change required.

29. Sentence 8: to provide employment and training to a popularity with the ability but not the opportunity.

    Which improvement should be made to Sentence 8?

    (A) Change *with* to *without*.
    (B) Change *popularity* to *population*.
    (C) Change *employment* to *employability*.
    (D) Change *not* to *knot*.

30. Sentence 12: BETA allowed a new group of entrepreneurs to enter the café business by providing reliable equipment at a lower price point.

    How can Sentence 12 be corrected?

    (A) Change *point* to *pointer*.
    (B) Change *by* to *buy*.
    (C) Change *allowed* to *allows*.
    (D) Change *reliable* to *unreliable*.

IF YOU FINISH BEFORE TIME IS CALLED, CHECK YOUR WORK ON THIS SECTION ONLY. DO NOT WORK ON ANY OTHER SECTION IN THE TEST.

Section 2

Time: 45 Minutes

Directions: On the following page, you'll find two articles that present arguments for and against "Right to Work" legislation. Analyze the two positions. Write an essay explaining which position you think is argued best. Be sure to use evidence from the articles to support your case.

- You must write only on the assigned topic.
- You have 45 minutes to write on your assigned essay topic.

On the RLA test, your essay will be scored according to its overall effectiveness. The evaluation will be based on the following features:

- Well-focused main points
- Clear organization
- Specific development of your ideas
- Control of sentence structure, punctuation, grammar, word choice, and spelling

Remember: You must complete all three sections to receive a score on the Reasoning through Language Arts Test.

To avoid having to repeat the Reasoning through Language Arts Test, be sure to observe the following rules:

- Before you begin writing, jot down notes or outline your essay. On your test day, an erasable noteboard will be provided at the test site.
- Reread your final copy to ensure that it is clear, well-ordered, and grammatically correct.
- Write on the assigned topic. If you write on a topic other than the one assigned, you won't receive a score for the Reasoning through Language Arts Test.
- Write your trial essay for this Diagnostic Test on a separate sheet of lined paper. On the actual test, you will have to write the essay in the window provided on the computer screen; rough work on the noteboard will not be scored. It is a basic word processor, but does not include spelling or grammar checkers. You need to spot your errors yourself and fix as many as possible within the time limit.

Article 1: For "Right to Work" Legislation

Unions have been around for more than a century. They were and are a reflection of the poor treatment workers received at the hands of corporations. This became especially urgent during the Great Depression. As the economy collapsed, companies slashed wages and increased the workload of individual workers. They treated their workers like disposable tools.

Since workers had little chance to fight back individually, unions rose to the occasion. Unions protect their workers from unsafe workplaces and arbitrary firing or layoffs. They negotiate reasonable pay scales for their workers. They also negotiate working conditions, working hours, and benefits with employers.

Many features of our working lives we owe to the union movement. Unions won workers the 40-hour workweek, overtime pay, paid holidays, retirement, and health benefits. The list goes on. In return for these negotiated benefits, unions ensure labor peace in the workplace.

To see what happens in a non-union workplace, all one needs to do is look at the fast-food industry or low-end department stores. Their workers often cannot get full-time work and cannot earn a living wage. The lack of full-time hours means workers rarely have benefits. Often they need to supplement their incomes with food stamps and social assistance. In effect, the government is subsidizing companies that offer low wages.

Now large companies and wealthy individuals are supporting "Right to Work" legislation. In many states, they are supporting politicians who want to undermine unions. They hope to undo decades of progress in the working and living conditions of workers. A new battle for the survival of unions, and living standards for all workers, has started. Just remember, the "Right to Work" laws mean the right to work for starvation wages.

Article 2: Against "Right to Work" Legislation

Unions certainly demand higher wages and benefits for their workers. This results in increased costs being passed on to customers, raising prices for all. It also has led to the transfer of jobs to countries like China, where wages are much lower. That, in turn, makes all of our industries less competitive, leading to further job losses down the road.

Unions succeed by bullying and blackmail. They threaten to shut down the workplace, schools, or police services to gain their demands. In effect, they are holding the public hostage, demanding the employers give in.

Unions have large cash reserves, and often make huge contributions to politicians to curry their favor. Since the unions can also promise large numbers of voters, politicians often give in. In the past, large unions also had connections to organized crime. It took decades for the justice system to end that.

Today, we have legislation governing working hours. Many states set minimum wages and guarantee safe working conditions. Anti-discrimination legislation makes unfair hiring practices illegal, and other legislation protects workers from arbitrary firing. Individuals have the right to sue companies for mistreatment; the fear of large settlements and bad publicity ensures fair treatment by companies.

In truth, union protection for the rights of workers is redundant today. Workers would be better off keeping the union dues for themselves and allowing employers to be more competitive.

IF YOU FINISH BEFORE TIME IS CALLED, CHECK YOUR WORK ON THIS SECTION ONLY. DO NOT WORK ON ANY OTHER SECTION IN THE TEST.

Mathematical Reasoning

This is a test of mathematics skills and will not cover all variations that can be tested on the GED® Mathematical Reasoning Test. The Practice Test in Chapter XII is longer and will be closer to the actual items on the test, but without knowing the basics, the more complex items will be very difficult for you. Take the time to do this Diagnostic Test seriously and check your answers and the explanations closely after completing the test.

For the Mathematical Reasoning Test, general calculator instructions are available on screen by clicking the Calculator Reference button. For an official calculator tutorial for the TI-30XS on-screen calculator, visit www.atomiclearning.com/ti30xs.

You will be provided with a list of mathematical formulas for your reference similar to the one provided on the following page.

IMPORTANT NOTE: The official formula sheet can be found online at www.gedtestingservice.com/uploads/files/15a95 1dfbdd875be5a7a73aa7912e2a0.pdf. Our version on the following page is a bit more thorough to help you as you study for the Mathematical Reasoning Test.

Formulas	
AREA of a:	
square	Area = side^2
rectangle	Area = length × width
parallelogram	Area = base × height
triangle	Area $= \dfrac{1}{2}$ base × height
trapezoid	Area $= \dfrac{1}{2} \times (\text{base}_1 + \text{base}_2) \times \text{height}$
circle	Area $= \pi \times \text{radius}^2$; π is approximately equal to 3.14
PERIMETER of a:	
square	Perimeter = 4 × side
rectangle	Perimeter = (2 × length) + (2 × width)
triangle	Perimeter = side$_1$ + side$_2$ + side$_3$
CIRCUMFERENCE of a: circle	Circumference $= \pi \times$ diameter; π is approximately equal to 3.14
VOLUME of a:	
cube	Volume = edge^3
rectangular solid	Volume = length × width × height
square pyramid	Volume $= \dfrac{1}{3} (\text{base edge})^2 \times \text{height}$
cylinder	Volume $= \pi \times \text{radius}^2 \times \text{height}$; π is approximately equal to 3.14
cone	Volume $= \dfrac{1}{3} \times \pi \times \text{radius}^2 \times \text{height}$; π is approximately equal to 3.14
COORDINATE GEOMETRY	distance between points $= \sqrt{(x_2 - x_1)^2 + (y_2 - y_1)^2}$; (x_1, y_1) and (x_2, y_2) are two points on a plane slope of a line $= \dfrac{y_2 - y_1}{x_2 - x_1}$; (x_1, y_1) and (x_2, y_2) are two points on the line
PYTHAGOREAN THEOREM	$a^2 + b^2 = c^2$; a and b are sides, and c is the hypotenuse of a right triangle
MEASURES OF CENTRAL TENDENCY	**mean** $= \dfrac{x_1 + x_2 + \ldots + x_n}{n}$, where x's are the values for which a mean is desired and n is the total number of values for x **median** = the middle value of an odd number of ordered numbers in a set, and halfway between the two middle values of an even number of ordered numbers
SIMPLE INTEREST	interest = principal × rate (entered as a decimal) × time
DISTANCE	distance = rate × time
TOTAL COST	total cost = (number of units) × (price per unit)

Time: 55 Minutes—25 Questions

Directions: Choose the best answer to each question. Following the instruction for each type of layout indicated, mark your answers on a separate sheet of paper.

On the 2014 GED® Mathematical Reasoning Test, an on-screen calculator is available for all but the first five questions. On the remaining questions, there is an icon to bring up the calculator if you need it, but remember that each diversion takes time and this is a timed test. Practice doing the items in the most time-efficient manner—without a calculator—to leave yourself some time at the end for reviewing items you are uncertain of and completing any items you may have skipped. For this Diagnostic Test, you do not need a calculator to answer any of the questions.

If a question is not standard multiple choice, the item type will be identified directly before the question.

1. Alvin was shopping for two pairs of jeans. Every store he went to seemed to have a sale. Store A was offering the $49.99 jeans for half off; Store B had the same jeans on sale for 50% off; Store C was offering "buy one get the second pair free"; and Store D had the same jeans for $25. Where should Alvin buy his jeans to get the best buy?
   - **(A)** Store A
   - **(B)** Store B
   - **(C)** Store C
   - **(D)** It doesn't matter.

Drop-down

2. Liz was getting serious about dieting and wanted to lose 12 pounds before the wedding, which was 12 weeks away. She was eating an average of 2,000 calories per day and would have to cut her overall intake by 3,500 calories for each pound she wanted to lose. She would have to cut out _____ calories of her diet each day to reach her weight-loss goal.
   - **(A)** 12
   - **(B)** 500
   - **(C)** 6,000
   - **(D)** 42,000

Fill-in-the-blank

3. Willie bought a new car that was guaranteed to average 36 miles per gallon in the city. For the second fill-up, the cost was $105.35 and the cost per gallon of gasoline was $3.01. If Willie knew how far he had traveled since he had first filled up the gas tank, what arithmetic operation should he use to calculate his average mileage per gallon? Enter your answer in the box below.

4. Georgina went shopping but discovered she had brought only $10 with her. She placed the following items into her shopping cart: bread for $2.49, a gallon of milk for $3.80, butter for $2.49, and a chocolate bar for $1.20. She wanted to make sure that she had enough money to pay for her purchases (excluding sales tax). She did a quick mental calculation and came up with an answer. What answer did she come up with?

   (A) She has enough money.
   (B) She should put the chocolate bar back.
   (C) She should buy a smaller container of milk.
   (D) She should buy a few buns instead of bread.

5. Paul was considering redecorating his rectangular living room. He measured the longest wall, the shortest wall, and the height of the room and recorded the following measurements:
   Long wall: 22 feet
   Short wall: 18 feet
   Height: 9 feet
   What assumptions can he make about the room, when planning the renovation?

   (A) The opposite walls will be parallel.
   (B) The long wall and the short wall will be perpendicular.
   (C) The outside walls will be perpendicular to the floor.
   (D) All of the above

Drop-down

6. In the following figure, the rotation of the triangle required for segment *BC* to remain parallel to segment *DE* would be _____.

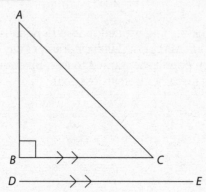

   (A) 45° around *B*
   (B) 90° around *C*
   (C) 135° around *A*
   (D) 180° around *C*

7. In a right triangle with base 30 inches and perpendicular side 20 inches, what is the length of the hypotenuse, in inches, to the nearest inch?

   (A) 34
   (B) 35
   (C) 36
   (D) 37

Fill-in-the-blank

8. An acceptable slope for a stairway is 8 inches of rise for each 12 inches of tread or run. A builder wants to build a house with a distance of 9 feet 6 inches between the first floor and the second floor. How many linear feet of room will the stairway occupy on the first floor? Enter your answer in the box below; you may use a decimal point.

9. Georgio wanted to paint the floor in his laundry room. The room measured 25 feet by 12 feet. If the paint he was going to use covered 450 square feet per gallon, how much paint would he use to cover the floor with one coat of paint?

    (A) $\frac{1}{2}$ gallon

    (B) $\frac{2}{3}$ gallon

    (C) $\frac{3}{4}$ gallon

    (D) 1 gallon

10. Sandy knows from experience that she can average 42 miles per hour on the drive from her home to her parents' home. They have invited her to dinner at 5 o'clock sharp to meet some special guests. Sandy calculates that if she leaves at 1:15 p.m., she will arrive on time. How far does Sandy live from her parents?

    (A) 157.5 miles
    (B) 168 miles
    (C) 175.5 miles
    (D) 186.5 miles

Fill-in-the-blank

11. Kelly and Frank were planning to have a swimming pool built in their backyard. The original dimensions were 60 feet long and 20 feet wide, with an average depth of 4 feet. One contractor said that he would build them a pool that would be 20% larger in surface area. How many more cubic feet of water would the larger pool hold? Enter your answer in the box below.

12. From the information in the following graph, what is the most you could save on a 20-gallon fill-up by traveling to the town with the lowest prices?

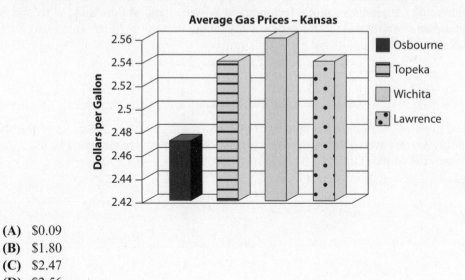

Average Gas Prices – Kansas

- ■ Osbourne
- ▤ Topeka
- ▢ Wichita
- ⊡ Lawrence

(A) $0.09
(B) $1.80
(C) $2.47
(D) $2.56

Questions 13 and 14 are based on the following information.

Surveys were taken regarding television-viewing habits and Internet usage as a percentage of population. The following results were tabulated.

Hours per Week of Television Viewing	
Country	Average Hours of Television Viewed per Week
United Kingdom	26
United States	28
Italy	27
Ireland	23
France	22
Germany	23

Internet Usage as a Percentage of Population	
Country	Internet Usage as a Percentage of Population
United Kingdom	74.4
United States	76.3
Italy	51.7
Ireland	67.3
France	69.3
Germany	75.3

13. From the results of the surveys, what conclusions could you reach?
    (A) People who watch a lot of television don't use the Internet a great deal.
    (B) People who use the Internet don't watch television very much.
    (C) Americans watch a lot of television and use the Internet.
    (D) Italians do not like to use the Internet.

14. One of the researchers said in an interview that American children were above average in weight because of the amount of time they spend watching television and using the Internet. How would you evaluate the researcher's statement?
    (A) The results do not support any such conclusion.
    (B) Anyone who watches a lot of television eats a lot of snacks.
    (C) The researcher was wrong because you shouldn't eat or drink near a computer.
    (D) Commercials on television make you want to eat more.

15. Angela got the following scores on her final exams:

Subject	Score (%)
Geography	91
History	87
Literature	88
Mathematics	72
Science	89

She had hoped for a 90% average and was disappointed in her mathematics score. How many percentage points higher would her mathematics score have to have been for Angela to have gotten her desired average?

    (A) 4.6
    (B) 6.4
    (C) 23
    (D) 85.4

16. Kelly's 11th-grade social studies class was conducting a political poll to determine the relative popularity of each of the major parties. They asked each person present in the class which party they would vote for in the next election and got the following results:
    Democrats: 28
    Republicans: 12
    Undecided: 3
    What conclusion could Kelly reach as a result of her poll?

    (A) The Democrats are going to win the next election.
    (B) The Republicans are going to win the next election.
    (C) Of the 43 people in the class, the majority support the Democrats.
    (D) Undecided people could swing the vote.

Hot Spot

17. The equation $y = mx + b$ has the slope m. If $m = 1$ and the line passes through the point $P(-1,3)$, what is the y-intercept? Mark the y-intercept on the coordinate-plane grid. To answer, blacken the appropriate oval on the grid below.

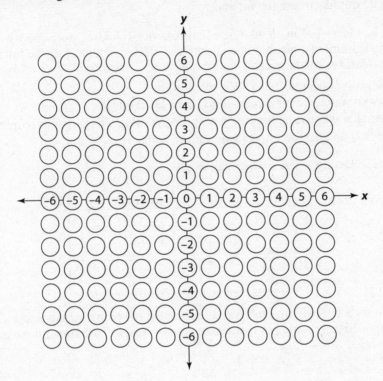

Drag-and-drop

18. Donald went shopping for clothes and was offered the following deal during a big sale: He could get 30% off the regular price for trousers, 45% off the regular price for shirts, and 50% off the regular price for overcoats. Donald needs four pairs of trousers, six shirts, and one overcoat. Complete the equation that could be used to calculate his total cost if the total spent is represented by T, the regular price of a pair of trousers is represented by P, the regular price of a shirt is represented by S, and the regular price of an overcoat is represented by C. Of the eight variables given below, drag the correct value into each box to complete the equation.

(To answer, write in the appropriate variable in each box to complete the equation.)

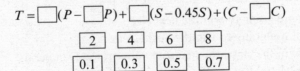

$$T = \boxed{}(P - \boxed{}P) + \boxed{}(S - 0.45S) + (C - \boxed{}C)$$

2	4	6	8
0.1	0.3	0.5	0.7

19. Francis wanted to write a series of equations to represent a group of parallel lines intersecting the y-axis in a sequence of points. What parameter would she have to change in each equation to get the required result?

    $y = mx + b$, where m is the slope and b is the y coordinate of the y-intercept.

    (A) y

    (B) m

    (C) x

    (D) b

20. Andy and a couple of his friends were sitting around watching a documentary about the pyramids in Egypt. Andy wondered how much paint it would take to paint the outside of a flat-sided pyramid, like the ones in the art sculpture outside their school. The program had said that one of the pyramids, said to be that of Sneferu, was 300 feet tall with a square base measuring 470 feet on each side. His friends looked up the formula for finding the lateral surface area of a pyramid and found it to be

    $A = \dfrac{PL}{2}$, where A is the surface area of the external slopes, P is the base perimeter, and L is the slant

    height. Approximately how many square feet would have to be painted to cover the external slopes of

    a flat-sided pyramid with these measurements?

    (A) 1,880

    (B) 220,900

    (C) 290,206

    (D) 358,234

Drop-down

21. Solve the following, where $a = 1$, $b = 6$, and $c = 5$.

    $$\frac{-b \pm \sqrt{b^2 - 4ac}}{2a} =$$

    The solution would be _____.

    (A) -5 or -1

    (B) $-\dfrac{5}{2}$ or $-\dfrac{1}{2}$

    (C) $-\dfrac{2}{5}$ or $-\dfrac{1}{3}$

    (D) 5 or 1

22. Solve the following system of equations for x:

    $$2x + 3y = 12$$
    $$3x + 4y = 6$$

    (A) $x = -30$

    (B) $x = -15$

    (C) $x = 15$

    (D) $x = 30$

23. What effect would doubling the value of c have on E in the equation $E = mc^2$ if the value of m remains constant?

    (A) E would double in value.
    (B) It would have no effect.
    (C) E would be four times its value.
    (D) E would be eight times its value.

Drop-down

24. Solve the following equation for d, where $a = 2$, $b = 5$, and $c = 2$.

$$d = \sqrt{b^2 - 4ac}$$

    d would equal _____.

    (A) 1
    (B) 2
    (C) 3
    (D) 4

25. In the equation $y = mx + b$, how would increasing b by 3 change the value of y if the other variables stay the same?

    (A) y would be 3 times larger.
    (B) y would be one-third of its value.
    (C) y would increase by 3.
    (D) y would decrease by 3.

IF YOU FINISH BEFORE TIME IS CALLED, CHECK YOUR WORK ON THIS SECTION ONLY. DO NOT WORK ON ANY OTHER SECTION IN THE TEST.

Science

The GED® Science Test is essentially a test of reading comprehension. You need to have some basic science knowledge, but you are not expected to memorize specific scientific information. For reading comprehension strategies, see "Reading Comprehension Strategies" (pages 9–17) in Chapter I. The Science Practice Test in Chapter XIII is longer and will be closer to the actual items on the test, but without knowing the basics, the more complex items will be very difficult for you. Take the time to do this Diagnostic Test and check your answers and the explanations closely after completing the test.

Time: 45 Minutes—25 Questions

Directions: Choose the best answer to each item. Mark your answers on a separate sheet of paper.

Questions 1 and 2 refer to the following passage.

All matter is made up of atoms, but atoms are made up of particles called electrons, neutrons, and protons. Because these are all so small that they cannot be seen by any ordinary means, there are theories about what they look like and how they behave. In the seventeenth and eighteenth centuries, scientists began to experiment with different substances and needed a plausible explanation for their behavior under certain circumstances. It was not until recently, with the development of scanning electron microscopes, that scientists could demonstrate that atoms were composed of two types of subatomic particles and each was differently charged. The negatively charged electrons form a cloud around the nucleus of the atom. Inside the nucleus are positively charged protons and neutrons, which have a neutral charge. Scientists believe that all the parts of the atom are in constant motion.

1. The nucleus of an atom is composed of

   (A) Electrons only
   (B) Protons only
   (C) Neutrons only
   (D) Protons and neutrons

2. Why would scientists assume that the description in the passage is the configuration of an atom?

   (A) They read about it in other scientific journals.
   (B) It is a similar configuration to the solar system.
   (C) This configuration would explain some of the observed behaviors of matter.
   (D) Atoms cannot be solid throughout.

Questions 3 and 4 are based on the following passage.

Have you ever picked up an old iron tool and found it covered with a flaky brown substance called rust? Have you ever wondered how it formed there? Rust, or ferric oxide, is formed by a chemical reaction between iron and the oxygen in air or water and can only be prevented by mechanically isolating the iron from oxygen. This is most commonly accomplished by completely coating the iron with a substance that will not allow oxygen to pass through it.

3. How can you prevent rust from forming?

    (A) Wash the iron with water.
    (B) Scrape the surface of the iron.
    (C) Cover the iron with a protective barrier, such as paint, to keep oxygen away.
    (D) Remove any hydrogen from near the iron.

Fill-in-the-blank

4. According to the passage, the scientific name for rust is _____. Enter your answer in the box below.

Questions 5 through 7 refer to the following passage.

Alvin's hobby is drag racing. He loves the feel of the car shooting away when he stomps on the accelerator and the sudden jerk when the parachute is deployed to slow him down. Janice, Alvin's friend, was telling him that drag racing is an example of Newton's First Law of Motion. She explained that the car will remain at rest until an unbalanced force acts on it. By depressing the accelerator, Alvin causes the engine to produce an unbalanced force through the rear wheels and the car takes off. Theoretically, the car would keep going forever, but Alvin releases the parachute, which causes an unbalanced force in the opposite direction and the car slows to a stop. Alvin looked at Janice and assured her that it was still fun.

5. Drag racing is an example of

    (A) A scientific experiment
    (B) The result of the effect of unbalanced forces
    (C) Newton's Third Law of Motion
    (D) Einstein's theory of Sequential Forces

6. A parachute slowing down a drag racer is an example of

    (A) Newton's First Law of Motion
    (B) Newton's Second Law of Motion
    (C) Effective braking
    (D) Good driving

Fill-in-the-blank

7. The _____ provides the power to accelerate the drag racer forward. Enter your answer in the box below.

Question 8 refers to the following passage.

The law of conservation of energy states that in an isolated system, the total amount of energy remains constant and, thus, energy cannot be created or destroyed. This really upset Hannah, who wanted to build a perpetual motion machine as her science project.

8. Why could Hannah not accomplish her objective?

   (A) There is no scientific basis for perpetual motion.
   (B) Energy cannot be created, so the machine could never produce any additional power.
   (C) The government would not allow it.
   (D) Energy cannot be destroyed, and this machine would destroy energy.

9. Laurie was very patient when she was asked to perform the following experiment: She was given a cube of ice, 6 inches on each side, in a glass container and asked to watch it until it changed its state and then to apply heat until it changed its state again. What would explain the second change of state?

   (A) Evaporation
   (B) Condensation
   (C) Melting
   (D) Sublimation

Question 10 refers to the following passage.

The cell is the smallest and most basic unit of life. Human beings, for example, have about 60 trillion to 100 trillion cells. On the other extreme, bacteria are only one cell and that one cell can infect a human being and make him sick. The size of the cell has nothing to do with its potential. An unfertilized ostrich egg cell is the largest known cell, weighing over 3 pounds, while an average cell weighs about 1 nanogram.

10. According to the passage, what is the weight of an unfertilized ostrich egg cell?

   (A) 1 nanogram
   (B) 1 pound
   (C) 10 trillion nanograms
   (D) 3 pounds or more

Questions 11 and 12 are based on the following passage.

DNA stores the basis of heredity in its genetic code. The DNA molecule is a double helix and is constructed in a way that it is capable of self-replication. All living creatures have cells comprised of DNA. Hereditary traits (called genes) are passed on from generation to generation through the DNA.

Heredity is the transmission of characteristics from one generation to the next. If your parents had red hair or blue eyes, there is a greater chance of your possessing these characteristics. If you have two ears and one nose and your parents had the same, that is part of being an organism commonly called a human being and not connected with the transmission of specific traits.

11. Heredity contributes to

   (A) Children of blue-eyed mothers always having blue eyes.

   (B) Parents with red hair having blonde children.

   (C) Parents passing some characteristics to their children.

   (D) Children looking exactly like their parents.

12. The basis of heredity is stored in the genetic code of

   (A) NaCl

   (B) H_2O

   (C) DNA

   (D) HCl

Question 13 is based on the following passage.

All species undergo gradual changes in order to be able to survive and reproduce in their environment. In the animal kingdom, the environment is often competitive and dangerous, and a life-form that is less likely to survive in that environment would leave fewer offspring and, thus, be less likely to pass on its traits to the next generation.

On the other hand, a life-form that is better suited genetically to a particular environment would be more likely to mate and reproduce, thus producing offspring with these advantageous traits. Because these traits assisted in their survival, their descendants stand a better chance of inheriting these traits and surviving to reproduce again.

There is a gradual but constant shift toward life-forms that are well adapted to their environment, and this can produce new species that differ from their ancestors.

13. Why are most animals living in their natural habitat most likely to have inherited traits from their parents that made this possible?

   (A) If they inherited traits that were counter-productive to survival, they probably wouldn't survive.

   (B) The parents would protect them against danger.

   (C) The children would move to a safer environment.

   (D) The children would learn new traits.

Fill-in-the-blank

14. Have you ever wondered why your friend has red hair and you have black hair? If you look at the members of your friend's family, there are probably a number of people with red hair. In your family, there are probably none, unless someone uses hair dye. Characteristics like hair color are hereditary and can be passed on from generation to generation through your genes.

    The means of transmission of characteristics like hair color is _____. Enter your answer in the box below.

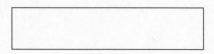

Questions 15 and 16 are based on the following passage.

Living organisms depend on each other for survival. Small fish depend on a supply of plankton for food. Larger fish depend on small fish to provide them with their food. Humans eat larger fish as a source of protein. Humans produce garbage, some of which finds its way into the waterways, providing food to the fish.

Ecosystems are composed of many factors. Among the living factors are the consumers and the producers. Producers such as plants create food through their internal processes. A plant can produce sugars using sunlight and carbon dioxide through a process called photosynthesis; consumers such as humans and cows can then eat the plants and survive. Animals that eat only plants are called herbivores, animals that eat meat are called carnivores, and animals that eat both are called omnivores.

Fill-in-the-blank

15. According to the passage, _____ and _____ are among the living factors of an ecosystem. Enter your answers in the boxes below.

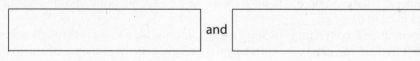

16. A herbivore's diet consists of

    (A) Only tasty recipes
    (B) Only plants
    (C) Only eggs
    (D) Parts of dead animals

Questions 17 and 18 refer to the following passage.

Alice has a new puppy and wants to train it to sit at her right side on command, but she has no idea how to do it. Her father, who used to train dogs, told her that a famous scientist named B. F. Skinner developed a system of changing the behaviors of animals that might help her. If she gave the dog a treat every time it obeyed the command, the chances of the dog obeying the command would increase until it would obey each time.

17. Which scientist developed the system that helped Alice train her puppy?

   (A) Einstein
   (B) Newton
   (C) Skinner
   (D) Abrams

18. How did Alice's father suggest she train her puppy?

   (A) Pick up the puppy and speak softly to it when it did what Alice wanted.
   (B) Ignore the puppy when it made a mistake.
   (C) Give the puppy a treat for doing the correct action.
   (D) Study books by famous scientists.

Drop-down

19. The passage below is incomplete. For each blank, choose the answer choices that best complete the sentences.

Harnessing the sun's energy to do work is an example of solar power, and it has the potential to provide much of Earth's energy requirements. Using photovoltaic cells, this solar energy can be directly converted into electricity. Some of us have used solar power without thinking about it. Photovoltaic cells often are used in (i) _____.

The other manner of converting the sun's energy into usable energy is through concentration. If you imagine a giant magnifying glass concentrating the energy from the sun on a point, you get the idea. The point would get so hot that, if it were flammable, it would burst into flames. The heat produced is a form of energy, but solar power is limited in use because (ii) _____.

Blank (i)	Blank (ii)
(A) calculators	**(A)** it is expensive
(B) washing machines	**(B)** it cannot be turned on and off at will
(C) radios	**(C)** appliances are not suited for it
(D) cars	**(D)** the sun doesn't shine constantly

Questions 20 and 21 are based on the following figure.

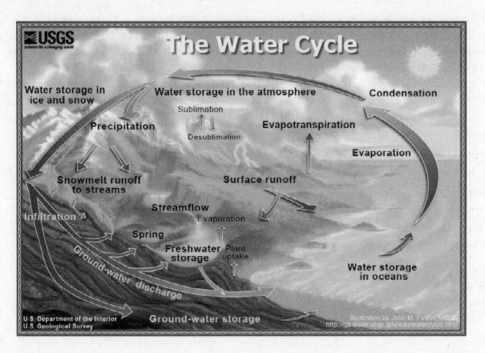

Hot Spot

20. Water exists in which of the following? Click on the diagram with your mouse to select all that apply.

    (To answer, write the letter of all answer choices that apply.)

    (A) Oceans
    (B) Ice and snow
    (C) Springs and streams
    (D) The atmosphere

21. A boater hits a rock in a body of water he has sailed before, without any problems in the past, because the water level is very low. According to the diagram, which part of the water cycle is creating this problem?

    (A) Condensation
    (B) Ground water storage
    (C) Insufficient ground water discharge
    (D) Runoff

Questions 22 through 24 refer to the following passage.

At first, there was a large cloud of dust and gases rotating through space around the center of the Milky Way (as a result of the Big Bang). This cloud was composed of helium and hydrogen gases. The gas cloud began to contract and rotate, gaining angular speed. This caused it to flatten into a disk, with most of the mass concentrated at the center where it began to heat up.

At the center, these conditions led to the nuclear fusion of hydrogen and helium, thus forming the star we know as the sun. Fragments rotating around this new star began to form bigger and bigger particles, which attracted other particles through gravitational attraction. The planets began to revolve around the sun, creating what we know as the solar system.

22. What was the chemical composition of the gaseous cloud that was rotating through space around the center of the Milky Way?

   (A) Dust
   (B) Chunks of rock
   (C) Hydrogen and helium
   (D) Oxygen and hydrogen

Fill-in-the-blank

23. Nuclear _____ formed the star known as the sun. Enter your answer in the box below.

24. The process that caused the particles to gather to form planets was

   (A) Centrifugal force
   (B) Centripetal force
   (C) Magnetism
   (D) Gravitational force

Question 25 is based on the following stimulus, an excerpt from www.jpl.nasa.gov/news/fact_sheets/LDSD.pdf.

Short Answer

Stimulus

The Red Planet is Different

Note: LDSD is an acronym for Low Density Supersonic Decelerators

Landing on Mars is not like landing on Earth, which has a dense atmosphere, or on the moon, which has no atmosphere. Mars has a tricky environment somewhere in-between: it has too much atmosphere to allow rockets alone to land heavy vehicles, as is done on the moon, but too little atmosphere to land vehicles from space purely with friction and parachutes, as is done on Earth.

In addition, parachutes for Mars surface-bound craft must be enormous, because the atmosphere is too thin to fill a parachute like those used on Earth. Even with large parachutes, powerful retro rockets or rugged airbags have been required to complete the landing. These are some of the factors that make delivering large payloads to the surface of Mars extremely difficult.

It is not practical to test new, unproven descent technologies at Mars. Instead, NASA intends to use the very thin air found high in Earth's stratosphere as a "local" test space that duplicates many of the most important aspects of Mars' low-density atmosphere.

Limits of Viking-Era Deceleration Techniques

NASA's current parachute-based deceleration system has been used since the Viking Program of the 1970s. This system has reached the limit of the amount of mass that it can deliver to Mars. Additionally, because of the extremely thin Martian atmosphere, regions at high elevations—such as mountainous areas and the high-altitude southern plains—will remain inaccessible until a new landing method can be developed and proven to work.

The new deceleration capabilities provided by NASA's Low Density Supersonic Decelerator (LDSD) project should permit landings at higher altitudes, with greater spacecraft masses and higher precision. A successful LDSD test program would bring these new technologies to sufficient readiness levels allowing them to be infused into potential future robotic and human mission designs.

25.

> PROMPT
>
> NASA is experimenting and testing ways of safely landing large loads on the surface of Mars. Explain why this development is important and what sorts of materials and people would be transported to Mars in the future. Include the problems and challenges of finding solutions to this problem in your answer.
>
> Type your response in the box (for this Practice Test, write your response on a separate sheet of paper). This short answer item may take you about 10 minutes to complete. See the answer explanation for tips on how your response can be self-scored.

IF YOU FINISH BEFORE TIME IS CALLED, CHECK YOUR WORK ON THIS SECTION ONLY. DO NOT WORK ON ANY OTHER SECTION IN THE TEST.

Social Studies

Section 1

Time: 40 Minutes—30 Questions

Directions: Choose the best answer to each question. Mark your answers on a separate sheet of paper.

Questions 1 through 5 refer to the following excerpt from U.S. History For Dummies, *2nd Edition, by Steve Wiegand, copyright 2009 by Wiley Publishing, Inc. Reprinted with permission of John Wiley & Sons, Inc.*

Christopher Columbus was born in Genoa, Italy, in 1451, the son of a weaver. In addition to running a successful map-making business with his brother, Bartholomew, Columbus was a first-class sailor. He also became convinced that his ticket to fame and fortune depended on finding a western route to the Indies.

Starting in the 1470s, Columbus and his brother began making the rounds of European capitals, looking for ships and financial backing for his idea. His demands were exorbitant. In return for his services, Columbus wanted the title of Admiral of the Oceans, 10 percent of all the loot he found, and the ability to pass governorship of every country he discovered to his heirs.

The rulers of England and France said no thanks, as did some of the city-states that made up Italy. The king of Portugal also told him to take a hike. So in 1486, Columbus went to Spain. Queen Isabella listened to his pitch, and she, like the other European rulers, said no. But she did appoint a commission to look into the idea and decided to put Columbus on the payroll in the meantime.

The meantime stretched out for six years. Finally, convinced she wasn't really risking much because chances were that he wouldn't return, Isabella gave her approval in January 1492. Columbus was on his way.

Partly because of error and partly because of wishful thinking, Columbus estimated the distance to the Indies at approximately 2,500 miles, which was about 7,500 miles short. But after a voyage of about five weeks, he and his crews, totalling 90 men, did find land at around 2 a.m. on October 12, 1492. It was an island in the Bahamas, which he called San Salvador. The timing of the discovery was good; it came even as the crews of the *Nina, Pinta,* and *Santa Maria* were muttering about a mutiny.

1. How did Columbus hope to gain fame and fortune?

   (A) By becoming a weaver
   (B) By becoming a successful map-maker
   (C) By becoming a first-class sailor
   (D) By finding a route to the Indies

2. Why did Columbus have trouble financing his voyage?

   (A) He made exorbitant demands.
   (B) He wanted to be Admiral of the Oceans.
   (C) He wanted 10 percent of the loot.
   (D) He wanted governorships for his heirs.

Fill-in-the-blank

3. Which country finally agreed to support Columbus? Enter your answer in the box below.

4. In which year did Columbus gain approval for his voyage?

   (A) 1451
   (B) 1470
   (C) 1489
   (D) 1492

5. Where was San Salvador located?

   (A) In the Indies
   (B) In the Bahamas
   (C) In Jamaica
   (D) In Trinidad

Questions 6 through 10 refer to the following excerpt from U.S. History For Dummies, *2nd Edition, by Steve Wiegand, copyright 2009 by Wiley Publishing, Inc. Reprinted with permission of John Wiley & Sons, Inc.*

In spite of his flaws, Washington was a born leader, one of those men who raised spirits and expectations simply by showing up. He was tall and athletic, an expert horseman and a good dancer. He wasn't particularly handsome—his teeth were bad, and he wasn't proud of his hippopotamus ivory and gold dentures, so he seldom smiled. But he had a commanding presence, and his troops felt they could depend on him. He was also a bit of an actor. Once while reading something to his troops, he donned his spectacles, and then apologized, explaining his eyes had grown dim in the service of his country. Some of his audience wept.

He also had an indomitable spirit. His army was ragged, undisciplined, and undependable, with a staggering average desertion rate of 20 percent. His bosses in Congress were often indecisive, quarrelsome, and indifferent. But Washington simply refused to give up. Just as important, he refused the temptation to try to become a military dictator, which he may easily have done.

One of the reasons many men loved him was that Washington was personally brave, often on the frontlines of battles, and always among the last to retreat. He was also incredibly lucky. In one battle, Washington rode unexpectedly into a group of British soldiers, most of whom fired at him at short range. They all missed.

Above all, Washington was a survivor. He drove the British army crazy (they called him "the old fox" even though he wasn't all that old), never staying to fight battles he was losing, and never fully retreating. He bought his new country time—time to find allies and time to wear down the British will to keep fighting.

Drag-and-drop

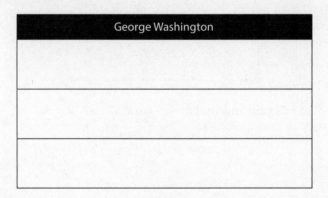

George Washington

6. Drag the characteristics that apply to George Washington into the boxes above.

   (To answer, write the letter of all answer choices that apply on your answer sheet.)

   (A) He raised spirits and expectations.
   (B) He was handsome.
   (C) He was an expert horseman.
   (D) He was a good dancer.

7. Which of these statements apply to how Washington felt about his dentures?

   (A) His teeth were bad.
   (B) He seldom smiled.
   (C) He wasn't proud.
   (D) He proudly displayed them.

8. Which of the following does NOT describe Washington's troops?

   (A) They had a staggering desertion rate.
   (B) They were indecisive and quarrelsome.
   (C) They had an indomitable spirit.
   (D) They were disciplined and dependable.

Fill-in-the-blank

9. The desertion rate among Washington's troops was _____ percent. Enter your answer in the box below.

10. Why did the British call Washington "the old fox"?

    (A) He was a survivor.
    (B) He drove them crazy.
    (C) He never fully retreated.
    (D) All of the above

Questions 11 through 15 refer to the following excerpt from U.S. History For Dummies, *2nd Edition, by Steve Wiegand, copyright 2009 by Wiley Publishing, Inc. Reprinted with permission of John Wiley & Sons, Inc.*

Unions weren't alone in their aspirations for improving the lives of working-class Americans. In Detroit, a generally unlikable, self-taught engineer named Henry Ford decided that everyone should have an automobile, and, thus, the right to go where they wanted, when they wanted. So, Ford's company made one model—the Model T. You could have it in any color you wanted, Ford said, as long as it was black. And because of his assembly-line approach to putting them together, you could have it relatively cheaply.

Ford's plan was a good one. The price of a Model T dropped from $850 in 1908 to $290 by 1924. As prices dropped, sales went up. Sales went from 10,000 in 1909 to just under a million in 1921. Within two decades, Ford and other car-makers had indelibly changed American life. The average family could now literally get away from it all, which created a new sense of independence and self-esteem. Because of the availability of the automobile, new industries, from tire production to roadside cafes, sprang up. And by the end of the 1920s, it could be persuasively argued that the automobile had become the single most dominant element in the U.S. economy.

When it came to getting from here to there, others were looking up to the skies. In December 1903, two brothers who owned a bicycle shop in Dayton, Ohio, went to Kitty Hawk, North Carolina. There they pulled off the world's first powered, sustained, and controlled flights with a machine they had built. Fearful of losing their patent rights, Orville and Wilbur Wright didn't go public with their airplane until 1908, by which time other inventors and innovators were also making planes. Unlike the automobile, however, the airplane's popularity didn't really take off until after its usefulness was proved in World War I.

11. Henry Ford believed that everyone should

    (A) Join a union
    (B) Be an engineer
    (C) Own an automobile
    (D) Have an improved life

12. What was Ford's greatest contribution to the auto industry?

    (A) The Model T
    (B) The assembly line
    (C) New industries
    (D) The U.S. economy

13. How did Ford increase sales of his automobiles?

    (A) By lowering prices
    (B) Through better advertising
    (C) By increasing tire production
    (D) By building roadside cafes

14. What impact did the availability of the automobile have on the U.S. economy?

   (A) It caused the Great Depression.
   (B) It changed American life.
   (C) It led to increased self-esteem.
   (D) It became a dominant element in the economy.

15. Why did the Wright Brothers become famous?

   (A) They owned a bicycle shop.
   (B) They built a machine.
   (C) They made the first powered, sustained flight.
   (D) They influenced World War I.

Questions 16 through 20 refer to the following political cartoon from GED® For Dummies, *by Murray Shukyn and Dale E. Shuttleworth, Ph.D., copyright 2003 by Wiley Publishing, Inc. Reprinted with permission of John Wiley & Sons, Inc.*

16. What is the direct impact of a rise in oil prices?

   (A) Sales of SUVs decrease.
   (B) People do more traveling.
   (C) Oil companies lose profit.
   (D) Gasoline prices rise.

17. When oil prices rise, the cost of living

    (A) Falls
    (B) Rises
    (C) Remains unchanged
    (D) None of the above

18. What adjective best describes the characters in the SUV?

    (A) Joyful
    (B) Surprised
    (C) Angry
    (D) Wasteful

19. What phrase does NOT describe the SUV?

    (A) Energy saver
    (B) Gas guzzler
    (C) Monster truck
    (D) Pollution machine

Drag-and-drop

Energy Crisis Solutions

20. Drag the solutions that the cartoon suggests for the energy crisis into the boxes above.

    (To answer, write the letter of all answer choices that apply on your answer sheet.)

    (A) Turn up the heat
    (B) Boil, not fry
    (C) Reduce lubrication
    (D) Buy smaller vehicles

Questions 21 through 25 refer to the following excerpt from U.S. History For Dummies, *2nd Edition, by Steve Wiegand, copyright 2009 by Wiley Publishing, Inc. Reprinted with permission of John Wiley & Sons, Inc.*

On August 23, 2005, a hurricane formed over the Bahamas and headed toward the southeastern United States. Called Katrina, it crossed Florida, picked up strength over the Gulf of Mexico, and made landfall in southeast Louisiana on August 29.

While Katrina's 125-mile-per-hour winds—sending beds flying out of hotel windows—and 10 inches of rain were bad enough, a storm surge of more than 28 feet devastated the Mississippi coastal cities of Gulfport and Biloxi. But the greatest damage was reserved for the region's largest city—New Orleans.

Nicknamed "the Big Easy," most of New Orleans is below sea level. Under Katrina's onslaught, levees supposed to protect the city gave way in more than 50 places, and 80 percent of the city was flooded. While most of New Orleans's 1.2 million residents were evacuated (many to the city of Houston, Texas), thousands either refused to leave or could not.

The disaster claimed more than 1,800 lives and destroyed 200,000 homes. Damage estimates ranged as high as $125 billion, making it the most expensive hurricane in U.S. history. It wasn't until October 11 that the last of the floodwaters were pumped out.

By then, a hurricane of criticism had whipped up over the federal government's response to the disaster. The criticism ranged from condemning the government's slow response in some areas with regard to the evacuation process to providing adequate temporary housing after the storm. There were also charges that the slow response was due, in part, to the fact that many of New Orleans's residents were poor African Americans. Bush's approval ratings sank to the lowest of his presidency—at least to this point.

21. The "Big Easy" refers to which of the following?

   (A) Florida
   (B) Louisiana
   (C) New Orleans
   (D) Houston

Drag-and-drop

Features of Hurricane Katrina

22. Drag the phrases that describe features of Hurricane Katrina into the boxes above.

    (To answer, write the letter of all answer choices that apply on your answer sheet.)

    (A) 125 mile-per-hour winds
    (B) Beds flying out of windows
    (C) 10 inches of rain
    (D) 28-foot surges

23. Why was New Orleans in danger?

    (A) It is located below sea level.
    (B) It is the region's largest city.
    (C) Thousands of residents refused to leave.
    (D) Hundreds of thousands of homes were destroyed.

24. What was the primary reason that the federal government was criticized?

    (A) Many residents were poor African Americans.
    (B) Bush's approval ratings dropped.
    (C) The evacuation process was slow.
    (D) The federal government was slow to respond.

25. How will Katrina be remembered in the United States?

    (A) People were evacuated to Houston.
    (B) It was the most expensive hurricane in U.S. history.
    (C) The floodwaters were pumped out.
    (D) There were $125 billion in damages.

Questions 26 and 27 are based on the following map.

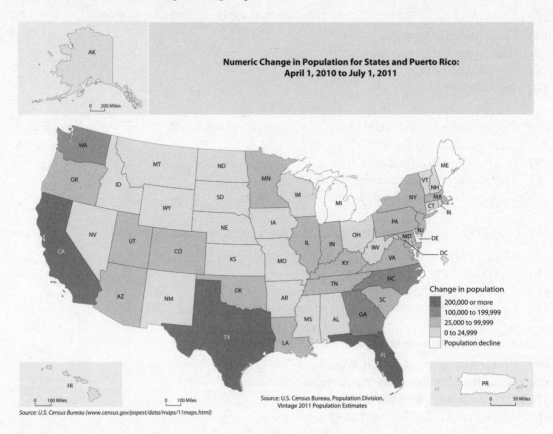

Numeric Change in Population for States and Puerto Rico:
April 1, 2010 to July 1, 2011

Change in population
- 200,000 or more
- 100,000 to 199,999
- 25,000 to 99,999
- 0 to 24,999
- Population decline

Source: U.S. Census Bureau, Population Division,
Vintage 2011 Population Estimates

Source: U.S. Census Bureau (www.census.gov/popest/data/maps/11maps.html)

26. Based on this map, which areas experienced declines in population between 2010 and 2011?

    (A) California, Texas, and Florida
    (B) Michigan and Maine
    (C) Montana, Wyoming, and Nebraska
    (D) Puerto Rico, Maine, and Michigan

Hot Spot

27. According to the map, which East Coast states had a change in population GREATER than 100,000?
    Click on the map with your mouse to select all that apply.

    (To answer, write the letter of all answer choices that apply on your answer sheet.)

    (A) North Carolina
    (B) South Carolina
    (C) Georgia
    (D) Florida

Questions 28 and 29 are based on the following diagram.

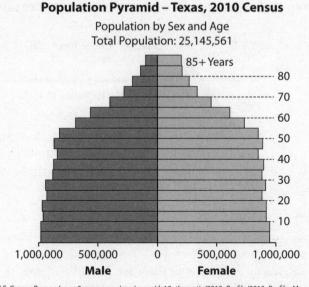

Population Pyramid – Texas, 2010 Census

Population by Sex and Age
Total Population: 25,145,561

Source: U.S. Census Bureau (www2.census.gov/geo/maps/dc10_thematic/2010_Profile/2010_Profile_Map_Texas.pdf)

28. How does the proportion of men to women change as the population ages?

    (A) There are more women than men.
    (B) The ratio of men to women remains about the same.
    (C) There are more men than women.
    (D) None of the above

29. How big of an age group does each bar in the pyramid represent?

    (A) One year
    (B) Five years
    (C) Ten years
    (D) None of the above

Question 30 is based on the following diagram.

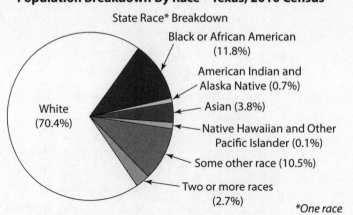

Population Breakdown By Race – Texas, 2010 Census

State Race* Breakdown

Black or African American (11.8%)

American Indian and Alaska Native (0.7%)

Asian (3.8%)

Native Hawaiian and Other Pacific Islander (0.1%)

Some other race (10.5%)

Two or more races (2.7%)

White (70.4%)

One race

Source: U.S. Census Bureau (www2.census.gov/geo/maps/dc10_thematic/2010_Profile/2010_Profile_Map_Texas.pdf)

30. The subtitle of this graph has an asterisk after the word *Race*. What does that mean?

   (A) There is an important explanatory note somewhere on the diagram.
   (B) Hispanic individuals are excluded from the calculations.
   (C) Most of the population is white.
   (D) This diagram does not give details of mixed race statistics.

IF YOU FINISH BEFORE TIME IS CALLED, CHECK YOUR WORK ON THIS SECTION ONLY. DO NOT WORK ON ANY OTHER SECTION IN THE TEST.

Section 2

Time: 25 Minutes

Read the following extract from a White House press release from December 4, 2013, containing remarks from President Obama on economic mobility. Using quotations from the President's speech and your own knowledge of American history and current events, you have 25 minutes to write an essay to discuss to what extent social and economic equality (or inequality) is an enduring issue in American history.

You may prepare rough notes before writing the essay, but only the final version will be scored. Pay attention to both your essay style and the proper use of English.

Remember, on the formal test, you will be working on a computer. Your rough notes will be done on an erasable noteboard. The only work evaluated will be what is entered into the computer.

Source: www.whitehouse.gov/the-press-office/2013/12/04/remarks-president-economic-mobility

THEARC
Washington, D.C.
11:31 A.M. EST

THE PRESIDENT: Thank you. (Applause.) Thank you, everybody. ...

Over the last two months, Washington has been dominated by some pretty contentious debates ...

But we know that people's frustrations run deeper than these most recent political battles. Their frustration is rooted in their own daily battles—to make ends meet, to pay for college, buy a home, save for retirement. It's rooted in the nagging sense that no matter how hard they work, the deck is stacked against them. And it's rooted in the fear that their kids won't be better off than they were... And that is a dangerous and growing inequality and lack of upward mobility that has jeopardized middle-class America's basic bargain—that if you work hard, you have a chance to get ahead. ...

It was Abraham Lincoln, a self-described "poor man's son," who started a system of land grant colleges all over this country so that any poor man's son could go learn something new. ...

... Teddy Roosevelt fought for an eight-hour workday, protections for workers, and busted monopolies that kept prices high and wages low.

When millions lived in poverty, FDR fought for Social Security, and insurance for the unemployed, and a minimum wage.

When millions died without health insurance, LBJ fought for Medicare and Medicaid.

Together, we forged a New Deal, declared a War on Poverty in a great society. We built a ladder of opportunity to climb, and stretched out a safety net beneath so that if we fell, it wouldn't be too far, and we could bounce back. And as a result, America built the largest middle class the world has ever known. And for the three decades after World War II, it was the engine of our prosperity. ...

... during the post-World War II years, the economic ground felt stable and secure for most Americans, and the future looked brighter than the past. And for some, that meant following in your old man's footsteps at the local plant, and you knew that a blue-collar job would let you buy a home, and a car, maybe a vacation once in a while, health care, a reliable pension. For others, it meant going to college—in some cases, maybe the first in your family to go to college. And it meant graduating without taking on loads of debt, and being able to count on advancement through a vibrant job market. ...

But starting in the late '70s, this social compact began to unravel. Technology made it easier for companies to do more with less, eliminating certain job occupations. A more competitive world lets companies ship jobs anywhere. And as good manufacturing jobs automated or headed offshore, workers lost their leverage, jobs paid less and offered fewer benefits. ...

And the result is an economy that's become profoundly unequal, and families that are more insecure. I'll just give you a few statistics. Since 1979, when I graduated from high school, our productivity is up by more than 90 percent, but the income of the typical family has increased by less than eight percent. Since 1979, our economy has more than doubled in size, but most of that growth has flowed to a fortunate few.

The top 10 percent no longer takes in one-third of our income—it now takes half. Whereas in the past, the average CEO made about 20 to 30 times the income of the average worker, today's CEO now makes 273 times more. And meanwhile, a family in the top 1 percent has a net worth 288 times higher than the typical family, which is a record for this country.

So the basic bargain at the heart of our economy has frayed. ...Some of you may have seen just last week, the Pope himself spoke about this at eloquent length. "How can it be," he wrote, "that it is not a news item when an elderly homeless person dies of exposure, but it is news when the stock market loses two points?"

... The problem is that alongside increased inequality, we've seen diminished levels of upward mobility in recent years. A child born in the top 20 percent has about a 2-in-3 chance of staying at or near the top. A child born into the bottom 20 percent has a less than 1-in-20 shot at making it to the top. He's 10 times likelier to stay where he is. In fact, statistics show not only that our levels of income inequality rank near countries like Jamaica and Argentina, but that it is harder today for a child born here in America to improve her station in life than it is for children in most of our wealthy allies—countries like Canada or Germany or France. ...

... And rising inequality and declining mobility are also bad for our families and social cohesion—not just because we tend to trust our institutions less, but studies show we actually tend to trust each other less when there's greater inequality. And greater inequality is associated with less mobility between generations. That means it's not just temporary; the effects last. It creates a vicious cycle. ...

... A new study shows that disparities in education, mental health, obesity, absent fathers, isolation from church, isolation from community groups—these gaps are now as much about growing up rich or poor as they are about anything else. The gap in test scores between poor kids and wealthy kids is now nearly twice what it is between white kids and black kids. Kids with working-class parents are 10 times likelier than kids with middle- or upper-class parents to go through a time when their parents have no income. So the fact is this: The opportunity gap in America is now as much about class as it is about race, and that gap is growing. ...

... But government can't stand on the sidelines in our efforts. Because government is us. It can and should reflect our deepest values and commitments. And if we refocus our energies on building an economy that grows for everybody, and gives every child in this country a fair chance at success, then I remain confident that the future still looks brighter than the past, and that the best days for this country we love are still ahead. (Applause.)

Thank you, everybody. God bless you. God bless America. (Applause.)

IF YOU FINISH BEFORE TIME IS CALLED, CHECK YOUR WORK ON THIS SECTION ONLY. DO NOT WORK ON ANY OTHER SECTION IN THE TEST.

Answer Key

Reasoning through Language Arts

Section 1

1. (A)	9. (A)	17. (D)	25. (B)
2. (D)	10. (D)	18. (B)	26. (C)
3. Mark Rutte	11. (B)	19. (D)	27. (D)
4. (C)	12. (C), (D)	20. (C)	28. (B)
5. (A)	13. (C)	21. (B), (C)	29. (B)
6. (B)	14. (B)	22. (C), (D)	30. (C)
7. (D)	15. (A), (C)	23. (C)	
8. (A)	16. (B)	24. (A)	

Mathematical Reasoning

1. (D)	14. (A)
2. (B)	15. (C)
3. division	16. (C)
4. (A)	17. (0,4)
5. (D)	18. $T = \boxed{4}(P - \boxed{0.3}P) + \boxed{6}(S - 0.45S) + (C - \boxed{0.5}C)$
6. (D)	19. (D)
7. (C)	20. (D)
8. 14.25	21. (A)
9. (B)	22. (A)
10. (A)	23. (C)
11. 960	24. (C)
12. (B)	25. (C)
13. (C)	

Science

1. (D)	8. (B)	15. producers; consumers	21. (C)
2. (B)	9. (A)		22. (C)
3. (C)	10. (D)	16. (B)	23. fusion
4. ferric oxide	11. (C)	17. (C)	24. (D)
5. (B)	12. (C)	18. (C)	25. See explanation
6. (A)	13. (A)	19. (A), (D)	
7. motor or engine	14. heredity	20. (A), (B), (C), (D)	

Social Studies

Section 1

1. (D)	9. 20	17. (B)	25. (B)
2. (A)	10. (D)	18. (D)	26. (D)
3. Spain	11. (C)	19. (A)	27. (A), (C), (D)
4. (D)	12. (B)	20. (B), (C), (D)	28. (A)
5. (B)	13. (A)	21. (C)	29. (B)
6. (A), (C), (D)	14. (D)	22. (A), (B), (C), (D)	30. (D)
7. (C)	15. (C)	23. (A)	
8. (D)	16. (D)	24. (D)	

Answer Explanations

Reasoning through Language Arts

Section 1

1. **(A)** President Obama states they are united on imposing costs on Russia in the form of sanctions.

2. **(D)** All of these choices are correct. President Obama clearly lists in his speech those very points as areas in which the Netherlands are contributing.

3. **Mark Rutte** The last name is mentioned near the beginning of President Obama's speech, while the first name is found at the end of the speech in the "thank you" section.

4. **(C)** The Netherlands took part with other NATO countries in placing Patriot Missiles in Turkey (C). While they did help fight piracy, their antipiracy efforts took place off the Horn of Africa, not off Mali (B). There is no mention of the Dutch assisting in Operation Desert Storm (A).

5. **(A)** The President states that sanctions will continue while discussions take place.

6. **(B)** The Netherlands are concerned about rising sea levels. While the other three choices may be of concern, they are not specifically mentioned in the text. Remember, you must pick the most correct answer based on the text.

7. **(D)** Of the specific choices offered, the only one that applies is choice (D), *serving in Afghanistan.*

8. **(A)** T-TIP refers to the Transatlantic Trade and Investment Partnership, an organization to increase trade between the United States and Europe. The other choices are things of concern to the Netherlands, or activities in which they are involved, but they do not answer the question.

9. **(A)** Connie expects an "A" because of the donations her father makes to the school. She does not care if (B) her father has a building named after him, or (C) if he receives an honorary degree, or (D) if he is introduced at a football game. None of those three choices is mentioned in the script.

10. **(D)** She states at the beginning that she needs that "A" to maintain her average for acceptance to graduate school. The other choices might apply but are not mentioned in the text.

11. **(B)** The village was located in a "province of Great Britain." Fort Christina (A) is wrong and the other choices are not mentioned.

12. **(C) and (D)** Van Winkle was not gallant and chivalrous (B); that applied to his forbearers. The fact that he descended from the Van Winkle clan (A) is not a personality trait.

13. **(C)** He was not in the least martial (i.e., warlike), choice (B), nor did he take part in the gossiping (D). The fact that he was henpecked (A) earned him sympathy, but did not account for his popularity.

14. **(B)** Van Winkle's marriage is described as a "domestic tribulation." Don't be fooled by choice (A). His wife, not his marriage is described as a "tolerable blessing." The other choices describe Van Winkle, not his marriage.

15. **(A) and (C)** The passage does not mention that he trained them to fight (D). Per the passage, the dogs didn't bark at him, but there is no mention of them not barking at the children (B).

16. **(B)** The text states that the village wives took his side in all family disputes.

17. **(D)** The text refers to educational travel programs. The rest of that paragraph is an elaboration of that idea.

18. **(B)** This is an example of a negative question. You need to examine the answer choices and find the one that is NOT mentioned in the passage. Retailing is the only service not mentioned in the text.

19. **(D)** All of the listed choices are in the text as constituencies for this business.

20. **(C)** The text mentions income is to be based "on a predetermined rate of commission per passenger."

21. **(B) and (C)** Blank (i): The correct answer is (B). The range met and exceeded all requirements. "Exceeds" is the present tense, unsuitable for statements using the past. Similarly, "will meet" is the wrong tense. Blank (ii): The correct answer is (C). Choices (A) and (B) are run-on sentences, with a comma splice in choice (B). Choice (D) contains a misspelling and has a comma splice.

22. **(C) and (D)** Blank (i): The correct answer is (C). Choice (A) could be used, but the subject-verb agreement is wrong. (B) uses the wrong pronoun, while (D) misuses the verb. Blank (ii): The correct answer is (D). Choice (A) uses a conditional verb, when the action is definite. Choices (B) and (C) both create a sentence fragment.

23. **(C)** Commas are needed to separate the phrase *including receipt of the fees* from the rest of the sentence.

24. **(A)** The word *basis* is used when it should be *basic*.

25. **(B)** There is a spelling error as indicated.

26. **(C)** This is a complex sentence. While it is correct as is, it is clearer if divided into two sentences, as per choice (C). The division is very much an improvement.

27. **(D)** The item is correct as written.

28. **(B)** This is a punctuation error for consistent serial punctuation. The comma after *equipment* should be changed to a semicolon.

29. **(B)** *Popularity* is misused. The proper word here is *population*.

30. **(C)** The verb *allowed* is the wrong tense. It should be *allows*.

Section 2

Although every essay will be unique, we provide a sample here to give you a better idea of what the test-graders expect to see in your essay. Compare the structure and development of this essay to yours.

As the test-graders read and evaluate your essay, they look for the following:

- Proper introduction
- Well-focused main points
- Evidence of clear organization
- Specific development of your ideas
- Clear references to the source texts and your own experience
- Correct grammar and proper sentence structure

- Necessary punctuation
- Appropriate use of vocabulary
- Correct spelling
- Proper linkage between paragraphs
- Clear summary

Sample Response

Article 1 certainly makes the better case. It is factual and supports statements with evidence. Few statements are purely opinion. The second article also states a clear position, but often uses unsupported arguments and biased wording.

Article 1 starts with the history and achievements of the union movement. These achievements are indisputable. They include protection against "unsafe workplaces and arbitrary firing or layoffs," to decent wages and benefits.

The articles have a different take on the current situation. The first argues unions are very important to workers today. The second article states that unions are no longer required. The second article then attacks union actions, calling them "bullying and blackmail." The terms used are an example of "loaded" words. They add a bias to the discussion. The article uses more terms like that. Two examples are "threaten to shut down" and "holding the public hostage." Calling negotiations with employers "bullying and blackmail" creates a negative image. It is supposed to turn readers against unions. The article does not have any factual evidence to back that position.

The second article also says unions have large cash reserves and make huge donations to "curry favor" with politicians. The article ignores the fact that companies also make political donations.

Finally, the second article argues that existing labor laws make union protection unnecessary. Yet laws can be changed by a vote at any time. How will workers be protected if companies can continue to argue their case before government representatives but there is no one to speak for workers?

The first article clearly explains why we still need unions. It reminds readers that many workers in non-union companies earn really low wages. These workers often rely on welfare and food banks to survive, despite having jobs. Current news reports continue to have stories about such workers.

The only area where the first article also uses a "loaded" expression is the final sentence, calling the "Right to Work" laws the right to work for starvation wages. While it may be true, it is also an emotionally charged phrase.

The better argued article is the first one. It supports its position with factual evidence and uses few emotionally charged statements. The second article also has some factual basis, especially the section about wages leading to outsourcing. But the rest of the argument often relies on biased phrases. Therefore, the better article is Article 1.

Evaluation of Sample Response

After reading through the sample essay once, reread it and answer the following questions about it.

- Is there a series of main points in this essay that clearly relate to the topic? (Underline the main points to check.)
- Does each paragraph have an introductory sentence or thought?
- Does each paragraph have a concluding sentence or thought?
- Do the sentences within each paragraph follow a logical sequence?

- Are the paragraphs organized in a natural flow from beginning to end? In other words, does each paragraph build on the previous one and lead to the next one?
- Have the ideas in the given topic and the first paragraph been developed throughout the essay?
- Are all the sentences grammatically correct?
- Are all the sentences properly structured?
- Are all the sentences correctly punctuated?
- Are all the words spelled correctly?

This particular sample essay would probably receive a fairly high score because it has all the attributes of a good essay that we list earlier in this section. It isn't perfect, but no one's asking you to write a perfect essay. Given the time frame, you are expected to produce a good first draft quality essay. The sample essay above clearly analyzes the two positions. It has a clear flow and uses linking phrases between paragraphs. The order of the content is effective. The writer also picks up on the use of bias and emotionally charged materials to influence a reader, as opposed to factual arguments. You can go through the checklist above and the essay, and tick off each requirement. While the essay is not perfect, it is satisfactory.

Look over the list of characteristics that the readers are looking for and try to determine whether your practice essay satisfies those requirements. Ask a friend to answer these same questions about your essay; then, rewrite your essay until you and your friend can answer yes to every question.

Remember: Your essay shouldn't be just a collection of grammatically correct sentences that flow from beginning to end. Rather, anything you write needs to be interesting and even entertaining to read. After all, no one wants to read a boring essay!

Mathematical Reasoning

1. **(D)** All the discounts and specials will produce the same price; thus, it doesn't matter from which store Alvin buys his jeans, as he would pay the same price at each.

2. **(B)** If Liz wanted to lose 12 pounds, she would have to cut $12 \times 3,500 = 42,000$ calories out of her diet in 12 weeks. Because there are 7 days in a week, she has $7 \times 12 = 84$ days to reach her goal. She would have to cut $42,000 \div 84 = 500$ calories out of her diet each day to reach her goal.

   If you wanted to try this problem using mental math, you could look at it this way: Because she wants to lose 12 pounds in 12 weeks, she would have to lose 1 pound per week. To lose 1 pound per week, she would have to cut out 3,500 calories per week or $3,500 \div 7 = 500$ calories per day.

3. **division** If Willie knows how far he has traveled on a tankful of gasoline and knows how many gallons he has used, he could find the average miles per gallon by dividing the distance by the fuel consumed. He could calculate the number of gallons of gasoline by dividing the total cost by the price per gallon. Although two operations are required, they are both division.

4. **(A)** If you added up the approximate costs of the items, you would get $2.50 + $4.00 + $2.50 + $1.20 = $10.20, which is more money than she has, but three of the approximations are a little more than the item's actual price (for example, the approximation for milk is a full $0.20 above the real price). The actual total is $9.98. Georgina has enough money.

5. **(D)** In a room, the basic assumptions are all of those stated; otherwise, the building would not be rectangular and the ceiling would be at different heights. If you have difficulty visualizing perpendicular and parallel planes, think of a regular room, and the concept may be easier to visualize.

6. **(D)** Rotating segment *BC* 180° around *C* would essentially place the triangle upside down and provide a line extended from the original segment *BC*, which is parallel to segment *DE*.

7. **(C)** To find the length of the hypotenuse, you first have to add the squares of the other two sides ($30^2 + 20^2 = 900 + 400 = 1,300$) and then find the square root of that number. The square root of 1,300 is 36.06, or 36 inches to the nearest inch.

8. **14.25** The slope is calculated by dividing the rise by the run, which is $\frac{8}{12} = \frac{2}{3}$. The rise is 9 feet 6 inches, or 114 inches. Next, create the equation $\frac{2}{3} = \frac{114}{\text{run}}$. Then $\text{run} = \frac{114 \times 3}{2} = \frac{342}{2} = 171$ inches. Converting 171 inches to feet, $\frac{171}{12} = \frac{57}{4} = 14\frac{1}{4} = 14.25$ feet.

9. **(B)** To find the area, multiply the length by the width, or $25 \times 12 = 300$ square feet. Because 1 gallon covers 450 square feet, you would divide the area by the coverage, or $\frac{300}{450} = \frac{2}{3}$. (Divide top and bottom by 150 to simplify the fraction.) Georgio would use $\frac{2}{3}$ gallon of paint.

10. **(A)** If Sandy leaves at 1:15 p.m. and arrives at 5 p.m., her travel time is 3 hours and 45 minutes or 3.75 hours. (Convert 45 minutes to a decimal by dividing it by 60.) She travels at an average of 42 miles per hour. To calculate the distance, multiply 3.75×42 to get 157.5.

11. **960** To calculate the original surface area, multiply the length by the width: $60 \times 20 = 1,200$. The new pool would be 20 percent larger in surface area, which would be $1,200 \times 0.20 = 240$ square feet larger. The new surface area would be $1,200 + 240 = 1,440$ square feet.

    To calculate the volume with the original dimensions, multiply the surface area by the depth: $1,200 \times 4 = 4,800$ cubic feet.

    To calculate the volume with the increased dimensions, multiply $1,440 \times 4 = 5,760$ cubic feet.

    To find the increased volume, subtract the larger volume from the smaller: $5,760 - 4,800 = 960$ cubic feet.

    The increased surface area would produce an increase in volume of 960 cubic feet.

12. **(B)** The highest price for gas is $2.56 in Wichita, and the lowest price for gas is $2.47 in Osbourne. The difference in the price per gallon is $2.56 - $2.47 = $0.09 per gallon. By buying 20 gallons at the lowest price, you would save $20 \times 0.09 = $1.80.

13. **(C)** From the tables, the country that watches the most television per week and has the highest Internet usage as a percentage of the population is the United States.

14. **(A)** The rest of the choices may be part of folklore or seem to be logical, but you were asked for an answer supported by the data and neither table mentions food or overeating. The answer for each question should be in the material presented and not be determined by prior knowledge or hearsay.

15. **(C)** Her present average is $(91 + 87 + 88 + 72 + 89) = 427$. $427 \div 5 = 85.4\%$ average. To get an average of 90%, she would need a total score of 450 ($450 \div 5 = 90\%$). $450 - 427 = 23$. Her mathematics score would have to be a total of 23 points higher to achieve a 90% average.

16. **(C)** The only factual data Kelly gathered was the number of people present in her class that day and their political preference. The sample is too small to make any other conclusion.

17. **(0,4)** Using the equation $y = mx + b$ and substituting $y = 3$, $m = 1$, and $x = -1$ and solving, the answer would be $b = 4$. The *y*-intercept would be the point (0,4) on a coordinate-plane grid.

Point $P(-1,3)$ has the coordinates $x = -1$ and $y = 3$. Remember that in writing the coordinates of a point, the first number is the value of x and the second number is the value of y for that point. Use the equation $y = mx + b$ and substitute $x = -1$, $y = 3$, $m = 1$:

$$3 = (1)(-1) + b$$
$$3 = -1 + b \qquad \text{(Isolate } b \text{ by adding 1 to both sides.)}$$
$$4 = b$$

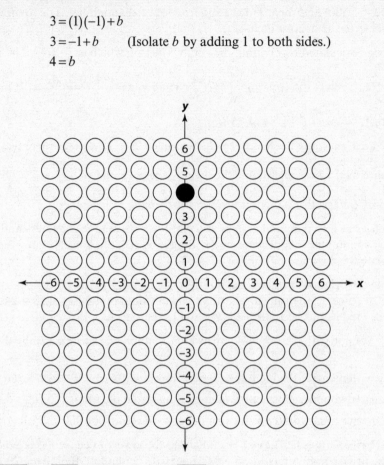

18. $T = \boxed{4}(P - \boxed{0.3}P) + \boxed{6}(S - 0.45S) + (C - \boxed{0.5}C)$

    You could read this equation as follows: The total cost is four times (the regular price of trousers less a 30% discount) plus six times (the regular price for shirts less a 45% discount) plus the regular price for a coat discounted by 50%. In mathematics, the parentheses indicate that the value in front of the parentheses is multiplied by each of the values inside the parentheses, which makes the first term read: 4 pairs of trousers at price P per pair of trousers less (minus) 0.3 (or 30%) off the price of a pair of trousers (discount) times the price of a pair of trousers.

19. **(D)** The slope, m, would need to remain the same if the lines were to be parallel and the y-intercept, b, would have to be different in each equation to produce a sequence of parallel lines.

20. **(D)** This is a problem requiring several steps and would be a good example to use with a calculator. If you look at the formula $A = \dfrac{PL}{2}$, which calculates the area of the lateral sides, you can calculate the area and the perimeter of the base from the information provided, but calculating the slant height will require another step.

Area of the base = 470 × 470 = 220,900 square feet

Perimeter of the base = 2(470 + 470) = 1,880 feet

You can use the Pythagorean theorem to find the slant height, which would correspond to the hypotenuse of a right triangle formed by the base and the height of the pyramid.

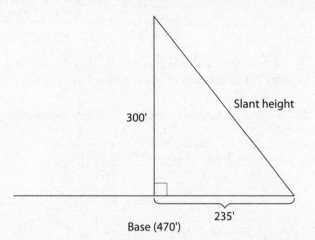

The right triangle would be formed by one-half the width of the base (235 feet) and the height. The reason for using one-half of the width of the base is that the triangle is formed by the height and the base intersecting at 90°, which is halfway across the base. The triangle formed this way is a right triangle.

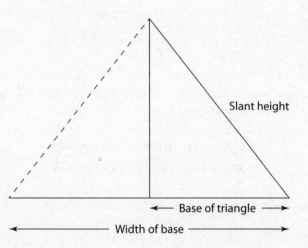

To calculate the slant height (the hypotenuse of the right triangle), you would have to calculate the square root of $235^2 + 300^2$, which is 235 × 235 + 300 × 300 = 55,225 + 90,000 = 145,225. The square root is one of two equal numbers that multiply together to form 145,225 as a product. Because both a negative number and a positive number, when squared, would create a positive product, the square root would be positive. The square root of 145,225 is approximately ±381.1.

Substituting in the equation:

$$A = \frac{PL}{2}$$
$$= \frac{(1,880)(381.1)}{2}$$
$$= 358,234$$

The lateral area that would have to be painted is approximately 358,234 square feet (the base is excluded; the ability to paint the base is severely limited because it is sitting on the ground).

21. **(A)** To evaluate $\frac{-b \pm \sqrt{b^2 - 4ac}}{2a} =$, substitute $a = 1$, $b = 6$, and $c = 5$ in the equation:

$$\frac{-b \pm \sqrt{b^2 - 4ac}}{2a} = \frac{-6 \pm \sqrt{6^2 - 4(1)(5)}}{2(1)}$$
$$= \frac{-6 \pm \sqrt{36 - 4(1)(5)}}{2(1)}$$
$$= \frac{-6 \pm \sqrt{16}}{2}$$
$$= \frac{-6 \pm 4}{2}$$
$$= \frac{-10}{2} \text{ or } \frac{-2}{2}$$
$$= -5 \quad \text{or } -1$$

The answers are –5 or –1.

22. **(A)** To solve this system of equations, you have to eliminate y, which you can do by multiplying the first equation by 4 and the second equation by 3:

$$4(2x + 3y) = 4(12) \rightarrow 8x + 12y = 48$$
$$3(3x + 4y) = 3(6) \rightarrow 9x + 12y = 18$$

Then subtract the first equation from the second:

$$9x + 12y = 18$$
$$-8x + 12y = 48$$
$$\overline{x = -30}$$

23. **(C)** If c became $2c$, then $(2c)^2$ would become $4c^2$ and E would become four times its value.

24. **(C)** To solve the equation $d = \sqrt{b^2 - 4ac}$, substitute $a = 2$, $b = 5$, and $c = 2$. This will produce $d = \sqrt{5^2 - 4(2)(2)} = \sqrt{25 - 16} = \sqrt{9} = 3$.

25. **(C)** If you add 3 to one side of an equation, you must add 3 to the other side to maintain the equality. This would increase the value of y by 3.

Science

1. **(D)** The center of the atom is called the nucleus and is composed of protons and neutrons.

2. **(B)** This item requires some familiarity with basic science. The configuration of the solar system and the atom are believed to be similar, but since atoms are too small to see, scientists have just theorized about their configuration based on the configuration of other structures that formed in similar manners.

3. **(C)** When iron combines with oxygen, rust forms. If iron is coated with a protective layer, such as paint, it won't come in contact with oxygen and rust cannot form.

4. **ferric oxide** The passage states that the scientific name for rust is ferric oxide. It is also known as iron oxide, but the question asks you to answer according to the passage.

5. **(B)** As Janice explained, this is an example of Newton's First Law of Motion, which deals with unbalanced forces.

6. **(A)** The parachute creates an unbalanced force in the opposite direction of the car's motion. This is clearly stated in the passage. Thus the answer would be Newton's First Law of Motion.

7. **motor** or **engine** The motor provides the power that propels the drag racer forward. *Engine* is also an acceptable answer.

8. **(B)** For a machine to be useful, it must do something, but according to the passage, energy cannot be created; thus, the machine would never produce any additional energy unless it converted some of its energy or matter into this additional energy, and then it would cease to exist as it used up its energy or matter. In any case, the theory applies to isolated systems, which don't exist in reality and would cause frustration in anyone attempting to create such a system.

9. **(A)** The heat in the room provides the energy needed to produce a change of state—in this case, from a solid to a liquid. Over time, there would be enough energy to change the liquid to a gas (water vapor) via evaporation.

10. **(D)** According to the passage, the weight of the ostrich egg cell is over 3 pounds.

11. **(C)** The passage states that heredity is the transmission of some characteristics from parents to their children.

12. **(C)** The passage states that DNA is the mode of transmission.

13. **(A)** A life-form that is well adapted to its environment stands the greatest chance of survival. If it were not well adapted, it would probably not survive in the environment. A fish born without gills would not survive in the water.

14. **heredity** Heredity is the means of transmission of characteristics from one generation to the next, and hair color is one such characteristic or trait.

15. **producers; consumers** The passage states that an ecosystem contains both producers and consumers. If one were missing, the ecosystem would be affected.

16. **(B)** By definition, herbivores eat only plants.

17. **(C)** The passage mentions that Alice's father told her about Skinner's work with animals.

18. **(C)** Alice's father suggested that she give the puppy a treat for performing the correct behavior.

19. **(A)** and **(D)** Blank (i): The small dark window in most calculators is a photovoltaic cell, which converts the energy from light into the power to run the calculator. If you need proof of this, cover the cell with your finger. Unless the calculator has a battery backup, the display will disappear. Blank (ii): When the sun doesn't shine, there is no source for the power.

20. **(A), (B), (C),** and **(D)** By carefully looking at the diagram, you'll see that water exists in all these locations.

21. **(C)** If there is insufficient ground water discharge that feeds the body of water, the water level will be low and the boat may hit a rock in the shallower water.

22. **(C)** The correct answer is hydrogen and helium because they're chemical elements. Choice (A) is mentioned in the passage, but dust is not a chemical element.

23. **fusion** The process mentioned in the passage is nuclear fusion. *Nuclear fission* may be a familiar term, but it involves the splitting of the atoms rather than the combining of atoms. Both produce immense amounts of energy but are different (opposite) processes.

24. **(D)** Gravity provided the attraction to gather the particles into planets, according to the passage. The particles were far enough away from the sun that they were attracted to the planets and not the sun.

25. This short answer item requires an essay response to be written in roughly 10 minutes. The first thing to remember is that this is an essay, and it should have an introduction and a conclusion. There should be no spelling or grammatical errors and the sentences should follow one another in a coherent pattern.

   The response will be scored on a 3-point scale. A 3-point response is well-crafted and uses data and information from the Stimulus. A 2-point response is reasonably well-crafted and includes partial support from the Stimulus but more than just a collection of quotes. A 1-point response is poorly crafted and contains only some evidence from the Stimulus. A 0-point response is poorly written and contains no supportive material from the Stimulus. If you just copy words from the Stimulus without interpreting or showing any understanding of what they mean, write it in a language other than English, or leave your response blank, your score will be not recorded.

Social Studies

Section 1

1. **(D)** Columbus hoped to gain fame and fortune by finding a route to the Indies. Although he was the son of a weaver, a successful map-maker, and a sailor, none of these is the best answer.

2. **(A)** According to the passage, Columbus was making exorbitant demands of his funders. Admiral of the Oceans, loot, and governorships are just examples of these demands.

3. **Spain** It was Queen Isabella of Spain who finally gave him support; he was refused by England, France, Portugal, and the Italian states.

4. **(D)** The queen gave her approval in 1492. The other dates are incorrect.

5. **(B)** Columbus named the island in the Bahamas, where he landed, San Salvador. He didn't reach the Indies or the other islands mentioned.

6. **(A), (C), and (D)** The qualities in choices (A), (C), and (D) are all cited in the passage. Choice (B) is directly contradicted in the passage ("He wasn't particularly handsome . . . ").

7. **(C)** The third sentence of the passage clearly states that Washington wasn't proud of his dentures. Although choices (A) and (B) are true, they do not relate to how he *felt* about his dentures. Choice (D) contradicts the passage.

8. **(D)** According to the passage, Washington's troops could not be described as disciplined and dependable. To the contrary, they were indecisive, quarrelsome, and prone to desertion. They also lacked a commanding presence or an indomitable spirit.

9. **20** The average desertion rate is stated directly in the passage as 20 percent. Washington's troops deserted in large numbers, compared to armies in modern times.

10. **(D)** Choices (A) through (C) all contributed to the British Army's description of Washington as "the old fox."

11. **(C)** Henry Ford believed that everyone should own an automobile. He also may have thought everyone should have a job and an improved life, but these are not mentioned in the passage. Joining a union or being an engineer is irrelevant.

12. **(B)** Ford's greatest contribution to the auto industry was the assembly line. As a result of the assembly line, more workers were employed and gained independence. This method of manufacturing also encouraged new industries, which strengthened the economy.

13. **(A)** Ford was able to sell more automobiles because he introduced cheaper prices. As a result, more tires were produced and roadside cafes opened, but these factors didn't influence sales. We don't know about his advertising efforts.

14. **(D)** The availability of automobiles became a dominant element in building the U.S. economy. A change in lifestyle and greater self-esteem were not the most important economic impacts. Cars certainly didn't cause the Great Depression.

15. **(C)** The Wright Brothers were famous for achieving the first powered, sustained flight by an aircraft. Owning a bicycle shop and building a machine didn't make them famous. Their invention may have had some influence on World War I, but the Wright Brothers were already famous by the time the war started.

16. **(D)** The rise in oil prices causes an increase in gasoline prices. Other choices—decrease in sales of SUVs and more travel—are not related directly to oil prices. Lost profit to oil companies is not a relevant choice.

17. **(B)** Higher oil prices cause a rise in the cost of living because many things become more expensive.

18. **(D)** The adjective that best describes the SUV characters is *wasteful*.

19. **(A)** The SUV cannot be described as an *energy saver* due to its poor gasoline mileage. The other terms are much more accurate.

20. **(B), (C), and (D)** Choices (B), (C), and (D) could help to solve the energy crisis.

21. **(C)** The third paragraph of the passage specifically states that New Orleans is nicknamed the "Big Easy."

22. **(A), (B), (C), and (D)** Choices (A) through (D) were all results of Hurricane Katrina.

23. **(A)** The major factor that put New Orleans in danger was that it is located below sea level. Thousands of people refusing to leave and the destruction of homes were results, not factors. Being the region's largest city is irrelevant.

24. **(D)** The federal government was slow to respond to the destruction of Katrina. The other choices, while true, were not the primary reason for criticism.

25. **(B)** Katrina will be remembered as the most expensive hurricane, so far, in U.S. history. Flood waters, evacuations, and damage costs were contributing factors to this expense.

26. **(D)** On mainland USA, Michigan and Maine show declines. Puerto Rico, on the inset, also shows decline.

27. **(A), (C), and (D)** North Carolina and Georgia had a population change between 100,000 and 199,000, and Florida had a change of 200,000 or more. South Carolina fell in the 25,000 to 99,000 range.

28. **(A)** The length of the horizontal bars indicates population size. The graph clearly shows that starting at age 65, the bars for women are longer than those for men.

29. **(B)** The numbering is every ten years, but there are two bars between numbers. Therefore, each bar represents an interval of five years.

30. **(D)** The asterisk refers to a note at the bottom of the chart: "one race." More detailed statistics will break down race further. Individuals may self-identify themselves as having parents of different race, and will be grouped by that. In this case, all mixed race individuals are grouped together.

Section 2

As the test-graders read and evaluate your essay, they look for the following:

- Proper introduction
- Well-focused main points
- Evidence of clear organization
- Specific development of your ideas
- Clear references to the source texts and your own experience
- Correct grammar and proper sentence structure
- Necessary punctuation
- Appropriate use of vocabulary
- Correct spelling
- Proper linkage between paragraphs
- Clear summary

Although every essay will be unique, we provide a sample response here to give you a better idea of what the test-graders expect to see in your extended response essay. Compare the structure of this sample response to yours.

Sample Response

Social and economic inequality is certainly an enduring issue in American history. It begins with the words of the constitution, "All men are created equal," and continues to the present day with various measures to promote equality. We have affirmative action and welfare programs, laws requiring equal treatment of all individuals, and prohibitions on discrimination.

Philosophically, America is all about freedom and social mobility. The Horatio Alger myth of the mailroom boy who becomes president is just one reflection of that. Implementing effective programs to accomplish that has had mixed success. Some social and economic inequalities have been overcome in various ways over the centuries in America. Lincoln freed the slaves and ensured voting rights to all. FDR supported and strengthened the union movement for the benefit of all workers in the 1930s and 1940s. LBJ, with his "Great Society" program, focused on eliminating poverty and ensuring equal opportunity for all, regardless of race.

As President Obama states in his speech, there is a long history of such government programs. Government funding, with the appropriate tax support, gave various administrations the funding to promote economic equality, to provide jobs, job training, and education for those who had none, and to promote health care for those who could not afford it. The programs also promoted social equality by supporting equal rights, voting laws, and enforcing antidiscrimination laws.

There has been political action over the last 250 years to support the lower class and promote advancement and upward mobility. However, as the history of the issue and these programs show, the problems never go away. As one attempt is made to better the situation, such as Lincoln's land grant colleges, other problems intensify. Enough pressure builds up and a president like FDR needs to bring in a "New Deal" to attack the issue once again. Johnson's "Great Society" and Nixon's continued support for those programs are all more of the same.

It seems that the end effect of all of these programs is both less and more than hoped for. On the one hand, people who cannot afford health care have Medicaid and Medicare. Hungry people have food stamps and welfare; some homeless have access to subsidized housing; and people eager for an education can access student loans. But in truth, the problems do not go away. Attacks by the infamous 1% on the tax base needed to support such programs are leading to significant cuts. Despite continuing high unemployment, some in government are blocking efforts to extend benefits. There are continuing attacks on the Affordable Care Act, along with vast cuts to income taxes that benefit mainly corporations and the wealthy. Many of the nation's elected representatives seem more interested today in perpetuating the division of wealth and opportunity than creating more equality. Obama's statistics on the lack of opportunity and upward mobility reinforce that view. The increasing disparity of wealth over the last five decades demonstrates that.

The President's speech states that various administrations have taken measures to solve issues of inequality and promote equal opportunity. He once again explains the dire need to do more to create equal opportunity, both economically and socially. Sadly that affirms the fact that social and economic inequality is indeed an enduring issue in American history.

Evaluation of Sample Response

After reading through the sample response once, reread it and answer the following questions about it.

- Is there a series of main points in this essay that clearly relate to the topic? (Underline the main points to check.)
- Does each paragraph have an introductory sentence or thought?
- Does each paragraph have a concluding sentence or thought?
- Do the sentences within each paragraph follow a logical sequence?

- Are the paragraphs organized in a natural flow from beginning to end? In other words, does each paragraph build on the previous one and lead to the next one?
- Have the ideas in the given topic and the first paragraph been developed throughout the essay?
- Are all the sentences grammatically correct?
- Are all the sentences properly structured?
- Are all the sentences correctly punctuated?
- Are all the words spelled correctly?

As far as this particular sample essay is concerned, a test-grader probably would have given it a high score because it has all the attributes of a good essay that we list earlier in this section. It isn't perfect, but no one's asking you to write a perfect essay. In the time you have available, only 25 minutes, you are expected to write a good first draft. Look over the list of characteristics that the readers are looking for, and try to determine whether your practice essay satisfies those requirements. Ask a friend to answer these same questions about your essay; then, rewrite your essay until you and your friend can answer yes to every question.

Remember: Your essay shouldn't be just a collection of grammatically correct sentences that flow from beginning to end. Rather, your essay needs to be interesting and even entertaining to read. After all, no one—not even a professional test-grader—wants to read a boring essay!

III. Reasoning through Language Arts Cram Plans

All study times are suggestions. You may need more or less time to complete the assignments, but complete the assignments.

Two-Month Cram Plan	
8 weeks before the test	**Study Time:** 1½ hours ❑ Read the "Introduction." ❑ Read Chapter I, "The 2014 GED® Test."
7 weeks before the test	**Study Time:** 3 hours ❑ Take the Reasoning through Language Arts section of the Diagnostic Test (Chapter II) and review the answer explanations. ❑ Note your errors. ❑ Based on your errors, identify difficult topics and item types. These are your targeted areas. ❑ Compare your extended response essay to the sample response and to the extended response checklist. This will show you areas that may need improvement.

6 weeks before the test	**Study Time:** 2½ hours
	❑ Read "Test Format," Chapter VII, Section A.
	❑ Read "Types of Questions in Sections 1 and 3," Chapter VII, Section B.
	   ❑ Read the material and do the examples.
	   ❑ Check the answer explanations and review any that you answered incorrectly.

5 weeks before the test	**Study Time:** 1½ hours
	❑ Read "Section 2: The Extended Response," Chapter VII, Section C.
	   ❑ Review Sections C.1 and C.2.
	   ❑ Write a practice essay on one of the given topics in Section C.3 and evaluate it, looking for ways to improve it.

4 weeks before the test	**Study Time:** 1 hour ❑ Read "Test Strategies," Chapter VII, Section D. ❑ Review and practice the strategies.

3 weeks before the test	**Study Time:** 3 hours
	❑ Read "Grammar Review," Chapter VII, Section E.
	   ❑ Read the material and do the examples.
	   ❑ Check the answer explanations and review any that you answered incorrectly.

2 weeks before the test	**Study Time:** 1 hour
	❑ Read "Practice," Chapter VII, Section F.
	   ❑ Answer the practice questions.
	   ❑ Check the answer explanations and review any that you answered incorrectly.

continued

7 days before the test	**Study Time:** 4½ hours ❏ Take the Reasoning through Language Arts Practice Test (Chapter XI) and review your answers. ❏ Based on your errors on the Practice Test, identify difficult topics and item types and their corresponding areas. Target these areas for extra review. ❏ Compare your extended response essay to the sample response and to the extended response checklist. This will show you areas that may need improvement.
6 days before the test	**Study Time:** 3 hours ❏ Review identified target areas. ❏ Review "Types of Questions in Sections 1 and 3," Chapter VII, Section B.
5 days before the test	**Study Time:** 1½ hours ❏ Review identified target areas. ❏ Review "Grammar Review," Chapter VII, Section E.
4 days before the test	**Study Time:** 1½ hours ❏ Review identified target areas. ❏ Redo "Practice," Chapter VII, Section F.1.
3 days before the test	**Study Time:** 1½ hours ❏ Review identified target areas. ❏ Redo "Practice," Chapter VII, Section F.2.
2 days before the test	**Study Time:** 2 hours ❏ Review the Reasoning through the Language Arts Practice Test (Chapter XI). ❏ Review the questions you missed and their answer explanations.
1 day before the test	❏ Relax . . . you are well prepared for the test. ❏ Have confidence in your ability to do well. ❏ Exercise to help relieve stress and improve sleep. ❏ Get a good night's sleep.
Morning of the test	**Reminders:** ❏ Have a good breakfast. ❏ Bring your admission ticket and photo ID with you. ❏ Try to go outside for a few minutes and walk around before the test. ❏ Most important: Stay calm and confident during the test. Take deep, slow breaths if you feel at all nervous. You can do it!

One-Month Cram Plan	
4 weeks before the test	**Study Time:** 4½ hours ❏ Read the "Introduction." ❏ Read Chapter I, "The 2014 GED® Test." ❏ Take the Reasoning through Language Arts section of the Diagnostic Test (Chapter II) and review the answer explanations. ❏ Note your errors. ❏ Based on your errors, identify difficult topics and item types. These are your targeted areas. ❏ Compare your extended response essay to the sample response and to the extended response checklist. This will show you areas that may need improvement.

3 weeks before the test	**Study Time:** 5 hours
	❏ Read "Test Format," Chapter VII, Section A.
	❏ Read "Types of Questions in Sections 1 and 3," Chapter VII, Section B.
	  ❏ Read the material and do the examples.
	  ❏ Check the answer explanations.
	❏ Gain experience reading fiction and nonfiction literary passages.
	❏ Read "Section 2: The Extended Response," Chapter VII, Section C.
	  ❏ Review Sections C.1 and C.2.
	  ❏ Write a practice essay on one of the given topics in Section C.3 and evaluate it, looking for ways to improve it.
	❏ Read "Test Strategies," Chapter VII, Section D.
	  ❏ Review and practice the strategies.

2 weeks before the test	**Study Time:** 4 hours
	❏ Read "Grammar Review," Chapter VII, Section E.
	  ❏ Read the material and do the examples.
	  ❏ Check the answer explanations and review any that you answered incorrectly.
	❏ Read "Practice," Chapter VII, Section F.
	  ❏ Answer the practice questions.
	  ❏ Check the answer explanations and review any that you answered incorrectly.

7 days before the test	**Study Time:** 4½ hours ❏ Take the Reasoning through Language Arts Practice Test (Chapter XI) and review your answers. ❏ Based on your errors on the Practice Test, identify difficult topics and item types and their corresponding areas. Target these areas for extra review. ❏ Compare your extended response essay to the sample response and to the extended response checklist. This will show you areas that may need improvement.
6 days before the test	**Study Time:** 3 hours ❏ Review identified target areas. ❏ Review "Types of Questions in Sections 1 and 3," Chapter VII, Section B.
5 days before the test	**Study Time:** 1½ hours ❏ Review identified target areas. ❏ Review "Grammar Review," Chapter VII, Section E.

continued

4 days before the test	**Study Time:** 1½ hours ❑ Review identified target areas. ❑ Redo "Practice," Chapter VII, Section F.1.
3 days before the test	**Study Time:** 1½ hours ❑ Review identified target areas. ❑ Redo "Practice," Chapter VII, Section F.2.
2 days before the test	**Study Time:** 2 hours ❑ Review the Reasoning through the Language Arts Practice Test (Chapter XI). ❑ Review the questions you missed and their answer explanations.
1 day before the test	❑ Relax . . . you are well prepared for the test. ❑ Have confidence in your ability to do well. ❑ Exercise to help relieve stress and improve sleep. ❑ Get a good night's sleep.
Morning of the test	**Reminders:** ❑ Have a good breakfast. ❑ Bring your admission ticket and photo ID with you. ❑ Try to go outside for a few minutes and walk around before the test. ❑ Most important: Stay calm and confident during the test. Take deep, slow breaths if you feel at all nervous. You can do it!

One-Week Cram Plan	
7 days before the test	**Study Time:** 4½ hours ❏ Read the "Introduction." ❏ Read Chapter I, "The 2014 GED® Test." ❏ Take the Reasoning through Language Arts section of the Diagnostic Test (Chapter II) and review the answer explanations. ❏ Note your errors. ❏ Based on your errors, identify difficult topics and item types. These are your targeted areas. ❏ Compare your extended response essay to the sample response and to the extended response checklist. That will show you areas that may need improvement.

6 days before the test	**Study Time:** 5 hours
	❏ Read "Test Format," Chapter VII, Section A.
	❏ Read "Types of Questions in Sections 1 and 3," Chapter VII, Section B.
	    ❏ Read the material and do the examples.
	    ❏ Check the answer explanations.
	❏ Read "Section 2: The Extended Response," Chapter VII, Sections C.1 and C.2.
	❏ Read "Test Strategies," Chapter VII, Section D.

5 days before the test	**Study Time:** 4 hours
	❏ Read "Grammar Review," Chapter VII, Section E.
	    ❏ Read the material and do the examples.
	    ❏ Check the answer explanations and review any that you answered incorrectly.
	❏ Read "Practice," Chapter VII, Section F.
	    ❏ Answer the practice questions.
	    ❏ Check the answer explanations and review any that you answered incorrectly.

4 days before the test	**Study Time:** 4½ hours ❏ Take the Reasoning through Language Arts Practice Test (Chapter XI) and review your answers. ❏ Based on your errors on the Practice Test, identify difficult topics and item types and their corresponding areas. Target these areas for extra review. ❏ Compare your extended response essay to the sample response and to the extended response checklist. That will show you areas that may need improvement.
3 days before the test	**Study Time:** 4 hours ❏ Review identified target areas. ❏ Review "Types of Questions in Sections 1 and 3," Chapter VII, Section B. ❏ Review "Grammar Review," Chapter VII, Section E. ❏ Redo "Practice," Chapter VII, Section F.
2 days before the test	**Study Time:** 2 hours ❏ Review the Reasoning through the Language Arts Practice Test (Chapter XI). ❏ Review the questions you missed and their answer explanations.
1 day before the test	❏ Relax . . . you are well prepared for the test. ❏ Have confidence in your ability to do well. ❏ Exercise to help relieve stress and improve sleep. ❏ Get a good night's sleep.

continued

Morning of the test	Reminders:
	❑ Have a good breakfast.
	❑ Bring your admission ticket and photo ID with you.
	❑ Try to go outside for a few minutes and walk around before the test.
	❑ Most important: Stay calm and confident during the test. Take deep, slow breaths if you feel at all nervous. You can do it!

IV. Mathematical Reasoning Cram Plans

All study times are suggestions. You may need more or less time to complete the assignments, but complete the assignments.

Two-Month Cram Plan	
8 weeks before the test	**Study Time:** 1½ hours ❏ Read the "Introduction." ❏ Read Chapter I, "The 2014 GED® Test."
7 weeks before the test	**Study Time:** 2 hours ❏ Take the Mathematical Reasoning section of the Diagnostic Test (Chapter II) and review the answer explanations. ❏ Note your errors. ❏ Based on your errors, identify difficult topics and item types. These are your targeted areas.

6 weeks before the test	**Study Time:** 2½ hours
	❏ Read "Test Format," Chapter VIII, Section A.
	❏ Read "Test Strategies," Chapter VIII, Section B.
	❏ Read "Math Review," Chapter VIII, Sections C.1.a–C.1.e.
	  ❏ Read the material and spend extra time on your targeted areas.
	  ❏ Do the examples and practice problems.
	  ❏ Check the answer explanations and review any that you answered incorrectly.

5 weeks before the test	**Study Time:** 2 hours
	❏ Read "Math Review," Chapter VIII, Sections C.1.f–C.1.m
	  ❏ Read the material and spend extra time on your targeted areas.
	  ❏ Do the examples and practice problems.
	  ❏ Check the answer explanations and review any that you answered incorrectly.

4 weeks before the test	**Study Time:** 2 hours
	❏ Read "Math Review," Chapter VIII, Section C.2.
	  ❏ Read the material and spend extra time on your targeted areas.
	  ❏ Do the examples and practice problems.
	  ❏ Check the answer explanations and review any that you answered incorrectly.

3 weeks before the test	**Study Time:** 1 hour
	❏ Read "Math Review," Chapter VIII, Section C.3.
	  ❏ Read the material and spend extra time on your targeted areas.
	  ❏ Do the examples.
	  ❏ Check the answer explanations and review any that you answered incorrectly.

2 weeks before the test	**Study Time:** 2½ hours
	❏ Read "Math Review," Chapter VIII, Section C.4.
	  ❏ Read the material and spend extra time on your targeted areas.
	  ❏ Do the examples.
	  ❏ Check the answer explanations and review any that you answered incorrectly.

continued

7 days before the test	**Study Time:** 3 hours ❏ Take the Mathematical Reasoning Practice Test (Chapter XII) and review the answer explanations. ❏ Note your errors. ❏ Based on your errors on the Practice Test, identify difficult topics and item types. Target these sections for extra review.
6 days before the test	**Study Time:** 1½ hours ❏ Review identified target areas. ❏ Review example and practice problems in "Math Review," Chapter VIII, Sections C.1.a–C.1.e.
5 days before the test	**Study Time:** 1½ hours ❏ Review identified target areas. ❏ Review examples and practice problems in "Math Review," Chapter VIII, Sections C.1.f–C.1.m.
4 days before the test	**Study Time:** 1½ hours ❏ Review identified target areas. ❏ Review examples and practice problems in "Math Review," Chapter VIII, Sections C.2 and C.3.
3 days before the test	**Study Time:** 1 hour ❏ Review identified target areas. ❏ Review examples in "Math Review," Chapter VIII, Section C.4.
2 days before the test	**Study Time:** 1½ hours ❏ Review the Mathematical Reasoning Practice Test (Chapter XII). ❏ Review the questions you missed and their answer explanations.
1 day before the test	❏ Relax . . . you are well prepared for the test. ❏ Have confidence in your ability to do well. ❏ Exercise to help relieve stress and improve sleep. ❏ Get a good night's sleep.
Morning of the test	**Reminders:** ❏ Have a good breakfast. ❏ Bring your admission ticket and photo ID with you. ❏ Try to go outside for a few minutes and walk around before the test. ❏ Most important: Stay calm and confident during the test. Take deep, slow breaths if you feel at all nervous. You can do it!

One-Month Cram Plan

4 weeks before the test	**Study Time:** 3½ hours ❏ Read the "Introduction." ❏ Read Chapter I, "The 2014 GED® Test." ❏ Take Mathematical Reasoning section of the Diagnostic Test (Chapter II) and review the answer explanations. ❏ Note your errors. ❏ Based on your errors, identify difficult topics and item types. These are your targeted areas.

3 weeks before the test	**Study Time:** 5 hours
	❏ Read "Test Format," Chapter VIII, Section A.
	❏ Read "Test Strategies," Chapter VIII, Section B.
	❏ Read "Math Review," Chapter VIII, Sections C.1 and C.2.
	    ❏ Read the material and spend extra time on your targeted areas.
	    ❏ Do the examples and practice problems.
	    ❏ Review the answer explanations.

2 weeks before the test	**Study Time:** 3½ hours
	❏ Read "Math Review," Chapter VIII, Sections C.3 and C.4.
	    ❏ Read the material and spend extra time on your targeted areas.
	    ❏ Do the examples.
	    ❏ Check the answer explanations and review any that you answered incorrectly.

7 days before the test	**Study Time:** 3 hours ❏ Take the Mathematical Reasoning Practice Test (Chapter XII) and review the answer explanations. ❏ Note your errors. ❏ Based on your errors on the Practice Test, identify difficult topics and item types. Target these sections for extra review.
6 days before the test	**Study Time:** 1½ hours ❏ Review identified target areas. ❏ Review the examples and practice problems in "Math Review," Chapter VIII, Sections C.1.a–C.1.e.
5 days before the test	**Study Time:** 1½ hours ❏ Review identified target areas. ❏ Review the examples and practice problems in "Math Review," Chapter VIII, Sections C.1.f–C.1.m.
4 days before the test	**Study Time:** 1½ hours ❏ Review identified target areas. ❏ Review the examples and practice problems in "Math Review," Chapter VIII, Sections C.2 and C.3.
3 days before the test	**Study Time:** 1 hour ❏ Review identified target areas. ❏ Review the examples in "Math Review," Chapter VIII, Section C.4.
2 days before the test	**Study Time:** 1½ hours ❏ Review the Mathematical Reasoning Practice Test (Chapter XII). ❏ Review the questions you missed and their answer explanations.

continued

1 day before the test	❏ Relax . . . you are well prepared for the test.
	❏ Have confidence in your ability to do well.
	❏ Exercise to help relieve stress and improve sleep.
	❏ Get a good night's sleep.
Morning of the test	**Reminders:**
	❏ Have a good breakfast.
	❏ Bring your admission ticket and photo ID with you.
	❏ Try to go outside for a few minutes and walk around before the test.
	❏ Most important: Stay calm and confident during the test. Take deep, slow breaths if you feel at all nervous. You can do it!

One-Week Cram Plan

7 days before the test	**Study Time:** 3½ hours ❑ Read the "Introduction." ❑ Read Chapter I, "The 2014 GED® Test." ❑ Take Mathematical Reasoning section of the Diagnostic Test (Chapter II) and review the answer explanations. ❑ Note your errors. ❑ Based on your errors, identify difficult topics and item types. These are your targeted areas.

6 days before the test	**Study Time:** 5 hours
	❑ Read "Test Format," Chapter VIII, Section A.
	❑ Read "Test Strategies," Chapter VIII, Section B.
	❑ Read "Math Review," Chapter VIII, Sections C.1 and C.2.
	    ❑ Read the material and spend extra time on your targeted areas.
	    ❑ Do the examples and practice problems.
	    ❑ Check the answer explanations and review any that you answered incorrectly.

5 days before the test	**Study Time:** 3½ hours
	❑ Read "Math Review," Chapter VIII, Sections C.3 and C.4.
	    ❑ Read the material and spend extra time on your targeted areas.
	    ❑ Do the examples.
	    ❑ Check the answer explanations and review any that you answered incorrectly.

4 days before the test	**Study Time:** 3 hours ❑ Take the Mathematical Reasoning Practice Test (Chapter XII) and review the answer explanations. ❑ Note your errors. ❑ Based on your errors on the Practice Test, identify difficult topics and item types. Target these sections for extra review.
3 days before the test	**Study Time:** 5½ hours ❑ Review identified target areas. ❑ Review the examples and practice problems in "Math Review," Chapter VIII, Section C.
2 days before the test	**Study Time:** 1½ hours ❑ Review the Mathematical Reasoning Practice Test (Chapter XII). ❑ Review the questions you missed and their answer explanations.
1 day before the test	❑ Relax . . . you are well prepared for the test. ❑ Have confidence in your ability to do well. ❑ Exercise to help relieve stress and improve sleep. ❑ Get a good night's sleep.
Morning of the test	**Reminders:** ❑ Have a good breakfast. ❑ Bring your admission ticket and photo ID with you. ❑ Try to go outside for a few minutes and walk around before the test. ❑ Most important: Stay calm and confident during the test. Take deep, slow breaths if you feel at all nervous. You can do it!

V. Science Cram Plans

All study times are suggestions. You may need more or less time to complete the assignments, but complete the assignments.

Two-Month Cram Plan	
8 weeks before the test	**Study Time:** 1½ hours ❑ Read the "Introduction." ❑ Read Chapter I, "The 2014 GED® Test."
7 weeks before the test	**Study Time:** 1½ hours ❑ Take the Science section of the Diagnostic Test (Chapter II) and review the answer explanations. ❑ Note your errors. ❑ Based on your errors, identify difficult topics and item types. These are your targeted areas.

6 weeks before the test	**Study Time:** 2 hours
	❑ Read "Test Format," Chapter IX, Section A.
	❑ Read "Types of Questions: A Detailed Look," Chapter IX, Section B.
	   ❑ Do the examples.
	   ❑ Check the answer explanations and review any that you answered incorrectly.
	❑ Read "Test Strategies," Chapter IX, Section C.

5 weeks before the test	**Study Time:** 1½ hours
	❑ Read "Science Review," Chapter IX, Section D.1.
	   ❑ Read the material and spend extra time on your targeted areas.
	   ❑ Do the examples.
	   ❑ Check the answer explanations and review any that you answered incorrectly.
	   ❑ Study the vocabulary.

4 weeks before the test	**Study Time:** 1½ hours
	❑ Read "Science Review," Chapter IX, Section D.2.
	   ❑ Read the material and spend extra time on your targeted areas.
	   ❑ Do the examples.
	   ❑ Check the answer explanations and review any that you answered incorrectly.
	   ❑ Study the vocabulary.

3 weeks before the test	**Study Time:** 1 hour
	❑ Read "Science Review," Chapter IX, Section D.3.
	   ❑ Read the material and spend extra time on your targeted areas.
	   ❑ Do the examples.
	   ❑ Check the answer explanations and review any that you answered incorrectly.
	   ❑ Study the vocabulary.

2 weeks before the test	**Study Time:** 2 hours ❑ General review of targeted areas. ❑ Review targeted areas of Chapter IX, paying particular attention to the vocabulary sections.

continued

7 days before the test	**Study Time:** 2½ hours ❑ Take the Science Practice Test (Chapter XIII) and review the answer explanations. ❑ Note your errors. ❑ Based on your errors on the Practice Test, identify difficult topics and item types. Target these sections for extra review.

6 days before the test	**Study Time:** 1 hour
	❑ Review identified target areas.
	❑ Review "Types of Questions: A Detailed Look," Chapter IX, Section B.
	   ❑ Redo the examples.
	   ❑ Check the answer explanations and review any that you answered incorrectly.

5 days before the test	**Study Time:** 1 hour ❑ Review identified target areas. ❑ Redo the examples and review the vocabulary in "Science Review," Chapter IX, Section D.1.
4 days before the test	**Study Time:** 1 hour ❑ Review identified target areas. ❑ Redo the examples and review the vocabulary in "Science Review," Chapter IX, Section D.2.
3 days before the test	**Study Time:** 1 hour ❑ Review identified target areas. ❑ Redo the examples and review the vocabulary in "Science Review," Chapter IX, Section D.3.
2 days before the test	**Study Time:** 1½ hours ❑ Review the Science Practice Test (Chapter XIII). ❑ Review the questions you missed and their answer explanations.
1 day before the test	❑ Relax . . . you are well prepared for the test. ❑ Have confidence in your ability to do well. ❑ Exercise to help relieve stress and improve sleep. ❑ Get a good night's sleep.
Morning of the test	**Reminders:** ❑ Have a good breakfast. ❑ Bring your admission ticket and photo ID with you. ❑ Try to go outside for a few minutes and walk around before the test. ❑ Most important: Stay calm and confident during the test. Take deep, slow breaths if you feel at all nervous. You can do it!

One-Month Cram Plan

4 weeks before the test	**Study Time:** 3 hours ❏ Read the "Introduction." ❏ Read Chapter I, "The 2014 GED® Test." ❏ Take the Science section of the Diagnostic Test (Chapter II) and review the answer explanations. ❏ Note your errors. ❏ Based on your errors, identify difficult topics and item types. These are your targeted areas.

3 weeks before the test	**Study Time:** 2 hours
	❏ Read "Test Format," Chapter IX, Section A.
	❏ Read "Types of Questions: A Detailed Look," Chapter IX, Section B.
	   ❏ Do the examples.
	   ❏ Check the answer explanations and review any that you answered incorrectly.
	❏ Read "Test Strategies," Chapter IX, Section C.

2 weeks before the test	**Study Time:** 3 hours
	❏ Read "Science Review," Chapter IX, Section D.
	   ❏ Read the material and spend extra time on your targeted areas.
	   ❏ Do the examples.
	   ❏ Check the answer explanations and review any that you answered incorrectly.
	   ❏ Study the vocabulary.

7 days before the test	**Study Time:** 2½ hours ❏ Take the Science Practice Test (Chapter XIII) and review the answer explanations. ❏ Note your errors. ❏ Based on your errors on the Practice Test, identify difficult topics and item types. Target these sections for extra review.

6 days before the test	**Study Time:** 1 hour
	❏ Review identified target areas.
	❏ Review "Types of Questions: A Detailed Look," Chapter IX, Section B.
	   ❏ Redo the examples.
	   ❏ Check the answer explanations and review any that you answered incorrectly.

5 days before the test	**Study Time:** 1 hour ❏ Review identified target areas. ❏ Redo the examples and review the vocabulary in "Science Review," Chapter IX, Section D.1.
4 days before the test	**Study Time:** 1 hour ❏ Review identified target areas. ❏ Redo the examples and review the vocabulary in "Science Review," Chapter IX, Section D.2.
3 days before the test	**Study Time:** 2 hours ❏ Review identified target areas. ❏ Redo the examples and review the vocabulary in "Science Review," Chapter IX, Section D.3.

continued

2 days before the test	**Study Time:** 1½ hours
	❏ Review the Science Practice Test (Chapter XIII).
	❏ Review the questions you missed and their answer explanations.
1 day before the test	❏ Relax . . . you are well prepared for the test.
	❏ Have confidence in your ability to do well.
	❏ Exercise to help relieve stress and improve sleep.
	❏ Get a good night's sleep.
Morning of the test	**Reminders:**
	❏ Have a good breakfast.
	❏ Bring your admission ticket and photo ID with you.
	❏ Try to go outside for a few minutes and walk around before the test.
	❏ Most important: Stay calm and confident during the test. Take deep, slow breaths if you feel at all nervous. You can do it!

One-Week Cram Plan	
7 days before the test	**Study Time:** 3 hours ❏ Read the "Introduction." ❏ Read Chapter I, "The 2014 GED® Test." ❏ Take the Science section of the Diagnostic Test (Chapter II) and review the answer explanations. ❏ Note your errors. ❏ Based on your errors, identify difficult topics and item types. These are your targeted areas.

6 days before the test	**Study Time:** 2 hours
	❏ Read "Test Format," Chapter IX, Section A.
	❏ Read "Types of Questions: A Detailed Look," Chapter IX, Section B.
	   ❏ Do the examples.
	   ❏ Check the answer explanations and review any that you answered incorrectly.
	❏ Read "Test Strategies," Chapter IX, Section C.

5 days before the test	**Study Time:** 3 hours
	❏ Read "Science Review," Chapter IX, Section D.
	   ❏ Read the material and spend extra time on your targeted areas.
	   ❏ Do the examples.
	   ❏ Check the answer explanations and review any that you answered incorrectly.
	   ❏ Study the vocabulary.

4 days before the test	**Study Time:** 2½ hours ❏ Take the Science Practice Test (Chapter XIII) and review the answer explanations. ❏ Note your errors. ❏ Based on your errors on the Practice Test, identify difficult topics and item types. Target these sections for extra review.
3 days before the test	**Study Time:** 2 hours ❏ Review identified target areas. ❏ Redo the examples and review the vocabulary in "Science Review," Chapter IX, Section D.
2 days before the test	**Study Time:** 1½ hours ❏ Review the Science Practice Test (Chapter XIII). ❏ Review the questions you missed and their answer explanations.
1 day before the test	❏ Relax . . . you are well prepared for the test. ❏ Have confidence in your ability to do well. ❏ Exercise to help relieve stress and improve sleep. ❏ Get a good night's sleep.
Morning of the test	**Reminders:** ❏ Have a good breakfast. ❏ Bring your admission ticket and photo ID with you. ❏ Try to go outside for a few minutes and walk around before the test. ❏ Most important: Stay calm and confident during the test. Take deep, slow breaths if you feel at all nervous. You can do it!

VI. Social Studies Cram Plans

All study times are suggestions. You may need more or less time to complete the assignments, but complete the assignments.

Two-Month Cram Plan	
8 weeks before the test	**Study Time:** 1½ hours ❑ Read the "Introduction." ❑ Read Chapter I, "The 2014 GED® Test."
7 weeks before the test	**Study Time:** 1½ hours ❑ Take the Social Studies section of the Diagnostic Test (Chapter II) and review the answer explanations. ❑ Note your errors. ❑ Based on your errors, identify difficult topics and item types. These are your targeted areas. ❑ Compare your extended response essay to the sample response, marking your essay with ways to improve it.

6 weeks before the test	**Study Time:** 1½ hours
	❑ Read "Test Format," Chapter X, Section A.
	❑ Read "Types of Questions in Section 1: A Detailed Look," Chapter X, Sections B.1–B.3.
	  ❑ Read the material and do the examples.
	  ❑ Check the answer explanations and review any that you answered incorrectly.

5 weeks before the test	**Study Time:** 1½ hours
	❑ Read "Types of Questions in Section 1: A Detailed Look," Chapter X, Sections B.4 and B.5.
	  ❑ Read the material and do the examples.
	  ❑ Check the answer explanations and review any that you answered incorrectly.

4 weeks before the test	**Study Time:** 1½ hours ❑ Read "Section 2: The Extended Response," Chapter X, Section C. ❑ Write a practice essay and evaluate it, looking for ways to improve it.
3 weeks before the test	**Study Time:** 1½ hours ❑ Read "Test Strategies," Chapter X, Section D. ❑ Review and practice the strategies. ❑ Gain experience reading historical passages (U.S. history, civics and government, economics, and geography).

2 weeks before the test	**Study Time:** 1 hour
	❑ Read "Practice," Chapter X, Section E.
	  ❑ Answer the practice questions.
	  ❑ Check the answer explanations and review any that you answered incorrectly.

7 days before the test	**Study Time:** 2½ hours ❑ Take the Social Studies Practice Test (Chapter XIV) and review your answers. ❑ Based on your errors on the Practice Test, identify difficult topics and item types and their corresponding areas. Target these areas for extra review. ❑ Compare your extended response essay to the sample response.

continued

6 days before the test	**Study Time:** 1½ hours
	❏ Review identified target areas.
	❏ Review "Types of Questions in Sections 1: A Detailed Look," Chapter X, Sections B.1–B.3.
5 days before the test	**Study Time:** 1½ hours
	❏ Review identified target areas.
	❏ Review "Types of Questions in Sections 1: A Detailed Look," Chapter X, Sections B.4 and B.5.
4 days before the test	**Study Time:** 1 hour
	❏ Review identified target areas.
	❏ Review "Section 2: The Extended Response," Chapter X, Section C.
	❏ Review "Test Strategies," Chapter X, Section D.
3 days before the test	**Study Time:** 2 hours
	❏ Review identified target areas.
	❏ Redo "Practice," Chapter X, Section E.
	❏ Answer the practice questions.
	❏ Check the answer explanations and review any that you answered incorrectly.
2 days before the test	**Study Time:** 2 hours
	❏ Review the Social Studies Practice Test (Chapter XIV).
	❏ Review the questions you missed and their answer explanations.
1 day before the test	❏ Relax . . . you are well prepared for the test.
	❏ Have confidence in your ability to do well.
	❏ Exercise to help relieve stress and improve sleep.
	❏ Get a good night's sleep.
Morning of the test	**Reminders:**
	❏ Have a good breakfast.
	❏ Bring your admission ticket and photo ID with you.
	❏ Try to go outside for a few minutes and walk around before the test.
	❏ Most important: Stay calm and confident during the test. Take deep, slow breaths if you feel at all nervous. You can do it!

One-Month Cram Plan

4 weeks before the test	**Study Time:** 3 hours ❑ Read the "Introduction." ❑ Read Chapter I, "The 2014 GED® Test." ❑ Take the Social Studies section of the Diagnostic Test (Chapter II) and review the answer explanations. ❑ Note your errors. ❑ Based on your errors, identify difficult topics and item types. These are your targeted areas. ❑ Compare your extended response essay to the sample response, marking your essay with ways to improve it.

3 weeks before the test	**Study Time:** 4½ hours
	❑ Read "Test Format," Chapter X, Section A.
	❑ Read "Types of Questions in Section 1: A Detailed Look," Chapter X, Section B.
	    ❑ Read the material and do the examples.
	    ❑ Check the answer explanations and review any that you answered incorrectly.
	❑ Read "Section 2: The Extended Response," Chapter X, Section C.
	    ❑ Write a practice essay and evaluate it, looking for ways to improve it.

2 weeks before the test	**Study Time:** 2½ hours
	❑ Read "Test Strategies," Chapter X, Section D.
	    ❑ Review and practice the strategies.
	❑ Gain experience reading historical passages (U.S. history, civics and government, economics, and geography).
	❑ Read "Practice," Chapter X, Section E.
	    ❑ Answer the practice questions.
	    ❑ Check the answer explanations and review any that you answered incorrectly.

7 days before the test	**Study Time:** 2½ hours ❑ Take the Social Studies Practice Test (Chapter XIV) and review your answers. ❑ Based on your errors on the Practice Test, identify difficult topics and item types and their corresponding areas. Target these areas for extra review. ❑ Compare your extended response essay to the sample response.
6 days before the test	**Study Time:** 1½ hours ❑ Review identified target areas. ❑ Review "Types of Questions in Sections 1: A Detailed Look," Chapter X, Sections B.1–B.3.
5 days before the test	**Study Time:** 1½ hours ❑ Review identified target areas. ❑ Review "Types of Questions in Sections 1: A Detailed Look," Chapter X, Sections B.4 and B.5.
4 days before the test	**Study Time:** 1 hour ❑ Review identified target areas. ❑ Review "Section 2: The Extended Response," Chapter X, Section C. ❑ Review "Test Strategies," Chapter X, Section D.

3 days before the test	**Study Time:** 2 hours
	❑ Review identified target areas.
	❑ Redo "Practice," Chapter X, Section E.
	    ❑ Answer the practice questions.
	    ❑ Check the answer explanations and review any that you answered incorrectly.

continued

2 days before the test	**Study Time:** 2 hours
	❏ Review the Social Studies Practice Test (Chapter XIV).
	❏ Review the questions you missed and their answer explanations.
1 day before the test	❏ Relax . . . you are well prepared for the test.
	❏ Have confidence in your ability to do well.
	❏ Exercise to help relieve stress and improve sleep.
	❏ Get a good night's sleep.
Morning of the test	**Reminders:**
	❏ Have a good breakfast.
	❏ Bring your admission ticket and photo ID with you.
	❏ Try to go outside for a few minutes and walk around before the test.
	❏ Most important: Stay calm and confident during the test. Take deep, slow breaths if you feel at all nervous. You can do it!

One-Week Cram Plan

7 days before the test	**Study Time:** 3 hours ❑ Read the "Introduction." ❑ Read Chapter I, "The 2014 GED® Test." ❑ Take the Social Studies section of the Diagnostic Test (Chapter II) and review the answer explanations. ❑ Note your errors. ❑ Based on your errors, identify difficult topics and item types. These are your targeted areas. ❑ Compare your extended response essay to the sample response, marking your essay with ways to improve it.

6 days before the test	**Study Time:** 4½ hours
	❑ Read "Test Format," Chapter X, Section A.
	❑ Read "Types of Questions in Section 1: A Detailed Look," Chapter X, Section B.
	    ❑ Read the material and do the examples.
	    ❑ Check the answer explanations and review any that you answered incorrectly.
	❑ Read "Section 2: The Extended Response," Chapter X, Section C.
	    ❑ Write a practice essay and evaluate it, looking for ways to improve it.

5 days before the test	**Study Time:** 3 hours
	❑ Read "Test Strategies," Chapter X, Section D.
	    ❑ Review and practice the strategies.
	❑ Gain experience reading historical passages (U.S. history, civics and government, economics, and geography).
	❑ Read "Practice," Chapter X, Section E.
	    ❑ Answer the practice questions.
	    ❑ Check the answer explanations and review any that you answered incorrectly.

4 days before the test	**Study Time:** 2½ hours ❑ Take the Social Studies Practice Test (Chapter XIV) and review your answers. ❑ Based on your errors on the Practice Test, identify difficult topics and item types and their corresponding areas. Target these areas for extra review. ❑ Compare your extended response essay to the sample response.

3 days before the test	**Study Time:** 5 hours
	❑ Review identified target areas.
	❑ Review "Types of Questions in Section 1: A Detailed Look," Chapter X, Section B.
	❑ Review "Section 2: The Extended Response," Chapter X, Section C.
	❑ Review "Test Strategies," Chapter X, Section D.
	❑ Redo "Practice," Chapter X, Section E.
	    ❑ Answer the practice questions.
	    ❑ Check the answer explanations and review any that you answered incorrectly.

2 days before the test	**Study Time:** 2 hours ❑ Review the Social Studies Practice Test (Chapter XIV). ❑ Review the questions you missed and their answer explanations.
1 day before the test	❑ Relax . . . you are well prepared for the test. ❑ Have confidence in your ability to do well. ❑ Exercise to help relieve stress and improve sleep. ❑ Get a good night's sleep.

continued

Morning of the test	**Reminders:** ❏ Have a good breakfast. ❏ Bring your admission ticket and photo ID with you. ❏ Try to go outside for a few minutes and walk around before the test. ❏ Most important: Stay calm and confident during the test. Take deep, slow breaths if you feel at all nervous. You can do it!

VII. Reasoning through Language Arts

A. Test Format

The Reasoning through Language Arts (RLA) Test evaluates your writing and reading skills. The items will test your ability to edit and revise workplace and informational documents. The RLA Test is 150 minutes long in total. It is divided into three sections and includes a 10-minute break. You have approximately 35 minutes for Section 1 (question-and-answer items) and 45 minutes for Section 2 (the extended response, also known as the essay). You are then allowed a 10-minute break, followed by approximately 60 minutes for Section 3 (more question-and-answer items). Please note that leftover time from one section cannot be transferred to another section. Each section is timed separately.

1. Sections 1 and 3 (Question-and-answer Items)

In Sections 1 and 3 of the RLA Test, you'll encounter four item types. For descriptions and examples of these item types, see Chapter I, "The 2014 GED® Test."

1. Multiple choice
2. Fill-in-the-blank
3. Drop-down
4. Drag-and-drop

> NOTE: For study purposes, all example items in this chapter are in the multiple-choice format.

Sections 1 and 3 measure your ability to use clear and effective English. It is a test of English as it should be written, not as it may be spoken. It also measures your grammar skills. Items that test your writing and grammar skills may ask you to identify or correct errors in a sentence or to select from a series of phrases to best complete a sentence. Your reading skills are also tested in Sections 1 and 3, revealing how well you read and how well you understand what you've read. The reading content will be at the high school level, with the expectation that you will show evidence of being ready to move on to college or further education. Reading passages will vary in length from 450 to 900 words, with vocabulary from literature as well as the sciences and founding documents from American history. The mix will be about 25% fiction passages and 75% nonfiction (informational) passages:

Fiction passages—The RLA Test may contain passages from the following fictional literature genres:

- **Drama:** Drama passages—excerpts from plays—tell a story using the words and actions of the characters. The stage directions describe the setting and costumes. Stage directions are usually shown in *italics* and can provide valuable information to assist in answering the items that follow the passage.
- **Prose fiction:** Prose fiction passages are excerpts from novels and short stories that the author creates from his or her imagination.

Nonfiction (informational) passages—Nonfiction passages will be chosen from the following categories:

- **Science:** Nutrition, heredity, living systems, the human body, energy, energy conservation, and so on.
- **Social studies:** Bill of Rights, political speeches, American civics, and so on.
- **Workplace and community documents:** These documents relate to employment and community-focused areas and may include
  - Business letters
  - Employer-related statements that describe company policies
  - Goal or vision statements that detail what an organization hopes to accomplish through its activities
  - Legal documents such as leases, purchase orders, bank statements, letters, and so on
  - Manuals that accompany a purchase or are used to define a set of operating procedures

2. Section 2 (Extended Response Item)

Section 2 is the extended response item. The extended response is basically a long essay. You will be assigned a topic based on an evaluation of two source texts. You will be asked to present an opinion or explanation regarding the content of those texts. Your analytical skills will be important here, as well as your ability to write clearly, with proper spelling and grammar.

You will write your essay on the same computer as the rest of the test. An erasable noteboard is provided for prewriting and drafting. However, only your typed essay will be considered by the scorers.

B. Types of Questions in Sections 1 and 3: A Detailed Look

1. Writing Skills

The four basic types of writing skills questions, which could be presented in any of the aforementioned formats, are detailed below, with examples. In each case, you will have a choice of four answer options.

a. Organization

Organization questions require you to edit and revise a document by adding, removing, or repositioning sentences. Skills tested include the following:

- Editing to ensure effective use of transitional words and conjunctive adverbs. *Note:* Conjunctive adverbs join two phrases, the first of which is followed by a semicolon and the adverb is followed by a comma.
- Editing so that words, phrases, and sentences support logic and clarity
- Editing to ensure proper capitalization and correct use of punctuation
- Editing to correct errors involving misused and misspelled words, eliminating nonstandard English
- Identifying and evaluating topic sentences and unity/coherence throughout

EXAMPLES:

> In the following paragraph, which sentence does NOT belong?
>
> (1) Since 1974, Can-Learn Study Tours has partnered with universities, colleges, school districts, voluntary organizations, and businesses. (2) They provide educational travel programs that meet the needs of their staff and clientele. (3) Financial incentives are important to the bottom line. (4) The programs explore artistic, cultural, historic, and environmental interests. (5) Professional development activities enhance international understanding and boost creativity.
>
> **(A)** Sentence 1
> **(B)** Sentence 2
> **(C)** Sentence 3
> **(D)** Sentence 4

The correct answer is **(C).** Sentence 3 does not relate to the general theme of educational travel programs and should be deleted from the paragraph.

In the following example, choose which sentence best serves as a topic sentence with which to begin the paragraph:

(1) The GED® test is an international testing program for adults who have been unable to complete high school. (2) The test covers what high school graduates are supposed to know about language arts, mathematics, science, and social studies. (3) It also measures reading comprehension, analytical abilities, writing ability, and other important skills. (4) Since 1942, millions of adults have earned GED® diplomas. (5) The GED® program is jointly sponsored by the American Council on Education and state, territorial, and provincial departments of education. (6) The GED® acronym stands for General Educational Development, a testing service for adult high school equivalency.

> Which sentence in the above passage should logically *begin* the paragraph?
>
> **(A)** Sentence 2: The test covers what high school graduates are supposed to know about language arts, mathematics, science, and social studies.
> **(B)** Sentence 4: Since 1942, millions of adults have earned GED® diplomas.
> **(C)** Sentence 5: The GED® program is jointly sponsored by the American Council on Education and state, territorial, and provincial departments of education.
> **(D)** Sentence 6: The GED® acronym stands for General Educational Development, a testing service for adult high school equivalency.

The correct answer is **(D).** It identifies the GED® acronym. To improve this paragraph, the sentences need to be reorganized in a logical order beginning with sentence 6.

In the following example, place the sentences in logical order.

(1) They are supposed to save trees by using air to dry your hands but the air is heated. (2) Perhaps the only solution is to leave with wet hands and let nature do the drying. (3) Most paper towels today are made from recycled paper and are a long distance from the original trees. (4) Hot-air hand dryers are a scam. (5) Heated air requires energy, and producing energy has a carbon footprint.

> A logical order for these sentences would be
>
> **(A)** 1, 2, 3, 4, 5
> **(B)** 2, 4, 5, 3, 1
> **(C)** 3, 5, 1, 4, 2
> **(D)** 4, 1, 5, 3, 2

The correct answer is **(D).** The best introductory sentence is number 4 and should be the first sentence in the paragraph. This sentence is logically followed by sentence 1. The most logical final sentence is 2. If you look carefully at the answer choices, after deciding that the most logical introductory sentence is 4, there is only one answer that can be chosen.

b. Sentence Structure

Sentence structure errors involve sentence fragments, comma splices, run-on sentences, improper coordination, improper subordination, dangling modifiers, parallelism, and interrupting phrases. Example questions can be found in the Grammar Review section, starting on page 125.

i. Sentence Fragments

Sentence fragments are the most common sentence structure errors. In a sentence fragment, the writer either left out a verb or a noun or misused a word, resulting in the same error. For example:

> John leaving his keys on the coffee table.

This sentence has a subject but not a proper verb. *Leaving* is an improper form of the verb. A corrected version is

> John left his keys on the coffee table.

Here is another example:

> Where the ball? I threw it to you.

The first sentence has no verb. A corrected version is

> Where is the ball? I threw it to you.

Here is one more example:

> Can't you do properly?

This sentence has no object, and thus we are not sure what the person spoken to is not doing correctly. A corrected version is

> Can't you do anything properly?

ii. Run-On Sentences

In a **run-on sentence,** two or more independent clauses (complete sentences) are joined but the necessary conjunction or punctuation is left out. For example:

> John forgot his keys he left them on the coffee table.

Some corrected versions are

> John forgot his keys; he left them on the coffee table.
> John forgot his keys. He left them on the coffee table.

Here is another example:

> Why don't you start your homework we have to leave early tomorrow?

A corrected version is

> Why don't you start your homework? We have to leave early tomorrow.

iii. Comma Splices

Another type of error is a **comma splice.** A comma splice occurs when two independent clauses (complete sentences) are joined by a comma rather than a conjunction, a semicolon, or a period. For example:

> Peter left the house, he slammed the door.

Some corrected versions are

> Peter left the house. He slammed the door.
> Peter left the house; he slammed the door.
> Peter left the house and slammed the door.

Here is another example:

> I turned the key, nothing happened.

Some corrected versions are

> I turned the key. Nothing happened.
> I turned the key; nothing happened.
> I turned the key, but nothing happened.

Here is another example:

> I've told you a thousand times, don't exaggerate.

Some corrected versions are

> I've told you a thousand times; don't exaggerate.
> I've told you a thousand times. Don't exaggerate.

Here is one more example:

> It was freezing in the kitchen, the windows were all closed.

A corrected version is

> It was freezing in the kitchen even though the windows were all closed.

iv. Improper Coordination

Improper coordination involves a conjunction error. For example:

John forgot his keys but left them on the coffee table.

And is used to indicate a continuation of action. A corrected version is

John forgot his keys and left them on the coffee table.

Here is another example:

Robert fixed the computer but a storm raged outside.

You cannot use a coordinating conjunction to join unequal ideas. One of these ideas is less important than the other. You have to decide where to place the emphasis. You could have two different corrected sentences, depending on that decision:

Either

Robert fixed the computer while the storm raged outside.

Or

The storm raged outside while Robert fixed the computer.

Here is one more example:

Turn off the radio while I can't hear you.

While usually indicates something to do with time. *Because* indicates causality. A corrected version is

Turn off the radio because I can't hear you.

v. Improper Subordination

Improper subordination is an error in linking two sentences where one contains an idea that is dependent upon the other. Like in the example above with Robert fixing the computer, you need to make sure that your sentences are in a sequence that makes sense in terms of what you are trying to emphasize. Some subordinating conjunctions are *after, before, because, since,* and *when.*

John forgot his car keys when he locked the car.

A corrected version is

When John locked the car, he forgot his car keys.

Or

John, when he locked the car, forgot his car keys.

Here is another example:

The dog ran away when I was delayed.

A corrected version is

When I was delayed, the dog ran away.

Or

The dog ran away because I was delayed.

Here is one more example:

The pilots all received their certification and they can all work on the newest aircraft.

A corrected version is

The pilots, since they received their certification, can all work on the newest aircraft.

vi. Dangling Modifiers

Another type of error is the **dangling modifier.** For example:

Having left his keys on the coffee table, the car could not start.

This sentence seems as though "the car" left his keys on the coffee table. A corrected version is

John could not start his car because he left his keys on the coffee table.

Here is another example:

Barking and running around, my ears hurt from the dog's barking.

The sentence seems to imply that his ears were barking and running around. A corrected version is

My ears hurt from the dog's barking and running around.

Here is one more example:

Falling and piling up on the road, my neighbor is complaining about the leaves.

The neighbor is not falling and piling up on the road. A corrected version is

My neighbor is complaining about the leaves falling and piling up on the road.

vii. Parallelism Errors

A **parallelism** error involves two unparallel verbs or phrases in the same sentence. For example:

Employers value punctuality, honesty, and behave friendly in their sales staff.

The three elements that make up the predicate are not parallel in structure. The first two elements are nouns (*punctuality* and *honesty*), while the third (*behave friendly*) is a verb and adverb. A corrected sentence would be:

Employers value punctuality, honesty, and friendliness in their sales staff.

In this sentence, all three elements of the predicate are nouns or act as nouns.

Here is another example:

Leaving dishes in the sink and having washed them once a week, left the kitchen looking messy.

The verbs *leaving* and *having washed* are unparallel. A corrected version is

Leaving dishes in the sink and washing them once a week left the kitchen looking messy.

Here is one more example:

Looking up the material in several reference books and having written new paragraphs took a lot of time.

Looking up and *having written* are unparallel. A corrected version is

Looking up material in several reference books and writing new paragraphs took a lot of time.

viii. Interrupting Phrases

Any phrase that interrupts the flow of the sentence should be omitted. If the thought is important, it can be restated as a complete sentence. For example:

This music is fantastic (don't you know) and everybody enjoys dancing to it.

The phrase *don't you know* is not needed in this sentence and interrupts the flow. The best option is to delete it, but if you really want to keep it, put it in parentheses.

c. Agreement

Agreement errors may involve subject/verb agreement, verb tense errors, and pronoun agreement errors. Example questions can be found in the Grammar Review section, starting on page 125.

i. Subject-Verb Agreement

Here's an example of a **subject/verb** error:

John and Mary is going to the movies.

The plural subject *John and Mary* requires a plural verb. A corrected version is

John and Mary are going to the movies.

ii. Verb Tense Errors

A **verb tense** error involves using a tense that is not the same as the other verb tenses in the sentence or paragraph. For example:

Peter gets up early, ate his breakfast, and leaves for school.

In this case both *gets* and *leaves* are present tense, while *ate* is past tense. All verbs must be in the same tense. A corrected version is

Peter gets up early, eats his breakfast, and leaves for school.

iii. Pronoun Reference Errors

Pronoun reference errors consist of agreement with antecedents, incorrect relative pronouns, pronoun shifts, and vague or ambiguous references. For example, pronouns must be the same gender and number as the nouns they refer to or replace.

Agreement with antecedents—A pronoun should agree with its antecedent (the noun it refers to). For example:

The players went to the game, and he was the first to leave.

In this case, *players* (the antecedent) is plural, while *he* (the pronoun) is singular. A corrected version is

The players went to the game, and they were the first to leave.

Another example:

> Everyone in class was busy reading their material.

Everyone is singular and cannot be followed by the plural pronoun *their*. *Their* should be changed to *his* or *her*.

> Everyone in class was busy reading his material.

Incorrect relative pronouns—Another pronoun reference error involves the incorrect usage of the relative pronoun. The relative pronouns are *who, whom, whose, which, what,* and *that*. For example:

> My brother, which lives in New York, is an engineer.

In this case, the pronoun *which* (used for inanimate objects) should be replaced with the pronoun *who* (used for people). A corrected version is

> My brother, who lives in New York, is an engineer.

Pronoun shift—Pronoun use should be consistent throughout a sentence. For example:

> The teacher gave us a lot of examples to make sure that you could learn about this topic.

In this sentence, the pronouns shift from first person, *us*, to second person, *you*. When you are writing sentences, ensure that your pronouns are consistent. A corrected version is

> The teacher gave us a lot of examples to make sure that we could learn about this topic.

Vague or ambiguous references—A pronoun should refer to a specific noun and not leave the reader wondering what is going on. For example:

> Harry, Joe, and Mohammed went to get ice cream cones, and by the look on his face you could tell he was really enjoying the treat.

The two pronouns, *his* and *he,* could refer to any one of the three people named, which is ambiguous and confusing to a reader. A corrected version is

> Harry, Joe, and Mohammed went to get ice cream cones, and by the look on Joe's face you could tell he was really enjoying the treat.

d. Mechanics

Mechanics problems may include capitalization, punctuation, or spelling errors. Example questions can be found in the Grammar Review section, starting on page 125.

i. Capitalization

Capitalization questions require that you understand the correct use of lowercase and capital letters with dates, places, times, titles, proper nouns, and adjectives. How can the following passage be corrected?

> I am pleased to comment on the relationship of our organization to Peta Jackson of the York Square employment Resource center (ERC). Since April 2002, the beatrice institute of technology has partnered with the York Square erc in recruiting candidates for our cafe equipment technician training program.

To correct this passage, all proper nouns should be capitalized as follows:

> I am pleased to comment on the relationship of our organization to Peta Jackson of the York Square Employment Resource Center (ERC). Since April 2002, the Beatrice Institute of Technology has partnered with the York Square ERC in recruiting candidates for our Cafe Equipment Technician training program.

ii. Punctuation

The use of proper punctuation refers to all usage, but especially the use of commas and colons. The comma is used to separate a series of three or more words, phrases, or clauses. The colon is used before a list of items or details.

How can the following sentence be improved?

> These programs have included educational travel programs, which explore the following artistic and cultural interests historic and archaeological themes environmental and wellness experiences and new service patterns.

The sentence can be corrected as follows:

> These programs have included educational travel programs, which explore the following: artistic and cultural interests, historic and archaeological themes, environmental and wellness experiences, and new service patterns.

iii. Usage Errors

Usage errors may involve the incorrect use of possessives, contractions, and *homonyms* (sound-alike words).

Possessives—Possessives show ownership. The following example contains an error in the use of the third person possessive pronoun. What change should be made to correct the sentence?

> This is an opportunity for adults to document and assess there prior learning.

To correct the spelling error, *there* should be replaced by *their*. *Their* is a possessive pronoun (showing belonging) and is required in this sentence. *There* is an indication of location in space or time.

Contractions—Contractions combine two words, leaving out a letter or letters and replacing them with an apostrophe. How would you correct the following sentence?

> Thank you for you're interest in our new company, which serves the rapidly expanding specialty coffee industry.

To correct this sentence, change *you're* (which means *you are*) to *your*. The pronoun *your* indicates ownership of the new company. The contraction is spelled correctly, but the usage is wrong.

> Remember that in essays, business letters, or other formal writing, contractions are considered poor style and inappropriate.

Homonyms—Homonyms are sound-alike words. They may be contractions or possessives, as mentioned earlier, or they may be other words that sound like one another but have different spellings and meanings. Consider the following three words, which are all pronounced similarly, but have different meanings: *knot, not,* and *naught.* For example:

The ship moved at three nots, but with the current, it was all for naught, and they did not arrive in time.

Which of the *not, knot,* or *naught* words is used incorrectly in the example above? In the above sentence, *nots* should be *knots;* a *knot* is a unit of speed.

Here is another example of a homonym usage error:

We have there approval for the purchase.

Which word, *their* or *there*, is correct in this case? The correct word to use in this case is *their. Their* indicates ownership, while *there* indicates a direction or location.

And here is one last example:

We have to many overdue bills.

Remember, there are three words that sound alike: *two, to,* and *too.* The correct version here is *too.*

Here is a partial list of common homonyms and their meanings. In some cases, you will see examples of the word used in a sentence. Learn these carefully. Not only are they common mistakes, but they are part of your essay evaluation on the extended response items on the Reasoning through Language Arts Test and the Social Studies Test.

accept except	To receive, admit, regard as true, say yes. *I accept your invitation.* Excluding. *Everyone is going to the party except Sally.* If not for the fact that; other than. *She always sleeps in except on Christmas morning.*
aid aide	To assist, help. *I need your aid in tying this parcel.* One who assists, helps. *Edwin was studying to become a nurse's aide.*
brake break	This stops a vehicle. *She applied the brake to the car.* A pause or injury. As a verb, to cause an injury in which something is torn or snapped. *Be careful! You might fall and break a bone.*
cereal serial	A food or a grain crop, such as wheat or oats. *Adam likes to eat cereal for breakfast.* Something that happens in sequence. Also means something which happens regularly, one part after the other, like a soap opera. *My grandfather used to watch the Buck Rogers serials at the movie theater every Saturday.*
cite site sight	To show the source for a quote or document in an essay. *Megan cited all of her sources at the end of her essay.* A location: *We visited the Google site regularly.* or *Waterloo was the site of a great battle.* The ability to see. Can also mean the targeting mechanism on a weapon. *After the accident, she lost her sight.* or *The sights on the rifle were inaccurate.*
dear deer	Darling or expensive or close. *My mother's present was very dear to her.* The animal. *We hunt deer because hunting is an exciting sport.*
feat feet	Achievement. *Winning a gold medal is a respectable feat.* What we walk on. *The wounded soldier struggled to get up on his feet.*
fir fur	A cone-bearing tree. *The fir tree grew straight and tall.* The thick hair covering an animal's body. *People are finally deciding not to wear fur as a fashion accessory.*
flour flower	Ground grain, fine powder. *We make pastries with flour.* Bloom on a plant. *They watered the flowers every day.*
gorilla guerrilla	The big ape. *The zoo's new gorilla exhibit is set to open this summer.* A warrior or a soldier who fights under cover, in secret. *It is very difficult to fight a guerilla army with conventional forces.*

groan	A sound one makes to express pain or disapproval. *After the bad joke, I could hear the audience groan.*
grown	Increased in size or stature. *It's so nice to see you after all these years; you have grown so much.*
here	At or in this place. *Please come here and help me lift the box.*
hear	To sense sounds with your ears. *Didn't you hear what I said?*
holey	Full of holes. *Swiss cheese is holey because of the way it is made.*
holy	Sacred. *Books like the Torah, the Bible, and the Quran are considered holy; they are the Word of God.*
wholly	Completely. *I wholly believe his story.*
knot	Something tied together, a jumble; also a nautical term used to measure speed. *The cruise ship travelled at 25 knots, trying to avoid a storm.*
not	Negative, refusal. *The captain did not want to get caught in that storm.*
naught	A zero, for nothing. *However, the storm changed directions and all the efforts were for naught.*
role	Part that one plays, serves. *Alvin played the role of Edwin in the play.*
roll	To move/turn in a circular motion. *Roll that barrel over here, please.*
soar	To rise far, fly. *The passengers could watch the storm clouds soar over the ship.*
sore	Hurt. *Some passengers fell as the ship rocked in the waves; they were sore for days.*
their	Belongs to them. *The crew worked hard to keep their ship and passengers safe.*
there	Location, in time or space. *When the storm hit, the ship was there, right in the center of it.*
they're	Contraction of *they are*. *No one is on deck. They're all trying hard to stay dry.*
two	The number. *The two passengers were too busy to go to the shelter.*
too	Also, more than, very. *It is too windy outside today to fly a kite.*
to	Toward, movement, or to indicate following verb is an infinitive (e.g., to buy, to go, to have). *I am going to the grocery store.*
weather	The climate at the moment. *The crew hoped the weather would clear up.*
whether	If. *Whether it cleared up or not, the trip would go on.*
your	Belongs to you. *Your backpack is hanging on the hook.*
you're	Contraction of *you are*. *You're going to take your camera with you on the trip.*

2. Reading Skills

As mentioned earlier, approximately 25 percent of the reading passages on the RLA Test are fiction, and the remaining 75 percent are nonfiction.

The four types of reading skills questions are described in detail in this section, along with examples of each question type. These questions will appear in various forms on the actual GED® test—multiple choice, drag-and-drop, drop-down, fill-in-the-blank—but for study purposes, all example questions in this chapter are in the multiple-choice format.

a. Comprehension

Comprehension questions test your ability to read a source of information, understand it, and restate it in your own words. Comprehension questions might ask you to choose the answer choice that rephrases what you've read without losing the meaning of the passage. Ideas from the passage can be summarized to demonstrate the meaning and implications of what the author suggests.

EXAMPLES:

The comprehension example questions are based on the following passage from "Gold Seekers of '49" by Edwin D. Sabin (1915).

It has taken Americans to build the Panama Canal, and it took the Americans to build California. These are two great feats of which we Americans of the United States may well be proud: the building of that canal, in the strange tropics 2,000 miles away across the water, and the up-rearing of a mighty State, under equally strange conditions, 2,000 miles away across plains and mountains.

On the Isthmus men of many nationalities combined like a vast family; each man, from laborer to engineer, doing his stint, without favoritism and without graft, toward the big result. So in California likewise a people collected from practically all the world became Americans together under the Flag, and working shoulder to shoulder—rich and poor, old and young, educated and uneducated, no matter what their manner of life previously—they joined forces to make California worthy of being a State in the Union.

What similarities does the author find between the building of the Panama Canal and the building of California into a prosperous state?

(A) Both were helped by the gold rush.

(B) Both were 2,000 miles away.

(C) In both places people worked hard together to create something great.

(D) People in both places prospered.

The correct answer is **(C)**. People worked together to create the Panama Canal and the state of California, an accomplishment to make them proud. Choices (A) and (B) are both mentioned in the passage but do not answer the question. Choice (D) may be partially true, but is not the best answer. It does not catch the flavor of the text, the feeling of pride in achievement.

Who built the Panama Canal?

(A) People of many nationalities

(B) The rich and the poor

(C) The young and the old

(D) All of the above

The correct answer is **(D)**. Per the passage, choices (A) through (C) all contributed to the successful completion of the Panama Canal.

b. Application

Application questions assess your ability to use the information in the passage in answering questions involving both stated and suggested information. Application questions often ask you to apply what you've learned in the passage to real-life situations.

EXAMPLES:

The application example questions are based on the following excerpt from remarks made by President Obama at the presentation ceremony for the Medal of Honor. Source: www.whitehouse.gov/the-press-office/2014/03/18/ remarks-president-presentation-ceremony-medal-honor.

…This ceremony reminds us of one of the enduring qualities that makes America great—that makes us exceptional. No nation is perfect, but here in America we confront our imperfections and face a sometimes painful past—including the truth that some of these soldiers fought, and died, for a country that did not always see them as equal. So with each generation we keep on striving to live up to our ideals of freedom and equality, and to recognize the dignity and patriotism of every person, no matter who they are, what they look like, or how they pray.

And that's why, more than a decade ago, Congress mandated a review to make sure that the heroism of our veterans wasn't overlooked because of prejudice or discrimination. Our military reviewed thousands of war records. They teamed up with veterans groups and museums to get this right. It was painstaking work, made even harder because sometimes our servicemembers felt as if they needed to change their last names to fit in. That tells a story about our past. But, ultimately, after years of review, these two dozen soldiers—among them Hispanic, African American and Jewish veterans—were identified as having earned the Medal of Honor. This is the length to which America will go to make sure everyone who serves under our proud flag receives the thanks that they deserve.

So this is going to be a long ceremony. We're going to read all 24 citations, because every one is a story of bravery that deserves to be told. But first, I want to take just a few minutes to describe the Americans behind these actions, the men these families know—the brilliant lives behind the smiling faces in those old photographs, and how they reflected all the beauty and diversity of the country that they served.

They were Americans by birth and Americans by choice—immigrants, including one who was not yet even a citizen. They grew up in big city neighborhoods like Brooklyn, rural communities like Hooper, Nebraska, small towns in Puerto Rico. They loved to fish and play baseball. They were sons who made their parents proud, and brothers who their siblings looked up to. They were so young—many in their early 20s. And when their country went to war, they answered the call. They put on the uniform, and hugged their families goodbye—some of them hugged the wives and children that they'd never see again.

They fought in the rocky hills of Italy, the blood-stained beaches of France, in the freezing mountains of Korea, the humid jungles of Vietnam. Their courage almost defies imagination. When you read the records of these individuals, it's unimaginable, the valor that they displayed. Running into bullets. Charging machine gun nests and climbing aboard tanks and taking them out. Covering their comrades so they could make it to safety. Holding back enemies, wave after wave, even when the combat was hand-to-hand. Manning their posts—some to their very last breaths—so that their comrades might live. …

Why was the President presenting Medals of Honor to soldiers so many years after the fact?

(A) To correct an injustice
(B) To acknowledge a change in criteria for the medal
(C) To garner more publicity
(D) Congress insisted

The correct answer is **(A).** While Congress had mandated a review (D), it did not insist on these particular medals being presented to these particular soldiers. While it may be great publicity (C), that is not the stated purpose of the passage. Certainly the criteria for the Medal of Honor have not changed (B). That means the medals were awarded to correct an injustice.

What does it take to qualify for the Medal of Honor?

(A) Great courage in the face of enemy action
(B) Risking one's life to save comrades
(C) Fighting on, even when the situation may be hopeless
(D) All of the above

In this instance, the correct answer is **(D)**, "All of the above." The medal winners were all involved in actions similar to the ones listed in choices (A), (B), and (C). While these actions may not have been listed very specifically, you can derive these generalizations from the text.

c. Analysis

By examining the style and structure of the passage, you should be able to draw conclusions, determine the tone of the passage, understand consequences, and make inferences. You have to be sure that the consequences you identify are based on the content of the passage, not on your own previous knowledge. Analysis questions might ask about cause-and-effect relationships, the type of language used, and presentation of details.

EXAMPLES:

The analysis example questions are based on the following passage, an excerpt from "All You Can Eat" by Murray Shukyn. The narrator is thinking of his friend Sandy while phoning a call center.

I thought of Sandy, who supervised a call center and wondered if it was a bank call center. Then I would understand why her job was so important. That was probably why she had to work so hard. I was beginning to appreciate Sandy's responsibilities.

"Operator forty-eight, can I help you?" a voice said.

"I lost my bank card," I said.

"Where did you lose your card?" operator forty-eight asked.

"If I knew that, I would go back and look for it," I replied.

"In what city did the loss occur?" operator forty-eight asked.

"The same city you're in," I immediately answered.

"You lost your card in Manila?" operator forty-eight said.

"No, I'm in Toronto," I said with a question in my voice. "Where are you?"

"In a call center in the Philippines. How can I help you?" operator forty-eight replied in a friendlier tone.

What phrase best describes Sandy's performance?

(A) Hard worker
(B) Thoughtful person
(C) Dedicated employee
(D) Careless supervisor

The correct answer is **(A).** According to the excerpt, choice (A) "hard worker" best describes Sandy's performance. She also may have been thoughtful (B), and dedicated (C), but these qualities are not mentioned in the passage. We have no reason to believe that she was careless (D).

> What is the main conclusion to be drawn from this passage?
>
> **(A)** People lose their bank cards.
> **(B)** Operators can be friendly.
> **(C)** Call centers don't always provide local service.
> **(D)** Callers should be patient.

The correct answer is **(C)**. From the passage we learn that the operator is located thousands of miles away. The other choices, while relevant, do not represent the main idea that the author wishes to convey.

d. Synthesis

Synthesis questions require you to identify and compare and contrast information from different parts of the passage. You should be able to integrate information from the passage to answer the questions. These questions measure your ability to understand the overall tone, point of view, style, purpose, and organization of the passage.

EXAMPLES:

The synthesis example questions are based on the following excerpt from "Beyond Good and Evil," written by Friedrich Nietzsche in 1886.

In what strange simplification and falsification man lives! One can never cease wondering when once one has got eyes for beholding this marvel! How we have made everything around us clear and free and easy and simple! how we have been able to give our senses a passport to everything superficial, our thoughts a godlike desire for wanton pranks and wrong inferences!—how from the beginning, we have contrived to retain our ignorance in order to enjoy an almost inconceivable freedom, thoughtlessness, imprudence, heartiness, and gaiety—in order to enjoy life! And only on this solidified, granite-like foundation of ignorance could knowledge rear itself hitherto, the will to knowledge on the foundation of a far more powerful will, the will to ignorance, to the uncertain, to the untrue! Not as its opposite, but—as its refinement!

> How does this passage predict the behavior of the "common man"?
>
> **(A)** People remain ignorant in order to enjoy life.
> **(B)** People love the freedom of not thinking too deeply.
> **(C)** There is a will to ignorance.
> **(D)** All of the above

The correct answer is **(D)**, "All of the above." Nietzsche states we have given ourselves a passport to everything superficial in order to enjoy life. He states this as a very clear generalization of human behavior.

> How would you describe Nietzsche's view of people in general?
>
> **(A)** People want to enjoy life.
> **(B)** People are generally shallow.
> **(C)** People lie to themselves.
> **(D)** Out of the foundation of ignorance grows a desire for knowledge.

These choices present a challenge. They require careful analysis because there's an element a truth in each of them. We can rule out choice (D) because nature makes it clear that this is an outgrowth of the foundation of the ignorance of most people. Therefore, it does not apply to people in general. Choices (A) and (B) are true but not the complete answer. Choice **(C)** is the best answer. It comes right at the beginning of the passage where Nietzsche states "what strange … falsification man lives!" In other words, most lives are falsifications. Most people lie to themselves, and out of that grows everything else.

C. Section 2: The Extended Response

The extended response item tests your writing and editing skills. It is basically a long essay. You will be presented with two readings, and be asked to analyze and evaluate them. Your essay will take a position based on these readings, and defend that position using information in the readings, as well as your own information. Below, we detail the steps to writing and editing an essay, followed by some suggestions for practicing for this portion of the test.

1. Writing

a. Steps to Writing a Passing Essay

1. Read the passages carefully. No credit is given for an essay written on another topic.
2. Plan the main points of the essay: an introduction, the main points, and a conclusion. The main points may need more than one paragraph.
3. Organize the material so it flows from beginning to end.
4. Make sure that the statement of purpose of the essay (the thesis) is contained in the introductory sentence of the first paragraph.
5. Turn the main points into sentences.
6. Reread paragraphs for continuity.
7. Enter the final essay into the computer.
8. Edit for mistakes in spelling and grammar.

b. Essay Structure

An effective essay should be organized, with effective text divisions and topic sentences. Your writing also should demonstrate unity and coherence.

This reminds us of the story of an old preacher who had a poor rural parish. He was able to present really sophisticated information to his parishioners without lecturing them or putting them to sleep. When he was asked how he managed that, he replied, "First, I tell them what I'm going to tell them. Then I tell them. Then I tell them what I told them." This is also a good approach to essay-writing. A good essay is comprised of an introduction (tell them what you're going to tell them), a body (tell them), and a conclusion (tell them what you told them).

Organization—One of the most important aspects of any essay is the organization of the ideas and the sentences that express those ideas. Once you have a list of main points, you have to decide on the order of ideas and which ideas belong together. Putting related ideas together makes dividing the essay into paragraphs a lot easier.

Effective text divisions—Your essay should be divided into paragraphs.

The **first paragraph** is the introduction. It should start by presenting the argument (your thesis statement) you intend to make in the essay. It should present all the basic evidence you intend to use to support your thesis or argument. It does not need to explain your evidence; that comes in the later paragraphs. In addition, it should catch the interest of readers and make them want to read the essay. This can be the hardest paragraph to write and deserves the most attention.

The **last paragraph** is the summary. This should sum up what was said or restate the point of view of the essay. It is the last paragraph to write because you have to know what you're going to summarize.

The **remaining paragraphs** should each contain one main thought. Like all paragraphs, they should start with an introductory sentence and finish with a summary sentence. That summary sentence might also provide a link to the first sentence of the next paragraph.

Forming new paragraphs—As you look at your rough material for the essay, join material that belongs together. You can do this by numbering the ideas or drawing boxes around related ideas or anything that is quick and keeps related ideas together. Mark some ideas as main points, and others as subpoints, which support the main points. Each idea forms the basis for one or more paragraphs. After you have sorted the points, you should write the introductory sentence. Your subpoints can now be put in order so that they flow and advance the topic of your essay. Once this is done, you can write your summary sentence and turn your subpoints into sentences.

Topic sentences—Each paragraph should begin with a topic sentence that states the main point of the paragraph and draws the reader into the material. A topic sentence has to be the most interesting sentence in the paragraph because it sets the tone and defines the topic of the paragraph.

Unity and coherence—A good essay is understandable and written about a single topic. If you're asked to write an essay about your favorite animal and you choose a Labrador Retriever, no matter how much you know about elephants, you can't write about elephants in this essay. Your essay about only Labrador Retrievers as pets would have unity. If you wrote clearly, your essay will have coherence or consistency. But if you interjected information about elephants into your Labrador Retriever essay, your essay would be disjointed.

2. Editing

After you write an essay or any other document, you come to the most important part of the job: editing. The following steps will help you edit your essay into an even better piece of work.

a. Adding

Read through your essay and your rough notes. Decide if there is any information you should add. The important consideration at this point is whether this additional information will improve the essay. If the information will improve your essay, include it. If not, leave it out.

b. Removing

Would your essay be improved by removing any information, words, or sentences? If there are facts that do not relate to the subject of your essay, delete them. Your essay should be about one topic and only one topic. If there is anything in the essay about another topic or something that does not add to your essay, leave it out.

c. Repositioning

Each paragraph of an essay should flow from beginning to end, and the essay itself should flow from beginning to end. If you have sentences that restrict this flow of ideas but are necessary to make the point of the essay, consider moving them. Ask yourself if there is a place in the essay where this sentence would add to the smooth flow of the paragraph. As a final check, make sure that each paragraph aids the smooth flow of ideas from beginning to end.

One way to check for flow is to read the introductory paragraph, and then the first and last sentence of each subsequent paragraph. Then read the concluding paragraph. What you have read should make perfect sense; if it does not, it is time for more editing. There is nothing wrong with moving words, sentences, or paragraphs to improve the essay.

3. Practice

For practice, write an essay on any two of the following three topics, using the plan suggested above:

- How would you organize an essay to convince someone that gun control is (or is not) a good idea?
- Pick an editorial or column from a newspaper. What methods does the editorial (or column) use to make its point?
- Find two articles, one for and one against a particular issue of your choice. Which article makes its argument most persuasively?

When you've completed your essays, you (or a friend) should evaluate each essay using the following questions:

- Does the essay focus on the assigned topic?
- Is the statement of purpose of the essay contained in the introductory sentence and paragraph?
- Does the essay flow in an organized manner?
- Do you support your point of view with specific examples?
- Do you always use correct English grammar, spelling, and punctuation?
- Do you use varied, precise, and appropriate choices of words?

If you can answer "yes" to each of these questions, you're well on your way to writing an essay that will receive at least a passing grade.

D. Test Strategies

1. Writing

Here are some strategies to help you succeed on the Reasoning through Language Arts writing skills items:

- **Brush up on your grammar skills.** Study Section E, "Grammar Review," in addition to any other grammar handbooks or resources you have available. (We list a few suggestions at the beginning of Section E.)

- **Read, read, read!** Reading is one of the best ways you can prepare for the Reasoning through Language Arts Test. Reading literature, magazines, and newspapers can expose you to proper grammar and writing structure.

- **Practice writing.** Start a journal or blog. Write stories.

- **Review the example questions.** There are example questions sprinkled throughout this chapter. Use your hand or a piece of paper to cover the answer and explanation while you're answering the question. After you answer the question, check your answer and, if it's right, read the explanation to reinforce the reasoning. If you got it wrong, read the explanation, reread the question to see where you went wrong, and reread the related grammar review material. If you're still struggling with a question, expand your reading until it all makes sense. Additional sample questions can be found online on the GED Testing Service® website: www.gedtestingservice.com/freepractice/download/GED_RLA/GED_RLA_PracticeTest.html. (Please note that this site is designed for use by educators and that GED Testing Service® is not affiliated with, and does not endorse, *CliffsNotes GED® TEST Cram Plan, 2nd Edition*.)

- **Take the practice test.** Take the Reasoning through Language Arts Practice Test (Chapter XI). Do so under test conditions—using a timer. Check your answers and review the explanations. Write your answers to the practice test on a separate sheet of paper, instead of directly in this book. That way you can take the practice test more than once.

2. Reading

To prepare for the reading skills items, you need to work on your reading and comprehension skills. Each passage and question should be read carefully to find the right answer. Here are a few tips to assist in preparation:

- **Read, read, read!** Read carefully as much fiction and nonfiction material as possible, including novels, plays, short stories, magazines, and newspapers. Visit the library for books and stories written about anything that interests you and read, read, and read some more. If you have trouble deciding what to read, follow your interests. Anything you read will make you a better reader.

- **Quiz yourself.** Ask yourself questions about what you've read. Try to understand the main ideas. Test yourself and your understanding by trying to explain those ideas to others.

- **Look it up!** Use a dictionary to discover the meaning of new words you find in your reading. To enrich your vocabulary, try to use these new words in a sentence or use them in conversation with family and friends.

- **Review the example questions and work the practice questions.** There are example questions in the Grammar Review section of this chapter (starting on page 125). More questions for practice appear at the end of this chapter. Work through these questions and check your answers. If you answered a question correctly, read the explanation to reinforce the reasoning. If you answered incorrectly, read the explanation, and then reread the question to see where you went wrong.

- **Take the practice test.** Take the Reasoning through Language Arts Practice Test (Chapter XI). Do so under test conditions—using a timer. Check your answers and review the explanations. Write your answers to the practice test on a separate sheet of paper, instead of directly in this book. That way you can take the practice test more than once.

E. Grammar Review

We've provided this grammar review to help you prepare for the RLA Test. This review will assist you in two ways:

- The material presented here can improve your ability to answer the items that require corrections.
- In writing your essay, correct grammar is a must; this section provides you with the basic information to write correct sentences.

Please keep in mind that this is a very general review. For additional grammar review, you can visit CliffsNotes.com (www.cliffsnotes.com/writing) or reference these other great CliffsNotes titles:

CliffsNotes English Grammar Practice Pack

CliffsNotes Verbal Review for Standardized Tests, 2nd Edition

1. Parts of Speech

a. Nouns

A noun is a word that names a person, place, thing, or idea.

EXAMPLE:

The cat was in the house looking for a mouse in the kitchen.

How many nouns are there in the sentence?

(A) One
(B) Two
(C) Three
(D) Four

The correct answer is **(D)**. There are four nouns in the sentence: *cat, house, mouse,* and *kitchen.*

A **proper noun** names a specific person, place, or thing and begins with a capital letter.

EXAMPLE:

I went to visit betty yesterday.

Change:

(A) *y* to *Y* in *yesterday*
(B) *I* to *i*
(C) *b* to *B* in *betty*
(D) No change needed

The correct answer is **(C)**. *Betty* is a proper noun and should begin with a capital *B*.

b. Pronouns

A pronoun stands in place of a noun in a sentence. You'll encounter several types of pronouns:

- **Personal pronouns** stand for nouns that name persons and things, such as *he, she,* and *they.* For example:

    Shakira arrived; *she* was late.

- **Possessive pronouns** indicate ownership and can be used to stand for nouns or used as adjectives. For example:

    His book was on the table beside the lamp.

    His is a possessive pronoun.

- **Intensive pronouns** can be used to emphasize a noun or another pronoun. For example:

    I myself will fix that tire.

    Myself is an intensive pronoun.

- **Reflexive pronouns** look like intensive pronouns but refer back to the subject of the sentence. For example:

    I will fix it myself.

    Myself is a reflexive pronoun in this sentence because it refers back to the subject of the sentence, *I.*

- **Interrogative pronouns** are used to introduce questions. For example:

    What did you want?

    What is an interrogative pronoun because it is used to introduce a question.

- **Indefinite pronouns** stand for unspecified persons or things. For example:

    No one can fix that rotten tire.

    No one is an indefinite pronoun because the noun that it stands for is not specified.

- **Demonstrative pronouns** point to nouns. For example:

    That is the garage where I got my tire fixed.

    That is a demonstrative pronoun because it points to a noun, *garage.*

- **Reciprocal pronouns** express the relationship between two or more nouns or pronouns. For example:

    Bill and the mechanic glanced from the flat tire to one another.

    One another is a reciprocal pronoun because it indicates that both *Bill* and the *mechanic* are related in their frustration over the tire.

EXAMPLES:

> *We often traveled the Grand Canyon on our vacation. No one else seemed to want to hike those trails, but we did and enjoyed each other's company while we were hiking.*
>
> How many pronouns are there in total in these sentences?
>
> **(A)** Four
> **(B)** Five
> **(C)** Six
> **(D)** Seven

The correct answer is **(C)**. There are six pronouns in these sentences: *we* (three times), *our, no one,* and *each other.*

> What type of pronoun is *no one*?
>
> **(A)** Personal pronoun
> **(B)** Indefinite pronoun
> **(C)** Reciprocal pronoun
> **(D)** Reflexive pronoun

The correct answer is **(B)**. *No one* is an indefinite pronoun because the person or persons whom it refers to are unspecified.

The next example question refers to the following passage.

(1) In order to open the door of the apartment, you should take the key provided by management in your right hand, or your left one if you're left-handed. (2) Stand so that your dominant hand is in front of the lock and insert it into the lock channel. (3) Make sure that the key goes all the way into the cylinder and turn the key clockwise, to the right, until a click is heard. (4) If there is a lot of noise in the hallway, you may miss the click, but be assured that the key can only be turned 45 degrees without forcing it. (5) At this point you may use either hand to turn the door handle clockwise until the door swings open.

> Which correction is needed to make the paragraph correct?
>
> **(A)** Sentence 2 should read: *Stand so that your dominant hand is in front of the lock and insert <u>the key</u> into the lock channel.*
> **(B)** Sentence 3 should read: *Make sure that the key goes all the way into the cylinder and turn the key <u>counterclockwise</u>, to the right, until a click is heard.*
> **(C)** Sentence 4 should read: *If there is a lot of noise in the hallway, you may miss the click, but be assured that the key can only be turned 45 degrees without forcing <u>him</u>.*
> **(D)** No change required.

The correct answer is **(A)**. The pronoun *it* refers back to the noun *hand* and that's incorrect. The noun *key* must be used in the sentence to make sense because most of the paragraph refers to the key. The other changes introduce grammatical errors into sentences that are already correct. For example, choice (C) has the correction of replacing the pronoun *it* referring to the noun *key* with *him,* which is a personal pronoun and should refer to a person.

c. Verbs

i. Verb Forms

Verbs are action words or state-of-being words.

A verb may consist of one word or two words. For example:

> The cat chased the mouse.
> The cat didn't have enough to eat.

In the first example, the verb is one word: *chased*. In the second example, the verb consists of two words: *didn't* and *have.* In this case, the first word, *didn't,* makes the verb negative.

A **transitive verb** is one that shows action and requires an object; **intransitive verbs** do not require objects in order to be understood. For example:

> The cat knocked over the vase.

The verb *knocked over* (a compound verb) is transitive because it requires the object *vase* to complete it. For example:

> The cat fell.

The verb *fell* is intransitive because there is no object, and the sentence makes sense.

A **linking verb** links the subject of the sentence to another word that relates to it. For example:

> The cat was sad.

The verb *was* is a linking verb because the subject *cat* is linked to the word *sad.*

A **predicate nominative** is a noun or pronoun after the verb *to be* in any form. For example:

> She is an astronaut.

She is the subject of the sentence. The word *astronaut* further identifies the subject and is in the nominative case. Since it makes up the predicate, it is called a predicate nominative. To test if this applies to a sentence, reverse the subject and the word you think is a predicate nominative. If it is a predicate nominative, you can reverse them without changing the meaning of the sentence.

ii. Verb Tense

The tense of a verb tells us when the action takes place.

Present tense describes actions that take place in the moment. For example:

> I am reading this book.

Past tense describes actions that took place before now. For example:

> I read this book yesterday.

Future tense describes actions that will take place in the future. For example:

- I will read this book tomorrow.

EXAMPLES:

> What is the verb in the following sentence?
> *The racing car rolled down the steep hill.*
>
> **(A)** steep
> **(B)** down
> **(C)** hill
> **(D)** rolled

The correct answer is **(D).** The word *rolled* indicates an action and is, thus, a verb. *Racing* is a form of a verb used as an adjective to modify car.

The next two sample questions refer to the company memo to all staff.

(1) Starting today, all staff members will finish consuming before the start of the business day and prior to going to their work stations. (2) The spilling of coffee on keyboards is creating an unexpected and unnecessary expense, which is starting to decrease our profits. (3) Anyone spilling coffee on his keyboard was expected to replace it at his own expense. (4) This also applies to water, tea, fruit juices, and any other liquids that can be carried to your workplace.

—Management

> What changes must be made to correct Sentence 1?
> **(A)** Replace *Starting* with *Start.*
> **(B)** Insert *coffee* between *consuming* and *before.*
> **(C)** Omit *stations.*
> **(D)** Omit *the start of.*

The correct answer is **(B).** *Consuming* is a transitive verb and needs an object to complete it. Because the entire memo is about coffee, it would seem reasonable to use *coffee* as the object of the verb.

> What changes must be made to correct Sentence 3?
> **(A)** Replace *Anyone* with *Everyone.*
> **(B)** Replace *it* with *him.*
> **(C)** Replace *was* with *will be.*
> **(D)** No change required.

The correct answer is **(C).** The verb *was expected* is in the past tense, which is the incorrect tense. Since the memo applies from this point forward, the sentence should be in the future tense. The correct version is *will be expected.*

iii. Sequence of Tenses

The verb tenses in a sentence should make sense chronologically. They should follow a logical sequence. You would never say,

> I had to take my dog to the vet today because he will be sick yesterday.

The sequence of events was as follows:

1. The dog got sick.
2. The dog had to be taken to the vet.

One correct option for these sentences is:

> My dog got sick yesterday, and I have to take him to the vet today.

In the corrected sentence, the verb tenses reflect the chronological order of events.

iv. Word Clues to Tense in Sentences

The verb tense in a sentence should make sense according to the clues in the sentence. For example:

> "Stop now!" the police officer will shout at the fleeing suspect.

Logically, if the police officer wanted the suspect to stop, the police officer would want the suspect to stop immediately and not sometime in the future. The sentence should read:

> "Stop now!" the police officer shouted at the fleeing suspect.

v. Word Clues to Tense in Paragraphs

The tense of a verb indicates the time an action took place. In a paragraph, the actions indicated should take place in a logical, sequential order. Check over your paragraph to make sure that the tenses indicate the time you want an action to occur.

d. Adjectives

Adjectives modify or describe a noun or pronoun and, by doing so, add information to the sentence. For example:

> I saw the red car go by again.

Red is an adjective modifying the noun *car* and adding information to the sentence. We now know that the car is red and not some other color.

EXAMPLES:

Which of the following improves the sentence by adding an adjective?

I love to go out in the woods in late autumn and look at the leaves.

(A) Replace *woods* with *trees.*
(B) Replace *late* with *the.*
(C) Insert *carefully* between *look* and *at.*
(D) Insert *colorful* between *the* and *leaves.*

The correct answer is **(D).** Inserting the adjective *colorful* before the noun *leaves* gives us some more information about the leaves. Choice (C) might give you more information, but it does not modify a noun and, thus, is not an adjective. (It is an adverb.)

Which of the following changes would emphasize the experience of being too close to race cars?

The race cars sped by, and the roar of the engines hurt my ears.

(A) Insert *red* before *cars.*
(B) Insert *cold* before *ears.*
(C) Insert *loud* before *roar.*
(D) Insert *finely tuned* before *engines.*

The correct answer is **(C).** The adjective *loud* emphasizes the sound made by the race cars as a result of being too close to them. Choices (A), (B), and (D) might make sense, but they do not answer the question.

Which of the following changes would emphasize the desolation of the cemetery?

The cemetery was bleak and desolate on that autumn day.

(A) Insert *early* before *autumn.*
(B) Insert *sunny* before *day.*
(C) Insert *well-kept* before *cemetery.*
(D) Insert *abandoned* before *cemetery.*

The correct answer is **(D).** Inserting the adjective *abandoned* before *cemetery* gives the reader a mental picture of a desolate place. Choices (B) and (C) would give the opposite image. The suggested change in choice (A) does nothing to emphasize the cemetery's desolation.

e. Adverbs

Adverbs modify a verb, an adjective, or another adverb; like adjectives, adverbs give the reader additional information. You can identify adverbs easily because they usually end in "-ly." For example:

> The child screamed constantly.

Constantly is an adverb modifying the verb *screamed,* adding the information that the child screamed all the time.

EXAMPLES:

Which of the following improves the sentence by adding an adverb?

Alvin hurt his leg and had to walk.

(A) Insert *carefully* after *walk.*
(B) Insert *Careless* before *Alvin.*
(C) Insert *right* between *his* and *leg.*
(D) No change required.

The correct answer is **(A)**. *Carefully* is an adverb modifying the verb (infinitive) *to walk* and providing the information as to how he had to walk. *Careless* and *right* are adjectives, not adverbs. (**Remember:** "-ly" endings identify adverbs.)

Which of the following improves the sentence by adding an adverb?

People stayed in their houses as the wind blew across the town.

(A) Insert *mercilessly* before *across.*
(B) Insert *cautious* before *people.*
(C) Insert *happily* after *stayed.*
(D) Insert *gentle* before *wind.*

The correct answer is **(A)**. The adverb *mercilessly* tells us how the wind was blowing and explains why people would have stayed in their houses. Choices (B) and (D) are adjectives. They modify nouns and could not be considered correct answers to the question even if they improved it. Choice (C) is an adverb, but it makes little sense in the context of the sentence. Remember to read the questions carefully before deciding on an answer.

Which of the following improves the sentences by adding an adverb?

Fishing is a wonderful sport. It gives you a chance to sit in a boat enjoying the scenery for hours on end.

(A) Insert *Fly* before *fishing.*
(B) Insert *seldom* before *gives.*
(C) Insert *quietly* after *sit.*
(D) Insert *not* before *enjoying.*

The correct answer is **(C)**. *Quietly* modifies the verb *to sit* and explains how you could enjoy the scenery for a long period of time. Choices (B) and (D) are wrong because they change the entire meaning of the sentence. Choice (A) is an adjective. It is important to understand the difference between adjectives and adverbs. Adjectives modify nouns, while adverbs can modify a verb, an adjective, or another adverb. Read this type of question carefully. Make sure you are clear on what is being asked.

f. Articles

The is a **definite article** that indicates one particular thing. For example:

The horse ran away from the farm in the morning.

Each of the *the*'s is a definite article because it modifies a noun and specifies which of all the things in the world the article refers to. It's a particular horse that ran away from a particular farm at a particular time of day.

A and *an* are **indefinite articles,** which do not indicate a particular thing. For example:

Did you leave a book on the table?

A is an indefinite article because it does not refer to a particular book but instead to any book. The articles *a* and *an* mean the same thing and are used the same way, as an indefinite version of *the*. Use *a* when it precedes a word beginning with a consonant (*b, s, c*) or any hard sound and *an* when it precedes a vowel (*a, e, i, o,* or *u*) or a soft sound. You would say *a book* but *an owl, a song* but *an appetite.*

EXAMPLE:

The next question refers to the following passage.

(1) There is great danger to the personal privacy in allowing governments to monitor and intercept the personal and business e-mails. (2) As the free society, we deserve privacy in our dealings with friends and associates. (3) It is unthinkable that the foreign government would demand to monitor our electronic correspondence. (4) When will we stop allowing our freedoms to slip away?

> What corrections are needed in this passage?
>
> **(A)** In Sentence 1, replace *the* with *our* between *to* and *personal* and between *intercept* and *personal.*
> **(B)** In Sentence 2, replace *the* with *a* between *As* and *free.*
> **(C)** In Sentence 3, replace *the* with *a* between *that* and *foreign.*
> **(D)** All of the above

The correct answer is **(D).** This is an excerpt from an editorial and, as such, it makes some specific references and some general references. The concerns it expresses about personal privacy are general, referring to all personal privacy. Similarly, references to *free society* and *foreign governments* are general, not specific. The articles should be revised to reflect these distinctions.

In Sentence 1, the sentence should read:

There is great danger to *our* personal privacy in allowing governments to monitor and intercept *our* personal and business e-mails.

Although privacy is a very specific concern, it's a personal concern and *our* makes a better sentence than *the* to indicate this.

Sentence 2 should read:

As *a* free society, we deserve privacy in our dealings with friends and associates.

The article should be the indefinite article *a;* although free society is normally considered a definite concept, the sentence talks about it as a general one.

Sentence 3 should read:

It is unthinkable that *a* foreign government would demand to monitor our electronic correspondence.

We have to replace the definite article with an indefinite article because the excerpt refers to foreign governments in general and not to a specific foreign government.

g. Conjunctions

Conjunctions are words that join other words or groups of words in a way that makes the sentence make sense. For example:

I looked all over the store for you, but I couldn't find you.

But is a **coordinating conjunction** that joins the two clauses *I looked all over the store for you* and *I couldn't find you* in a way that makes the sentence make sense. Other coordinating conjunctions are: *and, for, nor, or, so,* and *yet.*

There are special classes of conjunctions. **Subordinating conjunctions** make one clause subordinate to another. Examples of subordinating conjunctions are: *after, although, because, since, when,* and *whether.* For example:

Although I left early, I was still late for the play.

Although is a subordinating conjunction and is used to indicate that the important thought (represented by the main clause) is that I was still late for the play, and the less important idea (represented by a subordinate clause using the conjunction *although*) is that I left early.

Some conjunctions always act in pairs. Examples of these are: *as . . . as, both . . . and, either . . . or, neither . . . nor, not . . . but,* and *not only . . . but also.* For example:

I had neither the time nor the opportunity to shop for groceries.

Sometimes, specific adverbs can act as conjunctions for specific purposes:

Purpose	Example
addition	also
comparison	similarly
contrast	however
emphasis	namely
cause and effect	therefore
time	finally

For example:

I enjoyed reading the book; however, I found it much too long.

However is an adverb used as a conjunction here to indicate a contrast between the two clauses. The first clause indicates that the reader enjoyed reading the book, and the second clause indicates that the reader felt that the book was too long.

EXAMPLE:

The next question refers to the following passage on how to disassemble a computer.

(1) The first thing you must do is unplug the nonfunctioning computer. (2) Electricity is dangerous. (3) If you don't unplug the computer, not only will you be faced with sharp edges that can cut your fingers, but if you don't unplug it, you will also be faced with possible electrocution, which would interfere with your plans. (4) There are usually screws on one side of the computer, and if you remove them, the outer case should slip off and expose the inner electronics. (5) Set the outer shell aside. (6) You probably will never need it after dismantling the computer, but you should at least consider recycling it. (7) Inside is the frame containing a lot of electronic stuff and wires. (8) Disconnect all the wires and set them aside, but make sure that you keep them separate because they contain copper, which should be recycled. (9) Before all the wires are removed, take out all the electronic stuff by removing appropriate screws. (10) Don't worry about damaging anything because at this point, while there may be a lot of functioning parts, you probably couldn't reassemble them and the computer didn't work in the first place.

What changes should be made to make this a better set of instructions?

(A) Change Sentence 3 to read: If you don't unplug the computer, *not only will you be faced with sharp edges that can cut your fingers, but also with possible electrocution, which would interfere with your plans.*

(B) Change Sentence 6 to read: *You probably will never need it after dismantling the computer, yet you should at least consider recycling it.*

(C) Change Sentence 8 to read: *Disconnect all the wires but set them aside, but make sure that you keep them separate but they contain copper, which should be recycled.*

(D) Change Sentence 10 to read: *Don't worry about damaging anything because at this point, when there may be a lot of functioning parts, you probably couldn't reassemble them and the computer didn't work in the first place.*

The correct answer is **(A)**. *Not only* and *but also* are always used together; *also* is missing in the original. The other suggestions make the passage worse.

2. Parts of Sentences

The best way to recognize a correct sentence, or to write one, is to understand how sentences are created. Sentences consist of a subject and a predicate. The predicate consists of one or more of the following: a verb, a direct object, an indirect object, and any modifying phrases or clauses.

a. Subject

The subject of a sentence tells us what the sentence is about—a person, place, thing, activity, or idea. For example:

I love baseball.

This sentence is about me, and *I* is the subject of the sentence.

Baseball is my favorite sport.

Here the sentence is about baseball, and *baseball* is the subject of the sentence.

The complete subject is all the words associated with the subject. For example:

Slow, but always exciting, baseball is my favorite sport.

Slow, but always exciting, baseball is the complete subject because it consists of the bare subject, *baseball,* and all the words that modify it, which adds more interest to the sentence.

b. Predicate

The predicate tells what action the subject is doing or what state of being the subject is in. The **complete predicate** is the entire rest of the sentence excluding the subject. The **simple predicate** refers only to the verb, the action word. For example:

I wore my favorite jersey to the game.

The subject of the sentence is *I,* and the word that tells what the subject did, the action word, is *wore.* That is the simple predicate.

A simple predicate may consist of more than one word. It may have a helper word to show tense. For example:

The ship had left the dock when I arrived.

The subject of the sentence is *the ship,* and the words that tell what the ship did are *had left,* which is the simple predicate.

A complete predicate consists of all the words in the predicate. For example:

I noticed a lot of people waiting to see the doctor.

The subject of this sentence is *I.* The predicate is about *I.* The word that tells you what *I* did is *noticed.* *Noticed* is the verb, or bare predicate. The rest of the sentence, along with the verb, forms the complete predicate.

c. Object

The word or words that complete the action of the predicate are called the **direct object.** For example:

The boy bit the dog.

The subject of the sentence is *boy* and the word that tells what the boy did is *bite.* The word that answers the question "What did the boy bite?" is *dog. Dog* is the direct object.

An **indirect object** tells to whom or for whom the action is performed. For example:

Harry gave me the book.

The sentence is about *Harry.* The action performed by Harry is giving, which makes *gave* the simple predicate. The object that Harry gave is *the book,* and to whom he gave it is *me.* Therefore, *Harry* is the subject, *gave* is the simple predicate, *the book* is the direct object, and *me* is the indirect object. You can see this more clearly with a slight reordering of the words in the sentence: *Harry gave the book to me.* (**Note:** *To me* is no longer an indirect object in this revised example; it is the direct object.)

In the following examples, identify the function in the sentence of the underlined word.

EXAMPLES:

We all <u>went</u> to the park to watch the squirrels play.

(A) Subject
(B) Simple predicate
(C) Direct object
(D) Indirect object

The correct answer is **(B)**. *Went* is a word that indicates action and is a verb and the predicate of the sentence.

The green <u>book</u> lay on the table unread and unopened.

(A) Subject
(B) Simple predicate
(C) Direct object
(D) Indirect object

The correct answer is **(A)**. *Book* is a noun and the subject of the sentence.

I gave you the <u>basketball</u> after the last game.

(A) Subject
(B) Simple predicate
(C) Direct object
(D) Indirect object

The correct answer is **(C)**. *Basketball* is the word that indicates to what the action was directed and is the direct object. The answer to the question "To whom was the action directed?" is the indirect object *you*, but *you* is not the underlined word you are asked to identify.

d. Prepositional Phrases

A phrase is a group of two or more words that are related to each other. Prepositional phrases are made up of a preposition, its object, and any of the object's modifiers. For example:

I stored my CDs in the attic.

The words *in the attic* are related to each other because, together, they tell the reader where the CDs were stored.

A prepositional phrase will function as an adjective or an adverb. As an **adjective,** the prepositional phrase will answer questions such as *What kind?* or *Which one?* For example:

Napoleon was a man of action.

Of action is an adjective phrase that modifies the noun *man,* explaining what kind of man Napoleon was.

As an **adverb,** a prepositional phrase will answer questions such as *How? When?* or *Where?* For example:

Nancy spoke with enthusiasm.

With enthusiasm is an adverb phrase that describes how Nancy spoke; it modifies the verb *spoke.*

Remember that in writing your extended response essay, prepositional phrases can improve the essay by making it easier to understand, but when they're overused or incorrectly used, they can lower your score by making the essay difficult to read and understand.

e. Clauses

A clause is a group of related words containing a subject and a verb. There are two kinds of clauses: main clauses and subordinate clauses.

Main clauses can stand alone as sentences with the addition of appropriate punctuation. For example:

My dog barks a lot.

This is a group of words, all related to my dog, that contains a subject, *my dog,* and a verb, *barks,* and is a main clause because it expresses a complete thought.

Subordinate clauses depend on a main clause to make the sentence make sense. They are not complete sentences and cannot stand on their own. For example:

The dog that used to live with my sister barks a lot.

That used to live with my sister is a group of words that can't stand alone and is, therefore, a subordinate clause.

A **noun clause** acts like a single noun. It can be the subject of a sentence, the object, or a predicate nominative. For example:

Whatever I said should not have upset them.

Whatever I said is a group of words that replaces a noun and is, thus, a noun clause, and the subject of this sentence.

A noun clause can also be the object of a sentence. For example:

I understand what she is talking about.

What she is talking about is a clause that acts as a single noun, and is the direct object of *understand.*

A predicate nominative, in this case a single noun, is used to complete or restate the subject. For example:

Her favorite car is actually a convertible.

You can test this idea of completing the subject, because you could swap the subject *car* with the predicate nominative, *convertible,* without changing the meaning of the sentence. This is also referred to as a subjective completion.

An **adjective clause** acts as an adjective. For example:

Autumn, when the leaves are turning colors, is my favorite season.

When the leaves are turning colors is a group of words that modifies a noun *autumn.* It acts like an adjective, modifying *leaves,* and thus is known as an adjective clause.

An **adverb clause** acts as an adverb. For example:

> Frank won before I could show him my best moves.

Before I could show him my best moves is a group of words that modify the verb *won* and is, thus, an adverb clause.

3. Types of Sentences

a. Simple Sentences

Simple sentences consist of only one clause. For example:

> I went for a walk.

This sentence consists of only one clause: *I went for a walk.*

b. Compound Sentences

Compound sentences consist of two or more main clauses joined by a coordinating conjunction (*for, and, nor, but, or, yet, so*). **Note:** Coordinating conjunctions are always preceded by a comma. For example:

> I went for a walk, but it was still drizzling.

In this sentence, there are two main clauses, *I went for a walk* and *it was still drizzling,* each of which is independent and expresses a complete thought.

c. Complex Sentences

Complex sentences consist of one main clause and one or more subordinate clauses. For example:

> I couldn't go for a walk while the rain and wind were blowing across the field.

Here, there is one main clause, *I couldn't go for a walk,* and one subordinate clause, *while the rain and wind were blowing across the field,* which depends on the main clause to give it meaning.

d. Compound-Complex Sentences

Compound-complex sentences consist of two or more main clauses and at least one subordinate clause. For example:

> I went for a walk after the rain stopped, and I discovered that the ground was still very wet.

This sentence has two main clauses, *I went for a walk* and *I discovered that the ground was still very wet,* each of which expresses a complete thought and can stand alone, and one subordinate clause, *after the rain stopped,* which requires the main clauses to make its meaning clearly understood.

4. Voice

Active voice indicates that the subject performs the action of the sentence. For example:

> I listen to my favorite tunes every day.

Passive voice indicates that the subject has the action of the sentence performed on it. For example:

> My favorite tunes are listened to every day.

Avoid the passive voice unless absolutely necessary. It is considered to be one aspect of a poor writing style.

5. Agreement

When writing your extended response essay, as well as when correcting sentences, make sure that appropriate words agree with each other.

a. Subject-Verb Agreement

In a proper sentence, the subject agrees with the verb. For example:

> The boys have run away from the bear.

The boys is a plural noun/subject and requires a plural verb/predicate, *have run*. If the subject were singular, the sentence would read: *The boy has run away from the bear*.

b. Pronoun-Antecedent Agreement

Pronouns must agree with the nouns they replace. If a pronoun replaces a singular noun, it should itself be singular. For example:

> I brought my fishing rod.

My and *I* are both singular and agree with each other. If the subject were plural, it would read: *We brought our fishing rods.* The plural pronoun *our* agrees with the plural *we*.

6. Pronoun Reference

A pronoun must refer back to a noun. If you write a sentence or a paragraph with pronouns and the reader cannot figure out what the pronouns refer to, you'll quickly lose the reader's interest. For example:

> She wrote a letter to her about him that mentioned her but not his best friend.

This sentence has a lot of pronouns that do not refer to any nouns, making the sentence hard to understand.

7. Pronoun Case

Pronouns have a case depending on their function. The **subjective case** indicates that the pronoun is used as the subject of a sentence. For example:

> He sat in the chair.

He is a subjective pronoun because it is used as the subject of the verb *sat*.

The **objective case** indicates that the pronoun is the object of a verb or a preposition. For example:

> I had to leave without him.

Him is an objective pronoun because it is the object of the preposition *without*.

The **possessive case** indicates that the pronoun indicates ownership. For example:

> That is my umbrella.

My is a possessive pronoun since it indicates ownership of the *umbrella*.

8. Correcting Sentences

a. Sentence Fragments

A sentence without a subject or a predicate and/or that does not express a complete thought is considered a sentence fragment. In writing your extended response essay, make sure that each sentence is a complete sentence and not a sentence fragment. To make sure, ask yourself these questions:

- Does every one of my sentences have a subject?
- Does every one of my sentences have a verb?
- If I've used clauses in my sentences, is there a main clause for every subordinate clause?
- Can each of my sentences stand alone and make sense?

If you can answer "Yes" to every question, there are no sentence fragments in your essay.

b. Comma Splice and Fused Sentences

i. Comma Splice

If you join two perfectly good, but unrelated, main clauses or sentences together with a comma, you've created a comma splice, which is technically also classified as a run-on sentence. This common mistake creates a lot of confusion in the reader's mind. There is no place for comma splices in coherent writing. For example:

> The kite was blowing in the wind, the dog was running around.

These are two good, but unrelated, sentences. The best way to correct this error is to put a period after *wind,* put a capital *t* on *the,* and end up with two complete sentences. An alternative choice would be to replace the comma after *wind* with a semicolon. That too is grammatically correct. Which one you use is a matter of preference.

You could also turn this into a compound or complex sentence. A compound sentence contains two independent clauses. These clauses are of equal weight and meaning. A complex sentence contains a main clause and two or more dependent or subordinate clauses.

As a compound sentence, this sentence would read:

> The kite was blowing in the wind, and the dog was running around.

As a complex sentence, you need to rewrite the sentence somewhat. You need to make one of the two clauses a subordinate clause. For example:

> While the kite was blowing in the wind, the dog was running around.

In this case, one part of the sentence has been subordinated, or made less important, and dependent upon the other clause.

ii. Fused Sentences

The following is an example of a fused sentence:

> The kite was blowing in the wind the dog was running around.

Again, these are two good, but unrelated, sentences fused together. It is also called a run-on sentence because it runs on without proper punctuation. In this case, there is no punctuation of any kind. The correction would be the same as for a comma splice. Put a period after *wind,* put a capital *t* on *the,* and end up with two complete sentences. (The semicolon option works here as well.)

c. Misplaced and Dangling Modifiers

Words that modify are meant to give the reader additional information or a clearer picture of what is being written. Make sure that the word being modified and the modifier are close together, and make sure that a modifier can modify only one word. Don't put in modifiers if they have nothing to modify. For example:

> Feeling a headache coming on, Sally went to her bedroom and looked out the window bright and glowing in the late afternoon sky without a heavy curtain to shade the room.

If you tried to connect the modifiers with what they modified, it might look like this:

> Feeling a headache coming on, Sally went to her bedroom and looked out the window
> <u>Clearly modifies "Sally"</u>
>
> bright and glowing in the late afternoon sky without a heavy curtain to shade the room.
> <u>What does this modify?</u>   <u>What does this modify?</u>

In reading the sentence and answering the questions, you realize that the sentence doesn't make sense in its present form. If it were completely rewritten as follows, it still wouldn't be great literature, but at least the meaning of the words would be clear:

> Sally felt a headache coming on and went to her bedroom. She stood and looked out her window, which had no heavy curtain to shade the room. The sun outside shone bright and glowed in the late afternoon sky.

Remember also that too many modifiers make for very flowery prose, something generally considered to be a poor writing style.

d. Incomplete Sentences

If a sentence has all the requisite parts—subject and predicate—but still does not express a complete thought, it's considered incomplete. For example:

> I have always wanted.

This sentence has a subject, *I,* a predicate *have always wanted,* but makes no sense. It is incomplete.

Another example:

> After I buy a new lure, fishing is always.

This sentence has a subject, *fishing,* and a verb, *is,* but makes no sense. Fishing could be *wonderful, peaceful, productive, awful, boring,* or anything else you wanted to complete this incomplete sentence.

Another example:

> After gulping my morning coffee. I ran to the car, key in hand.

The first sentence is incomplete. It has words that go together, but no real verb. *Gulping* may look like a verb because it implies an action, but it isn't. Technically, it is a present participle because it is used as a verb and ends in *-ing*. If we rewrote the sentence as follows, it would be correct because *After gulping my morning coffee* is now used as an introductory phrase.

> After gulping my morning coffee, I ran to the car, key in hand.

e. Punctuation

i. End Punctuation

Periods are used to end sentences that tell us something. **Question marks** are used to end sentences that ask questions. **Exclamation points** are used to end sentences that call for emphasis, an interjection, or a command.

ii. Commas

Commas prevent the reader from misreading sentences. They're also used

- To join two main clauses with coordinating conjunctions (for example, *and* or *but*)
- After an introductory clause, word, or phrase
- Between items in a list
- Between adjectives (provided that they are separate and equal and modify the same noun)
- To set off a phrase or clause that does not restrict the meaning of the word it modifies
- To set off an appositive (a noun or noun phrase that renames the noun preceding it)
- To follow transitional words such as *however* and *nevertheless*
- To set off a contrasting phrase or clause
- To set off quotations
- To set off introductory elements (words, phrases, or clauses that begin a sentence)

Commas always come after:

- **Adverbial clauses:** For example
  Although we read that chapter twice, I still couldn't remember what it was about.
- **Long prepositional phrases:** For example:
  Before Charlotte got up and started to change her clothes, the doorbell rang.
- **Adverbial clauses that seem to modify the entire sentence:** For example:
  On the other hand, Fung did not complete all the questions in the assignment.
- **Any word or phrase that would confuse the reader:** For example:
  Before this summer, reading lists were not posted early.

An **appositive** is any information that is added to a sentence that explains a noun or pronoun. An appositive is separated from the rest of the sentence by commas. For example:

Jenny, the top graduate of her class, received a scholarship to Harvard.

Commas seem to have enough rules associated with their use to require a comma after every word! However, if you follow a simple rule, you won't overuse them: Use commas to make the sense of a sentence clear. As a general guide, use a comma whenever there is a natural break in the flow of a sentence. Beware of using so many commas that your sentences are hard to read because of the multiple pauses.

iii. The Semicolon

The semicolon joins independent clauses without the separation created by a period. It provides more sophisticated sentences than a series of short simple sentences separated by periods. Semicolons also are used with conjunctive adverbs (such as *therefore, nevertheless, besides, however,* and *otherwise*). Another use for the semicolon is to separate items with internal punctuation in a list. Here are some examples:

The line for the new roller coaster was extremely long; we waited in it for three hours!

I studied very hard for this test; however, my cold proved to be a huge distraction while I was taking it.

I believe three things about passing the test: No matter how hard I have to work, it will be worth it; I will be able to apply for that promotion; and no matter how long I live, I will know that this is one of my achievements.

In the first example, there is a connection between the long roller coaster line and the three-hour wait. By using the semicolon, that feeling is retained, whereas a period would create more distance.

iv. More Punctuation

Apostrophes are used to show possession or to indicate that a letter is missing. For example:

We can't find Heather's hat.

In the word *can't,* the apostrophe is used to show it is a contraction for the word cannot. The apostrophe in *Heather's,* shows that the hat in question belongs to Heather.

Quotation marks surround a direct quote:

"I can hardly wait to see the new Disney movie," said Lucy.

f. Capitalization

All sentences should start with a capital letter, but there are also other times when a word should be capitalized. A few of these are illustrated below.

Proper names are always capitalized. For example:

John, Mary, Paul, and Edward decided to go to a show.

Temperatures across Indiana dropped below zero.

Yellowstone National Park is a great place for a family vacation.

Titles are capitalized. For example:

Mr., Mrs., Ms., Major, Prince, and Dr.

Months and days of the week are always capitalized. For example:

June, March, and October

Monday, Tuesday, Wednesday, and so on

g. Spelling

Spelling is an issue in the RLA extended response item. If you misspell or misuse a word in your essay response, you may be marked down. In Sections 1 and 3 of the RLA Test, you'll be asked to correct some sentences of which a few will have spelling mistakes. The usual spelling mistakes that you're expected to correct consist of possessives, contractions, and *homonyms* (words that sound alike but are spelled differently, covered earlier on page 114).

For example:

Type of Error	Examples	Usage
Possessives	John's its	belonging to *John* belonging to it (**Note:** This is an exception, where the apostrophe is not used to show possession. *Its* is often confused with *it's*, the contraction of *it is*.
Contractions	o'clock wouldn't it's	contraction for *of the clock* contraction for *would not* contraction for *it is*

h. Nonstandard English

Nonstandard English is the kind of speech or writing that is likely to label someone as uneducated; it can also reflect a regional variation of speech. In the South, expressions like *y'all* are perfectly acceptable, but on a university campus, they are likely to attract snide comments. In some areas, *youse* (plural of *you*) is part of normal speech. Elsewhere it will make people wince. These types of regional speech patterns should be avoided where possible, unless used for particular effect. Avoid them on the RLA Test.

Example:

I seen he was going to be trouble. I just knowed it.

The sentence should start with *I saw*. The word *knowed* is supposed to be the past tense of *know*. The correct version is *knew*. The sentence should be rewritten this way:

I saw he was going to be trouble. I just knew it.

Example:

The dress was so hot, it was sick. When I told my friend the price, she was like, I want one too. LMAO.

This text is a mixture of slang, regional speech patterns, and texting shorthand. All of it is perfectly understandable and not uncommon in everyday speech. However, it also not Standard English. Unless it was used for effect, to create an image of the speaker, it should be avoided.

Correction:

That dress was so (elegant, beautiful, and so on—take your pick). When I told my friend the price, she told me she wanted one, too. That was a hilarious response.

Example:

I am going to try and win the casino jackpot.

The use of *and* is incorrect. One tries *to* do something.

Correction:

I am going to try to win the casino jackpot.

Example:

The future ain't what it used to be.

Ain't is another of those strange quirks of English. The contraction has been around since the 1700s. It shows up in common speech, cartoons, music, and even university speeches. However, in formal writing such as letters, essays, or job applications, *ain't* is inappropriate. The writer is automatically relegated to the category of illiterate. The *Oxford English Reference Dictionary* refers to it as a colloquialism and unacceptable. Like *LMAO* in the example above, this may be fine when you're talking to your friends but don't use it in formal writing.

Correction:

The future is not what it used to be.

F. Practice

1. Writing Skills

Directions: Correct the following sentences.

1. larry went to the dry cleaner every day at the same time to pick up the next day's clean shirt.

    (A) Change *every day* to *daily.*
    (B) Correct the spelling of *cleaner.*
    (C) Capitalize *larry.*
    (D) Change *day's* to *days.*

2. Our Teacher dislikes students who speek out in class.

    (A) Change *Teacher* to *teacher* and *speek* to *speak.*
    (B) Change *students* to *student.*
    (C) Change *class* to *classes.*
    (D) No change required.

3. Lets stop arguing so we can move forward and solve the problem.

    (A) Change *arguing* to *argueing.*
    (B) Insert a comma before *so.*
    (C) Change *Lets* to *Let's*
    (D) No change required.

4. My sister has a friend who comes from Oregon which is very far away from where she lives still they plan to meet at the corner store to drink coffee and eat a donut every year or so sometimes even sooner or later.

    (A) Insert a comma after *Oregon.*
    (B) Insert a period after *lives,* capitalize *still,* and insert a comma after *still.*
    (C) Omit *sometimes even sooner or later.*
    (D) All of the above

Directions: Correct the following passages to create correct, coherent passages.

Question 5 refers to the following paragraph.

(1) Unfortunately, her country was in financial trouble. (2) The Empress Dowager Cixi ruled China for 47 years. (3) She had spent money without thought for the future. (4) She was a very vain woman and always wanted to impress people with the wealth of her country. (5) When she was old and faced death, she decided that her tomb was not good enough for her and ordered it rebuilt.

5. To improve this paragraph, change the order of the sentences to:

   (A) 1, 2, 5, 4, 3
   (B) 2, 4, 1, 3, 5
   (C) 5, 3, 1, 2, 4
   (D) 3, 5, 2, 4, 1

Question 6 refers to the following sentence.

This Saturday at the recreation center, there will be a world-class lawn bowling tournament with people from all over the community who will arrive early in the morning and stay until late at night, playing this great game for all to watch.

6. What corrections must be made to the sentence to make it easier to read?

   (A) Divide the sentence into two after the word *tournament*.
   (B) Divide the sentence into two after the word *community* and replace the word *who* with *the players*.
   (C) Either choice (A) or choice (B).
   (D) No change required.

Question 7 refers to the following paragraph.

(1) My opponent, whom I have renamed Slowly Slowerton, does not believe in speed. (2) As your candidate for mayor, I would like to take the following position on the issue of speed limits. (3) I, on the other hand, want to remove speed limits altogether. (4) I am opposed to lowering the speed limit on the roads in our community to 12 miles per hour. (5) He wants a city where it is faster to walk to work than to drive. (6) Of course, there may be a few accidents, but we will just have to be more careful. (7) In this community, we will have to find ways of looking after one another rather than have city hall rule our lives with silly rules. (8) He wants every person who cannot speed-walk to always be late. (9) He wants you to waste time and gas in getting where you want to go.

7. What would be the best sentence order to produce a logically arranged speech?

   (A) 4, 1, 2, 8, 9, 3, 5, 7, 6
   (B) 7, 2, 4, 1, 3, 5, 9, 8, 6
   (C) 2, 1, 3, 4, 5, 8, 9, 6, 7
   (D) 2, 4, 1, 5, 8, 9, 3, 6, 7

Question 8 refers to the following paragraph.

(1) The meeting opened at 7 p.m. with Harold in the chair. (2) The first order of business was the reading of the minutes. (3) Since there were no additions or corrections, they were passed on a motion by Judy, seconded by Vivienne? (4) There was no new business to report.

8. Correct the punctuation in the paragraph.

   (A) In Sentence 1, change the period after *chair* to a question mark.
   (B) In Sentence 2, change the period after *minutes* to an exclamation point.
   (C) In Sentence 3, change the question mark after *Vivienne* to a period.
   (D) All of the above

2. Reading Skills

Directions: Choose the best answer to each question.

Questions 1 through 4 refer to the following passage.

Hybrids use both a small gasoline engine and a battery pack to operate. They generally obtain great fuel economy ratings. Hybrids generally get nearly 40 miles per gallon (mpg) in city driving, and some, like the Ford Fusion, do much better. It is rated at 51 mpg. The fuel consumption for gasoline cars decreases on highway driving, but hybrids tend to use more fuel. That is not entirely unexpected, since on longer trips the battery power needs to be supplemented with energy from the small gasoline engine. It cuts in more frequently, either as direct power or as a recharger for the battery pack. In city driving, quite often the gasoline motor is only used for shorter periods of time as a recharger.

But there is another option for people who want to reduce their fuel consumption: diesel engines. These engines are not the dirty, noisy old diesels of our parents' generation. At one time, you could hear a diesel Mercedes clattering half a block away. Now they are as quiet as any other vehicle, and concerted efforts have made the emissions as clean as any gasoline engine. As an added bonus, you get an engine that is reliable, with owners reporting hundreds of thousands of miles of trouble-free motoring. Even the old issue for drivers in northern states—difficult cold starts—is no longer a problem, thanks to modern fixes.

1. Which of the following does NOT describe hybrid vehicles?

   (A) Fuel-efficient
   (B) Especially energy-efficient on highway driving
   (C) Very noisy
   (D) Short-ranged

2. What is the definition of a hybrid vehicle?

   (A) A car that runs on gasoline
   (B) A car that runs on diesel
   (C) A car that runs on battery power with a small backup gasoline engine
   (D) A battery-powered vehicle

3. Within the context of the passage, what is the major advantage of switching to a diesel-powered vehicle?

   (A) A quiet motor
   (B) Great fuel mileage
   (C) A reliable engine
   (D) Really powerful motors

4. Why were diesel engines considered a problem 20 years ago?

   (A) They were noisy.
   (B) They gave off more air pollution than gasoline engines.
   (C) They were hard to start in the extreme cold.
   (D) All of the above

Questions 5 through 9 refer to the following excerpt from Murray Shukyn's short story "Just Another Day" (2008).

Sitting in his car on an empty street, alone, Irving knew that he had not handled that well. He had not handled many, many situations well. He was not a good father, even though he was a good provider. Out of the corner of his eye, he noticed a group of teenagers turning the corner. This group of boys and girls looked lively, speaking in loud voices. Automatically, he locked the doors of his car as they slowly approached. They seemed so happy, so carefree. Irving wished for the days he had been so happy, had so few responsibilities.

Irving Solnicki watched the group of teenagers approach him, walking, jostling each other, trading taunts and jokes. He watched them so intently, he did not notice the small, red, two-door car with the darkly tinted windows slowly cruise up behind him with headlights off and windows closed. Irving was watching the teenagers carefully. It was easier now; they were only about ten feet in front of his car. Suddenly, the group scattered and a few took refuge beside Irving's car door. The small, red, two-door car approached from the rear with the driver's window open. Irving noticed a glint of shiny metal protruding from the window of the car. He could not figure out what was happening. The teenagers scattering; the car with the metal pipe sticking out the window; and the dull thuds coming from the street were like a dream. Irving was not sure what to make of it until the red car pulled even with his, and he saw that the pipe looked like one of those automatic weapons he often saw on television. The passenger-side window of Irving's car shuddered, as a hole developed in it, with a rather loud bang. Irving Solnicki felt a sharp pain in his right temple and warmth oozing around it. He started to lift his hand to see what it was, but it just stopped as he slumped over the wheel, pressing on the horn button, creating a din in the quiet street with the scattering teenagers and the small, red, two-door car speeding away.

Suddenly, it was quiet except for a car horn loudly, soulfully lamenting in the night.

5. Why was Irving sitting alone in his car on an empty street?

   (A) He was resting his eyes.
   (B) He was waiting for someone.
   (C) He had not handled a family situation well.
   (D) He liked to watch teenagers.

6. Why would Irving lock his car doors as the teenagers approached?

   (A) He was afraid of teenagers.
   (B) It was an automatic reaction.
   (C) He was afraid of being happy.
   (D) He didn't want them to come into his car.

7. Why is it important to mention that Irving did not notice the small, red, two-door car approaching?

   (A) The red car will crash into Irving's car.
   (B) The red car is going to give the teenagers a lift.
   (C) A relative of Irving is driving the red car.
   (D) The red car is about to play an important role in the development of the story.

8. What was the glint of shiny metal sticking out from the car window?

   (A) A piece of pipe
   (B) A golf club
   (C) A gun
   (D) A camera

9. Why would the author describe the sound of the horn as lamenting?

 (A) Irving died from the gunshot.
 (B) Horns always sound sad.
 (C) Irving was singing a sad song.
 (D) The teenagers were frightened by the horn.

Questions 10 through 13 refer to the following passage from a course manual.

This course is based on a Prior Learning Assessment and Recognition (PLAR) model, which utilizes preparation for a standardized challenge examination as a component of the PLAR. In addition, candidates are guided through the creation of a portfolio, which can be evaluated by the college for admission or advanced standing. This is an opportunity for adults who have learned in informal as well as formal venues, to document and assess their prior learning. The course is intense and concentrated and is not meant for every applicant. Candidates who score low in the pretest, and who indicate educational gaps in the counseling interview, should be directed to remedial programs before beginning such a rigorous course. Those who score extremely well in the pretest might be advised to apply directly to take challenge examinations, such as the GED® examinations or other examinations as required by the college. This course is meant for candidates who will gain from review and remediation but do not require extensive teaching.

10. What does the course prepare candidates for?

 (A) A preparation program
 (B) The creation of a portfolio
 (C) The GED® test
 (D) A challenge examination

11. Who is eligible to enroll in the course as specifically mentioned in the passage?

 (A) Adult learners
 (B) High school students
 (C) College students
 (D) Recent immigrants

12. Where should candidates with low pretest scores be directed?

 (A) A counseling interview
 (B) A rigorous course
 (C) Remedial programs
 (D) Educational gaps

13. The course is NOT meant for candidates needing

 (A) Review
 (B) Remediation
 (C) Challenge examinations
 (D) Extensive teaching

Questions 14 through 18 refer to the following excerpt from the play Last Shrink Sitting *by Murray Shukyn (2005).*

> HOMELESS MAN: Hello, how are you?
>
> NORMAN: I'm fine thank you, and you?
>
> HOMELESS MAN: I feel the need for culture.
>
> NORMAN: That's nice. Excuse me.
>
> HOMELESS MAN: If you could give me the cost of a single ticket to a play, I could absorb some of the culture.
>
> NORMAN: I'm sorry. I don't have any change.
>
> HOMELESS MAN: Change? I don't want to go to an amateur production where they take up a collection at the end. Culture, man, real actors performing real plays!
>
> NORMAN: I really can't help you.
>
> HOMELESS MAN: Did you eat yesterday?
>
> NORMAN: Yes.
>
> HOMELESS MAN: Did you eat today?
>
> NORMAN: Yes.
>
> HOMELESS MAN: Then you're better off than me. Give me some money.
>
> NORMAN: No!
>
> HOMELESS MAN: Give me some money, and I won't hit you in the face.
>
> *NORMAN steps back. HOMELESS MAN approaches.*
>
> HOMELESS MAN: Give me ten dollars, and I won't hit you in the stomach.
>
> *NORMAN continues backing away with the HOMELESS MAN approaching at the same rate.*
>
> HOMELESS MAN: Give me twenty dollars so I won't cut myself and bleed on you. I could have terrible diseases, you know.
>
> NORMAN: *(turning)* You're nuts!
>
> HOMELESS MAN: Do you think I would live in an alley if I were the poster boy for mental health? Of course, I'm nuts. Give me some money or I'll go berserker all over you.
>
> *NORMAN turns and sprints out of the alley. The HOMELESS MAN just stands, staring after him.*
>
> HOMELESS MAN: Have a nice day. It was nice almost doing business with you.

14. In the closing line of the scene, why does the homeless man say, "It was nice almost doing business with you"?

    (A) Norman didn't buy anything from him.

    (B) The homeless man ran out of stock.

    (C) Norman wouldn't give him any money.

    (D) Norman wasn't interested in buying anything from the homeless man.

15. What can the reader infer about the homeless man?

    (A) He loves the arts.

    (B) He is very nervous about confronting Norman.

    (C) He's a poster child for mental health.

    (D) He is quite intelligent.

16. Why does the homeless man ask whether Norman had eaten in the last couple days?

    (A) He was asking Norman for money and wanted to prove a point.

    (B) He was concerned that Norman was not eating well.

    (C) Norman looked very thin and pale.

    (D) Norman's stomach was making strange noises.

17. Why does the homeless man say that he will cut himself?

    (A) He is suicidal.

    (B) He has nothing else to do with his knife.

    (C) He wants to make a point and is sure that Norman will understand.

    (D) He says that he will bleed all over Norman and might have terrible diseases.

18. Why wouldn't the homeless man accept change if it were offered?

    (A) He has a phobia of coins.

    (B) He wants to buy a ticket for a cultural event, and that costs more money.

    (C) He prefers eating in upscale restaurants, and they're more expensive.

    (D) He wouldn't want to use them because he collects coins.

3. Answers and Explanations

a. Writing Skills

1. **(C)** *Larry* starts a sentence and is a proper name. Both are reasons that it should begin with a capital letter. *Every day* and *daily* mean the same thing; there is no reason to change these words.

2. **(A)** *Teacher* does not fall into any of the groups of nouns that require capitals, and *speek* is spelled incorrectly.

3. **(C)** *Let's* stands for *let us,* and without the correction there is no subject for the sentence. *Arguing* is properly spelled, and a comma is not needed before *so.*

4. **(D)** The original sentence is a mess. It is too long and has extra words in it. To correct it, you would have to make all the suggestions given. When you're writing your essay, avoid long, complicated sentences—they're hard to read and often lead to errors.

5. **(B)** This order forms a coherent paragraph, which would read as follows:

    (2) The Empress Dowager Cixi ruled China for 47 years. (4) She was a very vain woman and always wanted to impress people with the wealth of her country. (1) Unfortunately, her country was in financial trouble. (3) She had spent money without thought for the future. (5) When she was old and faced death, she decided that her tomb was not good enough for her and ordered it rebuilt.

6. **(C)** In order to make this very long, complex sentence readable, it should be broken into smaller sentences. Following the instructions indicated by (C) would produce a paragraph reading as follows:

    Either:

    This Saturday at the recreation center, there will be a world-class lawn bowling tournament. People from all over the community will arrive early in the morning and stay until late at night, playing this great game for all to watch.

Or:

   This Saturday at the recreation center, there will be a world-class lawn bowling tournament with people from all over the community. The players will arrive early in the morning and stay until late at night, playing this great game for all to watch.

7. **(D)** Making the changes suggested in (D) would produce a paragraph like this:

   (2) As your candidate for mayor, I would like to take the following position on the issue of speed limits. (4) I am opposed to lowering the speed limit on the roads in our community to 12 miles per hour. (1) My opponent, whom I have renamed Slowly Slowerton, does not believe in speed. (5) He wants a city where it is faster to walk to work than to drive. (8) He wants every person who cannot speed-walk to always be late. (9) He wants you to waste time and gas in getting where you want to go. (3) I, on the other hand, want to remove speed limits altogether. (6) Of course, there may be a few accidents, but we will just have to be more careful. (7) In this community, we will have to find ways of looking after one another rather than have city hall rule our lives with silly rules.

   Sentences 8 and 9 are interchangeable in their order, but the rest need the order we show to create a strong flow of ideas and build toward the strong closing. The other suggestions would produce a paragraph without a strong opening or closing. Remember when you're writing your essay that having good opening and closing sentences is important.

8. **(C)** Sentence 1 is not a question and does not need a question mark. Sentence 2 is not an exclamation and does not need an exclamation point. However, in Sentence 3, Vivienne did second a motion. A question mark is incorrect in Sentence 3. Making that correction would produce the following passage:

   (1) The meeting opened at 7 p.m. with Harold in the chair. (2) The first order of business was the reading of the minutes. (3) Since there were no additions or corrections, they were passed on a motion by Judy, seconded by Vivienne. (4) There was no new business to report.

b. Reading Skills

1. **(B)** This is a tricky question. You can eliminate choice (A) quickly because hybrid vehicles are fuel-efficient. Choices (C) and (D) may or may not be correct, but they are not discussed in the context of hybrid vehicles and so are not possible answers. Choice B is the correct answer because the passage clearly states that hybrid vehicles are less efficient on highways than in city driving.

2. **(C)** At the beginning of the passage, hybrid vehicles are defined as cars that run on battery power with a small gasoline backup engine. They do not run on gasoline (A) or diesel (B), and they are definitely not a vehicle powered by battery power alone (D).

3. **(B)** This too is a somewhat tricky question. While quiet motors (A) and reliable engines (C) are a feature of modern diesels, in the context of the article these answers are incorrect. Remember that the key point of the article is fuel economy and fuel efficiency. Similarly, while diesel engines may be powerful (D), that is not mentioned in the text. The correct answer in the context of the passage is choice (B), great fuel mileage.

4. **(D)** The passage either suggests or directly mentions a number of issues with older diesel engines. They were indeed noisy (A), and hard to start an extremely cold weather (C). From the statements about improved emissions, you can deduce that the older diesel engines gave off far more pollutants (B). Therefore the correct choice is (D), all of the above.

5. **(C)** The first few sentences of the first paragraph tell you that Irving, as a father, had not handled a situation well.

6. **(B)** Locking the doors was an automatic reaction according to the first paragraph. Choice (A) may have been true, but it is not mentioned in the passage. Choice (C) has no connection to the passage.

7. **(D)** The red car plays an immediate role in the development of the story, and Irving's not noticing it makes it more powerful. Choices (A), (B), and (C) have nothing to do with the story.

8. **(C)** From the description in the passage and the subsequent events, the shiny metal object must have been a gun. The other choices are remotely possible but are not mentioned in the paragraph.

9. **(A)** Although the passage doesn't specifically state that Irving died, there are many clues to make that the best answer. The shot to the temple and the subsequent slumping over the wheel would indicate a fatal injury.

10. **(D)** The course prepares candidates for a standardized challenge examination as a component of the PLAR model. While it also is a preparation program (A), which includes a portfolio (B), these are not the best answers. Choice (C) is incorrect because the program assesses *prior* learning, and does not prepare students specifically for the GED® test.

11. **(A)** The passage tells us that this is a preparation course for adult formal and informal learners. Therefore, choice (A) is the correct choice. It is not available for high school (B) or college students (C). Recent immigrants (D) might qualify, but they must be adults not currently attending college.

12. **(C)** Those with low pretest scores are referred to "remedial programs" (C). A rigorous course (B) and educational gaps (D) are incorrect choices. The candidates might also be directed to a counseling interview (A), but that is not the best choice.

13. **(D)** According to the passage, the course is not meant for choice (D), those requiring "extensive teaching." It does, however, offer review (A), remediation (B), and preparation for challenge exams (C).

14. **(C)** The homeless man was asking for money, and Norman didn't give him any. The rest of the choices refer to a traditional manner of doing business, which does not describe the incident in the passage.

15. **(D)** At the beginning of the passage, the homeless man says he wants money to buy a ticket for a play, but that does not mean that he *loves the arts* (A). From his mannerisms, you can tell that he is certainly not nervous about confronting Norman, so choice (B) is incorrect. The homeless man himself states that he is not the poster child for mental health, so choice (C) is incorrect. However, the escalating action is quite calculated, and one could infer that despite any other issues, the homeless man is quite intelligent. Therefore choice (D) is the correct answer.

16. **(A)** To prove that he deserved money, the homeless man wanted to demonstrate to Norman that he was in a worse condition than Norman. The rest of the choices have no basis in the passage. Remember that you should select the best answer based on the material in the passage.

17. **(D)** The homeless man threatens Norman with giving him some unnamed terrible disease by bleeding on him. Choices (A) and (C) may or may not be correct, but they are not the best answers according to the passage. Choice (B) is wrong because the passage does not mention a knife, and although we can assume that in order to cut himself, the homeless man would need some instrument, there is not one in the passage.

18. **(B)** The homeless man says that he wants to buy a ticket to a professional cultural event, and they're expensive. Choices (A) and (D) might make sense if they were mentioned in the passage. Choice (C) has no basis in the passage.

G. A Few Reminders

Here are a few points to remember when taking the RLA Test:

- Read the items and text passages carefully.
- On items about text, all the information you need to answer the items is in the text. It is usually a matter of just how carefully you read the passage.
- On items asking for corrections, you need to know the writing skills we have reviewed in this chapter.
- When you are correcting written passages or writing your extended response essay, be careful to avoid slang or nonstandard English.

VIII. Mathematical Reasoning

A. Test Format

The Mathematical Reasoning Test will be administered on the computer. It is 115 minutes long. If you require a calculator to perform the calculations, one will appear on the computer screen for all but the first five items. Remember that a calculator is only an asset with difficult questions requiring complex calculations. Other times, it can slow you down, and this test is timed. Fortunately, you always have a "calculator" with you at all times: Your brain is capable of not only performing calculations but can estimate answers within a fair degree of accuracy. Practice using it. A calculator can help you calculate, not think.

The Mathematical Reasoning Test is comprised of the following item types:

- Multiple choice
- Fill-in-the-blank
- Drop-down
- Hot spot
- Drag-and-drop

Of these item types, the only one that is significantly different from the printed page is the hot spot item. On the computer screen, there will appear a graphic image and within that image there will be locations that will respond to a mouse click. You indicate your answer by clicking on the appropriate part of the graphic image. In the book, the closest that we can come is to have you mark or circle a point on a graphic image with your pen or pencil.

NOTE: For study purposes, all example and practice questions in this chapter are in the multiple-choice format.

The topics tested on the Mathematical Reasoning Test are listed below. An item on this test may be part of a series of questions based on a short text, graph, table, or a mathematical concept, or it may be a single question based on similar stimuli.

- Number operations and number sense
- Measurement and geometry
- Data analysis, statistics, and probability
- Algebra, functions, and patterns

NOTE: A list of common math formulas also will be provided to you for use on the Mathematical Reasoning Test. See page 34 for some of these formulas.

Often, with multiple-choice items, several of the answer choices are obviously incorrect. That makes it easier to choose the correct answer from the choices given because you can eliminate the obviously wrong answer choices. If you are struggling with a question, try this elimination approach first, because it improves your chances of guessing correctly. You don't have time to ponder every answer choice, so don't waste time on questions that are causing you trouble.

B. Test Strategies

Here are some strategies to help you succeed on the Mathematical Reasoning Test.

- **Make an educated guess.** Educated guesses are a little different from ordinary guesses. For multiple-choice questions, you'll be given four possible choices. If one is obviously wrong, you have three left to consider. If two are possibly wrong, you have a 50-50 chance of getting the right answer. If you do a bit of mental math, you often can choose the right answer on the basis of the approximate answer you came up with. If you work backward from an answer choice to the question and it doesn't work, it can't be the right answer.

  It is possible to answer all items on the Mathematical Reasoning Test within the given time frame. If you find a problem that's so complex that you need many minutes to try to figure it out, guess. You're better off guessing at one very difficult question and moving on than not finishing the test because you spent all your time on that one item.

- **Read carefully.** Math problems are little stories. Read them carefully. If you can visualize what's going on, you can probably solve the problem. Always be sure to answer the question from the information presented, not from what you may know or assume. For each question, there is a correct answer based on the information given, even if the correct answer is "Not enough information given" or "None of the above."

- **Pay attention to units of measurement.** Pay attention to units of measurement and note any changes in units. If you're asked for an answer in minutes, and the question gives time in hours, you need to do some converting.

- **Brush up on your math skills.** Study Section C, "Math Review," in addition to any other math review resources you have available (we list a few suggestions at the beginning of Section C).

- **Review and work the examples and practice questions.** There are examples and practice questions sprinkled throughout this chapter. Work through these and check your answers. If you answer a question correctly, read the explanation to reinforce the reasoning. If you answer incorrectly, read the explanation, and then reread the question to see where you went wrong. Additional sample questions can be found online on the GED Testing Service® website: www.gedtestingservice.com/freepractice/ download/Mathematical Reasoning_Math/Mathematical ReasoningMathPracticeTest.html. (Please note that this site is designed for use by educators and that GED Testing Service® is not affiliated with, and does not endorse, *CliffsNotes GED® TEST Cram Plan,* 2nd Edition.)

- **Use the on-screen calculator.** If an item requires several steps to solve, it's a good idea to use the calculator to save you time. You can find a manual for this calculator online at www.atomiclearning.com/ti30xs.

- **Use the Formula Sheet.** If you can't recall a formula from memory, check the Formula Sheet, which you can access on-screen during the test. As you study for the Mathematical Reasoning Test, refer to our Formula Sheet for common formulas (see page 34).

- **Take the Practice Test.** Take the Mathematical Reasoning Practice Test (Chapter XII). Do so under test conditions—using a timer. Check your answers and review the explanations.

C. Math Review

The purpose of this review is to get you familiar with the basic mathematic principles represented on the Mathematical Reasoning Test and to give you practice in applying them. All of the example and practice questions in this review are multiple choice because the majority of the questions on the Mathematical Reasoning Test are multiple choice.

For additional math review, you can visit CliffsNotes.com (www.cliffsnotes.com/math) or reference these other great *CliffsNotes* titles:

CliffsNotes Math Review for Standardized Tests, 2nd Edition
CliffsNotes Basic Math and Pre-Algebra Quick Review
CliffsNotes Algebra I Quick Review
CliffsQuickReview Geometry

1. Number Operations and Number Sense

The Mathematical Reasoning Test includes many items concerning basic number operations and number sense. Here are some tips that you should remember when you take the test:

- Remember that if the answer choices are very close, estimation may not be accurate enough to get the correct answer.
- Round your answers to the nearest number you can handle in your head. If you were asked to multiply 33 by 48, you could think 30×50, which equals 1,500. The correct answer is 1,584 but the estimated answer would be close enough to make sure that the answer you chose was in the right range.
- Round to the nearest multiple of 10 and compensate for the rounding error if needed. For example, if the question is 140 – 39, you can think of 140 – 40, which is equal to 100; then you can use that as an approximate answer or add the one back to get 101, which is the correct answer.
- Sometimes you're faced with two or more numbers, each of which has a series of zeros at the end. If you had to add 4,000 and 3,800, you could think about temporarily ignoring the last two zeros in each number. Then you would be adding 40 + 38, which equals 78. You can't really ignore zeros for very long. You have to put them back to arrive at the correct answer: 7,800.
- There are numbers that are just easier to work with for mental arithmetic. Say you were given the question, $15,270 \div 32$. If these numbers were $15,000 \div 30$, that would be a simple question. 15,270 and 15,000 are approximately equal, as are 32 and 30. You could try this approximation and see how it works in the question.
- If you are presented with a set of numbers to add, some of which are very close, such as in the following example, add the close ones (78 and 79) in your head first and then add the other number or numbers. You would then divide the total by the number of subjects:

> Darren is averaging his final scores and notices the following:
>
> English: 78%
> Mathematics: 93%
> Social studies: 79%
>
> If Darren were trying to maintain an 80% average, did he achieve his goal?

The numbers are very close except for the 93 in mathematics and could be about 80. Thus, his average score would be approximately 80%. The 93 would bring his average well above the 80% level.

a. Whole Numbers

Our system of whole numbers is based on ten. The first ten whole numbers are, in order, 0, 1, 2, 3, 4, 5, 6, 7, 8, 9. After that, the first digit indicates the number that is multiplied by ten and the second digit indicates the number that is multiplied by 1. So, 64 is (6 × 10) + 4, and it's also 60 + 4. Whole numbers do not include decimals or fractions. Because the units digit (the right-hand one) is always in order, we know that 48 is one larger than 47 and one less than 49. If you want to see relative size of a group of numbers, use a number line to illustrate them, and remember that every digit in a number determines its relative size.

Whole numbers can be factored. They can be expressed as a series of numbers or factors, which multiply together to form the number, even if the factors are the number itself and 1. For example:

$$6 = 2 \times 3 \text{ or } 6 \times 1$$
$$18 = 9 \times 2 = 3 \times 3 \times 2 \text{ or } 18 \times 1$$
$$11 = 11 \times 1$$

Whole numbers such as 11 are prime numbers. A **prime number** is a number greater than 1 that has no factors except itself and 1. Another example of a prime number is 13 because the only factors of 13 are 13 and 1.

You can factor any number by following some simple rules:

- A prime number can be divided only by itself and by 1.
- Any number ending in 0, 2, 4, 6, or 8 can be divided by 2.
- Any number ending in 0 or 5 can be divided by 5.
- Any number ending in 0 can be divided by 10.
- Any number whose digits add up to a multiple of 3 can be divided by 3. For example, with the number 66, if you add 6 + 6, you get 12, which is a multiple of 3, so you know that 66 can be divided by 3.
- Any number whose digits add up to a multiple of 9 can be divided by 9. For example, with the number 81, if you add 8 + 1, you get 9, which is a multiple of 9, so you know that 81 can be divided by 9.

These simple rules can make mental arithmetic a little easier on the Mathematical Reasoning Test, and may help you quickly eliminate some answer choices.

EXAMPLES:

> Andy made a wager with his classmates that he could tell them the prime factors of any number under 200 within 1 minute. To test his skill, Gloria asked him for the prime factors of 174. Andy smiled and told her the prime factors. What were the prime factors that Andy told Gloria?
>
> **(A)** 2, 2, 3, and 5
> **(B)** 2, 3, and 29
> **(C)** 3, 4, and 39
> **(D)** 2 and 87

The correct answer is **(B).** The prime factors of any number are the factors that can no longer be broken down into further factors. If you look at 174, you see that it ends in 4, so 2 is a factor. Then 174 ÷ 2 = 87, and 8 + 7 = 15, which is a multiple of 3. So, 87 is divisible by 3, and 87 ÷ 3 = 29, which is a prime number. Andy was lucky that one of the factors was a large prime number, or he could've ended up with a much longer string of prime factors.

Jessie is playing a new game called "What's That Number?" The announcer asks for a possible product of a whole number greater than 10 that is doubled and then multiplied by 5. Which answer would win the game for Jessie?

(A) 150
(B) 175
(C) 225
(D) 255

The correct answer is **(A)**. The operations of doubling a number (multiplying by 2) and then multiplying the product by 5 would be the same as multiplying by 10, and any number multiplied by 10 would end in 0, not 5. Therefore, choices (B), (C), and (D) are incorrect, as they all end in 5.

Donald was using a tape measure to measure the length of his room. The tape measure was 10 yards long, and his room was 21 feet long. How many feet longer was the tape measure than Donald's room?

(A) 3
(B) 7
(C) 9
(D) 11

The correct answer is **(C)**. Converting the length of the tape measure into feet, 10 yards = 10 × 3 = 30 feet. The length of Donald's room is 21 feet, so 30 – 21 = 9 feet. The answer in yards (which you weren't asked for) is 3 (choice A), and if you didn't pay attention to the units of measure, you might've just subtracted 21 – 10 = 11 (choice D). ***Remember:*** The numbers have to be in the same units *before* you can perform mathematical operations on them.

b. Integers

Integers are like whole numbers, but with one key difference: Integers also include negative numbers. Just remember: positive, negative, or zero—without decimal components. Integers can be added, subtracted, multiplied, and divided. *Note:* You cannot divide by zero. Division by zero is undefined.

There are two main subsets of integers. One subset is 1, 2, 3, and so on, where all the numbers are positive. The other main subset of integers is –1, –2, –3, and so on, where all the numbers are negative. Integers can be drawn on a number line, like this:

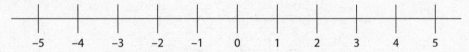

The positive integers are on the right side of the zero, and they increase in value, moving from the center to the right. The negative integers are on the left side of the zero, and they decrease in value moving from the center to the left.

One property of an integer is that it has an absolute value that is its distance from zero—in other words, it's always positive or zero. Absolute value is written as $|n|$. Thus, the absolute value of –4 is written as $|-4| = 4$.

Remember: Integers can be added, subtracted, multiplied, and divided as long as you watch the signs and don't divide by zero.

To add integers, the simplest way is to combine all the positive integers and all the negative integers and then combine the result. For example,

$$-5 + 3 + 7 = -5 + 10 = 5$$

To subtract integers, if there are only two integers and both are positive (for example, 8 – 2), the difference between them is 6. If the number you are subtracting is negative, however, (for example, 8 – –2), the minus sign becomes a plus sign and the negative sign is deleted: 8 – –2 = 8 + 2 = 10.

To multiply integers, you count the number of negative signs. If there is an even number of negative signs, the answer is positive. If there is an odd number of negative signs, the answer is negative. For example,

$$-3 \times -6 = 18$$
$$-3 \times 6 = -18$$

To divide integers, you have to keep track of the signs. If both the **divisor** (the integer dividing) and the **dividend** (the integer being divided) have the same sign, the **quotient** (answer) will be positive. If the divisor and the dividend have different signs, the quotient will be negative. For example,

$$36 \div 6 = 6$$
$$-36 \div -6 = 6$$
$$36 \div -6 = -6$$

Remember: You can't divide by 0.

Integers can be used in pairs to determine a location on a grid because a grid is just a series of perpendicular number lines. In this case, the first integer of the pair indicates the position with relation to the *x*-axis or the horizontal position. The second integer of the pair indicates the position with relation to the *y*-axis or the vertical position.

The point (5,–3) would appear as the following on the coordinate-plane grid:

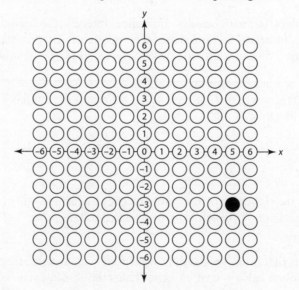

The simplest way to compare the size difference of two integers is to visualize them on a number line. This will give you clues about the relative value of the integers. The number to the right is always larger.

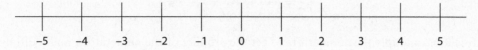

To subtract 8 from 5, start at 0 and count five spaces to the right and then count eight spaces to the left to arrive at −3.

$$5 - 8 = -3$$

EXAMPLES:

Robbie and Sandy are having a reading contest. Robbie has read 497 pages in a very long book, but Sandy has read 239 pages in one book and 261 pages in another book. Who is leading in the reading contest at the moment?

(A) It's a tie.
(B) Robbie
(C) Sandy
(D) Not enough information given

The correct answer is **(C).** Sandy has read 239 + 261 = 500 pages, and Robbie has read 497 pages. Choice (D) is incorrect; the question asks, "Who is leading in the reading contest at the moment?" which you can answer. You can eliminate choice (A) by completing the calculation. *Note:* The number of pages read is so close that approximations wouldn't give you the correct answer.

Two classmates are comparing their heights. Tom is 5 feet 11 inches tall, and Robert is 5 feet 9 inches tall. What is the height difference between Tom and Robert, in inches?

(A) 2
(B) 3
(C) 4
(D) 5

The correct answer is **(A).** The difference between the two heights is the difference between the inches because the feet are the same. The height difference is 11 − 9 = 2 inches.

c. Fractions

Fractions can be added, subtracted, multiplied, and divided.

In a fraction, the top number is called the **numerator** and the bottom number is called the **denominator.**

To add or subtract fractions, the denominators must be equal. You can make the denominators equal by multiplying each by a number that would produce denominators that are the same number. This number is called the **common denominator.** If you multiply the denominator by a number, you must multiply the numerator by the same number.

For example, to add $\frac{1}{2}$ and $\frac{2}{3}$, you need to get the denominators the same. Here's how:

$$\frac{1}{2}+\frac{2}{3}=\frac{1\times3}{2\times3}+\frac{2\times2}{3\times2}=\frac{3}{6}+\frac{4}{6}=\frac{7}{6}$$

To multiply fractions, multiply the numerators to get the product of the numerators, and multiply the denominators to get the product of the denominators. For example,

$$\frac{1}{2}\times\frac{2}{3}=\frac{1\times2}{2\times3}=\frac{2}{6}$$

To divide one fraction by another, **invert** (switch the numerator and denominator) the second fraction and multiply. For example,

$$\frac{1}{2}\div\frac{2}{3}=\frac{1}{2}\times\frac{3}{2}=\frac{3}{4}$$

Many fractions can be simplified—the numerator and the denominator can be divided by the same number until there is no number that will divide into each equally. Sometimes the only number that will divide evenly into the numerator and denominator is 1, and the fraction is called a **reduced fraction.** For example,

$$\frac{8}{16}=\frac{8\div8}{16\div8}=\frac{1}{2}$$

If the number is made up of a whole number and a fraction, it is called a **mixed number.** An example of a mixed number is $3\frac{1}{2}$.

If the numerator and denominator are both positive or both negative and the numerator is smaller than the denominator (for example, $\frac{1}{2}$), the fraction is **proper** and smaller than 1. If both the numerator and denominator are positive or negative and the numerator is larger than the denominator (for example, $\frac{5}{2}$), the fraction is **improper** and larger than 1. If either the numerator or denominator is negative, the fraction will be smaller than 1.

A mixed number can always be expressed as an improper fraction by multiplying the denominator by the whole number and using the product plus the old numerator as the new numerator. For example,

$$2\frac{1}{2}=\frac{(2\times2)+1}{2}=\frac{5}{2}$$

Any fraction has an endless number of equivalent fractions because multiplying the numerator and denominator of the fraction by the same (nonzero) number produces an equivalent fraction. Thus, $\frac{1}{2}=\frac{4}{8}=\frac{8}{16}$, and so on.

When two fractions have equal denominators, the one with the larger numerator is the larger fraction. When two fractions have equal numerators, the one with the larger denominator is the smaller fraction.

EXAMPLES:

Alex and José are looking for an apartment to share and find two buildings in the same area. Alex loves to cook and wants to live close to the supermarket so that he can shop each day for his groceries. José spends all his time reading and wants to be close to the library. If the supermarket is three blocks from one apartment and five blocks from a second apartment, what fraction would indicate the relative distance of the closer supermarket to the further supermarket for each apartment?

(A) $\dfrac{2}{5}$

(B) $\dfrac{1}{2}$

(C) $\dfrac{3}{5}$

(D) $\dfrac{5}{2}$

The correct answer is **(C)**. The closer apartment is three blocks away, the farther apartment is five blocks away, and the fraction would be the shorter distance over the farther distance or $\dfrac{3}{5}$.

Glen and Dave were looking for a deal on school sweatshirts for their baseball team. After a lot of shopping around, they narrowed it down to three suppliers. Supplier A offered them $\dfrac{1}{3}$ off each sweatshirt. Supplier B offered them $\dfrac{8}{25}$ off each sweatshirt. Supplier C offered them $\dfrac{3}{9}$ off each sweatshirt. Which supplier offered them the best deal?

(A) Supplier A
(B) Supplier B
(C) Supplier C
(D) Suppliers A and C

The correct answer is **(D)**. Suppliers A and C offered them the same discount because $\dfrac{1}{3}$ and $\dfrac{3}{9}$ are equivalent fractions. To compare the discounts, you must find the least common denominator. Since $\dfrac{1}{3}$ and $\dfrac{3}{9}$ are equivalent fractions, you can just compare $\dfrac{1}{3}$ and $\dfrac{8}{25}$. The least common denominator is 75: $25 \times 3 = 75$:

$$\text{Suppliers A and C:} \qquad \text{Supplier B:}$$
$$\frac{1}{3} \times \frac{25}{25} = \frac{25}{75} \qquad\qquad \frac{8}{25} \times \frac{3}{3} = \frac{24}{75}$$

As you can see, Suppliers A and C's discount is larger by $\dfrac{1}{75}$.

165

Sierra is entertaining three of her friends, and they decide to order pizza. Unfortunately, it arrives unsliced and she has to divide the pie so that each person gets an equal share. What fraction of the pizza would each piece be?

(A) $\dfrac{1}{6}$

(B) $\dfrac{1}{5}$

(C) $\dfrac{1}{4}$

(D) $\dfrac{1}{3}$

The correct answer is **(C)**. If Sierra has three friends over and wants all four people to share the pizza equally, then each person would get $\dfrac{1}{4}$ of the pizza. In working with fractions, the numerator of a fraction indicates the number of parts of a whole that are considered. In this case, each person was going to get one piece and the numerator would be 1. The denominator indicates the number the whole is divided into. In this case, the pizza was divided into four sections, one equal section for each person. Each person will get one of the four equal sections or $\dfrac{1}{4}$.

d. Decimals

Decimals or decimal fractions are fractions based on a denominator of ten or some power of ten. If we were to look at a number such as 23.345, we would know that the whole number is 23, which is 20 + 3 and the value of each digit gets bigger as you go from the decimal point to the left. The value of the numbers gets smaller as you go from the decimal point to the right.

Decimal	Equivalent Fraction
0.3	$\dfrac{3}{10} = \dfrac{300}{1,000}$
0.04	$\dfrac{4}{100} = \dfrac{40}{1,000}$
0.005	$\dfrac{5}{1,000}$
0.345	$\dfrac{345}{1,000}$

Decimals can be added, subtracted, multiplied, and divided just like whole numbers. To add or subtract decimal fractions, you must always keep the decimal points in line, which ensures that the place values of the numbers you're adding or subtracting are equal. Here's an example of aligning the decimals and adding:

$$\begin{array}{r} 34.782 \\ +\ 7.309 \\ \hline 42.091 \end{array}$$

To multiply decimal fractions, you have to remember that these are fractions and multiply using the rules of multiplication of integers. Here's an example:

$$\begin{array}{r} 3.7 \\ \times\ 2.4 \\ \hline 148 \\ 74 \\ \hline 888 \end{array}$$

But where do you put the decimal point? The simple answer is that you add the number of decimal places in the two multiples—in this case, two—and count off that number from the right. That would produce a product of 8.88. The reason for this is that $3.7 = 3\dfrac{7}{10} = \dfrac{37}{10}$ and $2.4 = 2\dfrac{4}{10} = \dfrac{24}{10}$. Multiplying the fractions, $\dfrac{37}{10} \times \dfrac{24}{10} = \dfrac{888}{100} = 8.88$.

To divide decimals, there is another approach. If you wanted to divide 36.6 by 2.4, you would write it as $36.6 \div 2.4$, which would become $366 \div 24$ (because you move all decimal points the same number of spaces to the right and then you divide). The quotient is 15.25. The long division is shown below.

$$2.4\overline{)36.6} \ \rightarrow \ 24\overline{)366.00} \begin{array}{l} 15.25 \end{array}$$

$$\begin{array}{r} 15.25 \\ 24\overline{)366.00} \\ \underline{24} \\ 126 \\ \underline{120} \\ 60 \\ \underline{48} \\ 120 \\ \underline{120} \end{array}$$

EXAMPLES:

> Max is shopping for clothes and sees a jacket he really likes. Store A has the jacket on sale for 40% off the regular price, and Store B is offering it for 60% of its regular price. If the jacket originally cost $49.99 in both stores, how much would Max have to pay for the jacket on sale at the lower price?
>
> **(A)** $19.99
> **(B)** $29.99
> **(C)** $39.99
> **(D)** $49.99

The correct answer is **(B)**. Looking at the two discounts, you'll notice that they're the same. If an item is discounted 40%, then the price is 60% of the original (100% − 40% = 60%). Max would then pay 60% of the original price for the jacket on sale: 0.6 × $49.99 = $29.99. Choice (A) is close to the dollar amount Max would save with the sale, which means that this problem requires you to pay close attention. You could estimate the answer by using 60% of $50, which is $30, making choice (B) just a penny away.

> José was shopping for school supplies and needed two binders. Looking at the binder display, he saw just the type of binder he needed. It cost $4.95, but the sign said that there was a $1.50 discount for buying two. If José bought two binders, how much would he pay for each binder after applying the discount?
>
> **(A)** $3.45
> **(B)** $4.20
> **(C)** $4.45
> **(D)** $4.95

The correct answer is **(B)**. If José received a discount of $1.50 for buying two binders, he would get a discount of $1.50 ÷ 2 = $0.75 per binder. This would reduce the price to $4.95 − $0.75 = $4.20.

> Sally has finished 0.6 of her reading course. If the total course is 10 months long, how many months does Sally have left?
>
> **(A)** 2
> **(B)** 3
> **(C)** 4
> **(D)** 5

The correct answer is **(C)**. Start by calculating 0.6 of 10, which is 0.6 × 10 = 6. But don't forget: This is how much Sally has *completed,* and you were asked how much time *remains* in the course, which is 10 − 6 = 4 months. You have to read even the simplest questions carefully to make sure that you're answering the question that is being asked.

e. Percentages

When you're working with percentages, you're really working with fractions whose denominators are always 100. To calculate a percentage, you can use the percentage as the numerator and 100 as the denominator, and use any of the common operations. Once you have the fraction, it can easily be turned into a decimal by dividing the denominator into the numerator.

If, for example, you are offered a discount of 40% at a store, they are saying that they will take $\frac{40}{100}$ or $\frac{4}{10}$ or $\frac{2}{5}$ of the price off the original price. Remember that fractions can be reduced by dividing the top number (called the numerator) and the bottom number (called the denominator) by the same number. In this case, we divide $\frac{40}{100}$ by 10 to get $\frac{4}{10}$ and then divide again by 2 to get $\frac{2}{5}$. Because 40% can be expressed as a fraction, it can also be expressed as a decimal fraction. For example, $40\% = \frac{40}{100} = 0.4$. This allows us to use percentages in different ways.

If the original price of the item was $100 and the discount was 40%, you could calculate the discount by multiplying $100 by $\frac{40}{100}$ or 0.4. In each case, the answer would be $40, which would be the discount.

i. Practice

Practice converting percentages to fractions to decimals by completing this table. Be sure to reduce fractions to their simplest form.

Percentage	Decimal	Fraction
34%	0.34	
		$\frac{3}{5}$
100%		
		$\frac{24}{25}$
	0.98	
75%		

ii. Answers

The table below shows the missing conversions:

Percentage	Decimal	Fraction
34%	0.34	$\frac{17}{50}$
60%	0.6	$\frac{3}{5}$
100%	1	1
96%	0.96	$\frac{24}{25}$
98%	0.98	$\frac{49}{50}$
75%	0.75	$\frac{3}{4}$

EXAMPLES:

Jeff is shopping for new shirts and notices a special sale. If he buys one shirt, there is a discount of 10% on it. If he buys two shirts, there is a discount of 30% off the second shirt. If he buys three shirts, there is a discount of 40% off the third shirt purchased, and the discount for four shirts or more is 50% off the most expensive shirt. Jeff sees four shirts he really likes but wants to save the most money he can.

Shirt 1 costs $59.95.

Shirt 2 costs $39.95.

Shirt 3 costs $29.95.

Shirt 4 costs $49.95.

Which shirt should Jeff buy fourth to save the most money?

(A) Shirt 1
(B) Shirt 2
(C) Shirt 3
(D) Shirt 4

The correct answer is **(A)**. The shirt bought last would create the biggest discount on that shirt and sensible Jeff would want to save by getting the biggest discount on his shirts. Because Shirt 1 is the most expensive, it would create the biggest savings if he bought it as the fourth shirt.

Carol is investing $200 she got for her birthday. Bank A offers her 3% simple interest for a year, while Bank B says it will invest her money in a certificate that will pay her no interest but a bonus of $5.75 after one year. Bank C offers Carol 2% simple interest for a year with a bonus of $2.50 after one year. Which bank will return the most money to Carol after one year?

(A) Bank A
(B) Bank B
(C) Bank C
(D) Not enough information given

The correct answer is **(C).** Bank A is offering her $200 × 0.03 = $6. Bank B is offering her $5.75. Bank C is offering her $200 × 0.02 = $4, plus a bonus of $2.50, for a total of $6.50, which is the greatest return on her money. Choice (D) can be eliminated quickly because there is enough information to get an answer.

f. Relationship of Basic Arithmetic Operations

Arithmetic operations are related to one another. Subtraction is the opposite of addition. Addition of positive numbers creates a sum larger than either of the numbers added. For example, if 5 + 1 = 6, then 6 – 1 = 5 and 6 – 5 = 1.

Here's another example: If you were adding the total bill for your grocery shopping, the sum would be larger than the price of each item. If you bought more than you could afford, subtracting items would make the sum of the items smaller. If Dave bought $20.04 worth of groceries but only had a $20 bill in his pocket, he would have to leave behind one or more items to reduce his total to $20 or less.

Addition and multiplication are related because multiplication is repeated addition of the same number (for example, 3 × 4 = 4 + 4 + 4 = 12).

Memorizing the multiplication tables is a far more efficient way of multiplying in your head, but if you get stuck, remembering that multiplication is repetitive addition of the same number can help. If you want to multiply 6 × 7 and you remember only that 5 × 7 = 35, you can figure out 6 × 7 by adding 7 to 35 to get 42.

Subtraction and division are related because division is repetitive subtraction of the same number. For example: 24 ÷ 6 = 24 – 6 = 18 – 6 = 12 – 6 = 6 – 6 = 0. We had to subtract 6 four times to arrive at zero. 24 ÷ 6 = 4. Again, memorizing the division tables is a more efficient way to divide, but keep this in mind if you're stuck on the test.

Multiplication and division are related and are opposite operations:

$$3 \times 4 = 12$$
$$12 \div 3 = 4$$

EXAMPLES:

Fernando was given a skill-testing question to answer in order to claim a prize at the local radio station. He was asked to calculate $23 + 45 - 59 - 45 + 59$. What should his answer be?

(A) 21
(B) 23
(C) 25
(D) 45

The correct answer is **(B)**. Because addition and subtraction are opposite operations, adding 45 and then subtracting 45 and subtracting 59 and then adding 59 have no effect on the 23. Remember to read questions carefully. In this case, if you read carefully, you noticed that 45 and 59 are both added and subtracted, leaving you with 23.

Josie was doing the mechanical arithmetic portion of a test and came across the following question:

$$46 \div 23 \times 54 \div 92 \div 54 \times 92 \times 23 = ?$$

What should her answer be?

(A) 2
(B) 23
(C) 46
(D) 54

The correct answer is **(C)**. Multiplication and division are opposite operations. In this case, the numbers 23, 54, and 92 are both multiplied and divided. Do all the multiplication and division before doing the addition and subtraction, leaving 46 as the answer. ***Remember:*** If addition/subtraction is mixed with multiplication/division, then the order of operations is always used.

g. Exponents

An exponent may be called a power, but no matter what it's called, it has a definite meaning and follows certain rules. N^e means a number, N, multiplied by itself (or "raised") e times and is usually read "N to the eth." You should be familiar with the following rules of exponents:

- The exponent tells you the number of times the number, or **base,** is to be multiplied by itself. For example, $6^3 = 6 \times 6 \times 6 = 216$.

- Any negative exponent means to divide by the number to that power. For example, $2^{-3} = \dfrac{1}{2^3}$.

- A number to the power of 0 equals 1. For example, $2{,}948^0 = 1$. Note 0^0 is not defined.

- Any number to the power of 1 equals the number. For example, $345^1 = 345$.

- To multiply two or more numbers involving exponents, if the base is the same, add the exponents to get the product. For example, $8^3 \times 8^7 = 8^{3+7} = 8^{10}$.

- To divide two numbers involving exponents with a common base, subtract the exponents to get the answer. For example, $5^8 \div 5^3 = 5^{8-3} = 5^5$.

- To raise an exponent to an exponent, multiply the exponents. For example, $(4^3)^2 = 4^{3 \times 2} = 4^6$.

- To raise two or more numbers in a product to a common exponent, raise each one to the exponent. For example, $(2 \times 3)^4 = 2^4 \times 3^4$ or 6^4.

- To raise a fraction to a power, raise the numerator and the denominator to the power. For example, $\left(\dfrac{3}{4}\right)^8 = \dfrac{3^8}{4^8}$.

There are a few other rules or laws of exponents, but these should take you through the Mathematical Reasoning Test.

EXAMPLES:

Solve the following equation for e: $2^e = 256$.

(A) 5
(B) 6
(C) 7
(D) 8

The correct answer is **(D).** In this equation, you're dealing with exponents. In this case, you're looking for a power of 2 that would equal 256. You can use a calculator to find the answer, or you can solve this problem manually as follows:

$2^1 = 2$
$2^2 = 4$
$2^3 = 8$
$2^4 = 16$
$2^5 = 32$

$2^6 = 64$

$2^7 = 128$

$2^8 = 256$

Thus, $e = 8$. In this case, the number 256 is an exact power of 2. If the number given were 257, the problem would have been extremely difficult and probably wouldn't appear on the Mathematical Reasoning Test.

Carlos is a whiz at math but a little lazy about helping around the house. His father offers to pay him $15 a week to rake the leaves each day. Carlos says that he won't work weekends but will take 2¢ for the first day and the square of yesterday's amount each day and would only accept the last day's pay. How much more than his father was offering would Carlos get on the last day for the first week's work?

(A) $0.32

(B) $640.36

(C) $655.36

(D) $672.36

The correct answer is **(B)**. This is a good question to use a calculator to find the answer. Exponential functions like this get large very quickly. In this case, you could create a table like the one below (since Carlos won't work weekends, you only need to calculate through Day 5).

Day	Amount (cents)
1	2
2	4
3	16
4	256
5	65,536

On the fifth day, Carlos would be owed 65,536 pennies or $655.36. But, his father had offered him $15 a week, so he would get $655.36 – $15.00 = $640.36 more than his father's original offer, choice (B). If you converted to dollars before the calculation, you would have gotten a different answer because the powers of a decimal get smaller and the units given were cents, not dollars. Always read carefully to ensure that you convert, if necessary, but at the right time.

h. Scientific Notation

Scientists often work in very large or very small numbers. They would waste a lot of time writing all those numbers each time they needed them, so they developed a system called scientific notation. Instead of writing 700,000,000, they could write 7.0×10^8 or $7.0 \times 100,000,000$. In scientific notation, the significant digits are always shown with the decimal point after the first digit multiplied by a power of 10 to keep the structured numbers equivalent. For example, 1,234,567 could be written in scientific notation as 1.234567×10^6.

If the number is greater than 1, the power of 10 is positive; if the number is less than 1, the power of 10 is negative.

EXAMPLES:

> Jason was working in a physics lab for the summer, but he could never figure out how big or small numbers written in scientific notation really were. In the last report he read, two items were 1.493×10^{-4} feet apart. If Jason just wanted to know how far apart they were using regular notation, what distance would he use in fe`et?
>
> **(A)** 0.0001493
> **(B)** 0.001493
> **(C)** 0.01493
> **(D)** 1.493

The correct answer is **(A)**. In order to switch scientific notation to regular notation, you multiply 1.493×10^{-4}, which would be 0.0001493. To solve this problem quickly, simply move the decimal point four spaces to the left since this is a negative power, as shown below.

$$1.493 \times 10^{-4} \longrightarrow 0.0001493$$
$$\phantom{1.493 \times 10^{-4} \longrightarrow 0.00}4\ 3\ 2\ 1$$

If this were a positive power, you would move the decimal point four spaces to the right: 14,930.

> Ahmed was researching the distance to the moon from Earth and found the figure: 238,857 miles from the center of the Earth to the center of the moon. His teacher asked him to write this in scientific notation. What number should Ahmed write?
>
> **(A)** 238,000
> **(B)** 238,857
> **(C)** 23.8×10^{5}
> **(D)** 2.38857×10^{5}

The correct answer is **(D)**. Scientific notation means writing the number with the decimal after the first number and multiplying by a power of 10. The simple way to do this is to count from right to left and increase the power by 1 for each digit. In this example, you would move the decimal point five places to the left and that would make 5 the power of 10. Note that choices (A) and (B) can be easily eliminated since they do not use scientific notation.

i. Ratios

A ratio is a fraction-like number that compares two quantities. In comparing ratios, the units must be the same. Like fractions, the numbers in a ratio always can be divided evenly by the same number to produce a simplified ratio (unless the ratio is already reduced).

The ratio of 5 to 8 may be written in different ways, such as 5:8, or $5 \div 8$, or $\frac{5}{8}$. The numbers 5 and 8 are the terms of the ratio.

If you divide one integer by another, you get a rational number or a ratio. If, for example, you divided 3 by 4, the result would be $\frac{3}{4}$ or 3:4.

Because ratios are fractions, the denominator can never be 0.

EXAMPLES:

> Abdul really likes soda. One day when it was on sale, he bought 25 cases of soda (20 cases of ginger ale and 5 cases of cola). What ratio of cola to ginger ale did Abdul buy?
>
> **(A)** 1:4
> **(B)** 20:25
> **(C)** 5:4
> **(D)** 4:1

The correct answer is **(A).** Abdul bought 5 cases of cola and 20 cases of ginger ale. A ratio compares numbers measured in the same units—in this instance, the unit is a case. When you compare the number of cases of cola bought to the number of cases of ginger ale bought, it's 5 to 20, usually written 5:20. Ratios usually are written in the lowest terms—that is, by dividing the numbers by any number or numbers that would divide equally into both. You'll notice that both 5 and 20 can be divided by 5 evenly. Thus, the ratio 5:20 becomes 1:4.

> Kelly and Gloria were having a contest to see who could read the most books in a month. In one month, Kelly read three books, one with 325 pages, one with 242 pages, and 115 pages of a third book. Gloria read two books, one with 505 pages and the other with 268 pages. What is the ratio of pages read by Kelly to pages read by Gloria?
>
> **(A)** 628:773
> **(B)** 682:773
> **(C)** 773:682
> **(D)** 773:628

The correct answer is **(B).** Kelly read a total number of pages of: 325 + 242 + 115 = 682. Gloria read a total number of pages of: 505 + 268 = 773. The ratio of pages read by Kelly to those read by Gloria is 682:773.

j. Proportions

An equation expressing the equality of two ratios is called a proportion and may be written in different ways: $\frac{a}{b} = \frac{c}{d}$ may be written $a:b = c:d$, or $a:b::c:d$ (read as "a is to b as c is to d"), where a and d are called the **extremes** and b and c are called the **means.** The product of the extremes equals the product of the means (that is, $ad = bc$) and is called **cross-multiplication.**

If one of the terms is unknown—for example, a, which could be represented by x—then $xd = bc$ and $x = \frac{bc}{d}$.

EXAMPLES:

> Alice just got a part-time job at a local restaurant, which prepares its sodas by mixing a concentrate with soda water. If the ratio of concentrate to soda water is 1 gallon of concentrate to 15 gallons of soda water, how many ounces of concentrate would Alice need to produce the Belly-Buster Special Soda, which is 32 ounces of pure delight?
>
> **(A)** 1
> **(B)** 2
> **(C)** 3
> **(D)** 4

The correct answer is **(B)**. The ratio of concentrate to soda water is 1:15. In order to solve this problem, we need to use a proportion. Adding 1 gallon of concentrate to 15 gallons of soda water would produce 16 gallons of Belly-Buster Special Soda. In this case, Alice doesn't need 16 gallons of soda but 32 ounces; 32 is double 16, so she can maintain the consistent units in the ratio. Then she can produce a proportion by multiplying the original ratio by 2 to produce 2:32. This means Alice needs 2 ounces of concentrate to produce 32 ounces of Belly-Buster Special Soda.

> Danny is tending bar at a local restaurant, and the manager has a new idea. He has put a tip container on the bar and has told Danny that he will divide tips this way: Seven parts go to the waiter, two parts go to the bartender, and one part goes to the manager. If the tip container contains $320 at the end of the night, what portion would go to Danny?
>
> **(A)** $23
> **(B)** $32
> **(C)** $46
> **(D)** $64

The correct answer is **(D)**. Each of the following gets a proportion of the tips. If you add up all the proportions, you get 10, which makes for easy calculation. The waiter would get $\frac{7}{10}$ of the tips. The owner would get $\frac{1}{10}$ of the tips, and Danny would get $\frac{2}{10}$ of the tips, or $\frac{1}{5}$. To solve, set up a proportion and solve for x, the amount of Danny's tips:

$$\frac{x}{320} = \frac{1}{5}$$
$$5x = 320$$
$$x = 64$$

k. Roots

If we consider the radical equation $\sqrt[e]{N} = R$, where N is a number or the base, e is the index of the root, and R is the root, we could read the equation as "the eth root of N is R." A root of such an equation is one of a predetermined number of factors that produce the product required. All this is good mathematics, but on the Mathematical Reasoning Test, you'll likely be asked to calculate nothing more than a square root or even a cube root without a calculator.

If the question is one for which a calculator appears on the computer screen, the work is done for you. If the concept of roots is still confusing, first try to remember that roots and powers are opposites. If you multiply 3×3, you get 9 or, to put it another way, $3^2 = 9$. If you're asked for the square root of 9, or which two equal factors multiply together to form a product of 9, you could either know or calculate the factors to be 3 and 3. The usual place to calculate roots is in problems about geometric measures. If you're given the area of a square, the length or width is the square root. If you're given the volume of a cube, each dimension is the cube root.

REMINDER: If you can't recall a formula from memory, check the Formula Sheet, which you can access on-screen during the test. As you study for the Mathematical Reasoning Test, refer to our Formula Sheet for common formulas (see page 34).

EXAMPLES:

Elana has always wanted a hot tub in the shape of a cube. Finally, after getting her first bonus on the job, she can afford it. She wants her hot tub to be able to hold 125 cubic feet of water, but she doesn't know how wide a tub that would produce. After some research, she figures it out. How wide will her hot tub be, in feet?

(A) 2
(B) 3
(C) 4
(D) 5

The correct answer is **(D)**. Because Elana wants the hot tub to be a cube, each dimension will be the cube root of the volume, which is 125 cubic feet. Mentally, you would know that $5 \times 5 \times 5 = 125$. This means that each dimension, including the width, would be 5 feet.

Alvin was shopping for new carpet. He needed a square carpet to cover a space about 9 feet by 8 feet. The store with the best prices sold square carpets by the square foot. The pattern Alvin preferred was marked at 81 square feet. If he chooses to buy this carpet, how much smaller or larger will it be than the space he had planned for the carpet?

(A) 9 square feet smaller
(B) 9 square feet larger
(C) 23 square feet larger
(D) 72 square feet larger

The correct answer is **(B)**. To calculate the dimensions of a square carpet, you would have to find the square root of the area. Remember that area equals length times width, and both the length and the width are equal in a square. The square root of 81 is 9, which means that the carpet would measure 9 feet on each side. The space that Alvin wanted to cover was 9 feet by 8 feet. The area of this space is $9 \times 8 = 72$ square feet. Subtracting the area Alvin wanted to cover from the total area of the carpet, $81 - 72 = 9$ square feet. It is important to know the dimensions of the carpet to see if it would approximately fit the space.

I. Selecting the Appropriate Operations

You may see a few questions on the Mathematical Reasoning Test asking you what operations you would use to solve a problem but not actually asking you to solve the problem. Some of these questions are simple.

If you wanted to calculate the area of a surface, you would multiply; if you wanted to calculate the perimeter, you would add and multiply. Knowing what operations to perform and the order in which to perform them is an important skill for the test.

EXAMPLES:

Donna bought a car that uses, on average, a gallon of gas for each 23 miles traveled in the city. If gas costs $3.07 a gallon, what operations would you use to calculate how far Donna could travel in the city, on average, with $20 of gas?

(A) Multiply then divide
(B) Divide then multiply
(C) Add then multiply
(D) Divide then add

The correct answer is **(B)**. To calculate how far Donna could travel for $20 of gas, we would first divide $20 by $3.07 to see how many gallons of gas she would use. Because she can travel 23 miles for each gallon, we would multiply the number of gallons by 23. The correct operations would be to divide and then multiply.

Doreen got a summer job on a farm gathering eggs. She was paid 2¢ an egg for her work. At the end of the day, she knew how many eggs she had gathered and her per-egg pay. How could she calculate her daily income?

(A) Add
(B) Subtract
(C) Multiply
(D) Divide

The correct answer is **(C)**. Doreen would calculate her daily income by multiplying the amount she was paid per egg by the number of eggs she gathered.

m. Methods for Calculating Your Answers

On the Mathematical Reasoning Test, you'll have to answer a series of questions requiring you to perform calculations with your brain, pencil and paper, and sometimes a scientific calculator. These calculations will involve whole numbers, fractions, decimals, and integers. The only way to become proficient in these calculations is to practice. Here are some questions to practice on. They're not anything like what you'll find on the test—they're just practice in different ways of calculating an answer.

First, look at the question, and then use your brain to estimate an answer. Next, calculate the answer using a pencil and paper. Finally, use a calculator to calculate the same question to two decimal places. Your first answer should be close to the second and third. If not, you might want to spend extra time on the next section of this review.

Remember: If more than one operation is present in a question, the order of operations is **p**arentheses, **e**xponents, **m**ultiply or **d**ivide (work left to right), and **a**dd or **s**ubtract (work left to right). The memory device for this is **PEMDAS**.

i. Practice

Question	Calculate Mentally	Calculate with Pencil and Paper	Calculate with Calculator
$2(15 - 6) + 23$			
$348 \div 29$			
$248 + 197 - 199$			
$21 + 24 \div 3 + (7 \times 16) - 3$			
$\sqrt{4^2 - 3(7+6)}$			
$6abc + d$, where $a = 4$, $b = 0.4$, $c = \dfrac{21}{5}$, and $d = 23$			
The length, in inches, of a wall 18 feet 7 inches long			
The amount of water, in cubic feet, a pool 24 feet long, 18 feet wide, and 5 feet 6 inches deep would hold when filled to the brim			
The length of the hypotenuse of a right triangle whose other two sides are 1 yard and 4 feet			
The square of the number of days in March			
$|-243| + 375$			
The square root of 20,736			
The average of 25, 18, 37, and 19			
What is the difference between the mean and the median of 19, 33, 9, and 24?			
What is the perimeter of a rectangle whose sides are 4 feet 6 inches and 2 yards, respectively?			
What is the area of a circle with radius 7 inches? ($\pi \approx 3.14$)			
$23 + (-48) \times 14 \div 7$			
The distance between the tip of George's thumb and his little finger when fully extended is about 8 inches. If he were trying to estimate the length of a board 4 feet 8 inches long, how many times would George have to span along the length?			
The average length of a song on Felix's iPod is 3 minutes 30 seconds. How many songs would he have to store to play for 1 hour and 15 minutes?			
$\dfrac{-27 + \sqrt{8^2 - 6(3-8)}}{27}$ (round to the nearest hundredth)			
$\sqrt{9^2 + 6^2}$ (round to the nearest hundredth)			
$38 + 6^3 - 25 - (17 + 26)$			
What time is 7 hours and 18 minutes after 1:24 a.m.?			
$256.46 \div 0.04$			
$2,494 \times 2.397$			
What is the perimeter, in inches, of a circular garden with a diameter of 2.5 yards? ($\pi \approx 3.14$)			
If a car travels an average of 35 mph and leaves at 1 p.m., when would it arrive after a 49-mile trip?			
Write the prime factorization of 256.			

ii. Answers

After you complete the table with all your computations in the preceding section, check your answers.

Question	Answer
$2(15 - 6) + 23$	41
$348 \div 29$	12
$248 + 197 - 199$	246
$21 + 24 \div 3 + (7 \times 16) - 3$	138
$\sqrt{4^2 - 3(7+6)}$	No answer. You cannot find the square root of a negative number.
$6abc + d$, where $a = 4$, $b = 0.4$, $c = \dfrac{21}{5}$, and $d = 23$	63.32
The length, in inches, of a wall 18 feet 7 inches long	223
The amount of water, in cubic feet, a pool 24 feet long, 18 feet wide, and 5 feet 6 inches deep would hold when filled to the brim	2,376 cubic feet
The length of the hypotenuse of a right triangle whose other two sides are 1 yard and 4 feet	5 feet
The square of the number of days in March	961
$|-243| + 375$	618
The square root of 20,736	144
The average of 25, 18, 37, and 19	24.75
What is the difference between the mean and the median of 19, 33, 9, and 24?	0.25
What is the perimeter of a rectangle whose sides are 4 feet 6 inches and 2 yards, respectively?	21 feet or 7 yards
What is the area of a circle with radius 7 inches? ($\pi \approx 3.14$)	153.86 square inches
$23 + (-48) \times 14 \div 7$	-73
The distance between the tip of George's thumb and his little finger when fully extended is about 8 inches. If he were trying to estimate the length of a board 4 feet 8 inches long, how many times would George have to span along the length?	7 times
The average length of a song on Felix's iPod is 3 minutes 30 seconds. How many songs would he have to store to play for 1 hour and 15 minutes?	21 songs (The mathematical answer is 21.43, but you cannot record 0.43 of a song if asked for the number of songs.)
$\dfrac{-27 + \sqrt{8^2 - 6(3-8)}}{27}$ (round to the nearest hundredth)	-0.64
$\sqrt{9^2 + 6^2}$ (round to the nearest hundredth)	10.82
$38 + 6^3 - 25 - (17 + 26)$	186
What time is 7 hours and 18 minutes after 1:24 a.m.?	8:42 a.m.
$256.46 \div 0.04$	6,411.5
$2,494 \times 2.397$	5,978.118
What is the perimeter, in inches, of a circular garden with a diameter of 2.5 yards? ($\pi \approx 3.14$)	7.85 yards
If a car travels an average of 35 mph and leaves at 1 p.m., when would it arrive after a 49-mile trip?	2:24 p.m.
Write the prime factorization of 256.	2^8

2. Measurement and Geometry

a. Perpendicular Lines

Two lines that intersect forming a right angle at the point of intersection are considered perpendicular to one another. We make some assumptions in everyday life pertaining to perpendicular lines:

- We assume that walls are perpendicular to the floor.
- We assume that the corners of a regular sheet of paper are formed by two perpendicular lines.
- We know that the corners of squares and rectangles are perpendicular.

In a triangle, if one of the angles is a right angle, the two sides forming the right angle are perpendicular and the triangle is called a **right triangle.** The side opposite the right angle is called the **hypotenuse.**

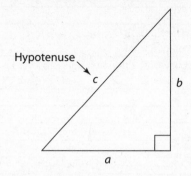

Use the Pythagorean theorem ($a^2 + b^2 = c^2$; a and b are legs and c the hypotenuse of a right triangle) to solve the following problem.

EXAMPLE:

> A right triangle has a hypotenuse of length 12 inches and one side of length 4 inches. What is the length, in inches, of the third side to two decimal places?
>
> **(A)** 11.31
> **(B)** 12.48
> **(C)** 13.13
> **(D)** 128

The correct answer is **(A).** The equation to calculate the sides of a right triangle is $a^2 + b^2 = c^2$, where $c =$ the length of the hypotenuse and a and b are the lengths of the other two sides. Substitute the known quantities into the equation and solve for b:

$$a^2 + b^2 = c^2$$
$$4^2 + b^2 = 12^2$$
$$16 + b^2 = 144$$
$$b^2 = 144 - 16$$
$$b^2 = 128$$
$$b = 11.31$$

b. Equations of Lines

Parallel lines are lines that never meet and are always the same distance apart and have the same slopes.

EXAMPLE:

If the equation of a line is $y = mx + 3$, where 3 is the y-intercept and m is the slope, what would be the effect of using different values for m?

(A) No effect
(B) A series of parallel lines
(C) A series of spoke-like lines passing through (3,0)
(D) A series of spoke-like lines passing through (0,3)

The correct answer is **(D).** Because the y-intercept is constant but the slope is variable, all lines would pass through the y-intercept (0,3) and look like the spokes of a wheel.

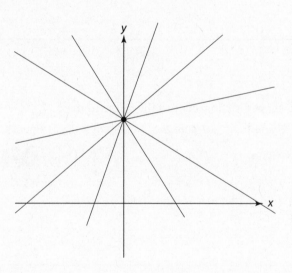

c. Geometric Figures

Two figures are **congruent** if one can be exactly slipped over the other, or superimposed. This can be accomplished by sliding, flipping, or rotating one to exactly fit over the other. If the two figures were triangles, when one triangle is superimposed on the other, each side would exactly fit over the corresponding side and each angle would fit exactly over the corresponding angle. If you did this with real triangles, you could not see the bottom triangle because it would be exactly and completely covered by the top triangle.

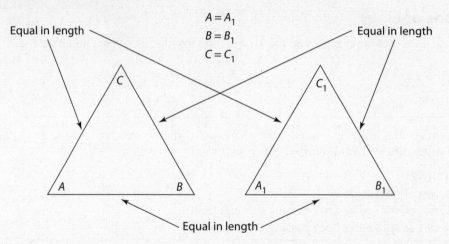

$$A = A_1$$
$$B = B_1$$
$$C = C_1$$

Equal in length

Equal in length

Equal in length

If the figures were rectangles, one would fit exactly over the other and each side would be exactly the same size as the corresponding side on the other. Because they are rectangles, the angles would all be right angles and would fit exactly.

EXAMPLE:

Which of the following shapes is congruent to the figure above?

Figure 1:   Figure 2:   Figure 3:   Figure 4:

(A) Figure 1
(B) Figure 2
(C) Figure 3
(D) Figure 4

The correct answer is (C). If you were to rotate the sample figure 90°, it would fit over Figure 3.

If two geometrical shapes differ only in size they are said to be **similar.** Corresponding sides of similar figures are all in the same ratio. Corresponding angles are congruent. For example:

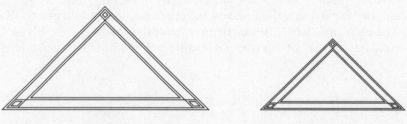

Triangle A   Triangle B

Triangle A is similar to Triangle B because it has the same shape, with corresponding angles equal in size. Here's another example:

Parallelogram A   Parallelogram B

The two parallelograms above are similar because they are identical in every aspect but size.

Some questions may ask you to describe or analyze a geometric figure.

EXAMPLES:

How would you describe the following figure?

(A) Two rectangles joined together
(B) A rectangle with a square missing
(C) A rectangle and a square joined together
(D) All of the above

The correct answer is **(D).** If you take a closer look at the given figure, you can see a rectangle joined to a square. Because a square is technically a rectangle, choices (A), (B), and (C) are all true. Thus, (D) is correct.

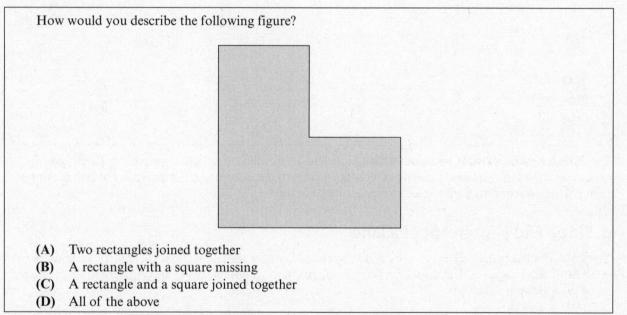

Describe the rotation of the following figure:

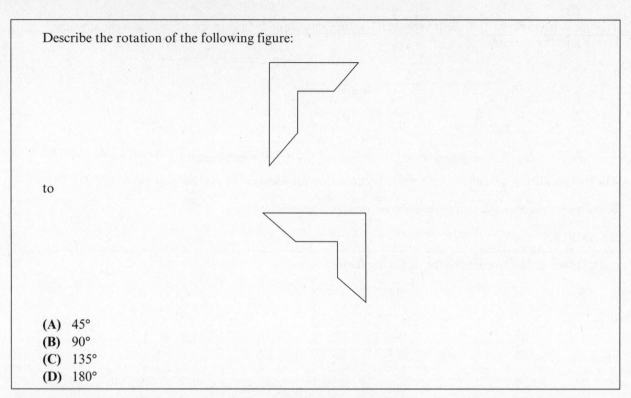

to

(A)   45°
(B)   90°
(C)   135°
(D)   180°

The correct answer is **(B).** If you have trouble visualizing this rotation, cut an approximate shape out of paper and try rotating around a point, using a protractor to measure angles. Or imagine holding the upper right corner and rotating counterclockwise about that corner.

d. Slope and *y*-Intercept of a Line

The **slope of a line** is defined as the rise divided by the run, where the **rise** is the vertical distance and the **run** is the horizontal distance. The slope of a line joining two known points (x_1, y_1) and (x_2, y_2) can be calculated using the following equation:

$$\text{slope of a line} = \frac{y_2 - y_1}{x_2 - x_1}$$

$$\text{Rise} \quad \left| \quad \text{Slope} = \frac{\text{Rise}}{\text{Run}} \right.$$

$$\text{Run}$$

The *y*-**intercept of a line** is the point on the graph where the line intersects the *y*-axis or where the coordinate *x* is 0. A very useful equation relating *y*-intercept and slope is $y = mx + b$, where *x* and *y* are coordinates of points on the line, *m* is the slope, and *b* is the *y*-coordinate of the *y*-intercept of the line.

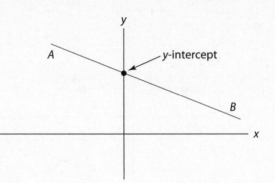

e. The Intersection of Two Lines

The **point of intersection** of two lines is the common point of the two lines, where they cross one another. At this point, both lines have a common point with the same coordinates.

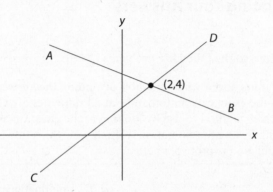

For example, line segment *AB* intersects line segment *CD* at point (2,4). This point would satisfy the equations of both lines.

Coordinates indicate points on a graph. By joining these points with segments, shapes can be drawn.

EXAMPLE:

Describe the geometric figure that would be formed by joining *A*(−3,3), *B*(3,3), *C*(1,−3), and *D*(−5,−3).

(A) Rectangle
(B) Square
(C) Parallelogram
(D) Trapezoid

The correct answer is **(C).** A quadrilateral with opposite sides parallel and opposite angles equal but not equal to 90° is called a **parallelogram.** If the opposite angles were right angles, the figure would be a rectangle, which is a special quadrilateral. The completed figure would look like this:

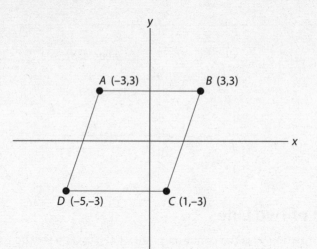

f. Methods for Calculating Your Answers

i. Practice

Estimate and calculate solutions to the following problems.

As you fill in the blank cells, think about which method of finding the answer would be simplest, easiest, and fastest. Not all questions require exact calculation and not all estimates are close enough to be used in finding the answer. Decide which method to use by looking at the question and the possible answers. If the answers are very different, usually an approximation will tell you which one is correct. If the answers are close together in value, a calculation is probably better.

	Problem	Information	What Is Asked?	Estimation	Calculation
Length	What would be the outside dimensions of a frame made to fit an 8-x-10-inch picture with a 1-inch border around it?				
Perimeter	What is the perimeter of a 3-x-2-yard carpet, in feet?				
Area	What is the area of a 9-x-12-foot rectangle, in square yards?				
Surface area	What is the surface area, in square feet, of a 50-foot-long circular pipe with a circumference of 36 inches? (**Note:** The surface area does not include the open ends of the pipe.)				
Volume	How many cubic feet of water will an aquarium measuring 2 feet in length, 1 foot 9 inches in depth, and 1 foot 6 inches in height hold?				
Angle measurement	On a compass, what direction is 90° clockwise from north?				
Capacity	If regular gasoline weighs 6.2 pounds per gallon, how much additional weight would filling a 21-gallon gasoline tank add to the overall weight of a car?				
Weight	If someone lost an average of 4.5 pounds per month, what would be his total weight loss from September 1 through June 30?				

ii. Answers

	Problem	Information	What Is Asked?	Estimation	Calculation
Length	What would be the outside dimensions of a frame made to fit an 8-x-10-inch picture with a 1-inch border around it?	Picture: Length = 8 inches Width = 10 inches Border = 1 inch on each side	Find outer dimensions of frame.	Length of picture + 2 inches (border top and bottom) by width of picture + 2 inches (border left and right side) is 10 inches by 12 inches.	8 + 2 = 10 10 + 2 = 12 Outside dimensions of frame are 10 inches by 12 inches.
Perimeter	What is the perimeter of a 3-x-2-yard carpet, in feet?	Length = 3 yards = 9 feet Width = 2 yards = 6 feet	Find perimeter Formula: $P = 2(l + w)$ P is the perimeter, l is the length, and w is the width.	Perimeter is 18 feet + 12 feet = 30 feet	$P = 2(l + w)$ $P = 2(9 + 6)$ $P = 30$
Area	What is the area of a 9-x-12-foot rectangle, in square yards?	Length = 12 feet = 4 yards Width = 9 feet = 3 yards	Find area Formula: $A = lw$, where A is the area, l is the length, and w is the width.	Area is $4 \times 3 = 12$ square yards	$A = lw$ $A = 4 \times 3$ $A = 12$
Surface area	What is the surface area, in square feet, of a 50-foot-long circular pipe with a circumference of 36 inches? (**Note:** The surface area does not include the open ends of the pipe.)	Surface area of pipe (cylinder) Length = 50 feet Perimeter = 36 inches = 3 feet	Find surface area Formula: $S = Pl$, where S is the surface area, P is the perimeter, and l is the length.	Surface area is $50 \times 3 = 150$ square feet	$S = Pl$ $S = 50 \times 3 = 150$
Volume	How many cubic feet of water will an aquarium measuring 2 feet in length, 1 foot 9 inches in depth, and 1 foot 6 inches in height hold?	Length = 2 feet Width = 1 foot 9 inches = 1.75 feet Height = 1 foot 6 inches = 1.5 feet	Find volume Formula: $V = lwh$, where V is the volume, l is the length, w is the width, and h is the height.	Volume: $V = 2 \times 1\frac{3}{4} \times 1\frac{1}{2}$ $= 2 \times \frac{7}{4} \times \frac{3}{2}$ $= \frac{42}{8}$ ≈ 5	Volume: $V = lwh$ $V = 2 \times 1.75 \times 1.5$ $V = 5.25$
Angle measurement	On a compass, what direction is 90° clockwise from north?			90° is one-quarter of the way around.	One-quarter turn from north is east.

continued

	Problem	Information	What Is Asked?	Estimation	Calculation
Capacity	If regular gasoline weighs 6.2 pounds per gallon, how much additional weight would filling a 21-gallon gasoline tank add to the overall weight of a car?	Weight of 1 gallon of gasoline = 6.2 pounds Capacity of tank = 21 gallons	Additional weight = capacity of tank multiplied by the weight of a gallon of gasoline	Additional weight = 21 × 6 = 126 pounds	Additional weight = 21 × 6.2 = 130.2 pounds
Weight	If someone lost an average of 4.5 pounds per month, what would be his total weight loss from September 1 through June 30?	Weight loss September through June = 10 months	Total weight loss = average monthly weight loss multiplied by the number of months	4 pounds × 10 = 40 pounds and 5 pounds × 10 = 50 pounds. Total weight loss will be between 40 and 50 pounds.	Total weight loss is 4.5 pounds × 10 = 45 pounds

3. Data Analysis, Statistics, and Probability

a. Data Analysis

Tables, charts, and graphs are methods of displaying information in an easy-to-see format. Displaying data in these formats makes trends and growth patterns more visible, allowing you to make inferences from the collected information.

The following example question asks you to interpret the data in the bar graph and make an inference.

EXAMPLE:

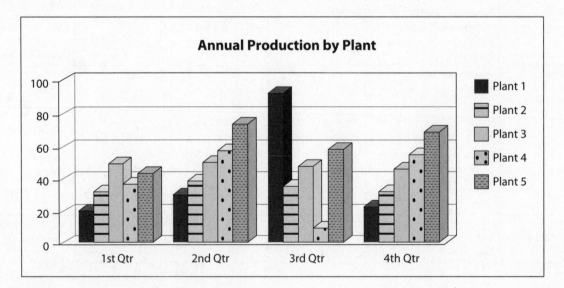

This bar graph indicates annual production by plant. One of the plants had a strike lasting two weeks. From the graph, which plant had the strike?

(A) Plant 1
(B) Plant 2
(C) Plant 4
(D) Plant 5

The correct answer is **(C)**. The bar graph for Plant 4 in the third quarter shows a dramatic drop in production compared to production in the other quarters. It is assumed that, during a strike, production would decrease, and that's indicated by choice (C).

The next three example questions are based on the data in the "Median Price of Houses in Florida" table.

EXAMPLES:

Median Price of Houses in Florida				
Year	Q1	Q2	Q3	Q4
2000	$126,015	$130,765	$133,991	$135,970
2001	$137,696	$142,006	$145,547	$146,467
2002	$148,697	$154,040	$158,942	$162,030
2003	$164,424	$169,112	$174,417	$179,306
2004	$184,309	$192,702	$199,771	$205,480
2005	$213,204	$222,668	$230,708	$235,610
2006	$237,739	$239,340	$237,046	$234,942
2007	$232,913	$230,821	$226,839	$215,170
2008	$200,817	$196,520	$189,640	$175,702
2009	$162,861	$167,915	$173,472	$171,657
2010	$166,100			

The following example question asks you to interpret the data in the table and draw a conclusion.

These figures represent median house prices in Florida for a 10-year period. Considering the numbers presented, what conclusion could you reach?

(A) In general, median prices rose during this 10-year period.
(B) Median prices stabilized in the last few years of this 10-year period.
(C) At the end of this 10-year period, median prices were at their lowest.
(D) During this 10-year period, housing in Florida was a bargain.

The correct answer is **(A)**. The median price for a house in Florida in the first quarter of 2010 was $166,100. In the first quarter of 2000, the median price was $126,015, which is lower than the 2010 price. Although you may have read about housing problems in Florida or noticed that there was a price bubble from 2003 to 2008, none of this was asked for in the question. You must answer the question based on only the information provided.

The following example question asks you to interpret the data in the table and evaluate an argument.

Consider the table of median house prices in Florida. In 2006, the Supreme Court ruled in favor of military recruiting on college campuses. Explain how this might have affected house prices.

Median house prices reached their peak in 2006 because:

(A) More young people joined the army.
(B) More people were looking for houses as an investment.
(C) There had been distress sales the years before.
(D) Not enough information given

The correct answer is **(D).** Any or all of the answers might be right, but none of them can be argued based on the data presented. You can use only the information presented to answer the question.

The following example question asks you to interpret the data in the table and determine how best this data could be represented graphically, a bar graph in this case.

Using the previous table of median house prices for the first quarter of the years 2000 to 2010, consider which of the following bar graphs would accurately represent the data.

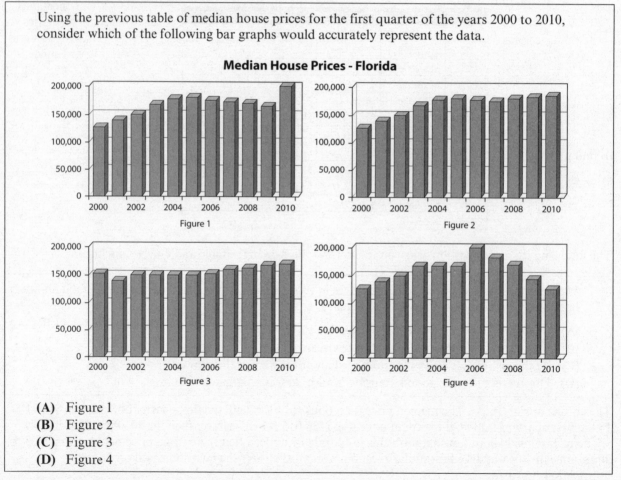

Median House Prices - Florida

(A) Figure 1
(B) Figure 2
(C) Figure 3
(D) Figure 4

The correct answer is **(D).** The most accurate representation is the graph in Figure 4. The other graphs show trends that are not apparent in the table data.

b. Statistics and Probability

Statistics are numerical data that describe a fact or an event. You are exposed to statistics in your everyday life—political polls, surveys, baseball batting averages, and so on. Statistics is also a process—making educated guesses about outcomes involving numbers.

One of the most familiar uses of statistics is to determine **probability**—the chance of some occurrence. Probability is expressed as a ratio (the number of favorable outcomes to the total number of possible outcomes). For example, the probability of drawing an ace from a well-shuffled standard deck of 52 cards is $\frac{4}{52} = \frac{1}{26}$, because there are 4 aces in a 52-card deck.

i. Mean, Median, and Mode

Mean, median, and mode are common statistics. The **mean** is the arithmetic average of a set of numbers; it is calculated by adding the items in the set and dividing by the total number of items in the set. The **median** is the middle number of an ordered list of numbers. To find the median number in a set, put the numbers in ascending order (smallest to largest). If the number of items in the set is odd, the middle number of the set is the median. If the number of items is even, average the two middle numbers to get the median. The **mode** is the number that appears most often in a set of numbers. There can be more than one mode or none at all.

Consider the following set of numbers:

$$90, 4, 30, 96, 25, 13$$

To find the mean, add the numbers:

$$90 + 4 + 30 + 96 + 25 + 13 = 258$$

And divide by 6 (the number of items in the set):

$$258 \div 6 = 43$$

To find the median, first place the numbers in ascending order:

$$4, 13, 25, 30, 90, 96$$

Because there are six items in the set, an even amount, you calculate the median using the average of the two middle numbers: 25 and 30:

$$(25 + 30) \div 2 = 27.5$$

Because no number occurs more than once in this set, there is no mode.

4. Algebra, Functions, and Patterns

a. Multiple-Use Equations

Recognize that a variety of problem situations may be modeled by the same function or type of function. An equation may have a specific meaning or use. For example, the equation of a straight line with slope $= m$ and y-intercept $= b$ is $y = mx + b$. It is also a linear equation, meaning that no power is greater than 1.

EXAMPLE:

What is the equation representing a straight line with slope of −4 and y-intercept of 5?

(A) −4x + y = 5
(B) 4x − y = 5
(C) 4x + y = 5
(D) −4x − y = 5

The correct answer is **(C)**. Using the equation $y = mx + b$ and substituting $m = -4$ and $b = 5$ produces $y = -4x + 5$ or $4x + y = 5$.

Here's another scenario. The equation for a parabola with vertex $(0, 0)$ is $y = ax^2$, which is a quadratic equation because there is a square of a variable.

EXAMPLE:

Solve the equation $y = ax^2$ for a, if $x = 4$ and $y = 8$.

(A) $\dfrac{1}{4}$

(B) $\dfrac{2}{8}$

(C) $\dfrac{1}{2}$

(D) $\dfrac{8}{4}$

The correct answer is **(C)**. If the equation is rewritten so that the variable is on the left side, it becomes

$$a = \frac{y}{x^2} = \frac{8}{4^2} = \frac{8}{16} = \frac{1}{2}.$$

b. Different Representations of Data

A question may ask you to choose the graph that best corresponds to a given table or may ask you which table corresponds to a given graph or chart.

i. Tables and Graphs

Tables such as the following can be drawn as graphs.

	1st Quarter	2nd Quarter	3rd Quarter	4th Quarter
East	20.4	27.4	90	20.4
West	30.6	38.6	34.6	31.6
North	45.9	46.9	45	43.9

This table would look like this, when drawn as a graph:

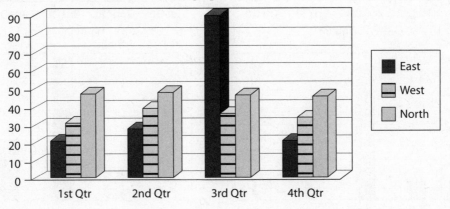

EXAMPLE:

Which bar graph represents the information in the following table?

1st Quarter	2nd Quarter	3rd Quarter	4th Quarter
25	75	50	20

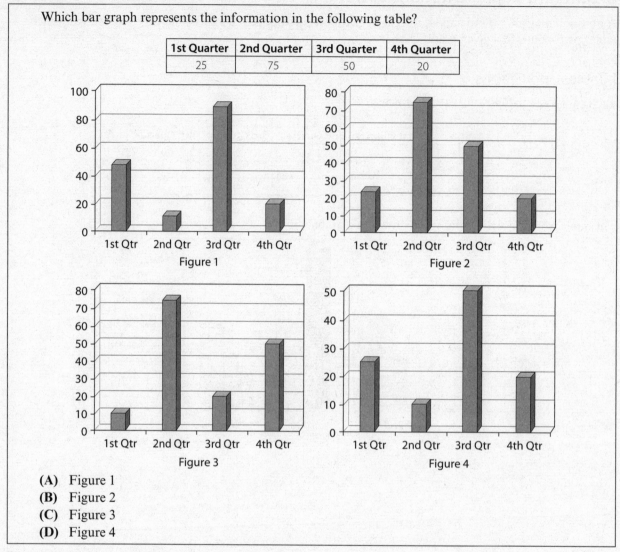

(A) Figure 1
(B) Figure 2
(C) Figure 3
(D) Figure 4

The correct answer is **(B).** Because each graph's *y*-axis is labeled in quantities, the heights of the bars can be compared. The one graph that represents the data in the table will become obvious.

ii. Different Types of Graphs

There are different types of graphs:

- Line graphs

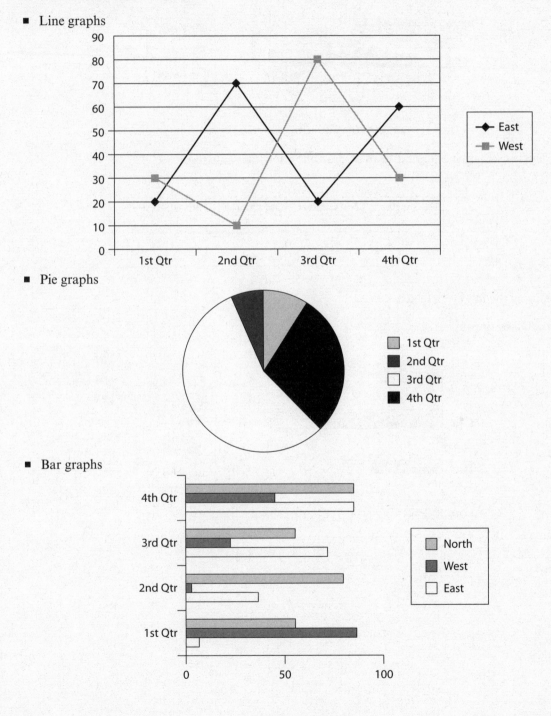

- Pie graphs

- Bar graphs

■ Area graphs

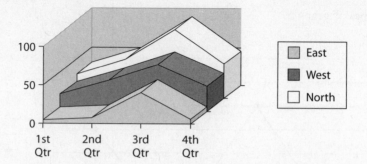

If the same data is used, different graphs can be drawn to show the same result.

	1st Quarter	2nd Quarter	3rd Quarter	4th Quarter
East	4	7	40	5
West	20	38.6	60	31.6
North	30	50	90	43.9

For example, using the following table:

A bar graph could be drawn:

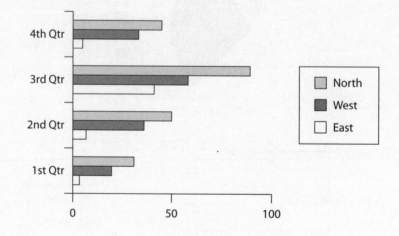

Or a line graph:

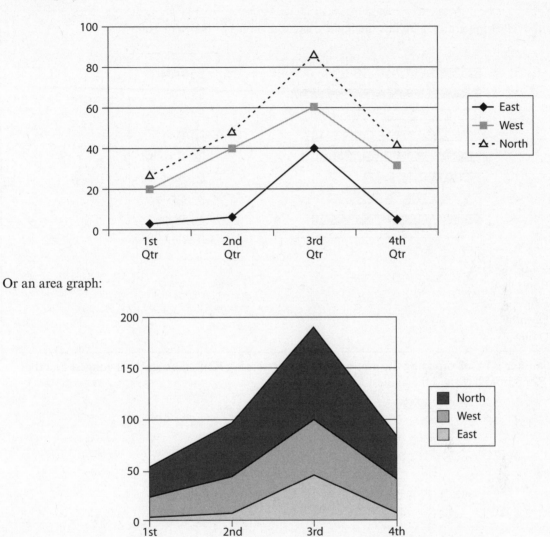

Or an area graph:

In an area graph, the height of each area for east, west, or north is the sum of all the data for each of east, west, and north (40 + 60 + 90 = 190 for the third quarter).

All these graphs present the same information and show the same trends because they were created from the same set of data. Any of them could form the basis for a question.

EXAMPLE:

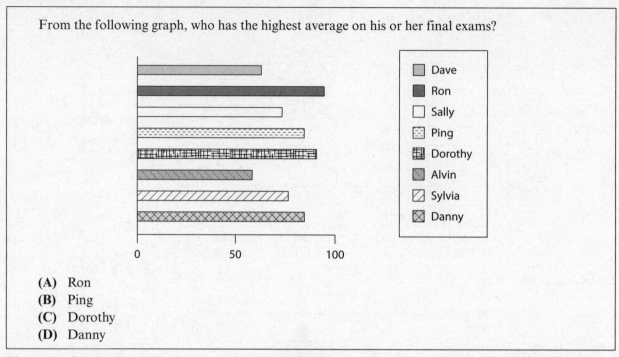

From the following graph, who has the highest average on his or her final exams?

Legend:
- Dave
- Ron
- Sally
- Ping
- Dorothy
- Alvin
- Sylvia
- Danny

(A) Ron
(B) Ping
(C) Dorothy
(D) Danny

The correct answer is **(A)**. Examining the graph, the bar representing Ron's average is the longest and that means that Ron would have had the highest average.

iii. Verbal Descriptions

A question may ask you to choose an answer from a series of verbal descriptions of a graph or may ask you which graph corresponds to a verbal description.

EXAMPLES:

If the following graph represents the number of pies eaten by each contestant in a pie-eating contest, which contestant won?

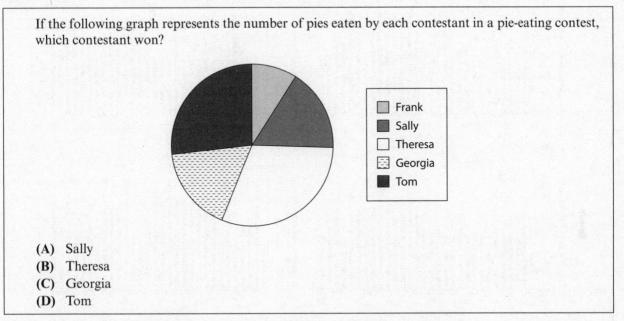

Legend:
- Frank
- Sally
- Theresa
- Georgia
- Tom

(A) Sally
(B) Theresa
(C) Georgia
(D) Tom

The correct answer is **(B).** Because the section of the pie graph representing the number of pies eaten by Theresa is the largest, she would have consumed the most pies and been the winner.

To convert a pie graph into a table of values, the angular measure of each segment would have to be measured and converted to percentages by comparing it with the number of degrees in a circle. Then the percentages would be used to calculate the individual numbers from the total number, if known. If the total number were not known, the specific data could not be found. This is beyond the scope of the Mathematical Reasoning Test.

Which of the following graphs best represents the following information?

The highest temperature reached in classroom 247 during the month of June was 78° Fahrenheit.

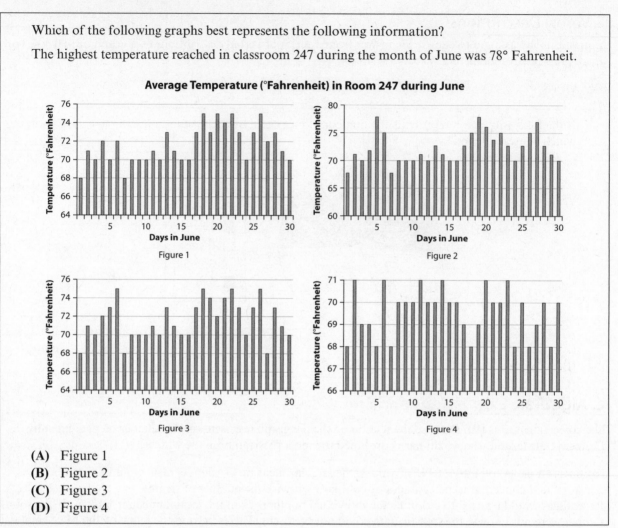

Average Temperature (°Fahrenheit) in Room 247 during June

Figure 1

Figure 2

Figure 3

Figure 4

(A) Figure 1
(B) Figure 2
(C) Figure 3
(D) Figure 4

The correct answer is **(B).** The graph in Figure 2 is the only one with temperatures of 78° on it. Looking carefully at the other graphs, the *y*-axis does not go as high as 78°; therefore, the temperature could not have reached 78°.

iv. Creating Equations

An equation can be created from a verbal statement or an equation can be read as a verbal statement. For example:

A merchant determines that the price that must be charged for an article in the store must equal the sum of the cost of the article, the markup in dollars required to show a reasonable return on investment, the total overhead costs for the store divided by the number of articles sold per month, and the bank charges incurred by the merchant for all the dealings with the bank including interest charges divided by the number of items. Translate the information given into an equation, indicating what each variable stands for.

$P = C + M + O + B$, where P = the selling price of an article, C = the cost of an article, M = the markup in dollars, O = the overhead costs divided by the number of articles sold in an average month, and B = the bank charges for running a business and including the interest on articles in stock but unsold divided by the number of items.

EXAMPLE:

Explain the equation $E = \dfrac{M}{G}$, where E is the average fuel consumption of a car, M is the number of miles traveled, and G is the fuel used to travel M miles.

(A) The average fuel consumption equals the number of gallons of gas used divided by the distance traveled.

(B) The average fuel consumption equals the distance traveled in a week divided by the fuel used.

(C) The average fuel consumption equals the distance traveled divided by the fuel used in a week.

(D) The average fuel consumption equals the number of miles traveled divided by the fuel used to travel that distance.

The correct answer is **(D)**. Reading the equation in English would be, "The average fuel consumption equals the number of miles traveled divided by the fuel used to travel that distance." The other answers do not reflect the information as presented in the equation.

c. Algebraic Expressions and Equations

You need to be able to create and use algebraic expressions and equations to model situations and solve problems. For example, you can use the following expression to find the area of two rectangular rooms with the same width: $A = (l_1 + l_2) \times w$, where A is the combined area of the two rooms, l_1 is the length of the first room, l_2 is the length of the second room, and w is the common width.

EXAMPLE:

A company is quoting a price for carpeting two rooms in a house. The first room is 18 feet by 12 feet, and the second room is 12 feet by 12 feet. How many square feet of carpeting would be required for these two rooms?

(A) 360

(B) 380

(C) 400

(D) 480

The correct answer is **(A)**. Using the equation $A = (l_1 + l_2) \times w$ and substituting, $A = (18 + 12) \times 12 = 360$ square feet. Be careful of answers that are close to the correct answer, especially if you're using mental math to approximate answers.

d. Applying Formulas

For some questions, you need to use a formula to find the answer. The formula to calculate the surface area of a cylinder (including the two caps) is $2\pi r^2 + 2\pi rh$, where r is the radius of the cylinder and h is the height.

EXAMPLE:

If the outside of a cylindrical fuel tank measuring 8 feet long and 4 feet across had to be painted with two coats of paint, and 1 gallon of paint will cover 360 square feet, how much paint, calculated to one decimal place, will be required to finish the job?

(A) 0.7 gallon
(B) 7 gallons
(C) 0.5 gallon
(D) 0.9 gallon

The correct answer is **(A)**. Using the formula $2\pi r^2 + 2\pi rh$ and substituting, the surface area to be painted is $(2 \times 3.14 \times 2 \times 2) + (2 \times 3.14 \times 2 \times 8) = 25.12 + 100.48 = 125.6$ square feet. Because two coats are needed, the area to be covered is $125.6 \times 2 = 251.2$ square feet. One gallon of paint will cover 360 square feet. The amount of paint needed is $251.2 \div 360 = 0.7$ gallon, to one decimal place.

e. Solving Equations

You need to be able to solve three types of equations: first-degree (linear), quadratic, and radical. Let's take these one at a time.

i. First-Degree (Linear) Equations

A first-degree (linear) equation can be solved by gathering all the variables on the left side and all the constants on the right, and then simplifying.

EXAMPLE:

Solve the following equation for g.

$$3g + 7 = 22$$

(A) 3
(B) 4
(C) 5
(D) 6

The correct answer is **(C)**. To solve the equation, gather the variable, g, on the left side and the constants on the right. This produces $3g = 22 - 7 = 15$ or $g = 5$.

ii. Quadratic Equations

A quadratic equation can have up to two **roots** (or two numbers or expressions) that satisfy the equation. A quadratic equation can have two different roots, two equal roots, or no root at all.

If a number or expression satisfies an equation, when it is substituted in the equation, both sides have the same value. A quadratic equation, $ax^2 + bx + c = 0$, can be solved using the formula $x = \dfrac{-b \pm \sqrt{b^2 - 4ac}}{2a}$, where x represents one root, a is the coefficient of x^2, b is the coefficient of x, and c is the constant term.

EXAMPLE:

Solve the equation $4x^2 + x = 2$ for x to two decimal places.

(A) −0.84 or 0.59

(B) $-\dfrac{1}{4}$ or 1

(C) 0.84 or −0.59

(D) 84 or 59

The correct answer is **(A)**. Use the formula $x = \dfrac{-b \pm \sqrt{b^2 - 4ac}}{2a}$ to find the values for x. Substituting,

$$x = \frac{-1 \pm \sqrt{1 - (4)(4)(-2)}}{2(4)}$$

$$= \frac{-1 \pm \sqrt{33}}{8}$$

$$= \frac{-1 \pm 5.74}{8}$$

$$= -\frac{6.74}{8} \text{ or } \frac{4.74}{8}$$

$$= -0.84 \text{ or } 0.59$$

iii. Radical Equations

$l = \sqrt{a^2 + b^2}$ is an equation containing a radical. It has a square-root sign, which is the opposite of squaring. In this equation, the unknown is not a power, so all you have to do is solve the expression inside the square-root sign and then find the square root of that result.

EXAMPLE:

If $a = 3$ and $b = 4$, solve the equation $l = \sqrt{a^2 + b^2}$ for l. The value of l is:

(A) 2

(B) 3

(C) 4

(D) 5

The correct answer is **(D)**. Substitute the values for a and b in the equation:

$$l = \sqrt{a^2 + b^2}$$
$$= \sqrt{3^2 + 4^2}$$
$$= \sqrt{9 + 16}$$
$$= \sqrt{25}$$
$$= 5$$

If the equation had been $l^2 = \sqrt{a^2 + b^2}$, then it would be:

$$l^2 = \sqrt{3^2 + 4^2}$$
$$= \sqrt{25}$$
$$= 5$$
$$l = \pm\sqrt{5}$$
$$\approx \pm 2.24$$

rounded to two decimal places. Remember that when you solve the equation, the answer could be either positive or negative, because squaring a negative number produces a positive number as a product.

EXAMPLE:

Solve the equation $y^2 = 16$ for y. The value(s) of y would be:

(A) 4

(B) ±4

(C) 5

(D) ±5

The correct answer is **(B)**. If $y^2 = 16$, then $y = \pm\sqrt{16} = \pm 4$.

f. Solving Systems of Linear Equations

To solve a system of linear equations, find a number by which to multiply the equations that will make the coefficients of one of the variables equal or opposites.

For example, consider the following system of linear equations:

$$4x - 6y = 28$$
$$2x + 5y = 18$$

If the first equation were multiplied by 1 and the second by 2, the equations would become

$$4x - 6y = 28$$
$$4x + 10y = 36$$

and subtracting the first from the second would produce

$$16y = 8 \text{ or } y = \frac{1}{2}$$

To find the value of x, substitute the value of y in either equation (let's use the first equation):

$$4x - 6\left(\frac{1}{2}\right) = 28$$
$$4x = 28 + 3$$
$$4x = 31$$
$$x = \frac{31}{4}$$

g. Direct and Indirect Variation

When the ratio of the values of two related variables always remains the same, the variables vary directly with each other. When the ratio of the values of two related variables vary inversely, the variables vary indirectly with each other.

Here's a simple example: If you arrive earlier by driving faster, your travel time and your speed vary indirectly. If you use more fuel by increasing your speed, then your speed and your fuel consumption vary directly.

If x varies directly as y, then $x = ky$ for some constant k.

EXAMPLE:

> A machine has been manufactured with a control mechanism to set the speed of the machine. If the control mechanism is moved up one step the speed doubles. If the control were moved from 1 to 3, what effect would that setting have on the machine?
>
> **(A)** The speed would double.
> **(B)** The speed would stay the same.
> **(C)** The speed would be four times faster.
> **(D)** The speed would be six times faster.

The correct answer is **(C)**. If the speed doubles for each one-step increment, the speed doubles again when you move from 2 to 3. This is an exponential increase. Therefore, a change from 1 to 3 would produce an increase in speed of $2 \times 2 = 4$.

Here's another example of variation:

> A politician notices that as the number of cars increases, the number of accidents increases, until a critical point where every square inch of road has cars on it and none of them can move. Then the number of accidents decreases substantially.

The first half of this statement is a direct variation. As the number of cars increases, the number of accidents increases. The second half of the statement is that, after a critical point, the number of accidents decreases because the cars cannot move. This is an indirect variation because the number of cars is increasing approaching the critical point, but the number of accidents is decreasing because of the extreme congestion.

You could represent an indirect variation by the equation $y = \dfrac{C}{x}$, where x and y represent the frequency of events and C is a constant.

EXAMPLE:

> The speed of a car determines the distance traveled in a specific time. If some event happened that slowed a car's speed to half on Wednesday from that on Tuesday, what effect would that have on the time required to make the trip?
>
> **(A)** It would remain the same.
> **(B)** The trip would take twice as long on Wednesday.
> **(C)** The trip would take half as long on Wednesday.
> **(D)** The trip would take one-and-a-half times as long on Wednesday.

The correct answer is **(B)**. Using the equation $y = \dfrac{C}{x}$ and substituting Tuesday's speed for x and Wednesday's

speed for y, you would obtain $y = \dfrac{C}{\frac{1}{2}x} = \dfrac{2C}{x} = 2\left(\dfrac{c}{x}\right)$, where y is the speed on Wednesday and C is the time

required for the trip. C would then equal 2, or twice as long.

IX. Science

A. Test Format

The Science Test is 90 minutes long and consists of six item types. For descriptions and examples of these item types, see Chapter I, "The 2014 GED® Test."

1. Multiple choice
2. Fill-in-the-blank
3. Drop-down
4. Drag-and-drop
5. Hot spot
6. Short answer

NOTE: For study purposes, all example questions in this chapter are in the multiple-choice format.

The content on the Science Test is based on the following subject areas, which are usually covered in high school science courses:

- **Physical science:** about 40 percent
  - Structure of atoms
  - Structure and properties of matter
  - Chemical reactions
  - Motions and forces
  - Conservation of energy and increase in disorder
  - Interactions of energy and matter
- **Life science:** about 40 percent
  - The cell
  - Molecular basis of heredity
  - Biological evolution
  - Interdependence of organisms
  - Matter, energy, and organization in living systems
  - Behavior of organisms
- **Earth and space science:** about 20 percent
  - Energy in the Earth system
  - Geochemical cycles
  - Origin and formation of Earth
  - Origin and formation of the universe

The Science Test is essentially a test of reading comprehension. It evaluates your ability to assess and interpret scientific information presented in provided text passages and visual materials. We've made all of the questions in this chapter multiple-choice items so you can gain a clearer picture of your strengths and weaknesses in various areas of science, and thus know where to concentrate in your studies. You need to have some basic science knowledge, but you are not expected to memorize specific scientific information. For reading comprehension strategies, see the "Reading Comprehension Strategies" section at the end of Chapter I, complete with example questions.

The short answer item is an essay with a provided stimulus (passage) and a prompt (directions). You are expected to write an essay response in about 10 minutes based on the information in the stimulus and the directions in the prompt.

B. Types of Questions: A Detailed Look

The questions on the Science Test are based on text or visual passages. Visual material may be graphs, tables, charts, or diagrams and may account for up to 60 percent of the items. Text passages will vary in length and may be followed by one or more questions.

1. Questions Based on Text

On the Science Test, you'll be presented with questions based on text passages. You have two choices in answering these questions:

- You can skim or read the passage and then answer the question.
- You can read the question and skim the answer choices looking for keywords, and then read the passage to find out which answer choice is correct.

The way you proceed depends on the passage and the question. If the question asks for specific information like a definition, you might want to skim the answer choices first and then go back to the passage to match an answer choice with the information presented.

Remember that in multiple-choice questions, you are provided with a series of answers, one of which is correct. If you must guess, the more incorrect answer choices you can eliminate, the better your chances of guessing the correct one. The fill-in-the-blank and short answer items require that you provide the answer, which means reading the passage far more carefully and understanding the question before responding. You can't guess at an answer if you have to supply the word or words needed to complete the item.

EXAMPLE:

The next question refers to the following passage.

If we wish to wash our clothes, we are faced with a chemical decision. Should we use detergent or soap to clean the apparel? The actual answer is affected more by the water used in washing than in the chemical we add to clean the clothes. Soap will form a scum in hard water and detergent will not. The actual cleaning may not be that different in soft water, but in hard water we would see a difference.

In washing clothes, the main determinant of how clean they will be after washing is

(A) The chemical added
(B) The amount of soap used
(C) The hardness of the water
(D) The brand of detergent used

The correct answer is **(C)**. According to the passage, soap will form a scum in hard water that will make the clothes look dirty. The other answer choices may have a ring of truth to them but cannot be backed up by information in the passage, and correct answers must be supported by the information in the passage.

2. Questions Based on Visual Materials

You'll also be presented with questions based on visual materials. Tables, graphs, and diagrams are visual representations of data or information and can be "read" if you do so carefully. Most people are more comfortable with reading words than visual material, but with practice you can do it.

a. Tables

A table presents data in a concise, organized manner. In a table, the information that is horizontal is said to be in *rows,* and the information that is vertical is said to be in *columns.* Tables have headings that tell you what the information in the table means. In the case of the table in the example questions below, the second column indicates the measurement and the unit of measurement. If you wanted to find the relative weight on Earth, you would look down the left column until you found Earth and then across the row until you found 150, which would be the relative weight in pounds.

In answering questions based on tables, read the headings first and then the question to understand what information you're looking for.

EXAMPLES:

The next two questions are based on the following table.

Relative Weights on Various Planets (rounded to the nearest whole pound)	
Planet	**Relative Weight (in pounds)**
Mercury	57
Venus	136
Earth	150
Mars	57
Jupiter	355
Saturn	160
Uranus	133
Neptune	169

On which planet would a person who weighs 127 pounds on Earth weigh the least?

(A) Venus
(B) Mars
(C) Saturn
(D) Uranus

The correct answer is **(B).** From the information in the table, a person would weigh the least on Mars because it has the lowest relative weight (57 pounds).

If the force of gravity on a person determines her weight, which planet has the largest force of gravity?

(A) Mars
(B) Saturn
(C) Uranus
(D) Neptune

The correct answer is **(D).** Weight is determined by the pull of gravity on the subject. You could correctly assume that the planet on which you have the greatest weight would have the highest pull of gravity. According to the table, a person would weigh the most on Neptune, so Neptune has the greatest force of gravity value.

b. Graphs

A chart or graph is a visual representation of data presented. Charts and graphs show relative information most easily. If you wanted to represent the data in the earlier table in the form of a chart or graph, you could do so as in the following figure.

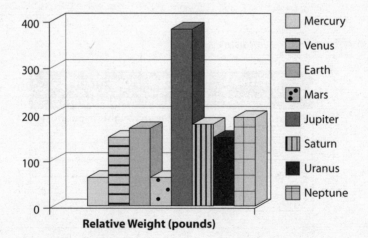

This type of graph is called a *bar graph* because the data is presented in the form of bars, each of which is proportional to the relative size of the data. Although the vertical axis is calibrated in the units given, it would be very difficult to give a definite answer to the size of any of the bars. Relative size is usually immediately apparent; absolute size is not.

EXAMPLE:

On which planet would you weigh the most?

(A) Mercury
(B) Mars
(C) Jupiter
(D) Saturn

The correct answer is **(C).** The bar representing the relative weight on Jupiter is the highest, which means that you would weigh the most on Jupiter.

If you wanted to represent the same data on a line graph, you would produce the following figure.

Relative Weight in Pounds on Various Planets

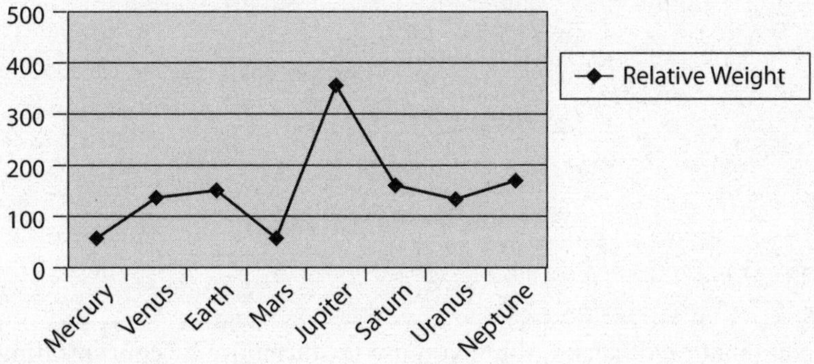

EXAMPLE:

On which planet would a car that weighs 2,000 pounds on Earth weigh the least?

(A) Venus
(B) Earth
(C) Mars
(D) Jupiter

The correct answer is **(C).** Of the choices given, the point on the line graph representing the lowest relative weight is Mars. Line graphs give an easy-to-understand picture of relative amounts.

The information represented by a *line graph* is relative and the position of points on the line can give you an indication of the size of the data. Unless you have an amazingly accurate graph, you couldn't read absolute data from the graph, but reading relative information is usually possible.

c. Diagrams

Diagrams can be read in a similar way to charts, graphs, and passages. The first thing you have to do when reading a diagram is to look for the title and then the labeling. In the following diagram, the title is "Lenses," which indicates that the diagram will be about a lens or lenses. The labels indicate the type of lens that the information presented is about. In the first case, the information presented is about a convex lens. Looking at the diagram, you can see that this type of lens refracts (bends) rays of light in a specific manner. Combining this with the other information about the behavior of rays of light passing through a particular type of lens would allow you to answer the question.

EXAMPLE:

The next question is based on the following diagram.

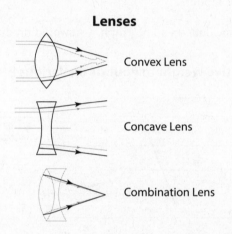

Lenses

Convex Lens

Concave Lens

Combination Lens

Which lens or combination of lenses would you use to start a fire by concentrating the rays of the sun on a piece of paper?

(A) Convex lens
(B) Combination lens
(C) Concave lens
(D) Either a convex or a combination lens

The correct answer is **(D)**. Either a convex lens or a combination lens would concentrate the rays of the sun on a spot, which would have the effect of concentrating the energy on that spot, raising the temperature, and increasing the possibility of setting fire to the paper. The concave lens would diverge the rays of light (spread them out).

C. Test Strategies

Here are some strategies to help you succeed on the Science Test:

- **Brush up on your science knowledge and vocabulary.** The Science Test requires a basic knowledge of the subject matter and a familiarity with the vocabulary of science. Study Section D, "Science Review"; some vocabulary terms are included there for all three science subject areas.

- **Read, read, read!** We've tried to give you a short introduction to each content area that may be on the test (see Section D). If you're familiar with a topic, you may want to read a bit to see if there is any new information on the subject. If a topic is unfamiliar to you, read and research as much as you need to get a general understanding of it. You can do this online by entering the topic in a search engine or doing a search at the library.

- **Review the example questions.** Example questions are sprinkled throughout this chapter. Use your hand or a piece of paper to cover the answer and explanation while you're answering the question. After you answer the question, check your answer and, if it's right, read the explanation to reinforce the reasoning. If you got it wrong, read the explanation, reread the question to see where you went wrong, and reread the related science review material. If you're still struggling with the question, expand your reading until it all makes sense. Additional sample questions can be found online on the GED Testing Service® website: www.gedtestingservice.com/freepractice/download/GED_Science/ GEDSciencePracticeTest.html. (Please note that this site is designed for use by educators and that GED Testing Service® is not affiliated with, and does not endorse, *CliffsNotes GED® TEST Cram Plan*, 2nd Edition.)

- **Use the scientific method.** One way to handle science questions is to try to think like a scientist by using what is commonly called the *scientific method*. Read more on this method below and follow it to help you answer Science Test questions.

- **Use the on-screen calculator when available.** On the Science Test, there is an expectation that you can apply mathematical reasoning to the subject matter. The on-screen calculator is provided on certain items where it would be useful to test-takers in answering those items. You can find a manual for this calculator online (www.atomiclearning.com/ti30xs).

- **Take the practice test.** Take the Science Practice Test (Chapter XIII). Do so under test conditions— using a timer. Check your answers and review the explanations.

The Scientific Method

The term *scientific method* is often used to describe how scientists go about investigating and experimenting. It is a method with several steps:

- The first step in investigating a phenomenon is formulating a question that you want to answer through research or experimentation.

- Second, you look at external research to formulate a hypothesis.

- Third, you test the hypothesis through experimentation and/or observation for the purpose of gathering evidence. To be scientifically valid, the evidence must be observable, measurable, and empirical. Sometimes evidence is gathered though a study of research done by others.

- Fourth, you analyze all the data gathered and, from that analysis, you can attempt to draw a conclusion.

Scientific Method Vocabulary

empirical: Developed through observation.

evidence: Material or data used to support or not support a theory.

experimentation: Carrying out experiments.

formulate a hypothesis: A prediction based on prior knowledge. In experimentation, hypotheses are supported or not supported based on the data obtained from the experiment.

investigating a phenomenon: Looking into something that has been observed.

measurable: Able to be measured in an accurate manner using a specific unit of measurement.

observable: Able to be observed (or perceived) by more than one person.

observation: Noticing or perceiving.

reproducible: Able to be reproduced more than once by more than one person.

scientifically valid: The application of a conclusion drawn from an experiment to a larger setting.

EXAMPLE:

Karen has been assigned a project by her science teacher with the advice that she should use the scientific method. What type of evidence should she gather?

(A) Observable
(B) Measurable
(C) Empirical
(D) All of the above

The correct answer is **(D)**. Evidence should be observable, measurable, and empirical.

D. Science Review

We've provided this basic science review to help you prepare for the Science Test. This is not a comprehensive review of each of the sciences. You should plan to do some reading on your own about the various subjects because the more reading you do, the more ideas and vocabulary you're exposed to.

For additional science review, you can visit CliffsNotes.com (www.cliffsnotes.com/sciences) or reference these other great *CliffsNotes* titles:

CliffsQuickReview Biology
CliffsNotes Chemistry Quick Review
CliffsQuickReview Earth Science
CliffsQuickReview Astronomy

1. Physical Science

Physical science studies the transference of energy within nonliving systems and includes chemistry and physics.

Chemistry is the branch of physical science concerned with the composition, behavior, structure, and properties of matter, as well as the changes matter undergoes during chemical reactions. *Matter* is a vague term for what things are made of, but in spite of the vagueness of the term, chemistry is an exact science with rules and theories.

EXAMPLES:

José is conducting an experiment in his lab. He wants to see if he can create the three states of water at different times. He could do that by

(A) Heating it to 212°F
(B) Cooling it below 32°F
(C) Leaving it at room temperature
(D) All of the above

The correct answer is **(D)**. Heating water to 212°F will turn it into steam (gas); cooling it below 32°F will turn it to ice (solid); and leaving it at room temperature will allow it to stay as water (liquid).

The next question is based on the following passage.

Have you ever wondered why some people sneeze during the spring and fall seasons? They may be suffering from allergies. An *allergic reaction* occurs when the person's body becomes *hypersensitive* to a substance that may normally be considered harmless, such as pollen or dust. These substances are called *allergens*. While people who do not suffer from allergies can tolerate these substances, allergic people have to try to avoid them or take some type of treatment to reduce their sensitivity.

A person suffering from allergies may sneeze when exposed to

(A) Cold
(B) Bad jokes
(C) Allergens
(D) Soap and water

The correct answer is **(C)**. Allergens are specifically referred to in the passage. In this question, skimming the passage after reading the question and answer choices might save you some time.

The next two questions refer to the following diagram and text.

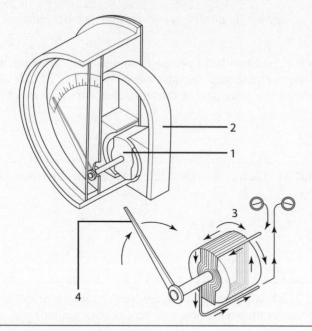

A galvanometer is an instrument for measuring extremely small currents. A coil is wound around an iron core (**1**) suspended between the poles of a horseshoe magnet (**2**). When a current flows in the coil, it induces a magnetic field in the core that causes it to move (**3**) in the field of the horseshoe magnet, registering as a deflection of the attached pointer (**4**).

A galvanometer is used for measuring

(A) Water pressure
(B) Wind velocity
(C) Direction of travel
(D) Extremely small currents

The correct answer is **(D)**. The galvanometer was designed to measure extremely small currents; this is stated in the passage beside the diagram.

The coil wound around the iron core is attached to the indicator needle and has a magnetic current induced in it when

(A) The pointer is wound up.
(B) A small current is passed through it.
(C) Static electricity is detected.
(D) It is plugged into the household current.

The correct answer is **(B)**. The passage states that the galvanometer measures an extremely small current; household current is not extremely small, and it is alternating current.

Physics is the branch of physical science that deals with understanding how the world and universe behave. Among other concepts, it includes matter and its movement through space and time, energy, force, and work.

There are **three laws of physics** that you should be aware of:

- **Newton's First Law of Motion** states that a body at rest will remain at rest unless acted upon by an external force. Every body moving in a straight line at a uniform velocity will remain so unless acted upon by an external force.

- **Newton's Second Law of Motion** states that a force acting on a body produces an acceleration that is inversely proportional to the mass of the object and directly proportional to the magnitude of the force.

- **Newton's Third Law of Motion** states that for every action there is an equal and opposite reaction. When a baseball player hits the ball with a bat, the ball has a certain amount of energy from being thrown. The swinging bat has energy from the efforts of the player. At the point of impact, the energy from the bat is transferred to the ball, provided that the energy from the bat is greater than that possessed by the ball, and the ball would reverse directions and proceed into the field. At the point and time of impact, there is an equal and opposite reaction on the ball from striking the bat.

EXAMPLE:

> Harvey is nailing together his deck. Every time he hits the nail with his hammer, he feels a shock in his wrist. What is the explanation based on a knowledge of physics?
>
> **(A)** Equal and opposite reaction
> **(B)** Rate of change of position
> **(C)** Body at rest remains at rest
> **(D)** Electrostatic forces

The correct answer is **(A).** When Harvey hits the head of the nail with his hammer, according to Newton's Third Law of Motion, the head of the nail is hitting back on the hammer and Harvey feels this force in his wrist. The other answer choices are associated with principles of physics, just not this one.

a. Structure of Atoms

Matter is composed of *atoms,* which can be visualized as a tiny solar system. At the center of this system is the *nucleus,* composed of *protons* (positively charged) and *neutrons* (electrically neutral) and responsible for most of the mass of the atom. *Electrons* (negatively charged), which travel at unbelievable speeds, exist outside the nucleus.

Atoms are electrically neutral, which means that they must have the same number of protons and electrons. *Nuclear force* holds the atom together in spite of the opposing charges. Electrons are thought to travel around the nucleus in a cloud-like atmosphere.

EXAMPLES:

> The number of protons in the nucleus determines what the atom is. Different elements have different numbers of protons and neutrons in their nuclei.
>
> What determines the name of a substance?
>
> **(A)** Hardness
> **(B)** State
> **(C)** Number of electrons
> **(D)** Number of protons

The correct answer is **(D).** Different elements have different numbers of protons in their nucleus.

The next two questions refer to the following passage and figure.

The explosion of the atomic bomb is an example of a nuclear chain reaction. In this reaction, a neutron strikes the nucleus of a uranium-235 atom. This neutron becomes part of the nucleus and forms uranium-236, which is very unstable and splits into two smaller nuclei. This splitting gives off a great deal of energy and releases several neutrons, which can continue the reaction. Under certain conditions, this can become a chain reaction, which can cause mass destruction if uncontrolled or, if properly controlled and monitored, power a nuclear generator.

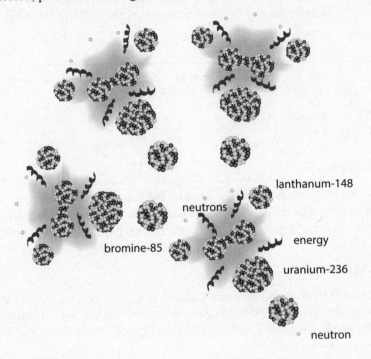

An atomic bomb is an example of

(A) A chemical reaction
(B) Formation of a solution
(C) A chain reaction
(D) Physical properties

The correct answer is (C). According to the passage, the atomic bomb is an example of a chain reaction. Both a text passage and a diagram are provided to make a complex concept a little simpler so that the questions can be answered. On the test, make sure that you pay attention to diagrams because they can clarify some complex ideas.

Nuclear reactions can be used to

(A) Power a nuclear generator
(B) Become a source of tremendous amounts of electric power
(C) Destroy cities
(D) All of the above

The correct answer is **(D)**. The power unleashed by a nuclear reaction can be used to aid civilization by providing a source of electricity and heat or destroy it in a nuclear firestorm.

b. Structure and Properties of Matter

Matter is composed of atoms. An *element* is made up of a single type of atom, and a *compound* is composed of two or more atoms that can interact with each other by transferring or sharing electrons, which creates *bonds*.

Solids, liquids, and gases may be composed of the same elements but differ in the distances between molecules and atoms. The energy that binds the atoms and molecules together is also different. A solid would have the least distance between atoms and molecules, and a gas would have the most; thus, a gas would have the least energy binding its atoms and a solid the most.

EXAMPLE:

Matter is composed of

(A) Forces

(B) Chemicals

(C) Molecules

(D) Electrons, protons, and neutrons, all of which comprise an atom

---

The correct answer is **(D)**. Matter is composed of atoms, which are composed of electrons, protons, and neutrons.

c. Chemical Reactions

When one set of chemical substances is transformed into another, the substances are said to undergo a chemical reaction. Chemical reactions can be *spontaneous* (requiring no input of energy) or *nonspontaneous* (requiring an input of energy). Chemical reactions can be *exothermic* (producing heat) or *endothermic* (requiring heat).

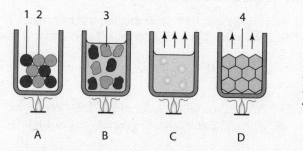

1 is aluminum sulfate
2 is potassium sulfate
3 is the addition of water
4 is alum

Heating aluminum sulfate and potassium sulfate produces no reaction (A).
If they are dissolved in water and heated until evaporation, alum is produced.

Alum is formed from aluminum sulfate and potassium sulfate. If the two chemicals are put together, nothing will happen (A). When water is added to *dissolve* the two chemicals (B), they form a *solution* (C), and with the addition of more heat until the liquid *evaporates,* alum is formed (D).

221

EXAMPLE:

> Donald wanted to create a reaction that would warm his small lab. What type of reaction would he want?
>
> **(A)** Atomic
> **(B)** Endothermic
> **(C)** Exothermic
> **(D)** Fusion

The correct answer is **(C)**. Exothermic reactions give off heat, which would warm his lab. Choices (A) and (D) would do more than warm his lab—they would destroy it!

d. Motions and Forces

When a *force* acts upon an object, *motion* is produced. If the force is positive and increasing, the object *accelerates*. If the force is constant, the object moves with constant velocity. If the force is negative and decreasing, the object decelerates.

EXAMPLE:

> Lois is driving along the road when she sees a stop sign in the distance. In order to stop in time, what should she do?
>
> **(A)** Open the windows.
> **(B)** Put the transmission in neutral.
> **(C)** Apply a negative force using the brakes.
> **(D)** Downshift the transmission.

The correct answer is **(C)**. Applying a negative force to a moving object will result in deceleration, which is what she wants. Choices (B) and (D) might eventually stop the car, but choice (C) is the best choice.

e. Conservation of Energy and Increase in Disorder

The *Law of Conservation of Energy* states that *energy* can be neither created nor destroyed. It only can be transformed from one form to another. This means that the total energy of the universe is constant.

Energy can be *kinetic* (the energy of motion), *potential* (the energy of position), or *electromagnetic* (the energy contained by a field).

In a *thermodynamic system,* the universe tends to become less organized and less orderly over time. *Entropy* is the amount of disorder in the universe; the higher the entropy, the greater the disorder.

EXAMPLE:

> Garry was making tea by warming up his water in a microwave oven. His younger brother came in to watch and asked Garry how the water was being heated to a boil. What explanation should Garry have given his brother?
>
> **(A)** The oven is heating the water.
> **(B)** The turntable is heating the water.
> **(C)** The magnetron is transferring energy to the water.
> **(D)** There are heating elements in the microwave oven.

The correct answer is **(C)**. The energy from the magnetron (the part that produces the energy) transfers the energy to the water, causing it to heat up and boil. This question depends on some general knowledge both of energy transfer and microwaves and the vocabulary associated with both.

f. Interactions of Energy and Matter

Any wave, including water waves, can transfer energy when they interact with matter. When the waves hit the shore, there is a transfer of energy from the wave to the shore. There are different types of waves, such as sound waves, seismic waves, light waves, and electromagnetic waves. Types of electromagnetic waves are radio waves, microwaves, infrared radiation, visible light, ultraviolet light, X-rays, and gamma rays.

Materials often are divided into two groups, depending on the ability for electrons to flow in them. *Conductors,* such as metals, allow the electrons to flow easily. In *insulators,* the electrons cannot flow. If you look at a piece of commercial cable, the middle is copper, a metal that is a good conductor, surrounded by a plastic or rubber material, which is an insulator. This product allows electricity to flow easily through the copper while protecting people from the electricity by surrounding it with an insulator.

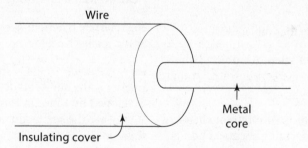

EXAMPLE:

> Karen spent the day at the beach and got sunburned. She wondered how she could get a burn when it wasn't even hot outside. Her doctor prescribed a cream for the burn and explained that the burn was caused by
>
> **(A)** Electromagnetic waves from space
> **(B)** Infrared waves from the sun
> **(C)** Ultraviolet light from the sun
> **(D)** Gamma rays

The correct answer is **(C)**. Sunburns are caused by ultraviolet rays from the sun. The other answer choices are wrong, but choice (B) is deceptive. If you didn't have some science background, you might associate *infrared* with heat, which would be technically correct, but not in the context of sunburn.

g. Vocabulary

The following are some physical science terms that you'll want to familiarize yourself with in preparation for the Science Test. Some of the terms on the list are included primarily because they appear in example questions in this chapter. As you do your reading in physical science, you may find terms that you do not understand. Look up the definitions and add them to your vocabulary list.

acceleration: The rate of change of velocity as a function of time.

allergen: Anything that causes an allergy.

allergic reaction: The body's reaction to an allergen.

atom: The smallest particle of an element that still retains the unique chemical properties of that specific element. It consists of a central nucleus surrounded by negatively charged electrons.

atomic number of an atom: Determined by the number of protons in the nucleus.

boiling point: The temperature point above which a substance exists as a gas and below which it exists as a liquid.

bonds: Force(s) holding together molecules.

center of gravity or center of mass: An object behaves as if all its weight or mass were concentrated at that point.

chemical reaction: The creation of different chemical substances by breaking or forming chemical bonds.

compound: A substance composed of more than one element.

conservation of energy: Total energy remains constant, and energy cannot be created or destroyed.

covalent bonding: The stable balance of forces between atoms when they share electrons.

density of a substance: Mass per unit volume.

dissolve: To create a solution by mixing soluble matter with water.

electrical force: Interaction of charged particles.

electromagnetic energy: Energy in the form of electrical and/or magnetic waves.

electromagnetism: What happens when moving particles with an electric charge interact.

electrons: Subatomic particles having a negative electric charge.

electrostatic forces: Interaction of charged particles at rest.

element: Made up of one type of atom.

endothermic reaction: A reaction that absorbs energy in the form of heat.

energy: $e = mc^2$ (mass × speed of light squared). Energy is the ability to do work. $e = mc^2$ is a formula developed by Einstein to show that matter and energy are the same and are related by a constant squared.

entropy: The degree of orderliness to any system.

evaporate: To transition from a liquid to a gas.

exothermic reaction: A reaction in which energy is released, often in the form of heat.

force: A push or pull that can change the state of motion of an object. If no net force is applied to an object, there will be no change in motion.

freezing point: The temperature point above which a substance exists as a liquid and below which it exists as a solid.

gamma rays: Electromagnetic radiation with short wavelength.

gaseous state: A substance is in a gaseous state when it expands to fill whatever container it is in.

gravitational potential energy: Energy that two objects have because of their mass and separation.

gravity: Every particle of matter in the universe attracts every other particle with a force that can be calculated mathematically.

hypersensitive: Allergic to common substances.

infrared radiation: Invisible electromagnetic radiation; can produce heat.

ion: An atom that has lost or gained electrons.

ionic bonding: An ionic bond is the bond formed by electrostatic attraction between ions with opposite charges in a chemical compound.

kinetic energy: Energy of motion.

light waves: Visible electromagnetic radiation.

liquid state: A substance is in a liquid state when it remains at a fixed volume but adapts to the shape of its container.

living system: A system that interacts with its environment and exhibits the characteristics normally associated with life.

magnetic force: Interaction of charged particles in motion.

magnitude: Relative size or length of a vector quantity.

matter: Matter is composed of atoms; it occupies space and has mass. The properties of matter are weight, volume, mass, and density.

microwaves: High-frequency electromagnetic waves.

molecule: An electrically neutral group of at least two atoms held together by a very strong bond.

motion: The action or process of moving.

neutrons: Subatomic particles that have no net electric charge.

nonliving system: A system that does not interact with its environment or show any of the characteristics normally associated with life.

nonspontaneous reaction: A chemical reaction that requires input of external energy.

nuclear chain reaction: Neutrons that are released as a result of nuclear fission collide with neighboring atomic nuclei, releasing them. The reaction continues exponentially, creating tremendous heat.

nuclear force: The force holding the nucleus of an atom together.

nucleus: The center of an atom; consists of protons and neutrons in most atoms.

potential energy: Energy of position.

products: Matter produced by a chemical reaction and usually having different properties from the reactants.

protons: Subatomic particles that have an electrical charge of +1 and are part of each atom.

quarks: Elemental particles that are a constituent of matter and combine to form composite particles such as protons and neutrons.

radio waves: Electromagnetic waves of medium frequency.

reactants: Substances initially involved in a chemical reaction.

scalar: A quantity that is described by its magnitude alone and has no direction, such as mass, length, time, or speed.

seismic waves: Shock waves in solid rock (often caused by earthquakes).

sensitivity: The ability to react to a stimulus.

solar system: The sun and all the planets revolving around it. Also includes the objects revolving around the planets like moons.

solid state: A substance is in a solid state when it maintains a fixed volume and shape.

solution: Homogeneous dispersal of two or more substances.

sound waves: Waves that produce sound.

speed: Magnitude of velocity without respect to its vector qualities.

spontaneous reaction: A chemical reaction proceeding without external energy input.

subatomic particles: Particles that are smaller than atoms.

thermodynamic system: A system that uses or produces heat.

transfer of energy: Energy can be transferred by heat transfer and doing work.

triple point: The temperature point at which a substance can exist as a gas, a liquid, and a solid.

ultraviolet light: Light with a shorter wavelength than visible light. Ultraviolet light can cause burns to skin.

uranium-235: A radioactive isotope of uranium used in bombs and as a fuel in nuclear reactors.

uranium-236: An isotope of uranium; radioactive waste.

vector: A quantity that has both magnitude and direction, such as velocity.

velocity: The rate of change of position and direction of an object.

visible light: Light that can be seen by the naked eye.

wave: A disturbance that moves from point to point in a medium without moving the points of the medium.

work: Force times distance.

X-rays: Electromagnetic radiation capable of penetrating solids.

2. Life Science

Life science studies living organisms and includes biology, ecology, and botany.

a. The Cell

The functional basic unit of life is the cell. There are many different kinds of cells, with the major division being between plant and animal cells. Although there are many organelles that are similar between the two types of cells, there are some common organelles, which are those internal structures of a cell that possess specialized functions. *Organisms* may range from *unicellular* (one cell) to *multicellular* (many cells). Most *bacteria* are unicellular and most animals are multicellular. Humans have about 60 trillion to 100 trillion cells.

EXAMPLE:

> An organelle is
>
> **(A)** A part of a cell possessing specialized functions
> **(B)** An organism
> **(C)** DNA
> **(D)** A formation of electron

The correct answer is **(A)**. An organelle is a part of a cell that has a specialized function.

b. Molecular Basis of Heredity

Children inherit traits from their parents; this is the example of genetics most familiar to all of us. Gregor Mendel, a nineteenth-century scientist (and monk), speculated that organisms inherit traits via unit factors. Today, we know that unit factors correspond to regions within the DNA of the organism that code for specific proteins.

DNA is a molecule comprised of repeating subunits called *nucleotides*. Nucleotides have one of four specific nitrogenous bases abbreviated with the letters G, C, T, and A. DNA (see next page) has the shape of a long twisted ladder (double-helix), a result of repeating nucleotides and bonding characteristics. The sequence of the bases in the repeating nucleotides is the genetic code, which serves as the blueprint for all life-forms.

EXAMPLE:

> Clara wants to grow the world's biggest cucumber. She has to decide where to put her money and efforts. Of the following, which would stand the best chance of growing a huge cucumber?
>
> **(A)** Special fertilizer
> **(B)** Enriched soil
> **(C)** Grow lights
> **(D)** Seeds from huge cucumbers

The correct answer is **(D)**. According to Mendel, offspring inherit their traits from their parents. The offspring, huge cucumbers, would inherit the "huge" gene from their huge cucumber parents. The other answer choices might have a small effect on the size of the plants, but the seeds would not carry the traits needed.

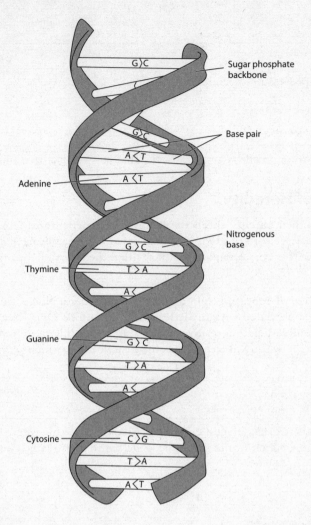

c. Biological Evolution

Any genetic change—small or large—in a population, inherited over several generations, is considered to be biological evolution. The change has to be at the genetic level (the genes show evidence of change) to be passed on from generation to generation.

EXAMPLE:

> Sylvia was tracing her family tree and was able to go back six generations and get photographs and paintings of the male members of her family. She noticed that each one of them was substantially taller than his peers. What could this indicate as a possibility for her male children?
>
> **(A)** They could speak English.
> **(B)** They could have long hair.
> **(C)** They could be taller than their peers.
> **(D)** They could be smarter than their peers.

The correct answer is **(C)**. If height is regarded as a genetic change and is noticeable over several generations, it is possible that the next generation of males would be taller than their peers. In evolution, there is no certainty. In this case, there was no genetic testing to determine if this was a change in the genes, but there is a strong possibility that Sylvia's male children could be taller than their peers based on the evidence.

d. Interdependence of Organisms

Living organisms depend on one another to remain alive, grow, and reproduce. Humans eat large fish, which consume smaller fish, which consume water plants and smaller fish, and so on. Water plants and humans are *interdependent*.

EXAMPLE:

> Lyle was trying to explain to his little cousin, Rose, that she should not try to kill all the ladybugs she sees, even if she is afraid of them. He told her that ladybugs eat large numbers of insects that eat the leaves of plants, and some of these leafy plants are eaten in salads by humans. Lyle tried to explain how living organisms are interdependent and thought Rose understood when she said that we shouldn't kill worms. Rose said that we depended on worms because
>
> **(A)** They are living creatures.
> **(B)** They produce compost, which can be used to grow vegetables.
> **(C)** They aerate the soil.
> **(D)** Some wild birds eat them.

The correct answer is **(B)**. The other answer choices seem reasonable, but they fail to show an interdependence between humans and worms. We all know the importance of worms in the soil. This is a case where some prior knowledge is important.

e. Matter, Energy, and Organization in Living Systems

Living systems or self-organizing systems of varying sizes interact with their environment by exchanging information and material-energy.

EXAMPLE:

The next question is based on the following passage.

> James Grier Miller, a scientist working in the field of living systems theory, suggested that systems have mutual interrelationships and that those interrelationships cross hierarchical levels. For example, the member countries of a supranational system such as the European Common Market benefit from the activities of each member nation. At the other end of the scale, a cell in a living system lives on the nutrients from its suprasystem or environment.

> A cell benefits from its environment because
>
> **(A)** The environment protects the cell from predators.
> **(B)** The environment provides nutrients to the cell.
> **(C)** It is better to live in a group than alone.
> **(D)** The environment's activities help the cells.

The correct answer is **(B)**. The passage states that "a cell in a living system lives on the nutrients from its suprasystem or environment." This is an example of an item in which it would be beneficial to read the question and then skim the passage. The word *environment* would then lead your eyes to the correct answer.

f. Behavior of Organisms

B. F. Skinner, an American psychologist, developed a theoretical basis for the behavior of organisms. He theorized that, through *conditioning,* an organism could be made to repeat an activity over and over again. He used rats in what was later to be called the "Skinner box" and was able to alter their behavior through a series of rewards or reinforcements for repeating the action. In this way, he was able to shape the organism's behavior.

We learn many behaviors in this way. If you go out in the rain wearing rubber boots, your feet don't get wet. Not getting your feet wet is a reward for wearing rubber boots. The next time it rains, you'll probably wear rubber boots because it's more comfortable than walking around with wet feet. However, being human, you may decide to go out in the rain wearing sandals and end up with wet feet. The reinforcement only increases the chance of something happening. It can't *guarantee* that it will happen.

EXAMPLE:

Amy was conducting an experiment to see if she could make a squirrel run around in circles through conditioning. Which of the following possible scenarios would likely prove successful?

(A) Put a harness and a leash on the squirrel and attach the end of the leash to a pole. When the squirrel is taken off the leash, it should run in circles.

(B) Wait until the squirrel runs in a circle and then give it a reward. After that, give the squirrel a reward each time it runs in a circle.

(C) Put the squirrel in a circular cage. When the squirrel is released from the cage, it will run in circles.

(D) Construct a model-train setup with a circular course. Put the squirrel on one car and leave the train running in circles for several hours. When the train stops, the squirrel will run in circles.

The correct answer is **(B)**. If you accept the theory of Skinner, then the reward should begin to shape the squirrel's behavior and repeated rewards would strengthen it. The other answer choices don't include any rewards, and, according to Skinner, some type of reward is necessary for conditioning to take place.

g. Vocabulary

The following are some life science terms that you'll want to familiarize yourself with in preparation for the Science Test. Some of the terms on the list are included primarily because they appear in example questions in this chapter. As you do your reading in life science, you may find terms that you do not understand. Look up the definitions and add them to your vocabulary list.

bacteria: One-celled organisms, some of which are capable of causing disease.

behavior of organisms: The way in which organisms act.

cell: The basic structural unit of all life-forms.

conditioning: To establish a particular repeated response in a subject.

diffraction: The slight bending of a ray of light as it passes over the edge of an object.

DNA: The molecule that transfers genetic traits in living creatures.

energy: The capacity or ability to do work.

environment: External physical conditions.

evolution: Changes from generation to generation in the gene pool through various genetic processes.

gene: Basic unit of heredity.

genetics: Science of heredity.

interdependent: Depend on each other.

lens: An optical device that allows light to pass through it and is capable of refracting or bending the light. A lens may be convex, concave, flat (plano), or a combination.

living systems: Self-organizing systems that can be referred to as alive and that interact with the environment.

molecular basis of heredity: The passage of characteristics from one generation to the next using DNA as the blueprint for life.

multicellular: An organism having many cells.

nucleotides: Groups of molecules linked together to form the building blocks of DNA.

organism: Individual life-form composed of mutually interdependent parts consisting of one or more cells.

refraction: The change in direction of a light wave when it passes from one medium to another—for example, from air to a glass lens.

reinforcement: A reward that increases the likelihood that a certain behavior will be repeated.

reproduce: To bear offspring.

self-organizing system: Process whereby structure appears within a system without external forces or influences.

traits: Characteristics determined through genetics.

unicellular: An organism having one cell.

3. Earth and Space Science

Earth and space science studies include geology, astrophysics, atmospheric science, hydrology, and geochemistry.

a. Energy in the Earth System

Earth has both internal and external sources of energy. The largest source of external energy is the sun, which provides vast amounts of energy. The outer core of Earth is *molten rock,* which has the potential to provide heat energy to Earth's surface.

EXAMPLE:

Quincy was designing a new subdivision and was looking for a different way of heating the houses that would be more efficient than each house having a furnace burning gas to produce heat. Which of the following methods would stand a good chance of working?

(A) Place solar panels on each roof with additional panels in the yards to create energy to heat water to circulate through the heating system of each house.

(B) Build large windmills to use the electricity generated to charge storage batteries, which could provide electricity to heat the houses.

(C) Drill deep enough into the earth to reach a temperature that would heat circulating water, which could be used to heat the houses.

(D) All of the above

The correct answer is **(D)**. Each of the systems would use energy that the earth is exposed to and transfer it where it's needed (to heat the houses). However, choice (C) is problematic: In order to get enough heat from the earth, we would have to drill deep enough (to the core). Because deep drilling is very expensive and almost impractical, choice (C) is not a reasonable answer.

b. Geochemical Cycles

Geochemical cycles are the movement between living and nonliving forms in the environment. Of all the elements that are involved in geochemical cycles, four are most important to us: carbon, nitrogen, phosphorus, and sulfur. These are important to us because, among other things, they allow the oceans to absorb carbon dioxide to slow global warming.

EXAMPLE:

The next question is based on the following passage.

Human beings are involved in biochemical cycles through their use of chemicals in daily life. *Fossil fuels* are carbon-based fuels; we use them daily as we commute to work. Before becoming gasoline or other petrochemicals, these carbon compounds were stored in the earth in relatively environmentally safe storage. By extracting the carbon-based oil, we move the carbon into a new pool. Here, it is converted to gasoline. When this is burned, carbon dioxide and carbon monoxide are created, which are released into the atmosphere. Once released into the atmosphere, these carbon compounds have the ability to raise the temperature of Earth by several degrees. This may not seem like much but affects agriculture, living conditions, and availability of land for habitation and animals. One universal hope is that forests and oceans can absorb the extra carbon compounds. There is also great concern that our clear-cutting of forests will just speed up this process.

One significant cause of global warming is the fact that

(A) The sun is getting closer to Earth.
(B) Cars are adding carbon compounds to the atmosphere.
(C) More heat is being reflected off Earth.
(D) Summers are getting longer.

The correct answer is **(B)**. The passage addresses the problems of converting carbon-based compounds in the earth to gasoline to be used in cars. The other answer choices are not mentioned in the passage and may or may not be relevant in general conversation, but the only answer choice that is relevant on the test is the one mentioned in the passage.

NOTE: One of the problems of reading widely in science is that some of the material read is conjecture or part of general knowledge, which cannot be used to answer questions on this test unless it is specifically mentioned in the passage.

c. Origin and Evolution of the Earth System

Earth is said to be 4.6 billion years old. At this time, it is thought that part of the solar system spun off and, through gravitational forces, became larger and more dense. This produced a large mass that moved through space in an orbit around the sun. As it moved, the material that came together to form the mass (Earth) cooled and solidified to form Earth's crust. It is thought that the moon was originally part of the mantle of Earth, before it spun off to orbit Earth.

Calculating Earth's age is very difficult. We all know how old we are because people were present at our birth and records were kept. There were no people present to observe the birth of Earth and, thus, no first-person records. We have to depend on other methods. One of these methods is radioactive dating, which determines the age of rocks. A different method is *carbon dating* of organic materials, such as bone, found in layers of rocks.

EXAMPLE:

The next question is based on the following passage.

> Carbon-14 dating helps us determine the age of any material that was once alive. Carbon-14 is a radioactive isotope, which decays from carbon-14 to nitrogen over the course of time. *Decay* is the spontaneous change from one nucleus to another through changes in the number of atomic particles. The rate of decay is constant and can give us an indication of age.
>
> While living organisms are alive, they consume carbon, some of which is carbon-14, either directly (in the case of plants) or indirectly (through consuming plants as food). Once an organism dies, it stops consuming carbon, and the process of radioactive decay of the carbon-14 becomes important because it is measurable.

How does carbon dating help estimate the age of a fossil?

(A) The fossil gives off carbon.

(B) The amount of carbon a fossil consumes can be measured.

(C) The rate of radioactive decay of carbon-14 is constant and measurable.

(D) The carbon-14 tells the scientist how old it is.

The correct answer is **(C)**. As stated in the passage, carbon-14 undergoes radioactive decay in a constant and measurable way. The other answer choices have no basis in the passage and some have no basis in fact, but you're looking for the best answer from the passage and that is choice (C).

d. Origin and Formation of the Universe

There are three main theories to explain the origin and evolution of the universe:

- **The Big Bang Theory:** In the beginning, all the matter in the universe was concentrated in an extremely dense, extremely hot ball until a huge explosion occurred, breaking the matter into pieces and expelling them in all directions. These pieces formed the stars and galaxies now known as the universe.

- **The Steady State Theory:** This theory states that the number of galaxies in the universe is a constant; as old galaxies disappear, new ones are formed.

- **The Pulsating Theory:** This theory states that the universe is constantly expanding and contracting, which means that it is pulsating.

EXAMPLE:

> Our universe was formed by an explosion, which blew particles out from a central hot mass.
> As these particles became concentrated by gravity, they formed solid and gaseous masses that
> became the stars and planets.
>
> Earth was originally formed by
>
> **(A)** Gases
> **(B)** An explosion
> **(C)** Space
> **(D)** Gravity

The correct answer is **(B).** The question asks what originally formed Earth, and the only specific choice that
is in the passage is choice (B). Choice (D) might be a possible answer if the question did not specify
"originally." Questions and answer choices must be read carefully. Gravity is mentioned in the passage but as
something that acted upon the particles after the original explosion.

e. Vocabulary

The following are some earth and space science terms that you'll want to familiarize yourself with in
preparation for the Science Test. Some of the terms on the list are included primarily because they appear in
example questions in this chapter. As you do your reading in earth and space science, you may find terms
that you do not understand. Look up the definitions and add them to your vocabulary list.

agriculture: Food production.

biosphere: The basic parts of the planet Earth that all
contain life—lithosphere (rock from the center to the
surface), hydrosphere (water), and atmosphere (air).

carbon compounds: Compounds based on the carbon
atom.

carbon dating: Determining the age of an object by
the amount of carbon-14 within it.

carbon dioxide: Gas formed during breathing or by
burning some substances.

carbon monoxide: Poisonous gas produced by
burning with insufficient air.

core: Center of Earth, thought to be made of nickel
and iron, with the outer core being liquid and a solid
inner core.

decay: Spontaneous change from one nucleus to another
through changes in the number of atomic particles.

external energy: Sources of energy outside Earth.

fossil fuels: Carbon-based fuels.

geochemical cycle: Changes in concentration of
various elements and compounds in the chemistry of
the earth.

habitation: Living space.

internal energy: Sources of energy within the earth.

mantle: The region between Earth's surface and
its core.

molten rock: Magma produced by active volcanoes.

orbit: Path.

origin of the universe: Theory of how the universe
was created.

radioactive isotope: An unstable isotope that
spontaneously emits radiation.

X. Social Studies

A. Test Format

The Social Studies Test is 90 minutes long. You have 65 minutes for Section 1 (the question-and-answer items) and 25 minutes for Section 2 (the extended response item, also known as the essay). Please note that leftover time from one section of the Social Studies Test cannot be transferred to the other. Each part is timed separately.

In Section 1 of the Social Studies Test, you'll encounter five item types. For descriptions and examples of these item types, see Chapter I, "The 2014 GED® Test."

1. Multiple choice
2. Fill-in-the-blank
3. Drop-down
4. Hot spot
5. Drag-and-drop

> NOTE: For study purposes, all example and practice questions in this chapter are in the multiple-choice format.

Social Studies questions assess your knowledge in the following subject areas:

- **U.S. history (20%):** Passages may have to do with the American Revolution, the Civil War and Reconstruction, industrial development, the Great Depression, immigration, the Cold War, current politics, and so on. World history will be a component in such areas as the development of democracy and the World Wars. Questions may be based on visual passages, including illustrations, maps, and charts. To prepare for this section, read articles and books concerning historical material.

- **Civics and government (50%):** These passages deal with civic life, government, and American politics. Passages may include issues of citizens' rights when they come into conflict with other societal values or needs, states' rights, as well as issues related to checks and balances in government, and the separation of powers. Material about civics and government may be found in newspapers and news magazines. Older issues can be found in libraries.

- **Economics (15%):** Economics is the study of how Earth's resources are used to create wealth, which is then distributed and used to satisfy the needs of mankind. It involves the world of banking and finance in both small businesses and large corporations. It includes the relationship between government and economics, theories of economics, and the economics of colonization. Economic articles may be found on the Internet and in newspapers, magazines, and books.

- **Geography and the world (15%):** Geography deals with the world's land masses, oceans, and other waterways. The impact of weather, environmental conditions, and the division and use of land are also a focus. To prepare for geographic questions, practice reading maps and answering questions about them. You also can read geography magazines, websites, and library books about topics of geographic interest.

The Social Studies Test assesses higher-level thinking skills. You are not required to try to remember facts, such as the year that the Declaration of Independence was signed. But you are expected to understand social studies principles, concepts, and events. The content will focus on two main themes applied to the four areas listed above. These themes are "Development of Modern Liberties and Democracy" and "Dynamic Responses in Societal Systems."

The first theme, "Development of Modern Liberties and Democracy," is more applicable to the history, civics, and civil rights topics. The content will focus on how democracy and human and civil rights developed in various societies and the development of modern ideas about government. Part of that will be an examination of the development of the American form of government, party politics, and the civil rights movement.

The second theme, "Dynamic Responses in Societal Systems," will apply more to the geography and economics content. You will look at how societies respond to particular stimuli, from variations in their resource base to variations of climate. You will look at the influence of natural events, as well as how countries and economies respond to economic issues. Topics will include the Scientific and Industrial revolutions, human migration, and basic economics.

B. Types of Questions in Section 1: A Detailed Look

The Social Studies Test measures your ability to understand and interpret concepts and principles in history, geography, economics, and civics. You're required to draw upon your previous knowledge of events, ideas, terms, and situations that may be related to social studies.

Items involving visual materials rely on graphs, maps, tables, political cartoons, diagrams, photographs, and artistic works. Graphs and charts demonstrate trends and relationships between different sets of information. It is important that you know how to read and interpret information presented in this format.

Here's a detailed look at each of the four question types, along with some example questions.

1. Comprehension Questions

Comprehension questions test your ability to identify information and ideas and interpret their meaning. You should be able to understand information presented in articles and excerpts, as well as in maps, charts, and graphs. This can involve determining the main point of the passage, restating the information, summarizing ideas, and identifying implications of this information.

EXAMPLES:

The comprehension questions are based on the following passage.

> Seventy-five percent of Americans are urban dwellers and, in spite of the booming economy, 30 percent of workers earn poverty or near-poverty wages. Low-wage workers are now the lowest paid in the industrialized world, with more than 20 percent of children in the United States living in poverty. The number of U.S. citizens who work more than one job has increased 92 percent between 1973 and 1997, with 43 percent of workers putting in more than 50 hours per week. Young entry-level workers without a college education saw their real wages fall by 20 percent between 1979 and 1997. On the other hand, the CEOs

(chief executive officers) of major corporations now earn 419 times more than the average salary of their employees. The richest 1 percent of the population now earns as much wealth as the bottom 95 percent.

Which of the following statements best summarizes this passage's central theme?

(A) Many Americans live in cities.

(B) The income of entry-level workers has increased.

(C) The income of CEOs has decreased.

(D) There is a major disparity between income levels.

The correct answer is **(D).** The "central theme" of the passage is the inequity that exists between the incomes of the richest citizens and the lowest wage earners. Choice (A), while true, does not represent the theme of the passage. Choices (B) and (C) are incorrect according to the passage.

According to the passage, what impact does a college education have on a worker's income level?

(A) There is no difference.

(B) The worker's income rises.

(C) The worker's income declines.

(D) The worker works more hours.

The correct answer is **(B).** The passage tells us that entry-level workers, without a college education, saw their income decrease by 20 percent. Therefore, by comparison, the college-educated workers must have seen a rise in income. The rest of the choices are either incorrect or not relevant.

Where do CEOs of major corporations fit among income earners?

(A) Top 20 percent

(B) About 43 percent

(C) At 75 percent

(D) Top 1 percent

The correct answer is **(D).** According to the passage, CEOs would occupy the top 1 percent of income earners. While they would also be in the top 20 percent (A), this is not the best answer. Choices (B) and (C) are incorrect.

2. Application Questions

Application questions assess your ability to use information and ideas in different ways to explore meanings or solve problems. You'll be asked to use the information from the passage to solve a problem in a different situation or context.

EXAMPLES:

The application questions are based on the following passage.

According to the United States Constitution, the responsibility for public education is divested to the states. Each of the 50 states has its own department of education, which delegates the actual operation of schools, from kindergarten through grade 12, to a number of local public school districts. One approach to school reform has meant that virtually every state has set standards of accountability for curriculum content and academic performance for students at each grade level and for each subject area. These results are typically made public, with comparison data across districts, so that communities can assess their district's performance in relation to other districts.

Who is directly responsible for the operation of public schools in the United States?

(A) Departments of education
(B) Local school districts
(C) State governments
(D) The House of Representatives

The correct answer is **(B).** Choice (B) is the best answer because local public school districts are directly responsible for the operation of public schools. Although the United States Constitution delegates responsibility to each of the 50 states, the actual operation of public schools is delegated to local school districts. Therefore, choices (A) and (C), while relevant, are not the best answers. Choice (D), the House of Representatives, is incorrect.

School reform is promoted by which of the following?

(A) Standards of accountability
(B) Curriculum content
(C) Academic performance
(D) Test scores

The correct answer is **(A).** According to the passage, choice (A), "standards of accountability," is the best answer. While these standards may involve curriculum content (B) and academic performance (C), these are but parts of the overall standards. Choice (D), while relevant, is not mentioned in the passage.

How do communities assess their school performance?

(A) Public awareness
(B) District's performances
(C) Local accountability
(D) Comparison of data

The correct answer is **(D).** The results of performance assessments are made public; therefore, choice (D), "comparison of data," is the best answer. While choices (A), (B), and (C) may be relevant factors, they are not the best answer to the question.

3. Analysis Questions

Analysis questions test your ability to break down information and understand how ideas relate to each other. This could involve comparing ideas and exploring their relationships. You need to know the difference between a fact, an opinion, and a hypothesis. You may be asked to find ideas not specifically stated or recognize a writer's historical point of view. What is the difference between a fact and an opinion? Why does an event happen and what are the results? What conclusion can you draw from the information presented?

EXAMPLES:

The analysis questions are based on the following passage.

With a land area of almost 2 million square kilometers and a population of about 96 million, Mexico shares borders with the United States to the north and Guatemala and Belize to the southeast. It is a representative, democratic, and federal republic with a government composed of legislative, executive, and judicial branches. The country is divided into 31 sovereign states, as well as the federal district in which the capital, Mexico City, is located.

Approximately 80 percent of the population is of mixed European and North American Indian or African slave ancestry (*mestizo*), while 10 percent is of purely indigenous descent (*indégena*). Mexicans are predominantly Roman Catholic Spanish-speakers, but more than 50 distinct indigenous peoples maintain their own languages and cultural traditions. The indigenous population is over-represented in the poverty statistics, in which 28 million Mexicans are estimated to live in extreme poverty, with an additional 12 million classified as poor.

What makes Mexico a federal republic?

(A) It has a population of 96 million.
(B) It is divided into sovereign states.
(C) It has a land area of 2 million square kilometers.
(D) The government is composed of three branches.

The correct answer is **(B)**. A federal republic is made up of a number of sovereign states forming a decentralized form of government. A population of 96 million (A) and a land area of 2 million square kilometers (C) are not directly related to being a federal republic. The fact that the government has three branches (D) is not relevant to the question.

Which term does NOT describe Mexican society?

(A) Multicultural
(B) Multilingual
(C) Homogeneous
(D) Indigenous descent

The correct answer is **(C)**. *Homogeneous* means "uniform in structure, essentially alike." All other answer choices are mentioned in the passages as descriptors of Mexican society. *Multicultural* (A) means many cultures, while *multilingual* (B) refers to multiple languages. *Indigenous descent* (D) is a term that may be used to describe the diversity of Mexico's population. So, choice (D) is included in choice (A).

Which segment of the population is the most impoverished?

(A) North American Indians
(B) African slaves
(C) Spanish speakers
(D) Indigenous peoples

The correct answer is **(D)**. According to the passage, choice (D) "indigenous peoples" are a minority that is over-represented in the poverty statistics. Spanish speakers (C) refers to the majority of citizens. North American Indians (A) and African slaves (B) are incorrect choices.

4. Evaluation Questions

Evaluation questions assess your ability to make judgments about the material's appropriateness, accuracy, and differences of opinion, as well as the roles that information and ideas play in influencing current and future decision-making. You should be able to judge the accuracy of material presented in the passage. Does the information represent a particular point of view? What determines the reasons for the decision-making? How are trends used to predict an outcome? How do you assess the accuracy of the facts presented?

EXAMPLES:

The evaluation questions are based on the following passage.

During the last decades, Hungary has experienced a process of transition, which has had far-reaching consequences for the economy and society as a whole. But it is important to underline that this process was initiated much earlier than in the neighboring countries. In the 1980s, a gradual process of democratization and of decentralization was introduced, and the private sector became increasingly significant. Dynamic entrepreneurs began to appear, and intellectuals were quite aware of new ideas and developments on the international scene.

It is not so surprising, therefore, that when the change of regime took place around 1990, Hungary went through the transition process at a particularly rapid pace. Drastic measures of privatization and economic reform were undertaken, as well as far-reaching institutional changes involving a large degree of decentralization. During the early 1990s, economic restructuring and the loss of export markets (especially in the Soviet Union) had serious adverse effects on the standard of living. There was a deep economic recession, with unemployment, poverty, and inequalities between regions and social groups appearing for the first time.

How did Hungary's economic changes compare to other Eastern European nations?

(A) They were more far-reaching.
(B) They were more important.
(C) They were more gradual.
(D) They were less significant.

The correct answer is **(A)**. According to the passage, Hungary's economic and social changes were "far-reaching" as compared to neighboring countries. They may also have been "more important" (B), but that is not the best answer. More gradual (C) and less significant (D) are incorrect choices.

What factors were responsible for changes in Hungary's society in 1990?

(A) Democratization
(B) Entrepreneurs
(C) Intellectuals
(D) All of the above

The correct answer is **(D)**. According to the passage, democratization, entrepreneurs, and intellectuals all contributed to changes in the economic and social order in 1990.

What was the chief reason for the decline in Hungary's standard of living in the early 1990s?

(A) Privatization
(B) Loss of export markets
(C) Economic reform
(D) Regional inequalities

The correct answer is **(B)**. The chief reason for decline in the standard of living was the loss of export markets. This resulted in a deep economic recession leading to unemployment and poverty. Privatization (A), economic reform (C), and regional inequalities (D) may also have had some impact, but they were not the chief reasons.

5. Chart or Table-based Evaluation and Analysis Questions

a. Tables

EXAMPLES:

Sex by Educational Attainment for the Population 25 Years and Over Clay County, Alabama								Two or More Races	
	Total*	One Race							
		White	Black or African American	American Indian and Alaska Native	Asian	Native Hawaiian and Other Pacific Islander	Some Other Race		Hispanic or Latino (any race)
Total:	9,673	8,064	1,415	25	0	0	70	99	219
Male:	4,582	3,838	645	17	0	0	35	47	91
Less than high school diploma	1,330	1,044	269	17	0	0	0	0	0
High school graduate, GED® diploma, or alternative	1,875	1,575	269	0	0	0	0	31	32
Some college or associate's degree	1,044	935	58	0	0	0	35	16	59

continued

Bachelor's degree or higher	333	284	49	0	0	0	0	0	0
Female:	5,091	4,226	770	8	0	0	35	52	128
Less than high school diploma	1,169	855	299	8	0	0	7	0	31
High school graduate, GED® diploma, or alternative	1,821	1,633	180	0	0	0	0	8	59
Some college or associate's degree	1,578	1,280	249	0	0	0	28	21	38
Bachelor's degree or higher	523	458	42	0	0	0	0	23	0

Source: U.S. Census Bureau, 2008–2012 American Community Survey 5-year Estimates.

*Except where noted, "race" refers to people reporting only one race. "Hispanic" refers to an ethnic category: Hispanics may be of any race.

By gender and race, what was the largest single group in Clay County, Alabama, in the period 2008–2012?

(A) White males
(B) Black females
(C) Hispanic or Latino males
(D) None of the above

The correct answer is **(D),** none of the above. If you examine the table, the largest single group is white females. There are 3,838 white males, 770 black females, and 91 Hispanic or Latino males. In this case, you need to determine the size of the groups in choices (A) through (C), and then see if any other group is larger.

How do men and women compare in this county in terms of completing a high school diploma or equivalent?

(A) A greater percentage of men have a high school diploma.
(B) A greater percentage of women have a high school diploma.
(C) Both are about the same.
(D) None of the above

The correct answer is **(A).** You need to work out the percentage of men with a high school diploma ($1,875 \div 4,582 = 40.9\%$) and women with a high school diploma ($1,821 \div 5,091 = 35.8\%$). As you can see, a greater percentage of men have a high school diploma. You can "guestimate" the answer: For men, you can round $1,875 \div 4,582$ to $2,000 \div 5,000$ and then simplify to $20 \div 50$, or roughly 40%. For women, you can round $1,821 \div 5,091$ to $1,800 \div 5,000$ and then simplify to $18 \div 50$, or roughly 36%. Why the arithmetic? Remember, there is an expectation in the Social Studies Test that you can apply mathematical reasoning to the subject matter.

Which group has the lowest percentage of people WITHOUT at least a high school diploma or equivalent?

(A) Black males
(B) Hispanic males
(C) White females
(D) Asian males

The correct answer is **(B)**. There are Hispanic males, but none without a high school or GED® diploma. Black males (A) and white females (C) all have a portion of their cohort without a high school or GED® diploma. Choice (D) Asian males can be excluded since, according to the statistics, there are no Asian males in the county.

b. Interpreting Charts

EXAMPLES:

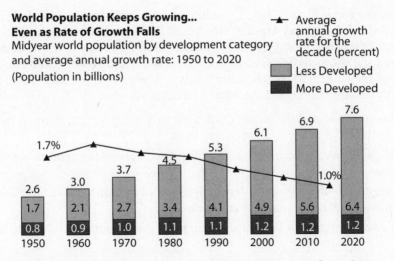

**World Population Keeps Growing...
Even as Rate of Growth Falls**
Midyear world population by development category and average annual growth rate: 1950 to 2020
(Population in billions)

Note: Figures for components may not add to total because of rounding.

Source: U.S. Census Bureau (www.census.gov/easystats/)

How has the average world growth rate by decade changed since the 1970s?

(A) Increased
(B) Decreased
(C) Remained the same
(D) None of the above

The correct answer is **(B)**. The world growth rate has decreased. There are three sets of data presented in this chart. You need to examine the entire graphic to determine which item represents world growth rates by decade. The line shows the world growth rate. The growth rate increased for the first decade shown and then declined for the entire rest of the period shown.

> How does the population growth rate for the more developed nations compare to that of less developed nations?
>
> **(A)** Developed nations have increased their proportion of the world's population.
> **(B)** Developed nations have decreased their proportion of the world's population.
> **(C)** Developed nations' proportion of the world's population has stayed about the same.
> **(D)** None of the above

The correct answer is **(B).** The key to answering this question correctly is the word "proportion." The question wants you to determine how the population of the developed world has changed compared to the less developed world. Since the world population has almost tripled in the time frame shown, and the developed nations' population only increased by 50%, clearly the developed nations' populations make up a smaller proportion of the world's population.

C. Section 2: The Extended Response

Of the 90 minutes for the Social Studies Test, 25 minutes are allocated for the extended response item. As with the Reasoning through Language Arts Test, the Social Studies extended response item is simply an essay. You need to read the two source documents provided, and then react to them. In the case of the Social Studies Test, there is a specific focus on "Enduring Issues in American History" and issues that reflect the founding principles of the United States. These are issues with which we as a society still have to deal. One document will usually be a quotation, and the other a related passage.

- As you read the quotation and the passage, you need to develop an argument on how the two items are related and how they both relate to an enduring issue.
- Start your essay with a clear statement on how these two source documents relate to each other and to an enduring issue.
- Support your arguments throughout with direct references to both of the source documents. Show their relationship to each other and to your argument.
- Draw on your own knowledge of American history and the issue in general to further support your arguments.

When you are ready to prepare your essay:

- Use the erasable noteboard to prepare a rough outline. Include the specific items from both source documents that you want to quote. Remember, you can copy from the source texts and paste them into your essay. Remember also to keep them short.
- Arrange your points in a logical order so that there is a clear building of the argument from your opening paragraph to the conclusion.
- Use proper linking words, phrases, and sentences between paragraphs to ensure proper flow. You can start a paragraph with "Further, . . ." or "We can also see that . . ." Either shows a linkage between what went before and what is to follow.
- Use proper formal English. You are writing an argumentative essay for an adult audience. Text shorthand, emoticons, or casual language are not acceptable.
- Choose your words carefully. Never assume the reader knows what you mean. The evaluation is based on what you write, not what you think the reader already knows.

When you write your essay:

- Put your key point(s) at the beginning of the first paragraph. Leave no doubt about your point of view. Then add, very briefly, the key reasons you think so.

- Expand on each of your reasons, using quotes from BOTH documents as well as your own knowledge.

- Ensure that you use all the worthwhile points you noted on your noteboard. If it does not appear in the word processing window on the computer, it will not be scored.

- Check your essay for grammar, spelling, and punctuation. These are also part of your evaluation. Make sure subjects and verbs agree, names are capitalized, and so on.

- Reread your final essay and make sure that it flows. Try reading it "out loud" (subvocally—not really aloud—the test monitors would likely have a fit if you did!) to yourself. If you stumble over what you have written, it needs a rewrite. Reread the introductory paragraph and every first sentence of the subsequent paragraphs. If they build logically to your conclusion, you are probably in good order. If not, rewrite, or at least, reorder the paragraphs.

The Social Studies extended response item tests a number of things. This item requires you to demonstrate that you can present a reasoned argument and extract evidence from the source documents to back that argument. You are expected to have some knowledge of history and social issues independent of the source documents, and you can use that knowledge appropriately as part of your response. Finally, the evaluators expect you to write clearly and persuasively and to do so with few mechanical mistakes.

D. Test Strategies

To improve your skills and get better results, try the following strategies before taking the Social Studies Test:

- **Read, read, read!** The best way to prepare for the reading-based questions is to practice reading excerpts or passages from a variety of documents. Following is a list of suggested reading to help you prepare. The important thing is to gain experience reading this type of material. The more you read, the better prepared you'll be when you encounter this type of material on the test.

  On the test, you will be presented with at least one passage of each of the following types of documents. You don't have to know all the details of what's in them, but you do have to become a bit familiar with the language so that you can answer the questions. Look up these types of documents at the library or online to become familiar with the way they are written.

  - Declaration of Independence
  - U.S. Constitution
  - Landmark Supreme Court cases
  - Consumer information guides
  - Political speeches
  - Almanacs

- **Get visual.** To prepare for visual materials questions, study the maps you see on television, in newspapers, and in magazines. Familiarize yourself with U.S. and world geography by studying a globe or an atlas. Study examples of charts and graphs in newspapers, magazines, and other texts to learn to understand what information is being presented or compared.

- **Quiz yourself.** Ask yourself questions about what you've read. Try to understand the main ideas so as to explain them to others.

- **Review the example questions and work the practice questions.** There are example questions in Section B of this chapter, and more questions for practice in Section E of this chapter. Work through these questions and check your answers. If you answered a question correctly, read the explanation to reinforce the reasoning. If you answered incorrectly, read the explanation, and then reread the question to see where you went wrong. Additional sample questions can be found online on the GED Testing Service® website: www.gedtestingservice.com/freepractice/download/GED_Social_Studies/GEDSocialStudiesPracticeTest. html. (Please note that this site is designed for use by educators and that GED Testing Service® is not affiliated with, and does not endorse, *CliffsNotes GED® TEST Cram Plan,* 2nd Edition.)

- **Use the on-screen calculator when available.** On the Social Studies Test, there is an expectation that you can apply mathematical reasoning to the subject matter. The on-screen calculator is provided on certain items where it would be useful to test-takers in answering those items. You can find a manual for this calculator online (www.atomiclearning.com/ti30xs).

- **Take the Social Studies Practice Test.** Take the Social Studies Practice Test (Chapter XIV). Do so under test conditions: a quiet room, no radio or other distractions. Use a timer and stick to the time limits. Check your answers and review the explanations.

E. Practice

Remember that Section 1 of the Social Studies Test does not measure your ability to recall information. It requires you to read a passage, analyze the information, evaluate its accuracy, and draw conclusions according to the printed text or visual materials contained in the passage. You then must choose the best answer to each question.

1. Questions

Questions 1 through 4 are based on the following passage excerpted from U.S. History For Dummies, *2nd Edition, by Steve Wiegand, copyright 2009 by Wiley Publishing, Inc. Reprinted with permission of John Wiley & Sons, Inc.*

The first Bank of the United States, whose majority stockholder was the federal government and which had helped the nation get a grip on its finances, had been created at the urging of Alexander Hamilton in 1790. But it had been allowed to expire in 1811, and a horde of state-chartered banks swarmed to take its place. In 1811, there were 88 state banks; by 1813, the number was 208, and by 1819, 392. Most of them extended credit and printed currency far in excess of their reserves; when the war came, most of them couldn't redeem their paper for a tenth of its worth.

In 1816, Congress chartered a second Bank of the United States, with capital of $35 million. The idea was to provide stability to the economic system by having a large bank that would serve as the federal government's financial agent. But the new bank's managers were corrupt, stupid, or both, and they lent money like mad to land-crazed Americans flocking to the West.

In 1819, land prices dropped, manufacturing and crop prices collapsed, and scores of overextended banks failed. The yahoos who were first put in charge of the second Bank of the United States finally got the boot; new management stepped in, clamped down hard on credit, and foreclosed on virtually all its debtors.

But the Panic of 1819, the nation's first widespread financial crisis, triggered strong resentment toward the Bank, which was nicknamed "the Monster." The Bank was particularly hated in the credit-dependent West, which saw it as a creature of rich financiers and speculators in New York and New England. The West's antipathy toward the bank drove a wedge between the regions.

1. Which of the following sentences summarizes the main point found in the first paragraph?

   (A) There were many state-chartered banks.
   (B) Alexander Hamilton helped the nation get a grip on its finances.
   (C) To protect the value of the currency, the country needed one federal bank.
   (D) Most banks extended credit and printed currency.

2. Which of the following sentences, adapted from the second paragraph, addresses the need for a stable financial system?

   (A) Congress chartered a second bank.
   (B) The new bank's managers were corrupt.
   (C) Land-crazed Americans flocked to the West.
   (D) A large bank would serve as the federal government's financial agent.

3. Which of the following conclusions can be drawn from the third paragraph?

   (A) Prices collapsed.
   (B) New management saved the Bank of the United States.
   (C) Yahoos got the boot.
   (D) Scores of banks failed.

4. Which of the following accurately describes the reason for resentment toward the bank?

   (A) Panic of 1819
   (B) Credit-dependent West
   (C) Creature of rich financiers
   (D) All of the above

Questions 5 through 8 are based on the following passage excerpted from U.S. History For Dummies, *2nd Edition, by Steve Wiegand, copyright 2009 by Wiley Publishing, Inc. Reprinted with permission of John Wiley & Sons, Inc.*

Even before the country's inception, Americans had been a hard-drinking bunch, and the social and private costs they paid for it had been high. But on January 16, 1920, the nation undertook a "noble experiment" to rid itself of the effects of Demon Rum. It was called *Prohibition,* and it was a spectacular failure.

There is some statistical evidence that Americans drank less after Prohibition began than they did before. But overall, the ban on booze was a bad idea. For one thing, it encouraged otherwise law-abiding citizens to visit *speak-easies* where alcohol was sold illegally. The number of "speaks" in New York City at the end of the decade, for example, was probably double the number of legal saloons at the beginning.

Gangsters like "Scarface" Al Capone and George "Bugs" Moran made fortunes selling bootleg booze, and they became celebrities doing it, despite the violence that was their normal business tool. Capone's Chicago mob took in $60 million a year at its peak—and murdered more than 300 people while doing it. But bullets weren't the gangsters' only tools. They also bought off or bullied scores of federal, state, and local officials to look the other way, which only added to public disrespect for law and government.

247

Part of the disrespect for government was well deserved. Even though Congress and a string of presidents paid lip service to the idea of Prohibition to make the anti-liquor lobby happy, many of the politicians were regular customers for the bootleggers. Congress provided only 1,550 federal agents to enforce the ban throughout the entire country, and criminal penalties for bootlegging were relatively light.

5. In the first paragraph, what is meant by "noble experiment"?

   (A) Hard-drinking bunch
   (B) Demon Rum
   (C) Prohibition
   (D) The right to vote

6. What was the result of Prohibition?

   (A) Americans drank less.
   (B) Booze was banned.
   (C) Citizens visited "speak-easies."
   (D) All of the above

7. Why did the public lose respect for law and government during Prohibition?

   (A) Gangsters became celebrities.
   (B) Officials were corrupted.
   (C) People were murdered.
   (D) Fortunes were made selling booze.

8. Who were the strongest supporters of Prohibition?

   (A) Congress
   (B) A string of presidents
   (C) Politicians
   (D) The anti-liquor lobby

Questions 9 through 12 refer to the following passage, which is excerpted from the Declaration of Independence.

In every stage of these Oppressions We have Petitioned for Redress in the most humble terms: Our repeated Petitions have been answered only by repeated injury. A Prince, whose character is thus marked by every act which may define a Tyrant, is unfit to be the ruler of a free people.

Nor have We been wanting in attentions to our British brethren. We have warned them from time to time of attempts by their legislature to extend an unwarrantable jurisdiction over us. We have reminded them of the circumstances of our emigration and settlement here. We have appealed to their native justice and magnanimity, and we have conjured them by the ties of our common kindred to disavow these usurpations, which would inevitably interrupt our connections and correspondence. They too have been deaf to the voice of justice and of consanguinity. We must, therefore, acquiesce in the necessity, which denounces our Separation, and hold them, as we hold the rest of mankind, Enemies in War, in Peace Friends.

We, therefore, the Representatives of the united States of America, in General Congress, Assembled, appealing to the Supreme Judge of the world for the rectitude of our intentions, do, in the Name, and by Authority of the good People of these Colonies, solemnly publish and declare, That these United

Colonies are, and of Right ought to be Free and Independent States; that they are Absolved from all Allegiance to the British Crown, and that all political connection between them and the State of Great Britain, is and ought to be totally dissolved; and that as Free and Independent States; they have full Power to levy War; conclude Peace, contract Alliances, establish Commerce, and to do all other Acts and Things which Independent States may of right do. And for the support of this Declaration, with a firm reliance on the protection of divine Providence, we mutually pledge to each other our Lives, our Fortunes and our sacred Honor.

9. Who was "the Prince" referred to in the first paragraph?

   (A) A tyrant
   (B) King George III
   (C) A free people
   (D) The ruler

10. What grievance was NOT directed at the British government in the Declaration?

   (A) Unwarrantable jurisdiction
   (B) Emigration and settlement issues
   (C) Lack of native justice
   (D) The right to keep slaves

11. What did the Colonies hope to gain from the Declaration?

   (A) To be free and independent states
   (B) To be absolved from allegiances to the Crown
   (C) To be able to wage war
   (D) All of the above

12. What does "divine Providence" refer to in the passage?

   (A) Our Fortunes
   (B) Our sacred Honor
   (C) The will of God
   (D) Acts and Things

Questions 13 through 16 refer to the following passage excerpted from U.S. History For Dummies, *2nd Edition, by Steve Wiegand, copyright 2009 by Wiley Publishing, Inc. Reprinted with permission of John Wiley & Sons, Inc.*

One of the most immediate problems was dealing with the menace posed by German submarines, or *U-boats,* in the Atlantic. Traveling in packs, the subs sank three million tons of Allied shipping in the first half of 1942 alone. But the Allies worked out a system of convoys and developed better anti-sub tactics. Most importantly, they built far more cargo ships than the Germans could possibly sink.

In the summer of 1942, Allied planes began bombing targets inside Germany. Eventually, the bombing would take a terrible toll. In 1943, 60,000 people were killed in the city of Hamburg, and the city of Dresden was all but destroyed.

In the fall of 1942, Allied armies, under a relatively obscure American commander named Dwight D. Eisenhower, launched an attack in North Africa against Hitler's best general, Erwin Rommel. The green American troops were whipped soundly at the Kasserine Pass in Tunisia. But in a return match—while

Rommel was in Germany—a combined U.S. and British force defeated the Germans at El Alamein and drove them out of Egypt.

From Africa, the Allies invaded Sicily, and then advanced into the Italian mainland. Mussolini was overthrown and eventually executed by his own people. But the German army poured troops into the country and it took until the end of 1944 for Italy to be completely controlled.

On the Eastern Front, meanwhile, the Russian army gradually had turned the tables on the invading Germans and begun pushing them back, despite staggering civilian and military losses. And in England, the Allies, under the leadership of Eisenhower, were preparing the greatest invasion force the world had ever seen.

13. What made the U-boats so effective in the Atlantic?

    (A) They had a system of convoys.
    (B) They had anti-sub tactics.
    (C) They built more ships.
    (D) They traveled in packs.

14. When did the Allies begin bombing inside Germany?

    (A) The first half of 1942
    (B) Summer of 1942
    (C) Fall of 1942
    (D) 1943

15. Where was General Eisenhower's first victory?

    (A) Tunisia
    (B) Egypt
    (C) Kasserine Pass
    (D) El Alamein

16. What happened on the Eastern Front?

    (A) Mussolini was overthrown.
    (B) The German army poured into the country.
    (C) The Russian army pushed back the Germans.
    (D) The Allies prepared for an invasion.

2. Answers

1. **(C)** This is an example of a comprehension question. To answer this question, you must understand the main idea of the paragraph. Be careful of answers such as (A), (B), and (D), which are mentioned in the paragraph but do not convey the main idea of the paragraph. Although they do provide information contained in the paragraph, they don't summarize the main idea.

2. **(D)** To answer this application question, you must understand the results of instability in the financial sector. Choices (A), (B), and (C) provide some information concerning attempts to obtain stability, but they don't address the application of the federal government's intervention to stabilize the financial system.

3. **(B)** This is an example of an analysis question. Choices (A), (C), and (D) involve conditions—such as collapsing prices, incompetent managers, and failing banks—that demonstrated the need for new management to save the bank.

4. **(D)** This is an example of an evaluation question. Choices (A), (B), and (C) describe points of resentment between the East and the West concerning the bank, which was nicknamed "the Monster" by its opponents. The Panic of 1819 resulted in a widespread financial crisis, which was blamed on the rich Eastern financiers by the credit-dependent West. Therefore, choice (D), which includes all these factors, is the correct choice.

5. **(C)** Choices (A) and (B) may be reasons for the imposition of Prohibition, but they are not the "noble experiment" referred to in the passage. Choice (D) is not mentioned anywhere in the passage.

6. **(D)** According to the second paragraph, choices (A), (B), and (C) all were a result of Prohibition. According to statistics, Americans drank less after Prohibition. But many citizens also visited "speak-easies" to get illegal alcohol even though "booze was banned." Therefore, Choice (D) is correct.

7. **(B)** Gangsters paid off or bullied corrupt federal, state, and local officials, causing the public to lose respect for law and government. As a result, gangsters used violence as a business tool to murder people, make illegal fortunes, and become celebrities.

8. **(D)** According to the fourth paragraph, the strongest supporters of Prohibition were the anti-liquor lobby. Presidents and members of Congress supported Prohibition only to gain political points with the anti-liquor lobby. Many politicians were, in fact, customers of speak-easies. Reread that paragraph carefully; it is easy to miss this point.

9. **(B)** Although King George III also may have been referred to as "a Tyrant" or "the ruler," the formal title for the King remains the best answer. Choice (C) is incorrect.

10. **(D)** There was no mention in the passage of "the right to keep slaves." All the other choices—jurisdiction, emigration, and justice—are grievances mentioned in the passage.

11. **(D)** According to the Declaration of Independence, the Colonies demanded to be free and independent, with no connection or allegiance to the Crown, and able to wage war and secure peace—all of which are covered in choices (A), (B), and (C).

12. **(C)** "Providence" may be defined as God's will, while "divine" pertains to God. Fortunes, sacred (or holy) Honor, and Acts and Things do not convey the correct meaning.

13. **(D)** According to the passage, the German U-boats sank three million tons of Allied shipping because they "traveled in packs." A system of convoys, anti-sub tactics, and building more ships all were ways that the Allies responded to the success of the U-boats.

14. **(B)** According to the passage, Allied bombing began inside Germany in the "summer of 1942." The other choices refer to different events during the war.

15. **(D)** General Eisenhower led the Allied army to victory at El Alamein after being defeated at the Kasserine Pass in Tunisia. This victory allowed the Allies to invade Sicily after driving the Germans out of Egypt.

16. **(C)** The Russian army was able to push back the Germans despite staggering civilian and military losses on the Eastern Front. The overthrow of Mussolini and the German invasion of Italy happened on the Western Front, as did planning for the Allied invasion of France.

XI. Reasoning through Language Arts Practice Test with Answer Explanations

This practice test is not related to the GED Ready™ – The Official Practice Test, produced and distributed by GED Testing Service LLC. GED Testing Service® has not approved, authorized, endorsed, been involved in the development of, or licensed the substantive content of this practice test.

REMINDER: In this practice test, we break the content out into two sections: Section 1 tests all content and Section 2 is the extended response item. On the actual GED® test, however, the Reasoning through Language Arts (RLA) Test is divided into three sections and includes a 10-minute break as follows:

- Section 1—approximately 35 minutes (question-and-answer items)
- Section 2—45 minutes (extended response item)
- 10-minute break
- Section 3—approximately 60 minutes (question-and-answer items)

On the actual RLA Test, the overall time for Sections 1 and 3 will total 95 minutes, but there is no set number of questions. The test is set up by selecting random items from a pool of potential items. Each item has a predetermined level of difficulty and each test will have the same potential score. Your job is to complete every item to the best of your ability and not worry if you end up with a couple of items more or less than your friend who also took the test.

Remember: Unused time cannot be transferred between sections of the RLA Test.

Although you will enter your answers and write your extended responses and short answer responses on the computer during the actual GED® test, you will need to use your own paper to record your answers and responses for this Practice Test.

Try to make your behavior on this Practice Test as close as possible to the actual test conditions. Observe the time constraints.

Answer all the questions. There is no deduction for wrong answers, and you get points for each right one. Some questions are worth more than 1 point, but that information might not be readily available to you while taking the test. The important thing is to get as many correct answers as you can and guess if you have to. Unanswered items do nothing to improve your score. If you need to, guess. The more wrong answer choices you can eliminate, the better your chances of guessing the correct answer. In multiple-choice items, if you can eliminate three choices, you will have a 100 percent chance of being correct! Unfortunately, for each choice you cannot eliminate, the odds go down.

Section 1

Time: 95 Minutes—57 Questions

Directions: Choose the best answer to each question. Following the instruction for each type of layout indicated, mark your answers on a separate sheet of paper.

If a question is not standard multiple choice, the item type will be identified directly before the question.

Questions 1 through 6 refer to the following excerpt from The Anti-Slavery Crusade: A Chronicle of the Gathering Storm, *by Jesse Macy, Volume 28 in the* Chronicles of America *series (1919).*

Women were not a whit behind men in their devotion to the cause of freedom. Conspicuous among them were Sarah and Angelina Grimke, born in Charleston, South Carolina, of a slaveholding family noted for learning, refinement, and culture. Sarah was born in the same year as James G. Birney, 1792; Angelina was thirteen years younger. Angelina was the typical crusader: her sympathies from the first were with the slave. As a child she collected and concealed oil and other simple remedies so that she might steal out by night and alleviate the sufferings of slaves who had been cruelly whipped or abused. At the age of fourteen she refused to be confirmed in the Episcopal Church because the ceremony involved giving sanction to words which seemed to her untrue. Two years later her mother offered her a present of a slave girl for a servant and companion. This gift she refused to accept, for in her view the servant had a right to be free, and, as for her own needs, Angelina felt quite capable of waiting upon herself.

Of her own free will she joined the Presbyterian Church and labored earnestly with the officers of the church to induce them to espouse the cause of the slave. When she failed to secure cooperation, she decided that the church was not Christian and she therefore withdrew her membership. Her sister Sarah had gone North in 1821 and had become a member of the Society of Friends in Philadelphia. In Charleston, South Carolina, there was a Friends' meeting-house where two old Quakers still met at the appointed time and sat for an hour in solemn silence. Angelina donned the Quaker garb, joined this meeting, and for an entire year was the third of the silent worshipers. This quiet testimony, however, did not wholly satisfy her energetic nature, and when, in 1830, she heard of the imprisonment of Garrison in Baltimore, she was convinced that effective labors against slavery could not be carried on in the South. With great sorrow she determined to sever her connection with home and family and join her sister in Philadelphia. There the exile from the South poured out her soul in an Appeal to the Christian Women of the South. The manuscript was handed to the officers of the Anti-slavery Society in the city and, as they read, tears filled their eyes. The Appeal was immediately printed in large quantities for distribution in Southern States.

1. What made Angelina Grimke an unusual anti-slavery activist?
   (A) Women did not become crusaders.
   (B) She came from a privileged, slave-owning family.
   (C) She refused confirmation as an Episcopalian.
   (D) Her sister was born in the same year as James G. Bernie, another anti-slavery crusader.

2. Why did Angelina reject the gift of the slave girl?

   (A) She was opposed to slavery.
   (B) She could perfectly well look after herself.
   (C) Her religion prohibited slave owning.
   (D) She wanted her sister to have the slave instead.

Drag-and-drop

3. The second paragraph states that she joined the Presbyterian Church in hopes of convincing the church to take an anti-slavery position. After some time, when she failed to convince church leaders, she decided they were not Christian and left the church.

   In that incident, which of the following characteristics would apply to Angelina's personality? Drag the terms that apply into the boxes above.

   (To answer, write the letter of all answer choices that apply on your answer sheet.)

   (A) Determined
   (B) Opinionated
   (C) Weak
   (D) Vacillating

4. How do you know that even at an early age Angelina was upset by slavery?

   (A) She became a Quaker.
   (B) She joined her sister in Baltimore.
   (C) As a child, she snuck out at night with home remedies for beaten slaves.
   (D) All of the above

5. Which of the following actions were part of Angelina's anti-slavery efforts?

   (A) She cut off contact with her family, except her sister.
   (B) She left the Episcopalian faith.
   (C) She moved to Philadelphia.
   (D) All of the above

6. Of the various actions outlined in the passage, which had the greatest effect on the anti-slavery campaign?

   (A) Her pamphlet appealing to Christian women in the South
   (B) Her work with the Quakers
   (C) Her efforts to change the Episcopalian Church
   (D) Her cutting off ties with her family

Questions 7 through 11 refer to the following excerpt from George Bernard Shaw's play Major Barbara *(1905). In this scene, Undershaft, a cannon manufacturer, meets Lomax and Barbara, members of the Salvation Army.*

UNDERSHAFT: One moment, Mr. Lomax. I am rather interested in the Salvation Army. Its motto might be my own. Blood and Fire.

LOMAX: *(shocked)* But not your sort of blood and fire, you know.

UNDERSHAFT: My sort of blood cleanses: my sort of fire purifies.

BARBARA: So does ours. Come down tomorrow to my shelter—the West Ham Shelter—and see what we are doing. We're going to march to a great meeting in the Assembly at Mile End. Come and see the shelter and then march with us. It will do you a lot of good. Can you play anything?

UNDERSHAFT: In my youth I earned pennies, and even shillings occasionally, in the streets and in public house parlors by my natural talent for step dancing. Later on, I became a member of the Undershaft Orchestra Society, and performed passably on the tenor trombone.

LOMAX: *(scandalized, putting down the concertina)* Oh I say!

BARBARA: Many a sinner has played himself into heaven on the trombone, thanks to the Army.

LOMAX: *(to Barbara, still rather shocked)* Yes; but what about the cannon business, don't you know? *(to Undershaft)* Getting into heaven is not exactly in your line, is it?

LADY BRITOMART: Charles!!!

LOMAX: Well; but it stands to reason, don't it? The cannon business may be necessary and all that; we can't get along without cannons; but it isn't right, you know. On the other hand, there may be a certain amount of tosh about the Salvation Army—I belong to the Established Church myself—but still you can't deny that it's religion, and you can't go against religion, can you? At least unless you're downright immoral, don't you know?

Fill-in-the-blank

7. Barbara invited Undershaft to the shelter to _____. Enter your answer in the box below.

Drag-and-drop

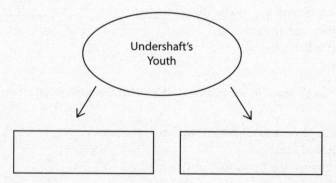

8. Drag the phrases that best describe how Undershaft survived as a youth into the boxes above.

   (To answer, write the letter of all answer choices that apply on your answer sheet.)

   (A) Playing the trombone
   (B) Step dancing in public houses
   (C) Playing in a church orchestra
   (D) Making cannons

9. What can Undershaft contribute to the band?

   (A) Trombone playing
   (B) Pennies
   (C) Marching
   (D) Step dancing

10. Why was Lomax less than thrilled by the idea of Undershaft joining the march?

   (A) Lomax could only offer pennies to the cause.
   (B) The marching band did not need a tap dancer.
   (C) Undershaft was in the "cannon business."
   (D) Undershaft was a member of the Established Church.

11. Why might Undershaft's motto be "Blood and Fire"?

   (A) He belonged to the Established Church.
   (B) He plays the trombone.
   (C) He makes cannons.
   (D) He marches for the Salvation Army.

Questions 12 through 15 refer to the following excerpt from Jack London's short story "In a Far Country" (1899).

The two shirks and chronic grumblers were Carter Weatherbee and Percy Cuthfert. The whole party complained less of its aches and pains than did either of them. Not once did they volunteer for the thousand and one petty duties of the camp. A bucket of water to be brought, an extra armful of wood to be chopped, the dishes to be washed and wiped, a search to be made through the outfit for some suddenly indispensable article—and these two effete scions of civilization discovered sprains or blisters requiring instant attention. They were the first to turn in at night, with scores of tasks yet undone; the last to turn out in the morning, when the start should be in readiness before the breakfast was begun. They were the first to fall to at meal-time, the last to have a hand in the cooking; the first to dive for a slim delicacy, the last to discover they had added to their own another man's share. If they toiled at the oars, they slyly cut the water at each stroke and allowed the boat's momentum to float up the blade. They thought nobody noticed; but their comrades swore under their breaths and grew to hate them, while Jacques Baptiste sneered openly and damned them from morning till night. But Jacques Baptiste was no gentleman.

12. Based on context, what does "scions of civilization" mean in the fourth sentence?

   (A) They were cultured men.
   (B) They were examples of civilized people.
   (C) They inherited rights to civilization.
   (D) They were products of civilization.

Drag-and-drop

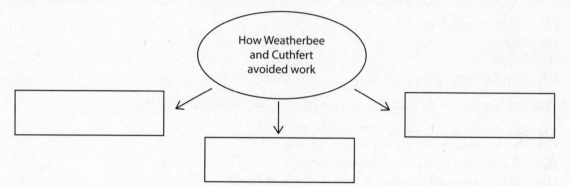

13. Drag the phrases that best describe how did Weatherbee and Cuthfert avoided work into the boxes above.

   (To answer, write the letter of all answer choices that apply on your answer sheet.)

   (A) By developing sprains or blisters
   (B) By being the first to turn in
   (C) By being busy chopping wood
   (D) By pretending to row

14. How did the rest of the party feel about the two men?

   (A) They admired them.
   (B) They hated them.
   (C) They encouraged them.
   (D) They laughed at them.

15. Which adjective best describes Weatherbee and Cuthfert?

   (A) Strong
   (B) Helpful
   (C) Lazy
   (D) Weak

Questions 16 through 20 refer to the following policy document.

   The management of Can-Learn International is vitally interested in the health and safety of its employees. Protection of employees from injury or occupational disease is a major continuing objective. Can-Learn International will make every effort to provide a safe, healthy work environment. All supervisors and workers must be dedicated to the continuing objective of reducing risk of injury.

Can-Learn International, as an employer, is ultimately responsible for worker health and safety. As President of Can-Learn International, I give you my personal promise that every reasonable precaution will be taken for the protection of workers.

The Occupational Health and Safety Act, which sets the standards for safe workplaces, is based on the internal responsibility system. This is a system of overlapping and concurrent duties of the employer, officers, directors, supervisors, and workers of Can-Learn International.

Supervisors will be held accountable for the health and safety of workers under their supervision. Supervisors are responsible for ensuring that machinery and equipment are safe and that workers work in compliance with established safe work practices and procedures. Workers must receive adequate training in their specific work tasks to protect their health and safety.

Every worker must protect his or her own health and safety by working in compliance with the law and with safe work practices and procedures established by Can-Learn International.

It is in the best interest of all parties to consider health and safety in every activity. Commitment to health and safety must form an integral part of this organization, from the president to the workers.

16. Who, within the company, is most interested in the health and safety of employees?

   (A) The workers
   (B) The union
   (C) The executive
   (D) The management

17. What is the objective of the policy?

   (A) To increase profitability
   (B) To increase productivity
   (C) To have a safe and healthy workplace
   (D) All of the above

18. Who is responsible for the safe operation of machinery?

   (A) The president
   (B) The supervisors
   (C) The directors
   (D) The workers

19. How can worker health and safety be protected?

   (A) By training workers adequately
   (B) By engaging in a responsibility system
   (C) By having concurrent duties
   (D) By complying with the law

20. What sets the standards for a safe workplace?

   (A) The Internal Responsibility System
   (B) Can-Learn International
   (C) The federal government
   (D) The Occupational Health and Safety Act

Questions 21 through 26 refer to an excerpt from John Masefield's military history, The Old Front Line *(1917).*

All that can be seen of it from the English line is a disarrangement of the enemy wire and parapet. It is a hole in the ground which cannot be seen except from quite close at hand. At first sight, on looking into it, it is difficult to believe that it was the work of man; it looks so like nature in her evil mood. It is hard to imagine that only three years ago that hill was cornfield, and the site of the chasm grew bread. After that happy time, the enemy bent his line there and made the salient a stronghold, and dug deep shelters for his men in the walls of his trenches; the marks of the dugouts are still plain in the sides of the pit. Then, on the 1st of July, 42 when the explosion was to be a signal for the attack, and our men waited in the trenches for the spring, the belly of the chalk was heaved, and chalk, clay, dugouts, gear, and enemy, went up in a dome of blackness full of pieces, and spread aloft like a toadstool, and floated, and fell down.

From the top of the Hawthorn Ridge, our soldiers could see a great expanse of chalk downland, though the falling of the hill kept them from seeing the enemy's position. That lay on the slope of the ridge, somewhere behind the wire, quite out of sight from our lines. Looking out from our front line at this salient, our men saw the enemy wire almost as a skyline. Beyond this line, the ground dipped towards Beaumont Hamel (which was quite out of sight in the valley) and rose again sharply in the steep bulk of Beaucourt spur. Beyond this lonely spur, the hills ranked and ran, like the masses of a moor, first the high ground above Miraumont, and beyond that the high ground of the Loupart Wood, and away to the east the bulk that makes the left bank of the Ancre River Valley made all that marshy meadow like a forest. Looking out on all this, the first thought of the soldier was that here he could really see something of the enemy's ground.

It is true, that from this hill-top much land, then held by the enemy, could be seen, but very little that was vital to the enemy could be observed. His lines of supply and support ran in ravines which we could not see; his batteries lay beyond crests, his men were in hiding places. Just below us on the lower slopes of this Hawthorn Ridge he had one vast hiding place which gave us a great deal of trouble. This was a gully or ravine, about five hundred yards long, well within his position, running (roughly speaking) at right angles with his front line. Probably it was a steep and deep natural fold made steeper and deeper by years of cultivation. It is from thirty to forty feet deep, and about as much across at the top; it has abrupt sides, and thrusts out two forks to its southern side. These forks give it the look of a letter *Y* upon the maps, for which reason both the French and ourselves called the place the "Ravin en Y" or "Y Ravine." Part of the southernmost fork was slightly open to observation from our lines; the main bulk of the gully was invisible to us, except from the air.

21. What is all that can be seen from the English line?

    (A) A cornfield
    (B) An abandoned mine shaft
    (C) A dome of blackness
    (D) A disarrangement of the enemy wire and parapet

22. Why could the soldiers not see the enemy's position?

    (A) The enemy had retreated.
    (B) The falling of the hill obstructed their vision.
    (C) The enemy was too far away.
    (D) It was too dark.

Fill-in-the-blank

23. In a phrase, describe how much of what was vital to the enemy could be seen from the English lines. Enter your answer in the box below.

24. Why was the gully called Y Ravine by the soldiers?

   (A) The gully looked like a *Y* on a map.
   (B) The gully before it had been named X Ravine.
   (C) Soldiers like to give geographical features familiar names.
   (D) The enemy commander's name started with *Y.*

Drag-and-drop

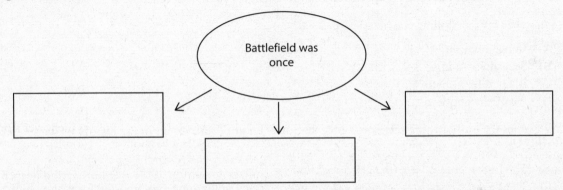

25. Drag that terms that, according to this passage, would have applied to the battlefield before the war into the boxes above.

   (To answer, write the letter of all answer choices that apply on your answer sheet.)

   (A) a cornfield
   (B) a valley
   (C) Ravines
   (D) Vast plains

Questions 26 through 31 refer to an excerpt from Criminology For Dummies, *by Steven Briggs, copyright 2009 by Wiley Publishing, Inc. Reprinted with permission of John Wiley & Sons, Inc.*

In 2006, former Enron CEO Jeffrey Skilling was convicted of securities fraud and conspiracy, among other charges, and was sentenced to over 24 years in prison. (You didn't think I could talk about white-collar crime without mentioning Enron, did you?) For many people in the corporate world, this case was a signal event, marking a change in historic sentencing practices for white-collar criminals.

Previously, most people probably believed that the more common treatment of white-collar criminals resembled what Martha Stewart received for her convictions in 2004: five months in a federal "country club" and five months of home detention.

This common viewpoint is important because one significant reason why society imprisons criminals is to deter other people from committing similar crimes. If the risk of serious punishment isn't real, people may be more likely to run the risk of conviction, especially when the payoff is millions of dollars in profit.

But there are legitimate reasons why white-collar criminals have received relatively light sentences in the past. Perhaps most importantly, such cases are often very difficult to prove. Sometimes law enforcement agencies make plea agreements to resolve cases instead of committing massive resources to lengthy and costly trials that may have uncertain outcomes. In addition, white-collar crimes often involve significant financial harm to victims, so prosecutors may be willing to negotiate away jail time in exchange for making the defendant pay money back to victims.

Sometimes the prosecutor doesn't agree to a short jail sentence, but the judge imposes the sentence on her own. One significant theory of punishment holds that jail or prison should be reserved only for people too dangerous to remain in society. The argument goes that, because white-collar criminals usually commit financial crimes, society shouldn't spend a lot of money incarcerating them. Instead, jails should house people who are violent risks to society. Judges who subscribe to this theory may also believe that the damage to the professional reputation of a white-collar criminal is sufficient punishment in itself, without sentencing the criminal to a lengthy prison sentence.

26. What was Jeffrey Skilling convicted of in 2006?

   (A) Impersonation
   (B) Securities fraud
   (C) Blue-collar crime
   (D) All of the above

27. Why does the author think the Enron prosecution is an important event in the history of white-collar crime?

   (A) The Enron crimes were on such a vast scale.
   (B) The Enron convictions resulted in long prison terms, something very unusual for white-collar crimes.
   (C) The courts did not take any plea bargains.
   (D) All of the above

28. Where did Martha Stewart NOT serve her sentence?

   (A) In a penitentiary
   (B) In a federal "country club"
   (C) In home detention
   (D) In a rehab center

29. According to the passage, what is one reason society imprisons criminals?

   (A) To fight crime
   (B) To punish criminals
   (C) To deter others
   (D) To gain a payoff

30. Why have white-collar criminals received light sentences?

   (A) Because their crimes are difficult to prove
   (B) Because they make plea bargains
   (C) To avoid costly trials
   (D) All of the above

31. Based on this passage, what kind of criminals receive the lightest penalties?

   (A) White-collar criminals
   (B) Violent criminals
   (C) Professional career criminals
   (D) Repeat offenders

Questions 32 through 36 refer to the following excerpt from the short story "Patricia" by Murray Shukyn (2010).

Patricia walks into the room. Furtively, she looks around, goes to the window and peers into the darkness. Relieved at what she doesn't see, she quickly leaves the room. Returning with a bright object in her hand, she places the nickel-plated revolver on the table, carefully inserts six bullets into the cylinder, clicks it shut, and nervously replaces it on the table at the ready.

Never again will she be a victim. Never again will that drunken lout strike her. Never again will she have to plaster makeup on herself to hide the bruises and welts resulting from a "discussion" with her live-in boyfriend.

Before he left, he gave her a preview of what was to come, and the stinging pain was all too fresh in her mind. She stared at her solution glistening in the light of the lamp, enticing her to pick it up just to feel the justice in the metal.

As she reached for it, she saw the headlights in the driveway. Her finger closed on the trigger as the door opened.

Never, ever again, she promised herself.

32. How would you characterize Patricia's state of mind as she waits?

   (A) Tranquil
   (B) Impatient
   (C) Determined
   (D) Stubborn

33. Why is the word *discussion* in quotation marks?

   (A) Patricia's boyfriend said, "discussion."
   (B) The author wants to emphasize the talks Patricia and her boyfriend had.
   (C) A discussion would not produce bruises and welts.
   (D) None of the above

34. What effect did the "preview" referred to in paragraph 3 have on Patricia?

   (A) It made her look forward to the continuation of the discussion.
   (B) It had no effect. She just patiently waited for his return.
   (C) It gave her time to polish her revolver.
   (D) It made her determined to stop the cycle of abuse.

Drag-and-drop

Order of Events

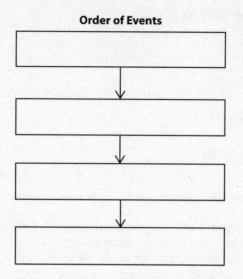

35. Drag the events into the boxes above so they are in chronological order.

    (To answer, write the letters of the answer choices in chronological order on your answer sheet.)

    (A) Headlights in the driveway
    (B) Patricia returns to room with revolver
    (C) Her boyfriend hit her
    (D) She loads the revolver

36. Why did Patricia promise herself, "Never, ever again"?

    (A) She was uncomfortable when her boyfriend went out alone.
    (B) The headlights coming up the driveway disturbed her sleep.
    (C) She didn't like to interrupt conversations.
    (D) She had had enough abuse and wanted it stopped.

Questions 37 through 40 refer to an excerpt from the novel All You Can Eat *by Murray Shukyn (2008).*

    This time I had to enter the bank and wait in line. The line was not too long, and I relaxed, looking at the poster decorating the wall. The interior of the bank was stark. There was one poster on every wall that didn't have an opening in it. Walls with doors or windows were bare. The tellers hid behind this huge counter with computers at each location. In front of the counter was a serpentine lineup device that made you cross parallel to the counter several times before arriving at the opening when you came face to face with a teller. It looked so sturdy that I just walked back and forth in front of the counter like a demented wanderer until I came to the end of the line. Within minutes, a young teller said, "Next," and it was my turn to do business with the bank.
    "What can I do for you today?" teller Jon inquired.
    "I lost my bank card," I said.
    "I'm sorry to hear that," Jon chirped in.
    "I need a new one," I answered.

"That makes sense," Jon added.

"What do I have to do to get one?" I asked.

"Let's see if you're known to this branch," he said, going over to one of the side offices and returning with a frown on his face. "Sorry, no one at the branch knows you."

"I've been dealing here for years," I said, getting slightly annoyed.

"But how often do you come inside the branch?" Jon asked.

"Oh, this is the first time," I said. "I use the ATM and the Internet."

"But those don't require real people. If everyone did that, I would be out of a job. Do you want me to be unemployed?" Jon asked.

"No, of course not. I just want a replacement bank card," I said. "The person at the call center said that you would give me one."

"Of course, they would. Do you know where this bank's call center is located? What do they know about what happens in a branch halfway around the world?" Jon said, slightly peeved.

"I just want to get a new bank card so that I can take money out of my account and take my girl-friend for coffee," I said.

"Some big spender. Why don't you take her out to dinner? There's this fabulous restaurant right around the corner. They do all their banking here. Come right up to the counter, call me by name, and carry on their business. Everyone knows them," Jon said.

37. Why would the narrator wander back and forth in front of the counter before speaking to a teller?

   (A) He was nervous.
   (B) He was waiting for his favorite teller.
   (C) All the tellers were busy.
   (D) The lineup was controlled by a serpentine device.

38. How would you describe the banking service the narrator receives?

   (A) Fast and pleasant
   (B) Impersonal and distant
   (C) Careless
   (D) None of the above

39. Why did Jon like the people from the restaurant right around the corner?

   (A) They come into the bank and call Jon by his name.
   (B) They serve good food.
   (C) Their prices are reasonable.
   (D) They bring Jon lunch when it's very busy.

40. Why would Jon be peeved about the location of the call center?

   (A) Jon applied for a job at the call center.
   (B) The call center is understaffed because of where it's located.
   (C) It's located halfway around the world.
   (D) Jon's manager likes call centers.

Questions 41 through 43 refer to the following business letter.

THE TRAINING RENEWAL FOUNDATION
750 Millway Ave., Unit 6
Concord, MA 12345

The Michael Di Base Charitable Foundation Inc.
70 Tigi Court, Suite 102
Vaughan, NY 54321

Dear Sir or Madam:

(i)_____ for your invitation to submit an initial letter of inquiry. The Training Renewal Foundation (TRF) is a nonprofit charitable organization located in the City of Vaughan. (ii)_____ mandate has been to serve disadvantaged youth and other displaced workers seeking skills, qualifications, and employment opportunities.

During 2006, TRF has joined with the Region of York Social Services & Housing Department to create the Employment Assistance and Retention Network (iii)_____ pilot project.

Foreign-trained professionals, trades people, (iv)_____ assisted in finding employment through the Community Development Investment Fund. Pre-employment training (v)_____ interpersonal skills, goal-setting, problem-solving, résumé preparation, computer literacy, educational upgrading, and parenting skills. Transferable (vi)_____ to achieve employment. To assist participants and their families, home computers, Internet connections, and telephone access are provided.

(vii)_____ 50 participants and their families have been assisted by EARN. A number of social assistance recipients (viii)_____ to secure employment. Others are pursuing (ix)_____

Thank you for considering the Training Renewal Foundation in your inaugural grant-making process.

Yours sincerely,

Dale E. Shuttleworth, Ph.D.
Executive Director

Drop-down

41. The paragraphs below are incomplete. For each blank, choose the answer choice that best completes the sentence.

(i) _____ for your invitation to submit an initial letter of inquiry. The Training Renewal Foundation (TRF) is a nonprofit charitable organization located in the City of Vaughan. (ii) _____ mandate has been to serve disadvantaged youth and other displaced workers seeking skills, qualifications, and employment opportunities.

During 2006, TRF has joined with the Region of York Social Services & Housing Department to create the Employment Assistance and Retention Network (iii) _____ pilot project.

Blank (i)	Blank (ii)	Blank (iii)
(A) I am writing to offer my gratitude	**(A)** Since it's incorporation in 1996, TRF's	**(A)** (EARN)
(B) Thank you	**(B)** Since its incorporation in 1996 TRF's	**(B)** EARN
(C) Thanks a bunch	**(C)** Since its incorporation in 1996, TRF's	**(C)** (EAaRN)
(D) Thanking you	**(D)** Since its incorporation in 1996, TRFs	**(D)** (earn)

Drop-down

42. The paragraph below is incomplete. For each blank, choose the answer choice that best completes the sentence.

Foreign-trained professionals, trades people, (iv) _____ assisted in finding employment through the Community Development Investment Fund. Pre-employment training (v) _____ interpersonal skills, goal-setting, problem-solving, résumé preparation, computer literacy, educational upgrading, and parenting skills. Transferable (vi) _____ to achieve employment. To assist participants and their families, home computers, Internet connections, and telephone access are provided.

Blank (iv)	Blank (v)	Blank (vi)
(A) entrepreneurs and managers are	**(A)** include confidence building,	**(A)** skills are assessed, accreditation is secured,
(B) entrepreneurs, and managers is	**(B)** including confidence building,	**(B)** skills are assessed, and accreditation secured
(C) entrepreneurs, managers are	**(C)** includes confidence building,	**(C)** skills are assessed and accreditation is secured
(D) entrepreneurs, and managers are	**(D)** includes confident building,	**(D)** skills are assessed and accreditation secured

Drop-down

43. The paragraph below is incomplete. For each blank, choose the answer choice that best completes the sentence.

(vii) _____ 50 participants and their families have been assisted by EARN. A number of social assistance recipients (viii) _____ to secure employment. Others are pursuing (ix) _____

Blank (vii)	Blank (viii)	Blank (ix)
(A) To date	**(A)** have already been able	**(A)** the following new certification; further education; or alternate employment opportunities.
(B) To date,	**(B)** have been already able	**(B)** the following: new certification; further education; or alternate employment opportunities.
(C) Too date,	**(C)** have been able already	**(C)** the following: new certification, further education, or alternate employment opportunities.
(D) Two date	**(D)** already have been able	**(D)** the following: New certification; Further education; or Alternate employment opportunities.

Questions 44 through 51 refer to the following passage regarding Training Interns in Education (T.I.E.).

(1) T.I.E. participants are educators from a variety of cultural backgrounds. (2) There selected through consideration of a wide range of criteria. (3) This includes the following examination of their academic documents; relevant experience in teaching or working with children and adolescents; and any references that they can provide.

(4) Intensive individual interviews were conducted with each potential participants to determine both their psychological suitability for working in schools and the level of their determination to succeed in the course. (5) Also they were questioned at length about their training and experience.

(6) The T.I.E. investigation of the successful participant's varied backgrounds found that, while academic training and teaching experiences differed in a variety of ways, the substance was very similar in terms of rigorously high expectations.

(7) The curriculum for the T.I.E. programme has been designed and modified to meet the unique needs of the participants. (8) The guiding aim was to give the participants a full understanding of the educational system and the proficiency to function in a culturally diverse schooling climate.

44. Sentence 1: T.I.E. participants are educators from a variety of cultural backgrounds.

Which change should be made to Sentence 1?

(A) Change *are* to *were*.
(B) Change *cultural* to *cultured*.
(C) Change *backgrounds* to *background*.
(D) No change required.

45. Sentence 2: <u>There selected</u> through consideration of a wide range of criteria.

 Which is the best way to write the underlined portion of Sentence 2?

 (A) Their selected
 (B) They are selected
 (C) Who are selected
 (D) No change required.

46. Sentence 3: This includes the following examination of their academic documents; relevant experience in teaching or working with children and adolescents; and any references that they can provide.

 Which punctuation changes should be made to Sentence 3?

 (A) Change the semicolon after *documents* to a comma.
 (B) Place a colon after *following* and replace the semicolons with commas.
 (C) Change the semicolon after *adolescents* to a comma.
 (D) Place a comma after *teaching*.

47. Sentence 4: Intensive individual interviews were conducted with each potential participants to determine both their psychological suitability for working in schools and the level of their determination to succeed in the course.

 Which change should be made to Sentence 4?

 (A) Change *were* to *was*.
 (B) Change the first *their* to *they're*.
 (C) Change *participants* to *participant* and change *their* to *his or her* in both places.
 (D) Change *course* to *coarse*.

48. Sentence 5: <u>Also they were questioned</u> at length about their training and experience.

 Which is the best way to write the underlined portion of Sentence 5?

 (A) They also were questioned
 (B) They were also questioned
 (C) They were questioned also
 (D) Also were they questioned

49. Sentence 6: The T.I.E. investigation of the <u>successful participant's varied backgrounds found that, while</u> academic training and teaching experiences differed in a variety of ways, the substance was very similar in terms of rigorously high expectations.

 Which is the best way to write the underlined portion of Sentence 6?

 (A) successful participants' varied backgrounds found that, while
 (B) successful participant's varied backgrounds found that while
 (C) successful participant's varied backgrounds found that; while
 (D) successful participants' varied background found that, while

50. Sentence 7: The curriculum for the T.I.E. programme has been designed and modified to meet the unique needs of the participants.

   Which correction should be made to Sentence 7?

   (A) Change *curriculum* to *curricula*.
   (B) Change *has been* to *had been*.
   (C) Change *programme* to *program*.
   (D) Change *needs* to *need*.

51. Sentence 8: The guiding aim was to give the participants a full understanding of the educational system and the proficiency to function in a culturally diverse schooling climate.

   What changes should be made to Sentence 8?

   (A) Change *a full* to *awful*.
   (B) Change *system* to *sistem*.
   (C) Change *to function* to *functioning*.
   (D) Change *was* to *is*.

Questions 52 through 57 refer to an adaptation of an excerpt from Green Business Practices For Dummies *by Lisa Swallow, copyright 2009 by Wiley Publishing, Inc. Reprinted with permission of John Wiley & Sons, Inc.*

(1) In response to the forest of chain stores peppering the landscape of any U.S. town in which people outnumber livestock an exploding number of self-described independent businesses are popping up. (2) Those who have weathered chain-store mania are banding together to crate their own retail force to be reckoned with. (3) From community groups to whole regional areas, hometown teams are committed to revitalizing their local economies. (4) In fact, independent business alliances across the U.S. are predicting that buy-local movements will make as big of an impact as buy-organic movements has in recent years. (5) Buying local can seem like a rather quaint idea, much like typewriters and poodle skirts. (6) Au contraire it's more than a movement; it's a revolution—an opportunity that's loaded with potential and serves as a key component of a sustainable business model.

52. Sentence 1: In response to the forest of chain stores peppering the landscape of any U.S. town in which people outnumber livestock an exploding number of self-described independent businesses are popping up.

   Which punctuation should be added to Sentence 1?

   (A) Add a comma after *response*.
   (B) Add a comma after *livestock*.
   (C) Remove the periods after *U* and *S*.
   (D) Place a comma after *self-described*.

53. Sentence 2: Those who have weathered chain-store mania are banding together to crate their own retail force to be reckoned with.

    Which change is required in Sentence 2?

    (A) Change *weathered* to *whethered.*
    (B) Change *chain-store* to *chainstore.*
    (C) Change *retail* to *retale.*
    (D) Change *crate* to *create.*

54. Sentence 3: From community groups to whole regional areas, hometown teams are committed to revitalizing their local economies.

    Which change is required in Sentence 3?

    (A) Change *economies* to *economy's.*
    (B) Change *are* to *were.*
    (C) Change *revitalizing* to *revitalising.*
    (D) No change required.

55. Sentence 4: In fact, independent business alliances across the U.S. are predicting that buy-local movements will make as big of an impact as buy-organic movements has in recent years.

    Which change should be made to Sentence 4?

    (A) Remove the comma after *fact.*
    (B) Change *alliances* to *alliants.*
    (C) Change *has* to *have.*
    (D) Remove the hyphen between *buy* and *local.*

56. Sentence 5: Buying local can seem like a rather quaint idea, much like typewriters and poodle skirts.

    Which change should be made to Sentence 5?

    (A) Remove the comma after *idea.*
    (B) Change *can* to *may.*
    (C) Change *typewriters* to *typeriters.*
    (D) No change required.

57. Sentence 6: Au contraire it's more than a movement; it's a revolution—an opportunity that's loaded with potential and serves as a key component of a sustainable business model.

    How can Sentence 6 be improved?

    (A) Place an exclamation point after *contraire* and capitalize the first *it's.*
    (B) Change the semicolon after *movement* to a comma.
    (C) Remove the apostrophe from the second *it's.*
    (D) Change *that's* to *thats.*

IF YOU FINISH BEFORE TIME IS CALLED, CHECK YOUR WORK ON THIS SECTION ONLY. DO NOT WORK ON ANY OTHER SECTION IN THE TEST.

Section 2

Time: 45 Minutes

Directions: On the following page, you'll find two articles that present arguments for and against laws regarding cyberbullying. One favors the approach of turning cyberbullying into a criminal offense, while the other argues such a step is not necessary. You have 45 minutes to write an essay response. Analyze both positions, explaining which argument is better supported. It does not matter whether you agree or disagree with the position. Be sure to use specific evidence from the two articles, and from your own life experience and knowledge, to support your response. Pay attention to the use of proper essay style, correct use of language and grammar, and presenting a properly ordered essay.

- You must write only on the assigned topic.
- You have 45 minutes to write on your assigned essay topic. This time is only for the extended response item (the essay). You may not return to Section 1 of the RLA Test.

Your essay will be scored according to its overall effectiveness. The evaluation will be based on the following features:

- Well-focused main points
- Clear organization
- Specific development of your ideas
- Control of sentence structure, punctuation, grammar, word choice, and spelling

Remember: You must complete all three sections in order to receive a score on the RLA Test.

To avoid having to repeat the RLA Test, be sure to observe the following rules:

- Before you begin writing, jot notes or outline your essay. On your test day, an erasable noteboard will be provided at the test site.
- For your final essay, use specific evidence to back up your position.
- Reread your final essay to ensure that it is clear, well-ordered, and grammatically correct.
- Write on the assigned topic. If you write on a topic other than the one assigned, you won't receive a score for the RLA Test.
- Stay on the assigned topic. If you drift off-topic, your score will be drastically reduced.
- Write your trial essay for this Practice Test on a separate sheet of lined paper. On the actual test, you will have to write the essay in the window provided on the computer screen; rough work on the noteboard will not be scored. It is a basic word processor, but does not include spelling or grammar checkers. You need to spot your errors yourself and fix as many as possible within the time limit.

Remember, your score on all three sections of the RLA Test will be combined for a final score. If that score is not a passing one, you will have to take the RLA Test over again. While it is possible to pass the RLA Test by doing brilliantly on just one or two of the sections, it is not likely. Study carefully.

Article 1: Cyberbullying Should Be a Criminal Offense

There is a great deal of evidence that cyberbullying is a serious issue. Studies show nearly a quarter of all teens have been bullied online. That has led to depression, failure at school, and feelings of helplessness and social isolation. In some infamous incidents, it has led to suicide. Current laws seem incapable of dealing with the issue, so the only solution is clearer and stronger laws specifically crafted to deal with this issue.

Cyberbullying is a subset of bullying. It uses communications technology to spread malicious rumors, demean, degrade, and harass victims in every way possible. Instead of physical attacks, these are emotional attacks based on some perception of blemish in an individual. The attacks eventually escalate from insults and harassment to threats of physical violence. Essentially, the victims are isolated and excluded from the community of their peers.

The ganging up by bullies is relentless, and the use of social media makes it inescapable. Victims all complain that there is no way to escape. Bullies tell their victims they are ugly, useless losers. They are told to drink bleach and die. They are taunted and urged to commit suicide. In more than 40 cases in recent years, the taunting and social isolation, combined with continuous harassment, have led to suicide. That should not be tolerated.

Cyberbullies pursue their victims by taking advantage of the Internet's anonymity. Some bullies attack directly, but others use fake accounts to mount their attacks. When one account is closed, they simply open a new one. Social media sites do close down some bullies, only to have the same bullies return on a new page. The anonymity of the Internet makes tracking down the bullies difficult, especially since media companies and ISPs are notoriously reluctant to reveal information about their customers. Police are also reluctant to become involved, arguing that there is no physical harm, no quantifiable damage, making it difficult to prove criminal activity.

Anti-bullying campaigns have not worked. Parents of bullies seem oblivious to the problem or unwilling or unable to control their children.

Some activities, harassment to threats of physical violence, are already criminal. Individuals could sue, based on libel and slander laws. But generally, most victims have neither the ability nor the financial resources to fight back at that level. The only solution is the criminal justice system. We must provide new, stricter laws to overcome the police's reluctance to act.

The only solution is for police to take action when victims file complaints. The state has the wherewithal, and the moral and ethical duty, to defend the weak. We need to give them the tools—the laws—to help them act.

Article 2: There Is No Need for Special Cyberbullying Laws

The essence of cyberbullying is harassment: insulting a target and pursuing that person with constant taunts and other demeaning attacks. However, insults and demeaning comments are not criminal. Is repeatedly calling someone a slut or loser acceptable? Certainly not. However, it is not a crime.

Unlike face-to-face bullying and the after-school fistfight, cyberbullies rarely physically hurt their victims. Most people are able to ignore it and get on with their lives.

Sadly, there have been infamous cases in which cyberbullying is linked with self-harm and even suicide of the victims. However, we need to be careful in assessing what happened. Correlation does not necessarily equate to causation. The victim may have underlying psychiatric or social issues. The cyberbullying may not be the sole cause of someone's suicide.

We must also be careful before we trample on the rights of free speech. Name-calling may not be pretty, but is it a crime? Telling someone to go hang themselves may be crude and tasteless, but it is not a crime.

Cyberbullying, and indeed all bullying, does become a crime when demeaning attacks are race- or religion-based. These are classified as hate crimes and are a criminal offense under existing laws. In such cases, no additional laws are required. In several cases that led to suicide, other issues were involved as well, including rape and extortion. Those are crimes and can already be dealt with by the criminal justice system, using laws already in place. No further laws are needed.

Cyberbullying is seen in terms of what it does to a person's sense of self-worth or reputation. Access to social media exacerbates the issue, increasing the anger against the perpetrators and the media. However, the media are not responsible for the bullying. Additional laws forcing social media sites to reveal, on request, the identities of their members are a gross invasion of privacy. If there is a reasonable belief that there is a crime being committed, a warrant can obtain the perpetrators' identities. No further laws are needed.

If someone feels that the name-calling, the taunting, and the threats go beyond acceptable, there are legal remedies available. Cyberbullying is already a crime under different headings: defamation, threatening, criminal harassment, even obscenity laws. In one case, posting images of an underage rape victim, also a victim of cyberbullying, resulted in charges of possession and distribution of child pornography.

One overlooked issue is that many cyberbullies are themselves minors. Perhaps the best control over such cyberbullies is the parents. They have the power to turn off access to social media and deal with their minor children. The fact that some parents do not act to stop their children from victimizing others is still not against the law. No law exists against bad parenting. Rather than adding more victims and creating more criminals, parental intervention should be emphasized. Social pressure on reluctant parents is the best tool. Make it unacceptable for parents to sit idly by.

We must balance individual rights against laws trying to control behavior. When cyberbullying crosses the line, there are criminal and civil remedies already in place. By using those effectively, we can control the issue. There is no need for additional laws.

IF YOU FINISH BEFORE TIME IS CALLED, CHECK YOUR WORK ON THIS SECTION ONLY. DO NOT WORK ON ANY OTHER SECTION IN THE TEST.

Answer Key

1. (B)	14. (B)	29. (C)	44. (D)
2. (A)	15. (C)	30. (D)	45. (B)
3. (A), (B)	16. (D)	31. (A)	46. (B)
4. (C)	17. (C)	32. (C)	47. (C)
5. (D)	18. (B)	33. (C)	48. (B)
6. (A)	19. (A)	34. (D)	49. (A)
7. march	20. (D)	35. (C), (B), (D), (A)	50. (C)
8. (A), (B)	21. (D)	36. (D)	51. (D)
9. (A)	22. (B)	37. (D)	52. (B)
10. (C)	23. very little	38. (D)	53. (D)
11. (C)	24. (A)	39. (A)	54. (D)
12. (D)	25. (A), (B), (C)	40. (C)	55. (C)
13. (A), (B), (D)	26. (B)	41. (B), (C), (A)	56. (B)
	27. (D)	42. (D), (C), (C)	57. (A)
	28. (D)	43. (B), (A), (C)	

Answer Explanations

Section 1

1. **(B)** The first two choices apply to some extent, and the third is true in itself. This is an instance where you need to pick the most correct answer, which is (B): She came from a privileged, slave-owning, family. The fact that she refused to be confirmed as an Episcopalian may or may not have had something to do with her anti-slavery sentiments, but that is never stated in the text (C). That her sister was born at the same time as another individual who became an anti-slavery crusader (D) is irrelevant. Her gender made her position unusual (A), but it is not the most important point.

2. **(A)** You can start by eliminating the obviously wrong options. There's nothing stated in the text to suggest that she wanted her sister to have the slave instead (D), nor that she belong to a religion that opposed slavery (C). Of the two remaining choices, you need to select the most important. In this case the most important option is the fact that she simply opposed slavery. The correct answer is (A).

3. **(A) and (B)** Of the terms—*determined, opinionated, weak, vacillating*—only the first two, *determined* and *opinionated,* apply.

4. **(C)** The proof lies in the fact that she snuck out at night with home remedies for injured slaves. The other suggestions happened once she was an adult, and therefore are irrelevant to this question.

5. **(D)** All of these activities were part of the Angelina's life as she was determined to fight against slavery.

6. **(A)** According to the text, her most effective action as an anti-slavery campaigner was writing a pamphlet appealing to Southern Christian women to join the fight against slavery.

7. **march** Barbara was recruiting people to march to the meeting and saw Undershaft as a candidate.

8. **(A) and (B)** Undershaft had an impoverished youth because he had to step-dance for pennies to survive. Like buskers or street performers today, back then, poor children danced as entertainment for people who might throw them pennies. This way of living was a bit above begging in that the children provided some entertainment for the money donated. He also played the trombone. There is no indication that the orchestra had any connections to a church. Making cannons is his adult career.

9. **(A)** Undershaft was a trombone player who could contribute his musical talents to the marching band. Pennies (B), marching (C), or step dancing (D) aren't contributions to the band.

10. **(C)** Lomax criticizes Undershaft for his work with that "cannon business." The fact that Undershaft could offer only pennies to the cause (A) and tap dance (B) may have mattered, but the main sticking point for Lomax was "that cannon business." That Undershaft was a member of the Established Church (D) is irrelevant because Lomax himself is a member.

11. **(C)** Undershaft's motto could be "Blood and Fire" because he is involved with "that cannon business." Cannons are used to kill people in war. Belonging to the church (A), playing the trombone (B), and marching (D) aren't related to blood and fire.

12. **(D)** In this context, the phrase "scions of civilization" means *the sons of,* or *products of, civilization.* Since the other members of the party were angry with these men because they rarely helped and frequently complained, the phrase also suggests that the product of civilization is weakness.

13. **(A), (B), and (D)** The author uses choices (A), (B), and (D) to describe Weatherbee and Cuthfert's behavior to avoid work. Choice (C) is wrong, since they never chopped wood.

14. **(B)** Because of Weatherbee and Cuthfert's behavior, the author tells us that the party hated the two men.

15. **(C)** According to the passage, the best adjective to describe the two men would be *lazy*. They also may have been weak, but the passage offers no evidence to substantiate it.

16. **(D)** The document states that "the management" is interested in the health and safety of employees. The other choices mentioned may feel the same way, but choice (D) is the best answer.

17. **(C)** The objective of the policy is to ensure a "safe, healthy work environment." Choices (A) and (B) are not relevant.

18. **(B)** The passage tells us that the supervisors have the major responsibility for the safe operation of machinery. The other choices—president (A), directors (C), and workers (D)—don't have direct responsibility.

19. **(A)** According to the passage, health and safety can be protected if the workers receive "adequate training."

20. **(D)** The standards are set by the Occupational Health and Safety Act.

21. **(D)** The first line states this answer. Although (A) and (C) are mentioned in the passage, neither is the best answer to the question.

22. **(B)** The first sentence of the second paragraph outlines the answer. The other choices are not mentioned in the passage.

23. **very little** The best phrase to describe what could be seen from the English lines is one directly from the passage: "very little." You can find the answer in the first sentence of paragraph 3: "It is true, that from this hill-top much land, then held by the enemy, could be seen, but very little that was vital to the enemy could be observed."

24. **(A)** The passage states that the ravine or gully looked like a *Y* on the map.

25. **(A), (B), and (C)** According to the passage, the battlefield was once a valley and cornfields. Part of it was ravines. There were no vast plains.

26. **(B)** The passage states that Skilling was convicted of "securities fraud." The other choices are not found in the passage.

27. **(D)** According to the passage, white-collar crimes were not usually punished with lengthy prison sentences (B). Usually the courts accepted plea bargains involving restitution and short prison terms. In this instance, because of the vast nature of the crime involved (A), the courts neither accepted nor offered plea bargains (C), and unusually long, harsh sentences were imposed.

28. **(D)** Martha Stewart did not serve her sentence in a rehab center. The other choices might be used to identify where she did serve her time.

29. **(C)** The passage states that society imprisons criminals to deter crime. Society may imprison criminals to fight crime and to punish, but these choices are not mentioned in the passage.

30. **(D)** In the passage, choices (A), (B), and (C) are all given as reasons for light sentences.

31. **(A)** White-collar criminals are treated more leniently than those who commit any other type of crime. The passage explains this treatment by stating that harsher penalties should be reserved for violent (B) and repeat offenders (D). Professional career criminals (C) are not mentioned in the passage.

32. **(C)** From the description of her feelings in the passage, especially in the last line, it is clear that Patricia was determined. Choices (B) and (D) may have been part of her state of mind at one time or another, but there is no indication of either idea in the passage.

33. **(C)** The interaction between Patricia and her boyfriend must have been violent to produce bruises and welts.

34. **(D)** The preview made her determined to stop it in any way that she could. The other choices might have been acceptable in another passage, but they have little relationship to this one.

35. **(C), (B), (D), (A)** The first event was her boyfriend hitting her—the "preview" of the physical abuse that was still to come. Patricia returns with the revolver, loads it, and then sees the headlights.

36. **(D)** Patricia had had enough of the abuse, as is indicated in the passage, and she wanted to end it forever.

37. **(D)** The lineup was controlled by a serpentine device according to the first paragraph in the passage. The other choices are not mentioned in the passage, although they might or might not be true. You must answer the questions using only the information in the passage.

38. **(D)** The service Jon provides to the narrator is certainly not fast and pleasant (A), nor is it impersonal and distant (B), or careless (C). If anything, it could be called confrontational or disdainful. In this instance, the correct answer is (D), none of the above.

39. **(A)** In the passage, Jon, the teller, makes a point of saying that the people from the restaurant come into the branch and call him by name when they get to the counter.

40. **(C)** The call center is located halfway around the world and that peeves Jon, although the exact reason for this is not given in the passage. The remaining choices are not mentioned in the passage.

41. **(B), (C), and (A)** For blank i, the simplest choice is the best one, *Thank you;* the subject, *I,* is understood. Choice (A), *I am writing to offer my gratitude,* is unnecessarily verbose (it is obvious that you are *writing* and *to offer my gratitude* is unnecessarily wordy); choice (C), *Thanks a bunch,* is too informal for a business letter; and choice (D), *Thanking you,* causes the sentence to not have a subject, making it a fragment (who is doing the thanking?). For blank ii, choice (C) is correct; the possessive form, *its,* is correctly used (*it's* is the contraction of *it is*), there's a comma after *1996,* and *TRF's* has an apostrophe to show possession. For blank iii, choice (A), *(EARN),* is correct; acronyms should be uppercase and enclosed in parentheses when following the fully spelled out phrase.

42. **(D), (C), and (C)** For blank iv, choice (D) is correct. A serial comma is needed after *entrepreneurs,* followed by *and,* and then using the verb *are.* For blank v, the correct answer is choice (C). The singular subject *Pre-employment training* requires the singular verb *includes,* and the correct word here is *confidence,* not *confident.* For blank vi, choice (C) is correct; *is* is properly used with the singular *accreditation.* Choice (A) includes *is,* but incorrectly uses commas after *assessed* and after *secured,* as if there will be one more item in the series.

43. **(B), (A), and (C)** For blank vii, choice (B) correctly spells *To* and uses a comma after *date.* For blank viii, choice (A), *have already been able,* correctly places the adverb (*already*) as close as possible to the verb it modifies (*been able*). For blank ix, choice (C) is correct; a colon is needed after *following* because it introduces a list, and the items in the list are in lowercase and properly separated with commas instead of semicolons.

44. **(D)** No change is required.

45. **(B)** These are homonyms. The proper form to use is *They are* or *They're.*

46. **(B)** To correct the punctuation, a colon should be added after *following* and the semicolons should be replaced with commas.

47. **(C)** The singular form *participant* is required to agree with the adjective *each*; in turn, both instances of *their* need to be changed to the singular *his or her* form as well.

48. **(B)** Changing the word order to *they were also questioned* is required to place the adverb close to the verb it modifies.

49. **(A)** The possessive plural *participants'* refers to the number of trainees involved in the program. Also, the comma after *that* is the correct way to set off the adverbial phrase *while academic training and teaching experiences differed in a variety of ways.*

50. **(C)** This is a spelling error. *Program* is the American spelling, as opposed to *programme,* which is used in Britain.

51. **(D)** The present tense of the verb *to be* or *is* is required to agree with the verb tense used in the rest of the paragraph.

52. **(B)** A comma after *livestock* is needed to separate the introductory section from the rest of the sentence.

53. **(D)** This sentence contains a spelling error. The verb *create* is required, not the noun *crate.*

54. **(D)** No change is required.

55. **(C)** Sentence 4 contains a subject-verb agreement error. The plural *have* is needed to agree with the plural subject *movements.*

56. **(B)** *May* is a less restrictive verb form than *can,* which means "to be able."

57. **(A)** The French term *au contraire* is an exclamation requiring an exclamation point. A new sentence should begin with a capital on *It's.*

Section 2

As the test-graders read and evaluate your essay, they look for the following:

- Proper introduction
- Well-focused main points
- Evidence of clear organization
- Specific development of your ideas
- Clear references to the source texts and your own experience
- Correct grammar and proper sentence structure
- Necessary punctuation
- Appropriate use of vocabulary
- Correct spelling
- Proper linkage between paragraphs
- Clear summary

Although every essay will be unique, we provide a sample response here to give you a better idea of what the test-graders expect to see in your extended response essay. Compare the structure of this sample response to yours.

Sample Response

Cyberbullying is a controversial issue, made worse because it is such an emotional issue. However, article 2, which argues against an extension of the law into this area, makes the stronger case. There are existing laws to deal with extreme cases, and less extreme cases can and should be dealt with through the schools and by parental intervention.

One justification for creating a new law to deal with cyberbullying is that the police do not have the willingness nor the tools to crack down on these bullies. However, in fact, such laws do exist. As article 2 points out, harassment is illegal. Slander is illegal. Posting sexual images, often used to embarrass and harass victims, is illegal. The problem is not a lack of law, but as article 2 points out, a lack of enforcement. The solution here is not more laws, but better education of those enforcing the criminal justice system. Police need to be reminded of what tools already exist, and prosecutors encouraged to prosecute.

Article 1, which supports the creation of cyberbullying legislation, points out that the anonymity of the Internet makes this kind of bullying difficult to deal with. However, rather than new laws, it would be a better approach to prosecute social media that permit such posts on their websites. Article 1 rightly points out that "the anonymity of the Internet makes tracking down the bullies difficult." Then why not take a much more direct approach and prosecute the websites that allow such postings? Article 2 does not support such a solution, but that is perhaps the weakest part of its argument. We should strengthen laws regulating websites, but we do not need additional criminal laws.

Article 2 points out that demeaning attacks that are "race- or religion-based" can be classified and prosecuted as hate crimes. Once again, the criminal laws are already in place.

Article 2 also raises the issue of the Right of Free Speech. This is a strong argument. I think it is important to balance individual rights. While people have the right to speak, that does not give them the right to speak in a manner that hurts other people. To that extent, I agree that there should be regulation. But we don't need to create more criminals. Regulation could apply penalties of bands from Internet sites and the like.

Then, there's the issue of parental involvement. Both articles mention that parents may not be able or willing to intervene to stop bullying. But as the second article points out, there's no law against bad parenting. When I was bullied, my parents met with the school principal and the parents of the bully. In my case, the intervention worked. That may not always be the case, but the point is parental intervention and school intervention can be effective.

On all the key points, article 2 makes the stronger case: There is no need for special cyberbullying laws. Existing laws can be useful if properly enforced. Parental involvement can be effective. And approaches controlling the websites, rather than criminalizing behavior, should be tried. When News media print libellous or slanderous material, they can be held accountable. The same should apply to social media websites in the cases of cyberbullying. While I do not agree with all the points raised in article 2, I believe it makes the stronger case.

Evaluation of Sample Response

After reading through the sample response once, reread it and answer the following questions about it.

- Is there a series of main points in this essay that clearly relate to the topic? (Underline the main points to check.)
- Does each paragraph have an introductory sentence or thought?
- Does each paragraph have a concluding sentence or thought?
- Do the sentences within each paragraph follow a logical sequence?
- Are the paragraphs organized in a natural flow from beginning to end? In other words, does each paragraph build on the previous one and lead to the next one?
- Have the ideas in the given topic and the first paragraph been developed throughout the essay?
- Are all the sentences grammatically correct?
- Are all the sentences properly structured?
- Are all the sentences correctly punctuated?
- Are all the words spelled correctly?

This particular sample response would probably receive a fairly high score. It certainly has all the attributes of a good essay that we list earlier in this section. It isn't perfect, but, considering the time limits, no one's asking you to write a perfect essay. However, you are expected to produce a good first draft quality essay. The sample response clearly meets the requirements: Analyze both positions, explaining which argument is better supported. It has a clear flow, and uses linking phrases between paragraphs. The order of the content is effective. The writer also acknowledges that the second article, while stronger, overlooks the potential solution of taking a much more direct approach and prosecuting the websites that allow such [cyberbullying] postings. You can go through the checklist and the essay, and tick off each requirement. While the essay is not perfect (for example, overuse of the phrase "points out"; spelling errors—*bands* should be *bans* and *libellous* should be *libelous*; improper capitalization—*Right of Free Speech* and *News*), it is satisfactory.

Remember: Your essay shouldn't be just a collection of grammatically correct sentences that flow from beginning to end. Rather, anything you write needs to be interesting and even entertaining to read. After all, no one wants to read a boring essay!

Although every essay will be unique, we provide a flowchart similar to what you might have written in your rough notes to prepare your response. This flowchart highlights some key points you could work into your response. You then build your essay around them. Compare this structure with what you wrote.

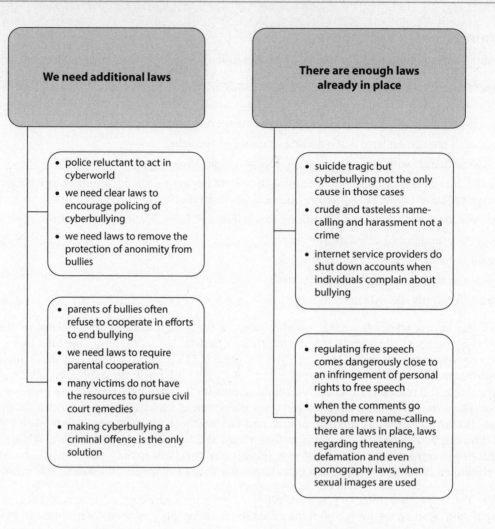

We need additional laws

- police reluctant to act in cyberworld
- we need clear laws to encourage policing of cyberbullying
- we need laws to remove the protection of anonimity from bullies

- parents of bullies often refuse to cooperate in efforts to end bullying
- we need laws to require parental cooperation
- many victims do not have the resources to pursue civil court remedies
- making cyberbullying a criminal offense is the only solution

There are enough laws already in place

- suicide tragic but cyberbullying not the only cause in those cases
- crude and tasteless name-calling and harassment not a crime
- internet service providers do shut down accounts when individuals complain about bullying

- regulating free speech comes dangerously close to an infringement of personal rights to free speech
- when the comments go beyond mere name-calling, there are laws in place, laws regarding threatening, defamation and even pornography laws, when sexual images are used

XII. Mathematical Reasoning Practice Test with Answer Explanations

This practice test is not related to the GED Ready™ – The Official Practice Test, produced and distributed by GED Testing Service LLC. GED Testing Service® has not approved, authorized, endorsed, been involved in the development of, or licensed the substantive content of this practice test.

Although you will enter your answers and write your extended responses and short answer responses on the computer during the actual GED® test, you will need to use your own paper to record your answers and responses for this Practice Test.

Try to make your behavior on this Practice Test as close as possible to the actual test conditions. Observe the time constraints.

Answer all the questions. There is no deduction for wrong answers, and you get points for each right one. Some questions are worth more than 1 point, but that information might not be readily available to you while taking the test. The important thing is to get as many correct answers as you can and guess if you have to. Unanswered items do nothing to improve your score. If you need to, guess. The more wrong answer choices you can eliminate, the better your chances of guessing the correct answer. In multiple-choice items, if you can eliminate three choices, you will have a 100 percent chance of being correct! Unfortunately, for each choice you cannot eliminate, the odds go down.

For the Mathematical Reasoning Test, general calculator instructions are available on screen by clicking the Calculator Reference button. For an official calculator tutorial for the TI-30XS on-screen calculator, visit www.atomiclearning.com/ti30xs.

For the Mathematical Reasoning Test, you will be provided with a list of mathematical formulas for your reference similar to the one provided on the next page.

IMPORTANT NOTE: The official formula sheet can be found online at www.gedtestingservice.com/uploads/files/15a95 1dfbdd875be5a7a73aa7912e2a0.pdf. Our version on the following page is a bit more thorough to help you as you study for the Mathematical Reasoning Test.

Formulas

AREA of a:	
square	Area = side^2
rectangle	Area = length × width
parallelogram	Area = base × height
triangle	Area $= \dfrac{1}{2}$ base × height
trapezoid	Area $= \dfrac{1}{2} \times (\text{base}_1 + \text{base}_2) \times \text{height}$
circle	Area = π × radius^2; π is approximately equal to 3.14
PERIMETER of a:	
square	Perimeter = 4 × side
rectangle	Perimeter = (2 × length) + (2 × width)
triangle	Perimeter = side$_1$ + side$_2$ + side$_3$
CIRCUMFERENCE of a: circle	Circumference = π × diameter; π is approximately equal to 3.14
VOLUME of a:	
cube	Volume = edge^3
rectangular solid	Volume = length × width × height
square pyramid	Volume $= \dfrac{1}{3} (\text{base edge})^2 \times \text{height}$
cylinder	Volume = π × radius^2 × height; π is approximately equal to 3.14
cone	Volume $= \dfrac{1}{3} \times \pi \times \text{radius}^2 \times \text{height}$; π is approximately equal to 3.14
COORDINATE GEOMETRY	distance between points $= \sqrt{(x_2 - x_1)^2 + (y_2 - y_1)^2}$; (x_1, y_1) and (x_2, y_2) are two points on a plane slope of a line $= \dfrac{y_2 - y_1}{x_2 - x_1}$; (x_1, y_1) and (x_2, y_2) are two points on the line
PYTHAGOREAN THEOREM	$a^2 + b^2 = c^2$; a and b are sides, and c is the hypotenuse of a right triangle
MEASURES OF CENTRAL TENDENCY	**mean** $= \dfrac{x_1 + x_2 + \ldots + x_n}{n}$, where x's are the values for which a mean is desired and n is the total number of values for x **median** = the middle value of an odd number of ordered numbers in a set, and halfway between the two middle values of an even number of ordered numbers in a set
SIMPLE INTEREST	interest = principal × rate × time (rate expressed as a decimal)
DISTANCE	distance = rate × time
TOTAL COST	total cost = (number of units) × (price per unit)

Time: 115 Minutes—50 Questions

Directions: Choose the best answer to each question. Following the instruction for each type of layout indicated, mark your answers on a separate sheet of paper.

On the 2014 GED® Mathematical Reasoning Test, an on-screen calculator is available for all but the first five questions. On the remaining questions, there is an icon to bring up the calculator if you need it, but remember that each diversion takes time and this is a timed test. Practice doing the items in the most time-efficient manner—without a calculator—to leave yourself some time at the end for reviewing items you are uncertain of and completing any items you may have skipped.

If a question is not standard multiple choice, the item type will be identified directly before the question.

1. Sally was shopping for a flat-screen TV. She had set a budget of $900 for the TV, delivery, and installation. As she shopped, she kept track of the prices in a table:

	Store A	Store B	Store C	Store D
TV	$1,200	$1,250	$1,500	$1,100
Discount	20%	30%	50%	10%
Delivery	$35	$0	$95	$0
Installation	$112.50	$0	$125	$0

Which store is offering Sally the best deal?

(A) Store A

(B) Store B

(C) Store C

(D) Store D

Fill-in-the-blank

2. Jan and Jean were very competitive friends. Jan announced that she was reading 398 pages of fiction each week. Jean said she could easily read $1\frac{1}{4}$ as many pages each week. Jan immediately challenged Jean to a one-week battle of the books. How many total pages would Jean have to read to win the challenge? Enter your answer in the box below, rounding your answer to the nearest whole page.

3. In a track-and-field event, five runners finished a race with the following times:

Runner	Time (seconds)
1	14.574
2	15.429
3	14.803
4	14.583
5	14.961

By how many seconds did the winner beat the second-place runner?

(A) 0.005

(B) 0.008

(C) 0.009

(D) 0.014

Questions 4 and 5 refer to the following passage.

Herbert was concerned about the cost of operating his car. Because the car was fairly new, his main concern was the cost of gasoline. He could document the distance he traveled each week, *D*, and the number of gallons of gasoline he used for this distance, *N*. He would also know the cost of gasoline per gallon that week, *C*. Herbert wants to figure out his annual cost of fuel per week.

Fill-in-the-blank

4. Write an equation that Herbert could use to calculate his weekly cost, *W*. Enter your answer in the box below.

5. What operations should Herbert use, and in what order, to estimate the cost of fuel per year for his car?

(A) Multiply the cost of gasoline per gallon by the number of weeks in a year.

(B) Divide the number of miles driven by 12 and multiply by the cost per gallon.

(C) Add the number of miles driven to the cost of gasoline and divide by the number of gallons used.

(D) Multiply the number of gallons used per week by the cost per gallon and then multiply by 52.

Fill-in-the-blank

6. Georgia won a contest in which she had to answer a skill-testing question before she was awarded the prize. The skill-testing question was to solve the following:

$$123 + 49 - 21 \times 8 \div 4 + 23 \times 2 =$$

What was the winning answer? Enter your answer in the box below.

7. Herbert was trying to figure out how much carpeting he would need to cover the floor of the square living room in his small apartment. He estimated that he would need 156 square feet of carpet to cover the floor. If his room was 12.5 feet long, how many square feet would Herbert have needed if he had calculated the amount using exact measurements?

   (A) 15.625
   (B) 156.25
   (C) 1,562.50
   (D) 15,625

Hot Spot

Question 8 refers to the following figure.

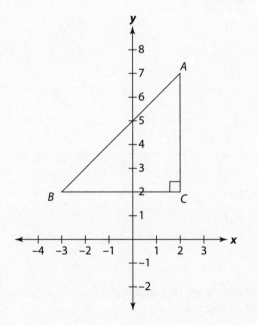

8. On the blank coordinate-plane grid below, mark the point where side *AC* would cross the *x*-axis if it were extended.

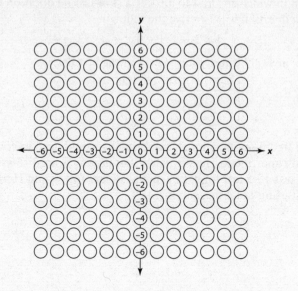

Drop-down

9. Find the length of the hypotenuse of the right-triangle *ABC*, where $\angle C = 90°$ and each side has an edge length as indicated in the diagram.

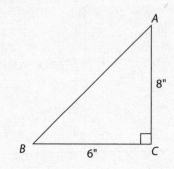

The length of $\overline{AB}$, in inches, is _____.

(A) 10

(B) 12

(C) 36

(D) 64

10. Find the point where a line with slope of 1 and *y*-intercept (0,4) intercepts a line through *P*(4,8) and *Q*(–2,–1). What is the point of intersection?

(A) (1,4)

(B) (4,1)

(C) (4,8)

(D) (8,4)

11. Ken wanted to carpet his apartment, except for the kitchen and bathroom. He summarized the size of the rooms in a table:

Room	Size (feet)
Living room	20 × 18
Dining room	12 × 14
Bedroom	18 × 24
Hallway	10 × 3

The flooring store was having a sale, but only 115 square yards of the carpet Ken really wanted were left at the sale price. If Ken buys the 115 square yards of carpet, how many square yards of carpet will be left over when he is done?

(A) 5
(B) 7
(C) 10
(D) 15

Fill-in-the-blank

12. If a plane could maintain an average speed of 575 miles per hour, how many hours would the 2,444-mile flight between New York City and Los Angeles take? Enter your answer in the box below, rounding to two decimal places.

13. The Smith family was considering buying a backyard swimming pool. The dimensions they settled on were 30 feet by 18 feet with an average depth of 3 feet. The salesperson told them that a pool with their specifications would cost them $126 per square foot of water surface. What would be the cost of the pool?

(A) $22,684
(B) $37,040
(C) $68,040
(D) $86,000

Questions 14–17 refer to the following table.

Country	Males		Females	
Percentage of 15+ Population Smoking Compared to Lung Cancer Death Rates (LCDR)				
	Smoker Prevalence (% Age 15+)	LCDR per 100,000 Smokers	Smoker Prevalence (% Age 15+)	LCDR per 100,000 Smokers
Austria	42	157.6	27	50.7
Finland	27	258.1	19	54.7
France	40	171.5	27	28.5
Germany	36.8	193.8	21.5	56.7
Israel	45	84.7	30	40.3
Japan	59	81.2	14.8	85.1
Norway	36.3	127.5	35.5	43.4
Portugal	38	107.1	15	45.3
Spain	48	143.8	25	21.6
Sweden	22	161.4	24	63.8
United States	28.1	305.7	23.5	157
Average	38.4	162.9	23.8	58.8

14. Looking at the table, which of the following are possible conclusions?

   (A) More smokers die of lung cancer in Finland than in any other country.
   (B) The fewest deaths among smokers are in Portugal.
   (C) The lowest percentage of 15+ female smokers is in Japan.
   (D) On average, 129.6 smokers per 100,000 die of lung cancer.

15. Which of the following graphs indicates that the lung cancer death rates (LCDR) for the selected countries are nearly equal?

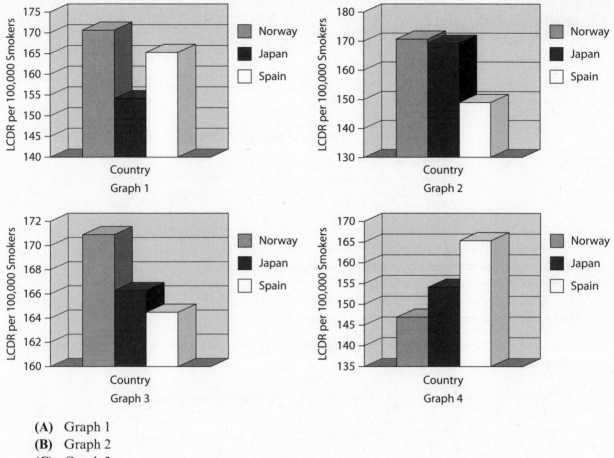

(A) Graph 1
(B) Graph 2
(C) Graph 3
(D) Graph 4

Drop-down

16. If everyone in Austria quit smoking, how would that affect the average percentage of people over the age of 15 who smoked in France?

The average smoker prevalence of persons 15+ who smoked in France would _____.

(A) increase by 63.42%
(B) decrease by 1.22%
(C) decrease by 4.78%
(D) remain the same

17. If the population of the United States age 15+ was 217,148,103, how many people age 15+ in the United States smoke? (Assume that the population is 50% female.)

    (A) 10,857,405
    (B) 14,028,419.75
    (C) 56,024,210.57
    (D) 62,418,092.36

18. Claudia's class of 34 students took a survey on likes and dislikes of dishes served in the school cafeteria. The results produced the following table:

Type of Dish	Number of Positive Responses
Meat	25
Fish	12
Vegetarian	2
Stew	18
Pasta	12

What conclusion could be reached from these survey responses?

    (A) Most people surveyed preferred easy-to-prepare dishes.
    (B) Pasta dishes received the most votes.
    (C) Meat dishes were the most popular.
    (D) Most people preferred dishes with pasta or fish.

19. Donald surveyed the alumni on the recording artists they enjoyed listening to and came up with the following results:

Artist	Genre	Total Number of Votes
ABBA	Pop	68
The Beatles	Rock, pop	137
Elvis Presley	Rock, pop, country	119
Madonna	Pop	103
Michael Jackson	Pop, R&B	146
Pink Floyd	Rock	87
Queen	Rock	74

Based on this limited survey, who are the most and least popular artists, respectively?

    (A) Michael Jackson and the Beatles
    (B) Elvis Presley and Pink Floyd
    (C) ABBA and Queen
    (D) Michael Jackson and ABBA

Drop-down

20. Consider the equation, $y = mx + b$, where m is the slope and b is the y-intercept. The result of substituting various values for b while keeping everything else the same would be _____.

    (A) a sequence of lines all going through the same point
    (B) a sequence of lines randomly scattered
    (C) a sequence of parallel lines
    (D) a sequence of perpendicular lines

Fill-in-the-blank

21. If an algebraic expression for the Pythagorean theorem is $l = \sqrt{a^2 + b^2}$, where l is the length of the hypotenuse and a and b are the lengths of the other two sides, what is the length, to one decimal point, of a side of a right triangle with a hypotenuse of 23 and a second side of 16? Enter your answer in the box below, rounding to one decimal place.

22. In the formula $d = \dfrac{-b \pm \sqrt{b^2 - 4ac}}{2a}$, solve for d to one decimal place if $a = 4$, $b = 11$, and $c = 3$.

    (A) −2.4 or −0.3
    (B) 2.6 or 0.5
    (C) 4.2 or 0.3
    (D) 25 or 195

23. A technician setting up a rock concert sound system was told that the volume level decreases in inverse proportion to the distance from the stage according to the following equation $I = k\dfrac{1}{r}$, where I is the volume, k is a constant, and r is the distance from the source, $r > 0$. If the sound level at the stage was 100, what would it be 10 feet from the stage?

    (A) 10
    (B) 100
    (C) 110
    (D) Not enough information given

24. In the following graph, what general trend can you discern?

Temperature Variation

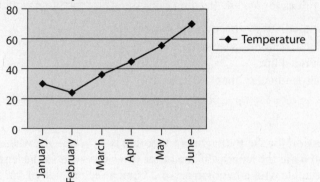

(A) The weather is nice in June.
(B) In general, the temperature rises toward summer.
(C) January is the coldest month.
(D) The least rainfall is in March.

Drop-down

25. In the equation $v - \dfrac{a}{ta} = F - \dfrac{v}{tv}$, the result of an increase in the value of F would _____ the value of the other side.

(A) increase
(B) decrease
(C) not change
(D) become one-half of t for

Fill-in-the-blank

26. What is the decimal equivalent of $\dfrac{1}{8}$? Enter your answer in the box below; do not round your answer.

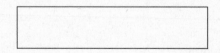

27. Alan was looking for a bargain in MP3 players. He passed by a store offering a 28% discount on an MP3 player priced at $49.99. How much would he save by buying the MP3 player at this store?

(A) $12
(B) $13
(C) $14
(D) $15

28. If you put the following fractions in order from smallest to largest, which one would be in third place in order of increasing size?

$$\frac{1}{2}, \frac{1}{6}, \frac{1}{7}, \frac{1}{4}, \frac{1}{9}, \frac{1}{8}, \frac{1}{3}, \text{ and } \frac{1}{5}$$

(A) $\frac{1}{8}$

(B) $\frac{1}{7}$

(C) $\frac{1}{4}$

(D) $\frac{1}{2}$

Drag-and-drop

29. You need to calculate the difference in volume, V, of two rectangular fish tanks. L_1, W_1, and D_1 represent the length, width, and depth, respectively, of the first fish tank. L_2, W_2, and D_2 represent the length, width, and depth, respectively, of the second fish tank. Complete the formula below by dragging the correct operation symbol into each box.

(To answer, write the appropriate operation symbol in each box to complete the formula. A symbol can be used more than once.)

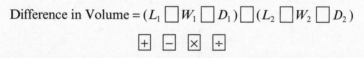

$$\text{Difference in Volume} = (L_1 \square W_1 \square D_1) \square (L_2 \square W_2 \square D_2)$$

30. If you calculated a result by multiplying a number by something and then adding to the product, what operations and in what order would you use to arrive back at the original number?

(A) Divide and then subtract
(B) Subtract and then divide
(C) Subtract and then multiply
(D) Add and then subtract

Fill-in-the-blank

31. Simplify the following expression: $25 + 36 \times 11 + 243 - 199$. Enter your answer in the box below.

32. Tom needed to buy six new shirts, each of which cost $24.99. Approximately how much would he spend for the shirts?

    (A) $120
    (B) $150
    (C) $175
    (D) $200

Hot Spot

Question 33 refers to the following figure.

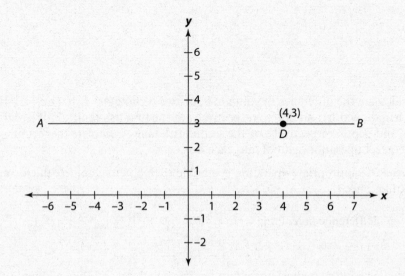

33. On the blank coordinate-plane grid below, mark the point where a line perpendicular to segment AB and passing through $D(4,3)$ would intersect the x-axis.

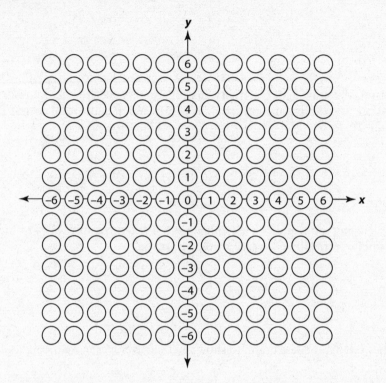

34. If each face of a standard die is 1.3 square inches in area, what would be the surface area of the die, in square inches?

   (A) 3.9
   (B) 5.2
   (C) 6.5
   (D) 7.8

35. Which of the following choices is an equation for the line $\overrightarrow{AB}$ with a slope of $\dfrac{3}{5}$ and y-intercept $(0,8)$?

   The equation needed is $y = mx + b$, where m is the slope and b is the y-intercept, and it is written in the form $ax + by + c = 0$.

   (A) $5x + 3y - 40 = 0$
   (B) $5x - 3y + 40 = 0$
   (C) $3x + 5y + 8 = 0$
   (D) $3x - 5y + 40 = 0$

36. Sally has a contract to tile around the outside of a swimming pool 75 feet long and 28.5 feet wide. If each tile is 9 inches square, how many tiles will it take to go around the entire edge of the pool?

    (A) 138
    (B) 238
    (C) 276
    (D) 280

37. A meter was installed 9 years ago. Electricity has consistently cost 16¢ per kilowatt hour since the meter's installation. The current meter reading is 67,015. What is the total cost of electricity since the meter was installed?

    (A) $1191.38
    (B) $4188.44
    (C) $7446.11
    (D) $10,722.40

38. Dawn has a large living room and can use either a 9-×-12-foot rug or a 10-×-14-foot rug. How much more floor, in square feet, will be covered by the larger rug?

    (A) 23
    (B) 32
    (C) 108
    (D) 140

39. The mathematics teacher made a graph to show the final averages in mathematics for the top seven students.

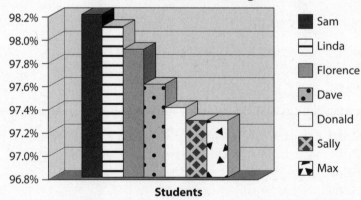

From the graph, what is the difference in average scores between the student who stood first and the one who stood fourth?

    (A) 0.3%
    (B) 0.4%
    (C) 0.5%
    (D) 0.6%

Questions 40 and 41 refer to the following tables.

Table 1: U.S. Dropout Rate 2003–2009	
Year	Total (%)
2003	10.9
2004	9.8
2005	10.7
2006	9.4
2007	8.7
2008	8.6
2009	8.4

Table 2: U.S. Unemployment Status (Ages 16 and Over)	
Year	Total (%)
2003	6.0
2004	5.5
2005	5.1
2006	4.6
2007	4.6
2008	5.8
2009	9.3

40. Table 1 details the dropout rate in the United States for the years 2003 to 2009.

    How would you describe the general trend shown in Table 1?

    (A) A lot of students dropped out of school.
    (B) School dropout rates have been increasing.
    (C) School dropout rates have been steady.
    (D) A higher percentage of students are staying in school each year.

41. Considering the data in Tables 1 and 2, what conclusion might be drawn about the relationship between unemployment rates and high school dropouts?

    (A) As unemployment rises, dropout rates decrease.
    (B) As unemployment falls, dropout rates decrease.
    (C) As unemployment rises, dropout rates increase.
    (D) Not enough information given

Fill-in-the-blank

42. At a sales meeting, the monthly average sales for January through June were posted for the top three salespeople. The summary is shown in the following table.

Monthly Average Sales			
	Salesperson 1	Salesperson 2	Salesperson 3
January	$4,569	$5,082	$3,997
February	$4,802	$5,385	$4,001
March	$4,207	$5,293	$4,099
April	$4,978	$5,583	$4,378
May	$5,049	$5,997	$4,997
June	$6,003	$6,104	$5,006

How much more in sales would the third highest salesperson have to accumulate from July to September in order to exceed the top-selling salesperson's January-to-June sales by at least $1? Enter your answer in the box below.

43. The ad for Car A claims that its highway mileage is 18.8 miles per gallon with diesel fuel. The ad for Car B claims that its highway mileage is 18.1 miles per gallon with regular gas; the ad claims that Car B is more economical. What conclusion could you reach?

(A) Car B is more economical.
(B) Car A is more economical.
(C) Both cars are equally efficient.
(D) Not enough information given

Question 44 refers to the following table.

Name	Average Number of Pages Read Monthly
Loren	483
Frank	398
Saul	501
Rachel	529
Noah	473
Arden	388

44. How many more pages did the person who read the greatest average number of pages read than the average of all the people in the table?

(A) 62
(B) 64
(C) 67
(D) 72

Fill-in-the-blank

45. Don drove 36 more miles than twice the number of miles that George drove. If you represented the number of miles driven by Don as D and the number of miles driven by George as G, what would the equation representing the statement be? Enter your answer in the box below.

Hot Spot

46. The formula of a line is $y = mx + b$. On the coordinate-plane grid below, plot the point with the y-coordinate equal to 3 on the line having m equal to $\dfrac{5}{2}$ and b equal to 8.

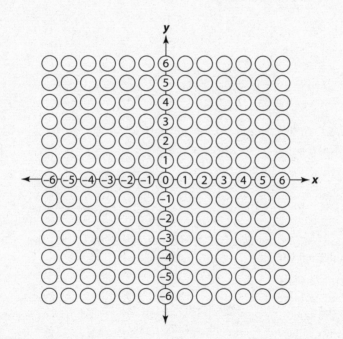

47. Harry is eating from a giant ice cream cone and wonders how much his cone would hold if it were filled with ice cream to the brim. He measures the cone and finds it to be 3 inches across the top and 5 inches high. How many cubic inches of ice cream, to one decimal place, would the cone hold?

(A) 11.6
(B) 11.8
(C) 16.7
(D) 18.1

48. Evaluate for K if $K = \dfrac{n}{r(n-r)}$, where $n = 12$ and $r = 8$.

   (A) $\dfrac{1}{12}$

   (B) $\dfrac{3}{8}$

   (C) $\dfrac{1}{4}$

   (D) $\dfrac{1}{2}$

49. Solve the following set of equations for y.

$$7x + 4y = 8$$
$$3x + 4y = 6$$

   The value of y is

   (A) $\dfrac{8}{9}$

   (B) $\dfrac{7}{8}$

   (C) $\dfrac{9}{8}$

   (D) $\dfrac{9}{6}$

50. How would doubling a affect the value of N in the equation $N = \sqrt{b^2 - 4ac}$ if initially $a = 3$, $b = 5$, and $c = 4$? (Consider only real values.)

   (A) N would be twice as large.
   (B) N would be half as large.
   (C) N would stay the same.
   (D) N would have no value.

Answer Key

1. (B)
2. 498
3. (C)
4. $W = N \times C$
5. (D)
6. 176
7. (B)
8. (2,0)
9. (A)
10. (C)
11. (A)
12. 4.25
13. (C)
14. (C)
15. (C)
16. (D)
17. (C)
18. (C)
19. (D)
20. (C)
21. 16.5
22. (A)
23. (D)
24. (B)
25. (A)

26. 0.125
27. (C)
28. (B)
29. Difference in Volume $= (L_1 \boxed{\times} W_1 \boxed{\times} D_1) \boxed{-} (L_2 \boxed{\times} W_2 \boxed{\times} D_2)$
30. (B)
31. 465
32. (B)
33. (4,0)
34. (D)
35. (D)
36. (D)
37. (D)
38. (B)
39. (D)
40. (D)
41. (D)
42. $6,967
43. (D)
44. (C)
45. $D = 2G + 36$
46. (–2,3)
47. (B)
48. (B)
49. (C)
50. (D)

Answer Explanations

1. **(B)** In order to figure out which store offers the best deal, you need to calculate the total price for each store. For Store A, the price after the discount is $960; this is above Sally's budget, so no further calculations are needed. For Store B, the price after the discount is $875; there are no delivery and installation charges, so the total price is $875. For Store C, the price after the discount is $750; the delivery charge is $95 and the installation charge is $125, so the total price is $750 + $95 + $125 = $970, which is above her budget. For Store D, the price after the discount is $990; this is above her budget, so no further calculations are needed. Store B offers the best total price, at $875, and is within Sally's budget.

2. **498** If Jan read 398 pages, Jean would have to read 497.5 pages for a draw. To win the challenge, however, Jean would have to read at least 498 pages. There are two ways to calculate this:

$$398 \times 1\frac{1}{4} = 398 \times \frac{5}{4} = \frac{398 \times 5}{4} = \frac{1,990}{4} = 497\frac{1}{2}$$

Or you can use the decimal equivalent of $1\frac{1}{4}$, which is 1.25:
$$398 \times 1.25 = 497.5 \approx 498$$

3. **(C)** This is a simple subtraction problem, but first, you have to put the times in order to determine the winner and the second-place runner's times:

Place	Runner	Time (seconds)
1st	1	14.574
2nd	4	14.583
3rd	3	14.803
4th	5	14.961
5th	2	15.429

With the times now in order, you can see that Runner 1 won the race with a time of 14.574, and Runner 4 was in second place with a time of 14.583. Simply subtract Runner 1's time from Runner 2's time to find the difference:
$$14.583 - 14.574 = 0.009$$
The winner won the race by 0.009 seconds.

4. $W = N \times C$ Multiply the gallons used per week by the cost per gallon to get the cost per week.

5. **(D)** Multiply the gallons used per week by the cost per gallon to get the cost per week: $W = N \times C$. Because there are 52 weeks in a year, multiply the cost per week by 52 to estimate the cost per year.

6. **176** Remember the order of operations, PEMDAS (parentheses, exponents, multiplication, division, addition, and subtraction). Look at the question:
$$123 + 49 - 21 \times 8 \div 4 + 23 \times 2 =$$
And organize it according to the order of operations:
$$123 + 49 - ([21 \times 8] \div 4) + (23 \times 2) = 123 + 49 - 42 + 46 = 176$$

7. **(B)** If the room was 12.5 feet long, the actual area to be covered would be 156.25 square feet, not 156 square feet.

8. **(2,0)** If side AC were extended down to the x-axis, it would cross at (2,0).

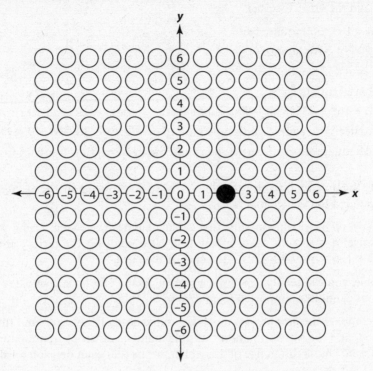

9. **(A)** $\overline{AB}$ is the hypotenuse. To find the length of the hypotenuse, you use the equation $l = \sqrt{a^2 + b^2}$, where l is the length of the hypotenuse, a is the length of $\overline{BC}$ or 6 inches, and b is the length of $\overline{AC}$ or 8 inches. Substituting, $l = \sqrt{6^2 + 8^2} = \sqrt{36 + 64} = \sqrt{100} = 10$ inches.

10. **(C)** Any values of x and y that satisfy the equations of both lines give the point of intersection.

The equation of a line with slope 1 and y-intercept of (0,4) is $y = mx + b$. Substituting, $y = x + 4$ or $x - y = -4$.

The equation of a line through (4,8) and (−2,−1) is $y = y_1 + \dfrac{(y_2 - y_1)}{(x_2 - x_1)}(x - x_1)$. Substituting,

$y = 8 + \dfrac{(-1-8)}{(-2-4)}(x - 4) = \dfrac{3x + 4}{2}$; or cross-multiplying, $2y = 3x + 4$ or $3x - 2y = -4$.

The equations are $x - y = -4$ and $3x - 2y = -4$.

Multiply the first equation by −2 to get $-2x + 2y = 8$. Then add the equations to solve for x:

$$\begin{array}{r} 3x - 2y = -4 \\ -2x + 2y = 8 \\ \hline x = 4 \end{array}$$

and substitute $x = 4$ into the first equation, $x - y = -4$, to get $y = 8$.

The point of intersection would be (4,8).

11. **(A)** To calculate the amount of carpet required for the apartment, you need to calculate the area of each room and add the areas together.

   Living room: 20 × 18 = 360 square feet

   Dining room: 12 × 14 =168 square feet

   Bedroom: 18 × 24 = 432 square feet

   Hallway: 10 × 3 = 30 square feet

   Total area = 360 + 168 + 432 + 30 = 990 square feet

   To convert square feet into square yards, you have to divide by 9. So, 990 ÷ 9 = 110 square yards.

   If he buys the 115 square yards of carpet, he would have 115 − 110 = 5 square yards of carpet left over.

12. **4.25** To calculate the time required for the flight, divide the distance by the average speed: 2,444 ÷ 575 = 4.25 hours (rounded to two decimal places).

13. **(C)** To find the cost of the pool, you must first calculate the surface area. Using the formula $A = l \times w$, substitute and solve: $A = 30 \times 18 = 540$ square feet. Next, multiply the surface area by the cost per square foot: 540 × 126 = $68,040. This is the cost of the pool.

14. **(C)** From the table, you can see that the lowest percentage of 15+ female smokers is in Japan. The rest of the conclusions cannot be supported from data in the table.

15. **(C)** In order to compare the graphs, you must first make note of the y-axis and the difference between the largest number and the smallest number, and the number of people represented by each division. For example, Graph 3 has a difference of 12, which means that each division on the y-axis represents 2 people.

16. **(D)** The number of smokers in each country is independent of the number of smokers in another country. Changing the percentage of smokers in Austria would not change the percentage of people in France who smoked.

17. **(C)** You can calculate the number of smokers in the United States as of the time this data was gathered by adding the number of male and female smokers 15+. To arrive at this number, using the assumption that males and females are equally represented in the population, divide the population by two to arrive at 108,574,051.5. Then the number of male smokers is 0.281 × 108,574,051.5 = 30,509,308.47 and the number of female smokers is 0.235 × 108,574,051.5 = 25,514,902.1. Adding the two numbers together would produce a sum of 56,024,210.57.

18. **(C)** The most popular dish selected by the 34 students was the meat dish, with 25 positive responses.

19. **(D)** Michael Jackson had the highest number of votes recorded, and ABBA had the least.

20. **(C)** If the slope remains the same and the y-intercept changes, the lines would be parallel but with different points of intersection with the y-axis.

21. **16.5** Using the equation $l = \sqrt{a^2 + b^2}$, substitute $l = 23$ and $a = 16$ to give you $23 = \sqrt{16^2 + b^2}$ or $529 = 256 + b^2$ (square both sides of the equation) or $b^2 = 529 - 256 = 273$. It follows that $b = 16.5$.

22. **(A)** If you substitute $a = 4$, $b = 11$, and $c = 3$ into the equation, you get the following:

$$d = \frac{-11 \pm \sqrt{11^2 - 4 \cdot 4 \cdot 3}}{2 \cdot 4} = \frac{-11 \pm \sqrt{121 - 48}}{8} = \frac{-11 \pm \sqrt{73}}{8} = \frac{-11 \pm 8.54}{8} = -2.4 \text{ or } -0.3$$

23. **(D)** Because no value is given for k, you have no way of calculating the volume.

24. **(B)** The value of temperature rises as the months pass from February to June on the graph.

25. **(A)** In this linear equation, increasing the value of one side increases the value of the other side.

26. **0.125** To convert a fraction into a decimal, you divide the top number (the numerator) by the bottom number (the denominator). So, $\frac{1}{8} = 1 \div 8 = 0.125$.

27. **(C)** To calculate the discount, it's easier to change the percentage into a decimal fraction ($28\% = 0.28$) and multiply it by the selling price to arrive at \$13.9972. But because this amount is in dollars and cents, the answer would round to \$14. Notice that you can round \$49.99 to \$50 to make the calculation simpler.

28. **(B)** If you remember that a fraction becomes larger as the denominator becomes smaller, the question is really "What is the third largest denominator?", which is 7. Therefore, the answer is $\frac{1}{7}$.

29. **Difference in Volume** $= (L_1 \;\boxed{\times}\; W_1 \;\boxed{\times}\; D_1) \;\boxed{-}\; (L_1 \;\boxed{\times}\; W_2 \;\boxed{\times}\; D_2)$ To calculate the difference, you would subtract the volume of the second fish tank from the volume of the first fish tank without worrying about the sign. If the first tank is smaller than the second, your answer would be negative, but since we are only interested in the absolute value, the sign of the difference has no bearing.

30. **(B)** Because multiplying and dividing are opposite operations and addition and subtraction are opposite operations, you would perform the opposite operations in the reverse order to arrive back at the original number—in other words, you would subtract and then divide.

31. **465** To do this calculation, remember the order of operations (PEMDAS). Multiply $36 \times 11 = 396$ first. Then add and subtract in order, left to right, to find the answer, 465.

32. **(B)** \$24.99 is approximately \$25, and six shirts costing \$25 each would cost $\$25 \times 6 = \$150$.

33. **(4,0)** The perpendicular line would intersect the *x*-axis at (4,0). This would appear on the coordinate-plane grid as follows:

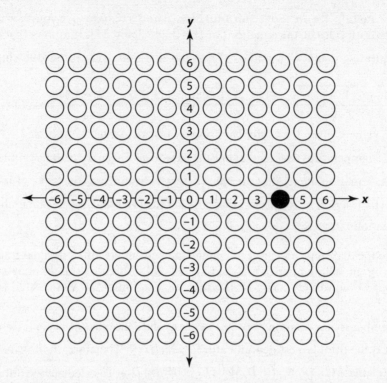

34. **(D)** If you could unfold a die, you would end up with six faces. It would look like this:

	1	
2	3	4
	5	
	6	

Since there are 6 faces, you multiply 6 by 1.3 to find the total surface area: 6 ×1.3 = 7.8

35. **(D)** Substituting in the equation $y = mx + b$ produces:

$$y = mx + b$$
$$y = \frac{3}{5}x + 8$$
$$5y = 3x + 40$$
$$3x - 5y + 40 = 0$$

36. **(D)** If each tile is 9 inches wide, it would be 0.75 feet wide. Tiling the 75-foot side would require 100 tiles: 75 ÷ 0.75 = 100. Tiling the 28.5-foot side would require 38 tiles: 28.5 ÷ 0.75 = 38. Tiling these two sides requires 100 + 38 = 138 tiles. And tiling all four sides requires 138 × 2 = 276 tiles. But that would leave a 9-×-9-inch space at each corner (see figure below), which would require four more tiles.

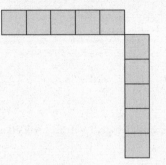

Corner of pool

The total number of tiles required would be 276 + 4 = 280 tiles.

37. **(D)** The meter reads 67,015. To find the total cost, multiply 67,015 × 0.16 to get $10,722.40.

38. **(B)** The area of the larger rug is 10 × 14 = 140 square feet, and the area of the smaller rug is 9 × 12 = 108 square feet. The larger rug will cover 140 − 108 = 32 more square feet.

39. **(D)** The student who stood first (Sam) received 98.2%, and the student who stood fourth (Dave) received 97.6%. The difference is 98.2 − 97.6 = 0.6%.

40. **(D)** The general trend visible in Table 1 is that dropout rates have decreased most years, which would mean that a higher percentage of students are staying in school.

41. **(D)** There is not enough information given to answer the question. Although, according to Table 2, there seems to have been a general decline in unemployment rates from 2003 to 2009, this doesn't correspond to the changes in dropout rates in Table 1. For example, 2005 shows a rise in dropout rates but a decrease in unemployment rates. Common knowledge may be that people who can't find work go back to school for further education or training, but that is not demonstrated by the statistics presented in Tables 1 and 2, and you can use only the information provided to answer the questions.

42. **$6,967** The top salesperson (Salesperson 2) sold $33,444, and the bottom salesperson (Salesperson 3) sold $26,478 in this period. If Salesperson 3 could increase his sales by $6,966, his sales would be equal with Salesperson 2's January-to-June total. In order to exceed it by $1, he would have to sell $6,967 from July to September.

43. **(D)** There is not enough information given to draw a conclusion. If the prices of regular gas and diesel fuel had been included, a conclusion might be possible.

44. **(C)** First, find the average of the average number of pages read monthly by adding them up and dividing by 6:

$$(483 + 398 + 501 + 529 + 473 + 388) ÷ 6 = 2{,}772 ÷ 6 = 462$$

The average of the averages is 462 pages. Rachel read an average of 529 pages, which is 67 pages more than the average of the averages: 529 − 462 = 67.

45. **D = 2G + 36** Equations read like sentences. $D = 2G + 36$ reads that the number of miles driven by Don is twice the number of miles driven by George plus 36 miles, which is what was asked.

46. **(−2,3)** To find the value of the x-coordinate, substitute into the equation $y = mx + b$:

$$3 = \frac{5}{2}x + 8$$

$$-5 = \frac{5}{2}x$$

$$-10 = 5x$$

$$x = -2$$

The point is (−2,3). The coordinate-plane grid would look like this:

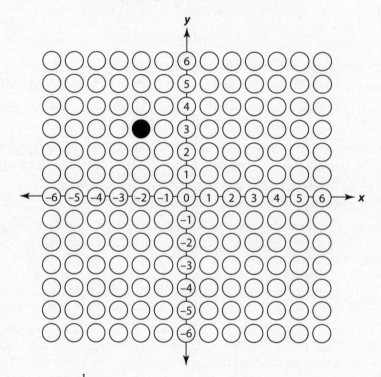

47. **(B)** The volume of a cone is $\frac{1}{3}\pi r^2 h$, or $0.3333 \times 3.14 \times 1.5 \times 1.5 \times 5 = 11.77$, or 11.8 to one decimal place.

48. **(B)** Substituting the values into the equation $K = \frac{n}{r(n-r)}$ produces $K = \frac{12}{8(12-8)} = \frac{12}{32} = \frac{3}{8}$.

49. **(C)** Subtract the two equations to solve for x:

$$\begin{aligned} 7x + 4y &= 8 \\ -3x + 4y &= 6 \\ \hline 4x &= 2 \\ x &= \frac{2}{4} \\ x &= \frac{1}{2} \end{aligned}$$

We get $x = \frac{1}{2}$.

Substitute $x = \frac{1}{2}$ in the first equation to find y:

$$7\left(\frac{1}{2}\right) + 4y = 8$$

$$3\frac{1}{2} + 4y = 8$$

$$4y = 8 - 3\frac{1}{2}$$

$$4y = 4\frac{1}{2} \text{ or } \frac{9}{2}$$

$$\frac{1}{4} \times 4y = \frac{1}{4} \times \frac{9}{2}$$

$$y = \frac{9}{8}$$

50. **(D)** Doubling the value of a and substituting in the equation would produce $N = \sqrt{25 - 96}$, which would require finding the square root of a negative number, which can't be calculated.

XIII. Science Practice Test with Answer Explanations

Although you will enter your answers and write your short answer responses on the computer during the actual GED® test, you will need to use your own paper to record your answers and responses for this Practice Test.

Try to make your behavior on this Practice Test as close as possible to the actual test conditions. Observe the time constraints.

Answer all the questions. There is no deduction for wrong answers, and you get points for each right one. Some questions are worth more than 1 point, but that information might not be readily available to you while taking the test. The important thing is to get as many correct answers as you can and guess if you have to. Unanswered items do nothing to improve your score. If you need to, guess. The more wrong answer choices you can eliminate, the better your chances of guessing the correct answer. In multiple-choice items, if you can eliminate three choices, you will have a 100 percent chance of being correct! Unfortunately, for each choice you cannot eliminate, the odds go down.

IMPORTANT NOTE: The actual GED® Science Test will contain two short answer items, but we only include one in this Practice Test. Short answer items are to be answered within the allotted 90 minutes. While these items are not timed separately, they do use a unique scoring system. The GED Testing Service® recommends that students spend roughly 10 minutes on each of the short answer items.

Time: 90 Minutes—50 Questions

Directions: Choose the best answer to each question. Following the instruction for each type of layout indicated, mark your answers on a separate sheet of paper.

If a question is not standard multiple choice, the item type will be identified directly before the question.

Questions 1 through 3 refer to the following passage.

Everything around us, including us, is composed of atoms. Atoms are the basic building block of matter and consist of parts (protons, neutrons, and electrons) but cannot be divided using chemicals. Electrons are negatively charged and move around the nucleus and account for most of the volume of the atom. Electrons are much smaller than protons or neutrons. Although electrons are bound to the nucleus, it is still possible to remove one or more electrons, resulting in ions of the original atom.

The nucleus is made up of protons and neutrons, which together create most of the mass of an atom. Protons are positively charged and bear a charge equal to an electron and, thus, are attracted to each other. Neutrons have no charge; consequently, the net charge of the nucleus is positive. If the number of neutrons in an atom is changed, an isotope of the atom is formed.

Atoms, isotopes, and ions are all related if they are formed from the same atom. If an electron has been removed from an atom to form an ion, that ion will have a positive charge. If an isotope of an atom is formed, it will still be electrically neutral but differ in mass since the atom is defined by the number of protons.

1. The nucleus of an atom is made up of
   - **(A)** Electrons and neutrons
   - **(B)** Protons and neutrons
   - **(C)** Electrons and protons
   - **(D)** Neutrons

2. An isotope of an atom is formed by a
   - **(A)** Change in the number of protons
   - **(B)** Change in the number of electrons
   - **(C)** Change in the charge of the atom
   - **(D)** Change in the number of neutrons

3. An ion of an atom would be formed by
   - **(A)** Chemical reaction
   - **(B)** Varying the number of electrons
   - **(C)** Varying the number of protons
   - **(D)** Varying the number of neutrons

Questions 4 through 6 are based on the following information.

Everything around us—whether it is living or not—is composed of matter, which is defined as anything that has mass and takes up space. Matter may belong to one of two classifications: One is based on physical state and the other is based on composition.

- **Classification based on physical state:** Matter exists in four states:
  - **Solid:** Matter existing in a solid state is rigid and almost totally incompressible.
  - **Liquid:** Matter existing in a liquid state is fluid and has very low compressibility.
  - **Gas:** Matter existing in a gaseous state is fluid and highly compressible.
  - **Plasma:** Matter that is partly ionized is called plasma. It does not have a definite shape or volume (like a gas), but under the influence of a magnetic field, structures may be formed.

Water can exist as a solid called ice, where it is rigid and almost impossible to compress without breaking it into finer and finer particles, which is not compressing but subdividing. If you apply heat to ice, it becomes water—a fluid that has very low compressibility. Apply more heat, and the water becomes steam, which is a gas and is highly compressible. Water is one form of matter that can exist in three states depending on pressure and temperature.

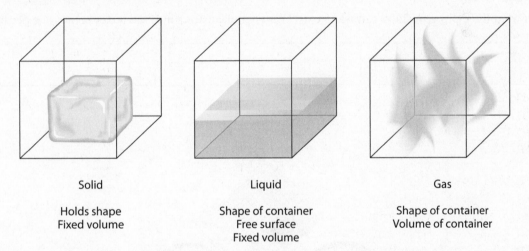

Solid	Liquid	Gas
Holds shape	Shape of container	Shape of container
Fixed volume	Free surface	Volume of container
	Fixed volume	

- **Classification based on composition of matter:** Matter also may be classified based on its compositions. An element is a substance that has atoms of all the same chemical nature. Examples of elements are oxygen and hydrogen.

Matter that is a homogeneous mixture throughout is called a solution. An example of a solution is salt added to water.

Matter that is formed by a mixture of two substances that remain the same but are mixed with one another is called a heterogeneous mixture. An example of a heterogeneous mixture is a combination of salt and pepper.

Fill-in-the-blank

4. In what four physical states can matter exist? Enter your answers into the boxes below, one per box.

5. In what physical state is matter highly compressible?

   (A) Liquid
   (B) Mixture
   (C) Gas
   (D) Solid

Fill-in-the-blank

6. In what three physical states can water exist? Enter your answers into the boxes below, one per box.

Question 7 refers to the following figure.

7. If the cyclist in the diagram wants to move forward, what must he do?

   (A) Lean forward in the seat
   (B) Push forward on the higher pedal
   (C) Push down on the lower pedal
   (D) Release the brakes

Questions 8 and 9 refer to the following figure.

8. Two boys are standing facing each other wearing inline skates. If Boy X pushes as hard as he can and Boy Y does nothing, what will be the result?

   (A) Both boys will remain in the same position.
   (B) Boy X will move backward.
   (C) Boy Y will move backward.
   (D) Both boys will move backward.

9. Boy X has a strange sense of humor. When Boy Y wants a turn pushing, Boy X turns his left foot 45 degrees, effectively creating a brake with his skates. What will happen if Boy Y pushes as hard as he can?

   (A) Both boys will move backward.
   (B) Boy X will move backward.
   (C) Boy Y will move backward.
   (D) Boy X will move slowly.

Question 10 refers to the following passage.

Energy is defined as the ability to cause change or do work. The two main forms of energy are potential (stored energy) and kinetic (energy due to motion). If you carried a 1-pound weight to the roof of a tall building and held it on the edge, it would possess potential energy because you carried it to the top of the building. If it accidentally fell, it would possess kinetic energy.

10. A basketball player is waiting for her teammates while holding a basketball in her hands. What type of energy does the basketball possess as she holds it?

    (A) Positional
    (B) Kinetic
    (C) Stationary
    (D) Potential

Question 11 refers to the following passage.

Most of the matter we're exposed to is really mixtures of substances and not pure ones. Pure substances have the same properties in any sample we find. It doesn't matter where the substance came from, it will always have the same chemical properties. Mixtures are composed of two or more substances, and a mixture's properties can vary from sample to sample depending on how much of each contributing substance it contains. Each sample, with varying ratios of components, will have differing properties.

11. The properties of a mixture can

    (A) Always be the same

    (B) Vary from sample to sample

    (C) Make them interesting to observe

    (D) Be the same as pure substances

Question 12 is based on the following stimulus, an excerpt from www1.eere.energy.gov/hydrogenandfuelcells/ pdfs/aluminium_water_hydrogen.pdf.

Short Answer

Stimulus

It should be emphasized that the hydrogen capacity values given in this paper for the aluminum-water reactions are for the materials only. There are, in addition, a number of on-board system requirements that would add more weight and volume. Some examples are containers for the fresh materials and the reaction products, a mechanism for unloading spent materials and loading fresh materials, a reactor that would allow controlled quantities of materials to react, devices for transporting solid and/or liquid materials between the different components, water recovery sub-systems (if used), heat exchangers, pressure control valves, etc. Some of these system components may prove to be very difficult to design and fabricate for reliability and longevity. The highly transient behavior of the fuel requirements for vehicles would be particularly difficult to accommodate with a chemical system that, once started, runs to completion. This is very different from a metal hydride, for example, where the thermodynamics of the material both supply and limit the equilibrium hydrogen pressure at a given temperature.

The current DOE hydrogen storage system capacity targets are a hydrogen gravimetric capacity of 6 wt.% and a hydrogen volumetric capacity of 45 g H2/L (27). It is clear from the analysis presented in this White Paper that no aluminum-water reaction system can meet these targets. Additional negative factors are the high cost of hydrogen from this process, and the amount of aluminum required for large-scale vehicular applications.

12.

> <u>PROMPT</u>
>
> There was some hope in the scientific community that vehicles could be powered by a reaction between aluminum and water. The results of the experiment seem to indicate otherwise. Explain why this reaction does not appear to be a solution to the environmental problems created by petrochemical-powered vehicles.
>
> Type your response in the box (for this Practice Test, write your response on a separate sheet of paper). This short answer item may take you about 10 minutes to complete. See the answer explanation for tips on how your response can be self-scored.

Question 13 refers to the following passage.

When we think of atoms, we visualize something like our solar system with particles orbiting around a central core. This may or may not be accurate, but it's the simplest way of thinking about atoms.

At the center of this system is the nucleus, where our sun would be in a diagram of the solar system. The nucleus is made up of protons and neutrons and makes up almost all the mass of the atom. Spinning around the nucleus are the electrons, which are much smaller and have little mass compared to the nucleus.

Protons bear a positive charge, electrons bear a negative charge, and neutrons are neutral. Atoms have an equal number of electrons and protons and are, thus, electrically neutral. Normally, like charges repel each other, but in the nucleus is a very powerful nuclear force that maintains stability in the nucleus.

13. The nucleus is composed of protons and neutrons held together by

   (A) Gravitational force
   (B) Centrifugal force
   (C) Nuclear force
   (D) Centripetal force

14. A car is traveling along a level road at a speed of 30 mph. Seeing a stop sign ahead, the driver decides to bring the car to a stop. What provides the force necessary to bring the car to a stop?

   (A) The driver's foot on the brake
   (B) The force of gravity
   (C) Wind resistance
   (D) Friction when the brakes are applied

15. The basic functional unit of life is the

   (A) Neutron
   (B) Proton
   (C) Molecule
   (D) Cell

Question 16 refers to the following passage.

An organism is comprised of one or more cells functioning as a stable unit and possessing all the characteristics of life. This definition excludes viruses because, in order to reproduce, viruses are dependent on the biochemical machinery of a host cell. Viruses have no metabolism of their own and, consequently, can neither synthesize nor organize the organic compound from which they are formed. Autonomous reproduction is, therefore, not possible, and viruses passively replicate using the machinery of the host cell. Viruses do have their own genes and can change just as organisms do.

16. Viruses are not considered the same as living organisms because

   (A) They make people sick.
   (B) They are not composed of molecules.
   (C) They depend on the host cell to reproduce.
   (D) They can replicate all by themselves.

Questions 17 and 18 refer to the following passage and figure.

Amino acids are involved in metabolism and are important to life. Amino acids join together to form proteins. The amino acids are linked in various configurations to form different proteins, and every protein can be identified chemically by the amino acids and their structure. Amino acids are very important for nutrition and human life. Without them, we would not have proteins.

Each amino acid can exist in two forms: left-handed (levo- or L) and right-handed (dextro- or D) versions. The following figure represents the two versions of alanine.

L-alanine

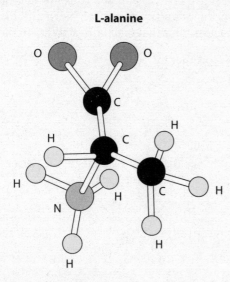

D-alanine

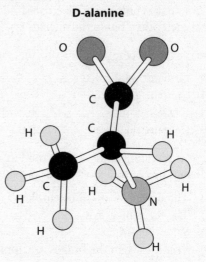

17. Proteins are formed by

   (A) Amino acid atoms
   (B) Cows
   (C) Linked amino acids
   (D) Chemical reactions of amino acids

18. What is the difference between a levo- and a dextro- amino acid?

   (A) The chemical bonds
   (B) The composition of the molecule
   (C) The way they're used in metabolism
   (D) The configuration of the atoms in space

Questions 19 and 20 refer to the following figure and passage.

Resulting Offspring from Breeding Tall and Short Plants

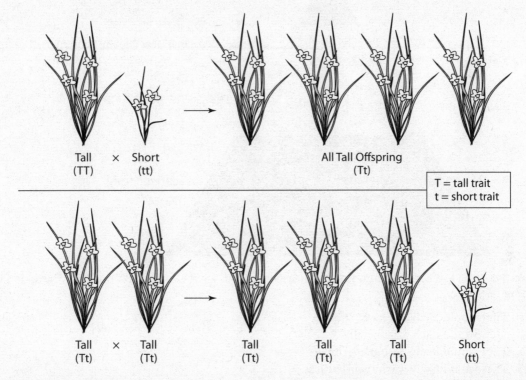

Tall × Short
(TT) (tt)

All Tall Offspring
(Tt)

T = tall trait
t = short trait

Tall × Tall
(Tt) (Tt)

Tall   Tall   Tall   Short
(Tt)   (Tt)   (Tt)   (tt)

Gregor Mendel was a scientist who was interested in how future generations of plants would carry traits of the first generation. He hypothesized that there were two types of traits: recessive and dominant. To test his hypothesis, Mendel cross-bred pea plants, mating two tall plants and then mating a tall plant with a short plant.

The two tall plants produced tall plants in the first generation of offspring but produced three tall and one short offspring in the second generation. The tall and the short produced all tall plants. He concluded that tall must be a dominant trait and short must be a recessive trait and that each plant contained both traits. The third generation produced a plant with the recessive trait—a short plant.

19. Mendel hypothesized that what two types of traits were involved in heredity?

(A) Tall and short
(B) Dominant and short
(C) Recessive and tall
(D) Dominant and recessive

20. Referring to the diagram, why would breeding a tall plant and a short plant produce all tall plants?

(A) Short plants cannot survive.
(B) Tall plants get more sun.
(C) The tall trait is dominant.
(D) The tall trait is recessive.

Question 21 refers to the following figure.

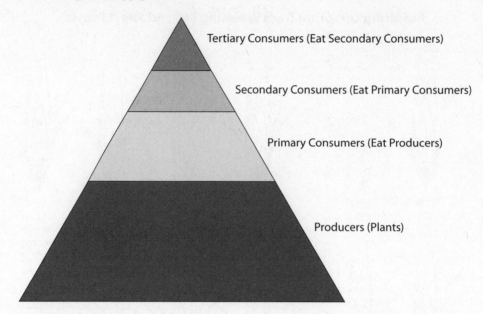

21. If lettuce were to become contaminated with salmonella, what effect would this likely have on salad-eating tertiary consumers?

   (A) They would likely eat fewer salads.
   (B) They would likely become ill.
   (C) They would likely become herbivores.
   (D) They would likely wash their lettuce.

Question 22 refers to the following diagram.

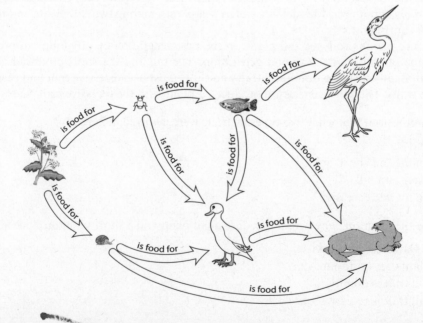

22. If snails suddenly disappeared, according to the diagram, what effect would this have?

    (A) Otters would grow thinner.
    (B) Insects would increase in number.
    (C) Otters would have to look for other food sources.
    (D) Otters would eat fewer fish.

23. If the hereditary traits of an organism are contained in the organism's DNA and if we could find a sample of DNA from a dinosaur, could the dinosaur be reproduced?

    (A) Yes, but you would need two dinosaurs from the same species.
    (B) Yes, but the infant dinosaur would be too large for a laboratory.
    (C) No, because DNA does not survive that long.
    (D) The experiment would have to be attempted to find out.

Question 24 refers to the following passage.

If a scientist wanted to produce an animal with the same nuclear DNA as another animal, she might use a process called reproductive cloning, also known as somatic cell nuclear transfer (SCNT). During this process, genetic material from the nucleus of the donor animal is transferred to an egg that has had its nucleus removed. This removes the genetic material from the egg and allows the introduced genetic material to exist. In order to stimulate cell division, the egg is subjected to electric current. When the egg matures slightly, it is implanted in a female host where it develops until it is ready to be born.

Drop-down

24. If a scientist wanted to clone an animal, she would start with _____.

    (A) SCNT
    (B) an egg
    (C) a somatic cell
    (D) genetic material from the donor

Question 25 refers to the following passage.

Every living thing is made of at least one cell. Human beings are made of many cells. These cells group together to form tissue and then eventually organs, which perform specific functions in the human body.

When two or more tissues work together, they form an organ, such as the stomach, heart, or skin. Each of these organs performs a specific task, which is dependent on all the other tasks performed by the other organs.

25. In the human body, cells group together to next form

    (A) Atoms
    (B) Legs and arms
    (C) Organs
    (D) Tissues

Questions 26 through 28 are based on the following figure and passage.

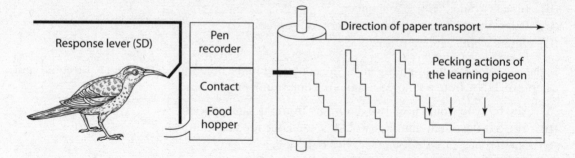

B. F. Skinner, a scientist, hypothesized that if an organism was given a reward for performing an action, that action would probably be repeated. In the diagram, the bird is rewarded with food for pecking at a lever. According to Skinner, a reward would increase the likelihood of the bird pecking at the lever again.

This theory can be useful in real life. If you're trying to teach your dog to heel and you give him a reward each time he heels after you give him a vocal instruction to do so, there is a greater likelihood that the dog will follow the instruction. After many attempts, the dog will have learned to heel at your command.

26. If you want to teach your dog to come when you call, one way of training the dog would be to

    (A) Yell at the dog whenever he fails to come.
    (B) Reward the dog for coming to you when you call him.
    (C) Call the dog until he comes to you.
    (D) Leave the dog outside until he learns to come when called.

27. In the diagram, the recorder shows that

    (A) The paper travels from right to left.
    (B) The bird will peck at the lever.
    (C) The pecking behavior increases with rewards.
    (D) The bird is pecking at the lever to make the paper move.

28. Joan and Henry have a young son who sucks his thumb. In order to teach him not to suck his thumb, what might they do?

    (A) Put heavy gloves on their son
    (B) Feed him only on days when he doesn't suck his thumb
    (C) Give him a meaningful reward whenever he doesn't suck his thumb
    (D) None of the above

Question 29 is based on the following figure.

The Skinner Box

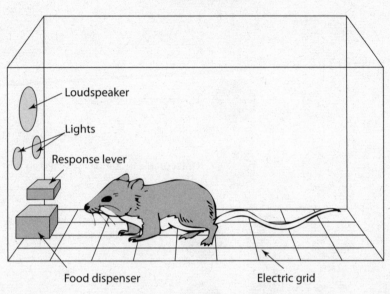

Loudspeaker

Lights

Response lever

Food dispenser

Electric grid

29. The Skinner box is used to condition small animals like rats. When the green light flashes and the rat hits the response lever, food is dispensed from the food dispenser. If the rat hits the response lever when the red light flashes, a mild shock is administered through the wire grid on the floor. The best explanation of why the rat would learn to press the response lever when the green light goes on is:

(A) The green light is more pleasant than the red one.
(B) The green light means go.
(C) The food is used as a reward for pressing the lever when the green light comes on.
(D) The mild shock is a reward for obeying instructions.

Question 30 is based on the following diagram.

Biological Evolution

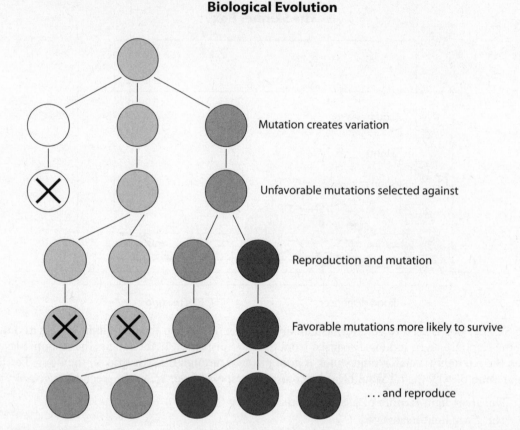

Mutation creates variation

Unfavorable mutations selected against

Reproduction and mutation

Favorable mutations more likely to survive

...and reproduce

30. In the preceding diagram, evolution says that favorable mutations are more likely to survive. If corn requires sunlight to thrive but tall plants are harder to harvest than short plants, which height of plants is more likely to survive?

(A) Short plants
(B) Both short and tall plants
(C) Whatever the farmer plants
(D) Tall plants

Question 31 is based on the following passage.

All the chemical reactions that take place in the body are collectively called metabolism. The reactions may be endergonic or exergonic. Endergonic reactions need a net input of energy to start the reaction. Exergonic reactions release energy. An example of an endergonic reaction is photosynthesis; the net input of energy is supplied by the sun. An example of an exergonic reaction is cell respiration, which burns food to release energy.

31. Metabolism is a collection of

    (A) Endergonic reactions
    (B) Exergonic reactions
    (C) Photosynthesis
    (D) All the chemical reactions taking place in the body

Questions 32 and 33 refer to the following passage.

Enzymes are catalysts, substances that start or speed up a chemical reaction without themselves being changed; they speed up reactions by providing an alternate path requiring lower activation energy for the reaction. These catalysts are very choosy, only catalyzing certain reactions.

Enzyme catalytic activity is affected by the following factors: temperature, pH, and concentration of catalyst and substrate. Some substances have the ability to slow down or stop the activity of the enzyme and are called inhibitors.

32. Enzymes are considered catalysts because they

    (A) Help reactions to occur
    (B) Make reactions easier to control
    (C) Take part in chemical reactions and emerge as different substances
    (D) Lower the energy required for the reaction to occur

Drag-and-drop

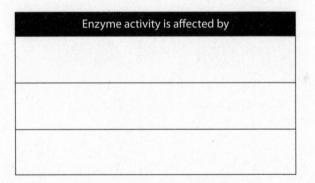

33. Drag the items that affect enzyme activity into the boxes above.

    (To answer, write the letter of all answer choices that apply on your answer sheet.)

    (A) pH
    (B) Concentration of catalyst
    (C) Concentration of substrate
    (D) Amino acids

Questions 34 through 36 refer to the following passage.

Cell theory states that all living organisms are made up of one or more cells, which are the basic unit of life and have the same basic chemical composition. Organisms may be unicellular or multicellular. Cell theory goes on to state that cells come from preexisting cells and that they are the basic unit of structure and function. Each cell contains DNA, which passes on hereditary information from cell to cell.

34. All living organisms are composed of

   (A) One or more cells
   (B) Life
   (C) Chemicals
   (D) Energy

Drop-down

35. The purpose of the DNA is to _____.

   (A) help the cell grow
   (B) provide the cell with energy
   (C) help the cell multiply
   (D) pass on hereditary information

36. An organism that is unicellular would

   (A) Have difficulty reproducing
   (B) Have only one cell
   (C) Contain multiple cells
   (D) Have no DNA

Question 37 refers to the following figure and passage.

DNA

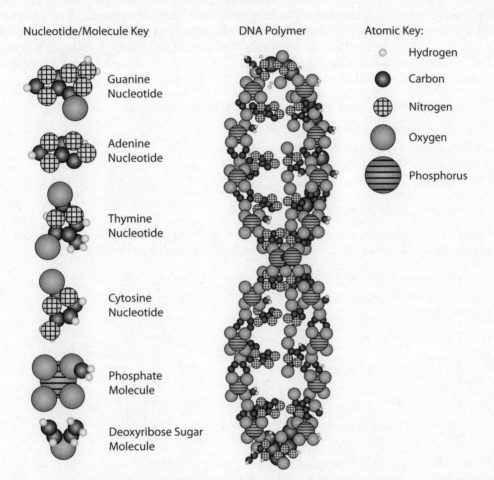

Nucleotide/Molecule Key

Guanine Nucleotide

Adenine Nucleotide

Thymine Nucleotide

Cytosine Nucleotide

Phosphate Molecule

Deoxyribose Sugar Molecule

DNA Polymer

Atomic Key:

Hydrogen

Carbon

Nitrogen

Oxygen

Phosphorus

We all carry the instructions for the characteristics of the next generation in our DNA. This is a large molecule forming a single chromosome in a cell. In humans, most cells have two copies of each of 23 different chromosomes. One of these copies comes from the father, and the other comes from the mother. The sex of the offspring is determined by a specific pair of chromosomes. Sometimes mutations occur in the DNA, but most of the mutations are insignificant.

37. Why do children often resemble both parents?

(A) Cells determine characteristics.
(B) They live with their parents.
(C) Both parents are involved in producing offspring.
(D) Both parents contribute characteristics through their DNA.

Question 38 refers to the following passage.

Sharks are considered dangerous fish, and most other fish prefer to stay out of their way. Not so with the remora, which is a suckerfish. Remoras are called suckerfish because their dorsal fins have modified to form a sucker or suction-cup-like appendage, which they can use to attach themselves to larger fish, such as a shark. The remora attaches itself to the shark and, because it's small and doesn't injure the shark with its sucker, neither benefits nor hurts the shark. The remora does benefit from this action because the shark provides protection (other fish seldom attack the shark) and the remnants of the shark's meals provide food for the remora.

38. The remora derives benefit from its association with the shark because

    (A) The remora does not have to learn to swim.
    (B) The shark provides food and protection for the remora.
    (C) Large fish are afraid of the remora.
    (D) The shark feeds the remora.

Questions 39 refers to the following passage and diagram.

When a heavier, unstable nucleus splits into two or more lighter nuclei releasing vast amounts of energy and two or three free neutrons, the process is known as nuclear fission.

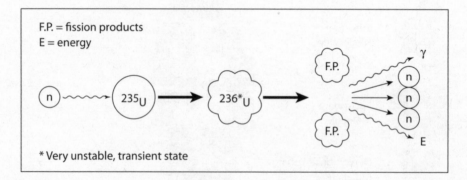

The free neutron can go on to produce other fissions producing free neutrons, which can produce many more fissions. This is known as a chain reaction and may or may not continue depending on a series of external conditions.

39. According to the diagram, what happens when a free neutron collides with an atom of U-235?

    (A) It changes to U-236.
    (B) It releases energy.
    (C) It releases free neutrons.
    (D) It assists in the creation of fission products.

Questions 40 through 42 refer to the following diagram and passage.

Car Strut

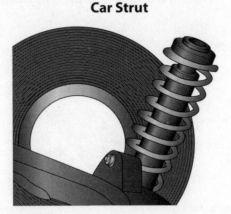

Springs are made of elastic materials (materials that can change in shape and then restore themselves). When you push down on a spring, the shape of the spring changes—it gets shorter. When you release the force that you've been applying, the spring restores itself to its former shape and size. This property is most useful in designing a car strut.

Roads are full of bumps and potholes. Bumps create a force upward on the tire, and the potholes create a condition where the force exerted upward by the road is suddenly released. Without something between you and the road, every bump and pothole would be reflected by a corresponding bump inside the car.

The spring in the strut acts as an intermediary and absorbs the forces of the bumps and potholes and returns to its former shape ready to begin work again.

40. How does the strut act to produce a smooth ride in the car?

   (A) It acts on the shock absorber to smooth out the movements of the shock absorber.
   (B) It absorbs the forces from irregularities in the road.
   (C) It creates forces that make the road smoother.
   (D) It bounces back and forth.

41. Why is a car spring considered an elastic material?

   (A) It can bounce.
   (B) It can stretch and then restore itself.
   (C) It is made of rubber.
   (D) It can change its shape and then restore itself.

42. Why do cars require springs?

   (A) To help the motor work efficiently
   (B) To help the driver keep his attention on the road
   (C) To smooth out the ride
   (D) To make sure that the brakes stop the car

Questions 43 and 44 refer to the following diagram and passage.

Producing Electricity from the Sun's Energy

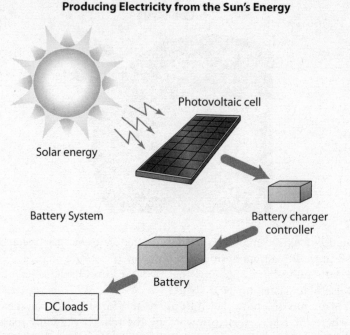

A great deal of energy is delivered by the sun to Earth every sunny day. For millennia, people just enjoyed the heat and light and didn't think about harnessing that energy. With the reducing supplies of oil and the environmental impact of combustion on Earth, people are turning to the sun for answers.

Science has given us the ability to convert energy from the sun into electricity through the use of photovoltaic cells. These cells can be mounted on rooftops or set up in fields. In any case, they'll produce electrical power—but the next question is what to do with that electrical power.

Rooftop photovoltaic cells can produce electricity for the use of the building every day when the sun is shining, but during the dark hours of the day, no electricity is produced. The simplest solution is to feed the electricity into the electric grid during the day and extract electricity from the grid during the dark hours of the day. Many local governments are promoting this system through subsidies for solar producers.

43. How can we use the free energy from the sun to run our appliances now?

   (A) Plug them into wall sockets
   (B) Insist that our local electric authority investigate solar power
   (C) Convert the energy with photovoltaic cells
   (D) Put our appliances outside in the sun

44. How is government trying to promote the increased use of solar energy?

   (A) By building huge solar generation plants
   (B) By passing laws to require people to use solar energy
   (C) By paying people and companies to produce solar electricity
   (D) By making the use of solar power an election platform

Question 45 refers to the following diagram and passage.

Hot Spot

Oxygen Cycle Reservoirs and Flux

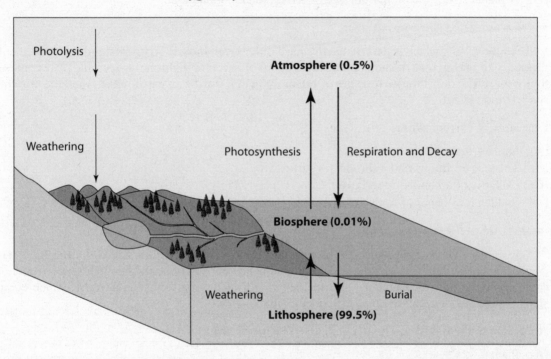

The largest oxygen reservoir is within Earth's crust and mantle. The largest oxygen source is photosynthesis. Oxygen is lost to the atmosphere through respiration and decay, where oxygen is consumed and carbon dioxide is released.

45. What are opposite processes in the oxygen cycle according to the diagram and passage? Click on the diagram with your mouse to select the opposite processes.

    (To answer, write the letter of the answer choice that applies.)

    (A) Respiration and decay
    (B) Photosynthesis and weathering
    (C) Photolysis and burial
    (D) Photosynthesis and respiration and decay

Question 46 is based on the following passage.

The planet we know as Earth was originally a massive object that attracted more matter by gravitational force. As the inner part of this mass became hotter and hotter, the metals began to melt and sink to the middle of this mass, creating a metallic core. It is thought that another planet crashed into the forming Earth and the collision released a hunk of mass that became the moon.

46. How do scientists think that the moon was formed?

    (A) A gigantic space rock was attracted to Earth's gravitational field.
    (B) The mass of the moon attracted material to form a ball.
    (C) A mass of molten material spun around Earth until it became solid.
    (D) A planet struck the molten surface of Earth, releasing material.

Question 47 refers to the following passage.

The lithosphere, which is part of Earth's hard outer layer, moves. To understand this movement, it is necessary to realize that the lithosphere is made up of seven or eight major tectonic plates and several minor ones. The only time we're aware of the movement is during an earthquake, when the movement is sudden and violent.

47. One cause of earthquakes is

    (A) Underground vibrations
    (B) Volcanic eruptions under the earth's surface
    (C) Collapse of an underground cave
    (D) Sudden movement of one of the tectonic plates

Question 48 refers to the following passage.

One of the most accepted theories of how the universe was formed is called the Big Bang Theory. According to the Big Bang Theory, something happened billions of years ago. In essence, from nothing came all of the universe's matter and time began. All of the matter in the universe, which comprises stars, planets, moons, and so on, is explained by the theory.

48. According to the Big Bang Theory, the universe came from

    (A) Planets
    (B) Rocks
    (C) Nothing
    (D) Space junk

Question 49 refers to the following passage.

Under Earth's crust is a hot molten layer, and if an opening develops, the hot magma escapes along with ash and gases. Volcanoes can be classified as active or dormant. Some volcanoes have not erupted in historical times and are called extinct. An active volcano may be erupting or likely to erupt in the near future and poses the greatest danger to people and animals in the area. Scientifically speaking, any volcano that has erupted in the last 10,000 years is considered active; using this definition, there are around 500 active volcanoes on Earth. There are around 50 active volcanoes in the United States, but few of these erupt in any one year. It is estimated that around 500 million people on Earth live close to active volcanoes.

49. What is an active volcano, from a scientific point of view?

    (A) One that has never erupted
    (B) One that is currently erupting
    (C) One that is releasing hot gases
    (D) One that has erupted in the last 10,000 years

Question 50 refers to the following figure.

The Carbon Cycle

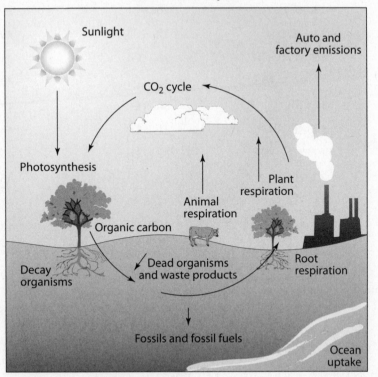

50. Looking at the illustration above, how would reducing emissions from cars and factories affect the overall amount of carbon dioxide in the atmosphere?

   (A) It would reduce the amount of carbon dioxide in the atmosphere.
   (B) It would increase the amount of carbon dioxide in the atmosphere.
   (C) It would leave the amount of carbon dioxide in the atmosphere unchanged.
   (D) It would interfere with photosynthesis.

Answer Key

1. (B)
2. (D)
3. (B)
4. solid, liquid, gas, plasma
5. (C)
6. solid, liquid, gas
7. (B)
8. (D)
9. (C)
10. (D)
11. (B)
12. See explanation.

13. (C)
14. (D)
15. (D)
16. (C)
17. (C)
18. (D)
19. (D)
20. (C)
21. (B)
22. (C)
23. (D)
24. (D)
25. (D)

26. (B)
27. (C)
28. (C)
29. (C)
30. (D)
31. (D)
32. (D)
33. (A), (B), (C)
34. (A)
35. (D)
36. (B)
37. (D)
38. (B)

39. (D)
40. (B)
41. (D)
42. (C)
43. (C)
44. (C)
45. (D)
46. (D)
47. (D)
48. (C)
49. (D)
50. (A)

Answer Explanations

1. **(B)** The nucleus of the atom is made up of protons and neutrons according to the passage. The other choices are impossible combinations of the possible parts in the atom.

2. **(D)** Altering the number of neutrons creates an isotope, which will have a different mass. If it were possible to change the number of protons, a different element would be formed.

3. **(B)** An ion of an atom would be formed by varying the number of electrons. Varying the number of protons would form another element. Varying the number of neutrons would form an isotope. Chemical reaction would have little effect on the electrons.

4. **solid, liquid, gas, plasma** The four physical states of matter are solid, liquid, gas, and plasma. Solutions and mixtures are not states, but part of a classification system.

5. **(C)** Matter is highly compressible in a gaseous state. Liquids (A) can be slightly compressed, solids (D) are not compressible, and mixture (B) is not a state.

6. **solid, liquid, gas** Ice is the solid form, water is the liquid, and steam is the gas.

7. **(B)** Pushing forward on the higher pedal creates a downward force that is translated by the chain and the transmission in the rear wheel to a forward motion. Pushing down on the lower pedal would have little effect because it is at a point where there will be no rotation of the pedals.

8. **(D)** Assuming that neither skate will stick on the floor as it rolls, the force applied by Boy X should cause both boys to move; because they are facing each other, they will each move backward.

9. **(C)** If Boy X locks his skates by turning his foot, all the force applied by Boy Y will move Boy Y backward, but Boy X will not move.

10. **(D)** The basketball would possess potential energy while she holds it because of its position above the floor. If she dropped it or threw it, it would possess kinetic energy, but she didn't. Choices (A) and (C) are not types of energy.

11. **(B)** Because a mixture is made of two or more substances, each of which can be added in differing amounts, the properties of a mixture can vary from sample to sample. Choice (A) refers to pure substances and is a reminder to read passages carefully.

12. This short answer item requires an essay response to be written in roughly 10 minutes. The first thing to remember is that this is an essay, and it should have an introduction and a conclusion. There should be no spelling or grammatical errors and the sentences should follow one another in a coherent pattern.

   The response will be scored on a 3-point scale. A 3-point response is well-crafted and uses data and information from the Stimulus. A 2-point response is reasonably well-crafted and includes partial support from the Stimulus but more than just a collection of quotes. A 1-point response is poorly crafted and contains only some evidence from the Stimulus. A 0-point response is poorly written and contains no supportive material from the Stimulus. If you just copy words from the Stimulus without interpreting or showing any understanding of what they mean, write it in a language other than English, or leave your response blank, your score will be not recorded.

13. **(C)** The force holding the nucleus together is a nuclear force. The other choices, while they are examples of forces, have nothing to do with the nucleus. This is one example when skimming the passage after reading the question might prove beneficial. The only force mentioned in the passage is nuclear force, which is the correct answer.

14. **(D)** Applying the brakes in a car creates a frictional force, which brings the car to a halt. Choice (A) seems possible, but it doesn't describe a force—it describes a position.

15. **(D)** The cell is the basic functional unit of life. This should be common knowledge from your basic science knowledge and reading.

16. **(C)** The passage states that viruses depend on the host cell to reproduce. Choice (A) may be correct, but it doesn't answer the question. Choices (B) and (D) are false statements. Always read the question carefully to make sure that the information given in the answer you choose answers the question that is asked. The information may be correct, but if it doesn't answer the question, it isn't the correct answer.

17. **(C)** Proteins are formed by amino acids linking together. The other choices are wrong, although some of them do contain the words *amino acid.* Always read the choices carefully. Some may contain familiar words and still not answer the question or be wrong.

18. **(D)** Looking carefully at the diagram, you'll notice that the two forms differ in their configuration in space.

19. **(D)** Mendel hypothesized that there were two types of traits—dominant and recessive—which answers the question. The other choices are incorrect because both types of traits are not mentioned.

20. **(C)** Mendel said that the tall trait was dominant and, thus, would produce tall plants when bred with a short plant. This is a question that depends on your understanding of scientific vocabulary. If you understand the difference between *dominant* and *recessive,* the question is easy to answer; if you don't, it becomes very difficult. If you look carefully at the diagram, you'll see that all offspring plants contain both traits (Tt), but because the tall trait is dominant, they're all tall.

21. **(B)** Salmonella is an organism that can cause illness in humans, who are tertiary consumers. Washing the lettuce doesn't always destroy the salmonella, and herbivores eat lettuce.

22. **(C)** Otters depend on snails as part of their diet. If there were no more snails, the otters would have to look for other sources of food.

23. **(D)** The best answer is that the experiment would have to be attempted. What is presented is a question that might lead to a hypothesis. The hypothesis could lead to a series of investigations that might lead to an experimental design. Choices (A) and (C) are two of the questions that would have to be investigated but are not yet answers. Choice (B) is wrong because labs can be built in any size.

24. **(D)** According to the passage, the scientist would start with genetic material from the donor.

25. **(D)** The cells group together to form tissues. Then two or more tissues working together form an organ. You may have been tempted to choose choice (C), organs. The key word in the question stem is "next." According to the passage, the order is cells, then tissues, and then organs.

26. **(B)** According to Skinner, rewarding the dog will increase the chances of the dog coming when called. Choices (A) and (D) are cruel and wouldn't work. Choice (C) will just wear out the owner.

27. **(C)** The graph shows an increase in pecking behavior with the passage of time as the bird is rewarded for pecking.

28. **(C)** It is difficult to teach someone *not* to do something—according to Skinner, a reward increases the likelihood of the organism repeating an action. Joan and Henry are trying to get their son not to do something, which is decreasing the likelihood of an event. They have to find another way. Choice (A) might work but is unlikely and doesn't follow any of the material presented. Choice (B) is cruel and neglectful.

29. **(C)** Pushing the lever when the green light comes on produces food for the rat, which is a reward for pushing the lever at the appropriate time and would increase the frequency of the rat doing so at the right time.

30. **(D)** Tall plants are more likely to thrive and reproduce than short plants.

31. **(D)** According to the passage, metabolism is collectively all the chemical reactions taking place in the body. You often can understand scientific vocabulary by looking for clues in the sentence or passage. In this case, metabolism is defined in the passage.

32. **(D)** Enzymes lower the energy required for the reaction to occur. This answer is a summary of the first part of the passage.

33. **(A), (B), and (C)** The first three choices are factors that do affect enzyme activity. Amino acids, choice (D), are not mentioned in the passage.

34. **(A)** The passage states that all living organisms are composed of cells. The other choices are incorrect but may sound plausible if you just skimmed the passage.

35. **(D)** DNA passes on hereditary information from cell to cell. The other choices might sound plausible if you didn't read the passage.

36. **(B)** Sometimes a scientific word can be understood if you look at the parts of it. *Uni* means one; so, *unicellular* means having one cell. When you come across an unfamiliar word on the Science Test, try to see if you understand any part of the word so you can make an educated guess at its meaning.

37. **(D)** According to the passage, the instructions for the characteristics of the offspring are contained in the DNA of both parents. Choices (A) and (C) are partially correct, but choice (D) is more accurate and complete. Always look for a complete answer that is supported by the passage.

38. **(B)** The remora's food and protection are provided by the shark. Choice (D) is wrong because the remora feeds off the remnants of the shark's meals. If the remora were not there, the excess food would just remain in the ocean for other organisms to eat, but the shark does not directly feed the remora. Choices (A) and (C) have no basis in the passage or in fact.

39. **(D)** A fission reaction can continue without outside help because it produces the free neutrons needed to continue by the reaction itself.

40. **(B)** The strut absorbs the forces created by the irregularities in the road. Always read the question and choices carefully to make sure that you're answering the question correctly. Shock absorbers may be part of the process, but they are not mentioned in the diagram or the passage, so Choice (A) is wrong as an answer.

41. **(D)** A spring can change its shape and then restore itself. The car spring absorbs irregularities in the road by compressing and changing its shape, but then the energy present through the change in shape acts upon the spring to restore it to its original shape.

42. **(C)** The springs in the car smooth out the ride by absorbing the forces presented by the road.

43. **(C)** Photovoltaic cells have the ability to convert the energy from the sun into electricity. One hint, aside from the context of the passage, is that *photo* refers to light and *voltaic* refers to electricity. Choice (B) is a good idea, but it would take time to implement and the question refers to *now*.

44. **(C)** Offering subsidies to people usually increases the number of people who buy into a particular project. Photovoltaic cells are expensive; subsidies help defray the cost.

45. **(D)** Photosynthesis and respiration and decay are opposite processes. According to the diagram, photosynthesis is the production of oxygen from energy and carbon dioxide, and respiration and decay lead to carbon dioxide.

46. **(D)** According to the passage, a planet struck Earth's surface, releasing a hunk of the surface, which flew into space to form the moon. The other choices may sound plausible if you haven't read the passage. The answer to the question is always included in the passage or the illustrative material.

47. **(D)** The best answer to the question is choice (D). The others may sound reasonable or semi-reasonable, but the only one mentioned in the passage is choice (D), and the answer must be based on the passage.

48. **(C)** The answer, "nothing," is clearly stated in the third sentence of the passage.

49. **(D)** A volcano that has erupted in the last 10,000 years is considered active by scientists. Choices (B) and (C) might be correct from a layperson's point of view, but the scientific view supports choice (D).

50. **(A)** The diagram shows carbon dioxide being emitted into the atmosphere by automobiles and factories. If this amount were to be reduced, it would reduce the amount of carbon dioxide in the atmosphere. It would take a dramatic reduction of all forms of carbon dioxide emissions to interfere with photosynthesis.

XIV. Social Studies Practice Test with Answer Explanations

This practice test is not related to the GED Ready™ – The Official Practice Test, produced and distributed by GED Testing Service LLC. GED Testing Service® has not approved, authorized, endorsed, been involved in the development of, or licensed the substantive content of this practice test.

The Social Studies Test is divided into two sections: Section 1 contains question-and-answer items and Section 2 is the extended response item. On the actual GED® test, there is no set number of questions in Section 1. Also, please note that Section 1 and Section 2 are timed independently, and there is not a break between the two sections.

Although you will enter your answers and write your extended responses and short answer responses on the computer during the actual GED® test, you will need to use your own paper to record your answers and responses for this Practice Test.

Try to make your behavior on this Practice Test as close as possible to the actual test conditions. Observe the time constraints.

Answer all the questions. There is no deduction for wrong answers, and you get points for each right one. Some questions are worth more than 1 point, but that information might not be readily available to you while taking the test. The important thing is to get as many correct answers as you can and guess if you have to. Unanswered items do nothing to improve your score. If you need to, guess. The more wrong answer choices you can eliminate, the better your chances of guessing the correct answer. In multiple-choice items, if you can eliminate three choices, you will have a 100 percent chance of being correct! Unfortunately, for each choice you cannot eliminate, the odds go down.

Section 1

Time: 65 Minutes—50 Questions

Directions: Choose the best answer to each question. Following the instruction for each type of layout indicated, mark your answers on a separate sheet of paper.

If a question is not standard multiple choice, the item type will be identified directly before the question.

Questions 1 through 7 refer to the following excerpt from U.S. History For Dummies, *2nd Edition, by Steve Wiegand, copyright 2009 by Wiley Publishing, Inc. Reprinted with permission of John Wiley & Sons, Inc.*

The Pilgrims (actually, they called themselves "the Saints" and everyone else "the Strangers," and weren't dubbed Pilgrims until much later by one of their Leaders) were mostly lower-class farmers and craftsmen who had decided the Church of England was still too Catholic for their tastes. So they separated themselves from the Church, thus resulting in everyone else calling them "Separatists." This did not please King James I, who suggested rather forcefully that they rejoin or separate themselves from England.

The Separatists we're concerned with did just that, settling in Holland in 1608. But after a decade of watching their children become "Dutchified," the English expatriates longed for someplace they could live as English subjects and still worship the way they wanted. The answer was America.

After going back to England and negotiating a charter to establish a colony, taking out a few loans, and forming a company, a group of 102 men, women, and children left England on September 16, 1620, on a ship called the *Mayflower.* (A second ship, the *Speedwell,* also started out, but sprang a leak and had to turn back.) The *Mayflower* was usually used for shipping wine between France and England. Its cargo for this trip was decidedly more varied than usual. Although the Pilgrims didn't really pack any smarter than had the Jamestown colonists, they did show some imagination. Among the things they took to the wilderness of North America were musical instruments, all kinds of furniture, and even books on the history of Turkey (the country, not the bird). One guy even brought 139 pairs of shoes and boots.

Despite a rough crossing that took 65 days, only one passenger and four crewmen died, and one child was born. After some preliminary scouting, they dropped anchor in a broad, shallow bay we know as Plymouth. (No evidence exists to indicate they landed on any kind of rock.)

1. Who were the Pilgrims in the passage?
   - (A) Strangers
   - (B) Lower-class farmers
   - (C) Church leaders
   - (D) The Dutch

2. Why did they want to separate from the Church of England?
   - (A) It was too strange.
   - (B) It was too forceful.
   - (C) It was too saintly.
   - (D) It was too Catholic.

Drop-down

3. The Separatists first settled in _____ .

   (A) Holland
   (B) England
   (C) America
   (D) France

Drop-down

4. To establish a colony, the Separatists required _____ .

   (A) a crew
   (B) Permission
   (C) the King's blessing
   (D) a charter

Drop-down

5. The *Mayflower* had previously been used for _____ .

   (A) springing a leak
   (B) shipping wine
   (C) forming a company
   (D) negotiating a charter

6. What did the Pilgrims bring with them on the voyage?

   (A) musical instruments
   (B) furniture
   (C) books
   (D) All of the above

7. Where did the *Mayflower* actually land?

   (A) France
   (B) England
   (C) Plymouth
   (D) Turkey

Questions 8 through 10 refer to the following political cartoon from GED® For Dummies *by Murray Shukyn and Dale E. Shuttleworth, Ph.D., copyright 2003 by Wiley Publishing, Inc. Reprinted with permission of John Wiley & Sons, Inc.*

Drop-down

8. According to the cartoon, cell phones are _____.

    (A) a wonderful invention
    (B) an aid to communication
    (C) a medical breakthrough
    (D) injurious to health

9. What is the best way to describe the cell phone user in the cartoon?

    (A) Foolhardy
    (B) Talkative
    (C) Considerate
    (D) Courageous

10. The cartoon suggest that cell phones represent a risk to our health. Where does that idea come from?

    (A) Going to the movies
    (B) Scientific research
    (C) Urban legends
    (D) Popular opinion

Questions 11 through 14 refer to the following excerpt from U.S. History For Dummies, *2nd Edition, by Steve Wiegand, copyright 2009 by Wiley Publishing, Inc. Reprinted with permission of John Wiley & Sons, Inc.*

Despite the widespread publicity surrounding the tragedy in Boston, cooler heads prevailed for the next year or two. Moderates on both sides of the Atlantic argued that compromises could still be reached.

Then the powerful but poorly run British East India Company found it had 17 million pounds of surplus tea on its hands. So the British government gave the company a monopoly on the American tea business. With a monopoly, the company could lower its prices enough to undercut the smuggled tea the colonists drank instead of paying the British tax. But even with lower prices, the colonists still didn't like the arrangement. It was the principle of the tax itself, not the cost of the tea. Shipments of English tea were destroyed or prevented from being unloaded or sold.

On December 16, 1773, colonists poorly disguised as Native Americans boarded three ships in Boston Harbor, smashed in 342 chests of tea, and dumped the whole mess into the harbor, where, according to one eyewitness, "it piled up in the low tide like haystacks." No one was seriously hurt, although one colonist was reportedly roughed up a bit for trying to stuff some of the tea in his coat instead of throwing it overboard.

King George III wasn't amused by the colonists' lack of respect. "The die is now cast," he wrote to his latest prime minister, Lord North, who had succeeded Townshend upon his sudden death. "The colonies must either submit or triumph."

11. Based on the passage, the British East India Company is best described as

(A) Powerful
(B) Poorly run
(C) A monopoly
(D) All of the above

12. How did the colonists avoid the tax on tea?

(A) They gained a monopoly.
(B) They had surplus tea.
(C) They smuggled tea.
(D) They undercut prices.

13. What did the colonists NOT do in 1773?

(A) Disguise themselves as Native Americans
(B) Amuse King George
(C) Smash chests
(D) Board ships

Drag-and-drop

Order of Events

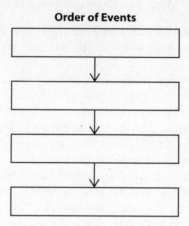

14. Drag the events that led to the Boston Tea Party to the flow chart above, placing them in chronological order.

    (To answer, write the answer choice letters in the order that the events occurred.)

    (A) British government gave tea monopoly to British East India Company
    (B) Boston Tea Party
    (C) Americans smuggle tea to avoid taxes
    (D) British East India Company has 17 million pounds of surplus tea

Questions 15 through 19 refer to the following excerpt from U.S. History For Dummies, *2nd Edition, by Steve Wiegand, copyright 2009 by Wiley Publishing, Inc. Reprinted with permission of John Wiley & Sons, Inc.*

Jefferson set to work at a portable desk he had designed himself, and a few weeks later produced a document that has come to be regarded as one of the most eloquent political statements in human history. True, he exaggerated some of the grievances the colonists had against the king. True, he rather hypocritically declared that "all men are created equal," ignoring the fact that he and hundreds of other Americans owned slaves, whom they certainly didn't regard as having been created equal.

Overall though, it was a magnificent document that set forth all the reasons America wanted to go its own way—and why all people who wanted to do the same thing should be allowed to do so. After a bit of tinkering by Franklin, the document was presented to Congress on June 28.

At the demand of some Southern representatives, a section blaming the king for American slavery was taken out. Then, on July 2, Congress adopted the resolution submitted by Lee. "The second day of July, 1776, will be the most memorable epoch [instant of time] in the history of America," predicted John Adams. He missed it by two days, because America chose to remember July 4 instead—the day Congress formally adopted the Declaration of Independence, or as one member put it, "Mr. Jefferson's explanation of Mr. Lee's resolution."

15. What did Jefferson produce at his desk?

    (A) A document
    (B) Political statements
    (C) Human history
    (D) A list of grievances

16. What did Jefferson ignore in his writing?

(A) All the reasons America had for going its own way
(B) The fact that all men are created equal
(C) The fact that some Americans owned slaves
(D) The Americans' grievances against the king

17. What section had to be taken out?

(A) The tinkering done by Franklin
(B) The section blaming the king for slavery
(C) The resolution from Lee
(D) The section referring to the most memorable epoch

Fill-in-the-blank

18. When was the document presented to Congress? Enter the correct date (month, day, and year) in the box below.

Fill-in-the-blank

19. Who submitted the final resolution? Enter the correct last name in the box below.

Questions 20 through 24 refer to the following excerpt from the Declaration of Independence (1776).

For cutting off our trade with all parts of the world:
For imposing taxes on us without our consent:
For depriving us, in many cases, of the benefits of trial by jury:
For transporting us beyond seas to be tried for pretended offenses:
For abolishing the free system of English laws in a neighboring province, establishing therein an arbitrary government, and enlarging its boundaries, so as to render it at once an example and fit instrument for introducing the same absolute rule into these colonies:
For taking away our charters, abolishing our most valuable laws, and altering, fundamentally, the forms of our governments:
For suspending our own legislatures, and declaring themselves invested with power to legislate for us in all cases whatsoever:
He has abdicated governments here, by declaring us out of his protection and waging war against us.
He has plundered our seas, ravaged our coasts, burnt our towns and destroyed the lives of our people.
He is at this time transporting large armies of foreign mercenaries to complete the works of death, desolation, and tyranny, already begun with circumstances of cruelty and perfidy scarcely paralleled in the most barbarous ages, and totally unworthy the head of a civilized nation.

He has constrained our fellow-citizens, taken captive on the high seas, to bear arms against their country, to become the executioners of their friends and brethren, or to fall themselves by their hands.

He has excited domestic insurrections among us, and has endeavored to bring on the inhabitants of our frontiers the merciless Indian savages, whose known rule of warfare is an undistinguished destruction of all ages, sexes, and conditions.

Drag-and-drop

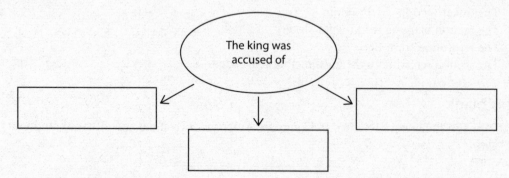

20. Drag the offenses that the king was accused of, according to the document, into the boxes above.

    (To answer, write the letter of all answer choices that apply on your answer sheet.)

    (A) Cutting off trade
    (B) Imposing taxes
    (C) Transporting Americans overseas for trial
    (D) Banning foreign mercenaries from America

21. Where did the king abolish the free system of English laws?

    (A) In the Thirteen Colonies
    (B) In Great Britain
    (C) In a neighboring province
    (D) In foreign lands

22. According to the passage, what was the king NOT guilty of?

    (A) Taking away charters
    (B) Waging war
    (C) Abdicating government
    (D) Encouraging freedom of speech

23. The king forced his will upon the colonies largely with the help of

    (A) Foreign mercenaries
    (B) The British Army
    (C) Merciless savages
    (D) Fellow citizens

24. What had the king encouraged among the colonists?

(A) Death and desolation
(B) Domestic insurrections
(C) Barbarous ages
(D) Undistinguished destruction

Questions 25 through 29 refer to the following passage.

From the 1960s, Japan has made massive economic progress based largely on manufacturing industries with a move toward tertiary industry. By 1997, only 5.5 percent of the working population was employed in primary industry, with 31.9 percent in secondary industry and 61.8 percent in tertiary industry. A period of continuous economic growth came to an end in 1997, leading to calls for industrial and commercial restructuring. This coincided with increasing attention being paid to globalization, particularly to the impact of new information and communication technologies, which brought reforms in education.

Demographically, Japan has witnessed intensive urbanization and consequent rural depopulation. The government is concerned with the implications of a falling birth rate, the trend toward nuclear families and an aging population. Across the country, educational expectations have been heightened, with parents wishing to see their children attend prestigious schools followed by prestigious universities and, hopefully, attain high-status jobs. Increasingly, expectations have been high for both males and females. Social mobility, maintaining high living standards, and education have been seen to be closely linked.

Traditionally, the centralized administration has been strong in Japan, but in recent years important steps have been taken to deregulate and decentralize many areas of the public sector, including education. A package of laws designed to promote decentralization was passed in July 1999, with implementation beginning April 2000.

Such broad trends are reflected in national, regional, and local policies for educational reform. In 1996, the second Hashimoto Cabinet designated educational reform, alongside governmental administration, the economic structure, the financial system, the social welfare system, and the fiscal structure, as one of the government's major areas for reform. More recently, the Obuchi Cabinet took up education as a major agenda item and, in March 2000, established the National Commission on Educational Reform, a private discussion group of eminent citizens advising the prime minister.

Hot Spot

25. Which of these graphs best represents the percentage of working people in various sectors of the economy in Japan in 1997? Click on the appropriate graph with your mouse to select.

(To answer, write the letter of your answer choice.)

(A) Graph 1
(B) Graph 2
(C) Graph 3
(D) Graph 4

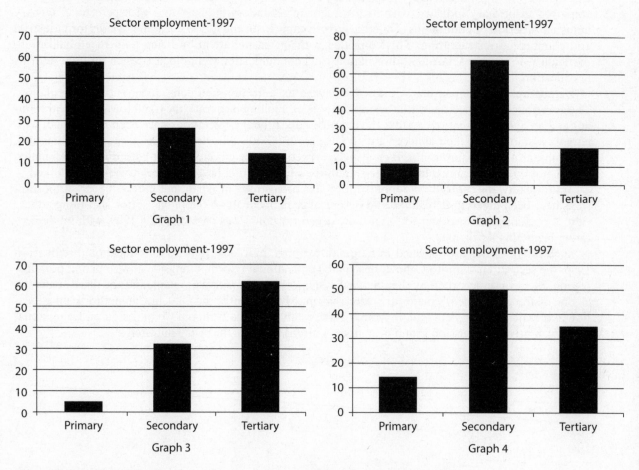

26. Which of the following has affected the demography of Japan since 1997?

(A) Urbanization
(B) Falling birth rate
(C) Aging population
(D) All of the above

27. What do Japanese parents most want their children to achieve?

   (A) Education
   (B) Nuclear families
   (C) High-status job
   (D) Increased living standards

28. What has the Japanese government traditionally been known for?

   (A) Deregulation
   (B) Social mobility
   (C) Prestigious schools
   (D) Centralized administration

29. What was NOT a major area of reform for the government in 1996?

   (A) Educational policies
   (B) Economic structure
   (C) Financial system
   (D) Sports and recreation

Questions 30 through 32 refer to the following graph from the U.S. Bureau of Justice Statistics.

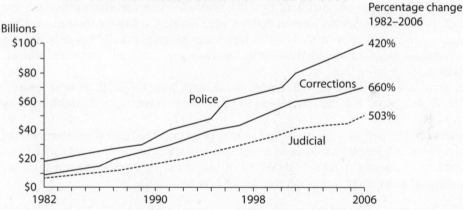

U.S. Criminal Justice Costs from 1982 to 2006

Fill-in-the-blank

30. According to the graph, which service sector experienced the largest percentage of growth from 1982 to 2006? Enter your answer in the box below.

31. What was the cost of the judicial system in 2006?

    (A) About $40 billion
    (B) About $50 billion
    (C) About $60 billion
    (D) About $80 billion

32. How have cost patterns changed for U.S. criminal justice from 1982 to 2006?

    (A) There has been a slight increase.
    (B) There has been a slight decrease.
    (C) There has been a significant increase.
    (D) No change has been noted.

Questions 33 through 36 refer to the following excerpt from U.S. History For Dummies, *2nd Edition, by Steve Wiegand, copyright 2009 by Wiley Publishing, Inc. Reprinted with permission of John Wiley & Sons, Inc.*

Gearing up of the industry needed to wage a global war on two fronts was handicapped by a lack of manpower. More than 15 million Americans eventually served in the military. Training and supplying them was a staggering challenge. It took more than 6,000 people to provide food, equipment, medical services, and transportation to 8,000 soldiers. In addition, many raw materials, such as rubber, manila fiber, and oil, were in short supply. And to top it off, President Roosevelt was a great leader, but not a great administrator.

Nevertheless, Americans rose to the occasion. When FDR called for the production of 50,000 planes in a year, it was thought to be ridiculous. By 1944, the country was producing 96,000 a year. Technology blossomed. When metals became scarce, plastics were developed to take their place. Copper was taken out of pennies and replaced with steel; nickel was removed from nickels. War-inspired pragmatism even affected fashions: To save material, men's suits lost their pant cuffs and vests, and women painted their legs to take the place of nylons.

Other sacrifices were made as well. Gasoline and tires were rationed, as were coffee, sugar, canned goods, butter, and shoes. But the war proved to be more of an economic inconvenience than a real trial for most people.

Of course, all that military hardware had a hefty price tag. The federal government spent about $350 billion during World War II—or twice as much as it had spent *in total* for the entire history of the U.S. government up to that point. About 40 percent of that came from taxes; the rest came through government borrowing, much of that through the sale of bonds.

33. Which shortage most impacted America's ability to wage a global war?

    (A) Shortage of manpower
    (B) Shortage of training
    (C) Shortage of medical services
    (D) Shortage of food

Fill-in-the-blank

34. By 1944, America was producing _____ planes each year. Enter the correct number in the box below.

Fill-in-the-blank

35. _____ was used to solve the metals shortage. Enter the correct material in the box below.

36. How did rationing affect most people?

   (A) It was a real trial.
   (B) It was a hardship.
   (C) It had no effect.
   (D) It was an inconvenience.

Questions 37 through 40 refer to the following hypothetical newspaper column.

Hillary Clinton, U.S. Secretary of State, arrived in Canada for the G8 Summit yesterday with her verbal guns blazing. She does not agree with Prime Minister Harper on several issues and used her style of gunboat diplomacy to tell him so publicly.

Canada has advised NATO that it will withdraw troops from Afghanistan. This goes against American policy and Clinton told Harper so in public. Most disagreements of this type are sorted out behind closed doors. Clinton chose the public arena to try to whip Canada into American shape. The war has been unpopular in both countries, but that did not stop the U.S. from advocating more troops.

Although the Americans are embroiled in their own healthcare problems, Clinton gave Harper her views on abortion and maternal health and tried arm-twisting to solve their differences.

Harper is also in trouble with Clinton's America for convening a meeting on the Arctic Ocean. It seems our sovereignty has its limits with our neighbors.

Canadians are now wondering if this was the opening salvo in an invasion by coercion or just a misstep in what has been peaceful coexistence. Only time will tell.

37. How did Hillary Clinton arrive at the G8 Summit?

   (A) By Air Force One
   (B) With verbal guns blazing
   (C) With gunboat diplomacy
   (D) From Afghanistan

38. How are disagreements usually settled?

   (A) At NATO
   (B) In public
   (C) Through peaceful coexistence
   (D) Behind closed doors

39. What is Harper's policy on Afghanistan?

   (A) Withdraw troops
   (B) Advocate more troops
   (C) Offer healthcare assistance
   (D) Support abortion and maternal health

40. What did the disagreement between Clinton and Harper concern?

   (A) Troop withdrawal
   (B) Views on abortion
   (C) Arctic sovereignty
   (D) All of the above

Questions 41 through 44 refer to the following chart excerpted from Green Business Practices For Dummies, *by Lisa Swallow, copyright 2009 by Wiley Publishing, Inc. Reprinted with permission of John Wiley & Sons, Inc.*

Greening of Existing Industries	
Traditional Industry Sector	**Niche Marketing Riding the Green Tidal Wave**
Accounting, business consulting, and legal services	Sustainability reporting, environmental management systems, and green business design and support
Appliances	Energy Star certification
Automobiles	Hybrids, electrics, scooters, recyclable components
Clothing	Ecofashion (hemp and organic textiles, recycled clothing)
Financial products	Socially responsible investment, microfinance
Grocery	Organics and naturals
Housing	Green buildings
Lawn and garden	Nontoxic and bio-based products
Medical care	Naturopathy, acupuncture
Travel and tourism	Ecotourism
Wood products	Sustainably harvested forestry, reclaimed wood products

41. Traditional industries are trying to become "greener." What one feature do most of the listed industries have in common?

   (A) Most of these industries promote more oil and gas exploration.
   (B) Most of these industries promote energy conservation.
   (C) Most of these industries have switched to off-shore production.
   (D) Most of these industries promote the use of nuclear power.

42. How is clothing impacted by the greening of its industry?

   (A) Hemp fabric
   (B) Organic textiles
   (C) Recycled material
   (D) All of the above

43. How does the automotive industry show that it is "greener" today?

   (A) Produce hybrid cars
   (B) Use more recyclable components
   (C) Produce electric vehicles
   (D) All of the above

44. Which industry can be affected by naturopathy?

   (A) Appliances
   (B) Medical care
   (C) Lawn and garden
   (D) Wood products

Questions 45 through 47 refer to the following graph.

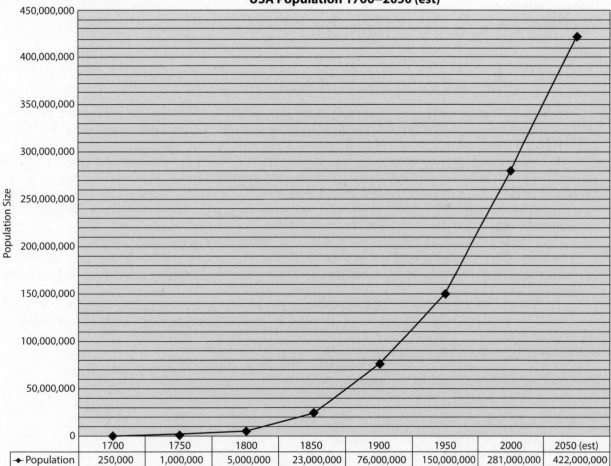

USA Population 1700–2050 (est)

	1700	1750	1800	1850	1900	1950	2000	2050 (est)
Population	250,000	1,000,000	5,000,000	23,000,000	76,000,000	150,000,000	281,000,000	422,000,000

45. According to the graph, between what years was the rate of growth the fastest?

    (A) Between 1700 and 1750
    (B) Between 1750 and 1800
    (C) Between 1900 and 1950
    (D) Between 1950 and 2000

46. In approximately what year did the population reach 200 million?

    (A) 1960
    (B) 1970
    (C) 1980
    (D) 1990

47. Using the graph data, what was the approximate population of the USA in 1925?

    (A) 80 million
    (B) 90 million
    (C) 110 million
    (D) 140 million

Questions 48 through 50 refer to the following excerpt from U.S. History For Dummies, *2nd Edition, by Steve Wiegand, copyright 2009 by Wiley Publishing, Inc. Reprinted with permission of John Wiley & Sons, Inc.*

Obama held a narrow lead through most of the summer. But as Election Day grew closer, the country's staggering economy came to dominate the campaign, and voters decided Obama was better equipped to deal with it.

It was a convincing victory. Obama won the popular vote in every section of the country but the South. He carried states no Democratic candidate had carried in 30 or 40 years. Obama's campaign leaned heavily on 21st-century technology and techniques, from sending Election Day voting reminders to cellphones to using Web sites to raise money and organize grassroots efforts. Obama also galvanized young voters and minorities to vote in record numbers.

"If there is anyone out there who still doubts that America is a place where all things are possible, who still wonders if the dream of our founders is alive in our time, who still questions the power of our democracy, tonight is your answer," Obama said in his Election Night victory speech in Chicago's Grant Park.

In 1858, the buying and selling of human beings was legal in America. In 1958, segregation and discrimination based on race was widespread. In 2008, an African American was elected 44th president of the United States.

The country had come a long way.

48. What had the most impact on the campaign?

    (A) The lack of leadership
    (B) The Iraq War
    (C) The heat of summer
    (D) The economy

49. What assured Obama's convincing victory?

    (A) Technology and techniques
    (B) Voting reminders
    (C) Grassroots efforts
    (D) All of the above

50. Why had the country come a long way?

    (A) Because of the dream of its founders
    (B) Because of the power of democracy
    (C) Because of the election of the first African-American president
    (D) Because of the selling of human beings

IF YOU FINISH BEFORE TIME IS CALLED, CHECK YOUR WORK ON THIS
SECTION ONLY. DO NOT WORK ON ANY OTHER SECTION IN THE TEST.

Section 2

Time: 25 Minutes

Read the quote, the Second Amendment to the Constitution, and the commentary that follows it. You have 25 minutes to write an essay to discuss how these two excerpts reflect an enduring issue in American history, using the commentary and your own knowledge.

You may prepare rough notes before writing the essay, but only the final version will be scored. Pay attention to both your essay style and the proper use of English.

Remember, on the formal test, you will be working on a computer. Your rough notes will be done on an erasable noteboard. The only work evaluated will be what is entered into the computer.

Second Amendment to the United States Constitution

A well regulated Militia, being necessary to the security of a free State, the right of the people to keep and bear Arms, shall not be infringed.

Commentary

On December 15, 1791, Congress adopted the Second Amendment, enshrining the right to bear arms in the American Constitution.

However, the American Constitution is a living document. While the text is fixed, interpretations of the meaning change over time. In 1876, the Supreme Court ruled that the Second Amendment referred to the government's right to arm people as part of a well-regulated militia. It does not give unlimited rights to individuals to bear arms. A 1939 Supreme Court ruling expanded on that. It decided that both the Federal government and the states could limit gun ownership outside the needs of a "well-regulated militia."

Those rules, in the 1800s, applied throughout the United States. According to a recent book by Adam Winkler, law professor at UCLA, the "Wild West" was not so wild. Western towns, famous for tales of gunslingers, actually banned the carrying of either open or concealed weapons. Most western towns required people to check their guns before entering town, much the way we would check our coats at a fine-dining restaurant.

Interpretations of the Second Amendment fall into several categories. The oldest interpretations argue that the amendment must be considered together with the issue of States' Rights. The phrase "the people" is interpreted as "the state," rather than individuals. The right to bear arms does not apply to individuals. It applies to the states, to ensure that the states have the right to have a National Guard or state militia. This legal interpretation allowed states to organize armed militias. State governments often needed such forces to recapture fugitive slaves or put down slave uprisings prior to the Civil War. Another consideration also favored this interpretation. However, there was an issue: if individuals did have the right to bear arms, freed slaves, as citizens, also would have the right to bear arms. That was a less than popular concept. After the Civil War, some southern states brought forward legislation to prohibit blacks from owning firearms.

The limitation on the rights of individuals to bear arms also fits historical facts. At the time of the writing of the Constitution, Americans were very leery of the establishment of a permanent standing army. They preferred that the state call upon the people to form an army, a militia, as the need arose. However, individuals must have weapons with which to train to form such a militia. A further, somewhat later, interpretation expanded that position. It argued that indeed individuals have the right to bear arms, but only insofar as participating in an organized militia.

Today, the Courts interpret the amendment to mean that individuals have a blanket right to bear arms. The phrase "in a well regulated militia" is meant only as an example, and not as a restriction. In recent years, the Courts have put forward the concept, "the natural right to self-defense." The most recent Court rulings have reinforced the idea that individuals have the right to bear arms, regardless of any linkage to the militia.

People today see the Second Amendment in terms of individual rights, not group rights. This interpretation continues to push the envelope. The gun lobby argues criminal background checks are an unwarranted incursion of individual rights. It argues that the state cannot limit gun ownership, or even where guns may be carried. Tracking the sales of weapons, or a waiting period before receiving them, becomes an infringement of individual rights. As a result, in many states it is now legal to bring a gun to a movie theater, national park, or even a school.

Is it perhaps time to revisit the issue? Today, anyone can carry a military-grade rifle with magazines holding twenty rounds or more. U.S. schools have allowed teachers to carry guns in school. People may carry guns to national parks, even where hunting is prohibited. Colleges and universities are under pressure to allow students to carry weapons. Some states have even made it legal to carry guns in airports and bars. Considering that there are more gun deaths per capita in the U.S. than any other nation in the world, many think these freedoms have gone too far. Perhaps it is time to look at an older interpretation of the Second Amendment.

IF YOU FINISH BEFORE TIME IS CALLED, CHECK YOUR WORK ON THIS SECTION ONLY. DO NOT WORK ON ANY OTHER SECTION IN THE TEST.

Answer Key

Section 1

1. (B)
2. (D)
3. (A)
4. (D)
5. (B)
6. (D)
7. (C)
8. (D)
9. (A)
10. (B)
11. (D)
12. (C)
13. (B)
14. (C), (D), (A), (B)
15. (A)
16. (C)
17. (B)
18. June 28, 1776
19. Lee
20. (A), (B), (C)
21. (C)
22. (D)
23. (A)
24. (B)
25. (C)
26. (D)
27. (C)
28. (D)
29. (D)
30. Corrections
31. (B)
32. (C)
33. (A)
34. 96,000
35. plastic
36. (D)
37. (B)
38. (D)
39. (A)
40. (D)
41. (B)
42. (D)
43. (D)
44. (B)
45. (B)
46. (B)
47. (C)
48. (D)
49. (D)
50. (C)

Answer Explanations

Section 1

1. **(B)** According to the passage, the Pilgrims were lower-class farmers and craftsmen.

2. **(D)** The Pilgrims wanted to separate because they found the Church of England to be "too Catholic." The other choices—strange, forceful, and saintly—were not given as reasons for separation.

3. **(A)** When the Separatists left England, they first settled in Holland. It was only later that they went to America in the New World.

4. **(D)** To establish a new colony, a charter had to be negotiated with England. The other choices—a crew, permission, and the King's blessing—although factors, are not the best answer.

5. **(B)** Before it was used to carry Pilgrims, the *Mayflower* had carried wine between France and England.

6. **(D)** Musical instruments, furniture, and books are all mentioned in the passage as items that were taken by the Pilgrims on the voyage.

7. **(C)** The Pilgrims first landed at a broad, shallow bay now known as Plymouth.

8. **(D)** The cartoon depicts cell phones as being health risks due to brain tumors, radiation, and careless driving. The other choices are not mentioned in the cartoon.

9. **(A)** The cell phone user is foolhardy in that he is operating dangerously—his eyes are closed, he's on the phone, and he doesn't have either hand on the steering wheel. Talkative, choice (B) may seem like a good answer, but it is not the best answer; it's possible that the person on the other end of the phone call is doing most or all of the talking.

10. **(B)** Scientific research indicates that cell phones may represent a risk to one's health. Movies, urban legends, and popular opinion are incorrect choices.

11. **(D)** The author uses choices (A) through (C) to describe the British East India Company.

12. **(C)** The colonists engaged in tea smuggling to avoid the tax.

13. **(B)** The actions of the colonists in 1773 certainly wouldn't have amused King George, as he was losing control of the colonies.

14. **(C), (D), (A), (B)** The events took place in the following order: (C), Americans smuggle tea to avoid taxes; (D), British East India Company has 17 million pounds of surplus tea; (A), British government gave tea monopoly to British East India Company; (B) Boston Tea Party.

15. **(A)** Jefferson produced a document at his desk. The other choices may have been part of that document, but they were not the final product.

16. **(C)** In writing the document, Jefferson failed to acknowledge that some Americans owned slaves. The other choices were all related to the theme of the document and, therefore, were not ignored by Jefferson.

17. **(B)** To satisfy Southern delegates, the section "blaming the king for slavery" was removed from the document. Contributions by Franklin and Lee remained. John Adams recognized that the document would be a "memorable epoch."

18. **June 28, 1776** On June 28, 1776, the document was actually presented to Congress. Although they formally adopted the Declaration of Independence on July 4, 1776, this does not answer the question posed.

19. **Lee** According to the passage, Lee (Richard Henry Lee, a delegate from Virginia) submitted the final resolution.

20. **(A), (B), and (C)** Choices (A), (B), and (C)—cutting off trade, imposing taxes, and transporting Americans overseas for trial—are correct. The Crown never banned foreign mercenaries (D).

21. **(C)** The passage states that the king abolished the free system of English laws "in a neighboring province."

22. **(D)** The king certainly could not be accused of encouraging freedom of speech among the colonists. The other choices are all accurate.

23. **(A)** According to the document, the king hired foreign mercenaries to wage war on the colonists. Of course, the British Army was also involved, but that is not the best answer.

24. **(B)** The passage states that the king encouraged "domestic insurrections" in efforts to put down the rebellion.

25. **(C)** Graph 3 shows the proper proportions of employment. Primary is lowest and tertiary is greatest.

26. **(D)** Choices (A), (B), and (C) all describe Japan's demography since 1997.

27. **(C)** According to the passage, Japanese parents most want their children to achieve "high-status jobs." Education would be just a contributing factor to attaining a high-status job.

28. **(D)** Traditionally, Japan has been known for its centralized form of governance.

29. **(D)** The passage does not mention sports and recreation as being a major area of reform. The other choices—educational policies, economic structure, and financial system—are all listed as areas of reform.

30. **Corrections** According to the graph, Corrections (at 660 percent) shows the largest percentage of growth. This compares to Judicial at 503 percent and Police at 420 percent.

31. **(B)** The graph tells us that about $50 billion was spent on the judicial system in 2006.

32. **(C)** Cost patterns have shown a significant increase from 1982 to 2006.

33. **(A)** The passage states that a "lack of manpower" most affected America's ability to wage a global war. Although training, food, and medical services are mentioned, they are not the best answer.

34. **96,000** According to the passage, the U.S. was producing 96,000 planes a year by 1944.

35. **plastic** Because there was a shortage of metal, plastic was used as a replacement.

36. **(D)** According to the passage, the war was "more of an economic inconvenience than a real trial for most people," not a real trial or a hardship.

37. **(B)** According to the passage, Hillary Clinton arrived at the G8 Summit "with verbal guns blazing." Choices (A) and (C)—Air Force One and gunboat diplomacy—while mentioned, are not the best answer. Arriving from Afghanistan (D) is incorrect.

38. **(D)** The passage states that disagreements are usually settled "behind closed doors."

39. **(A)** The passage states that Harper, as prime minister of Canada, intends to withdraw troops from Afghanistan. He certainly is not advocating more troops. The other choices don't relate to Afghanistan.

40. **(D)** Choices (A), (B), and (C) were all issues of disagreement between Clinton and Harper.

41. **(B)** According to the chart, efforts to conserve energy feature in most "greening."

42. **(D)** According to the chart, choices (A), (B), and (C) all relate to the greening of the clothing industry.

43. **(D)** According to the chart, the automobile industry is promoting all of the choices and options: producing hybrid cars, using more recyclable components, and producing electric vehicles.

44. **(B)** Naturopathy is listed as a marketing niche for the medical care industry.

45. **(B)** If you look at how much the population increased, you will note that in the second 50-year period (between 1750 and 1800), the population increased by a factor of five. None of the other 50-year periods show this great of an increase. The actual rounded values are shown at the bottom of the graph. The slope of the line shows you the rate of growth; the actual numbers confirm it.

46. **(B)** If you draw an imaginary line down from the point where the 200 million population mark crosses the population graph line, it would hit the date a little before the division between 1950 and 2000. The year 1975 is the midpoint between 1950 and 2000. The 200 million mark crosses a little before this midpoint, so 1970 is your best choice.

47. **(C)** If you draw a line upward from the 1925 point (the year 1925 falls at the divider line between the 1900 and 1950 sections on the *x*-axis), it crosses the population growth line at about the 110 million mark.

48. **(D)** According to the passage, it was the economy that most influenced the outcome of the campaign.

49. **(D)** Obama's victory was assured by all the choices—technology and techniques, voting reminders, and grassroots efforts.

50. **(C)** For the first time in U.S. history, an African American had been elected president. The country had, indeed, come a long way.

Section 2

As the test-graders read and evaluate your essay, they look for the following:

- Proper introduction
- Well-focused main points
- Evidence of clear organization
- Specific development of your ideas
- Clear references to the source texts and your own experience
- Correct grammar and proper sentence structure
- Necessary punctuation
- Appropriate use of vocabulary
- Correct spelling
- Proper linkage between paragraphs
- Clear summary

Although every essay will be unique, we provide a sample response here to give you a better idea of what the test-graders expect to see in your extended response essay. Compare the structure of this sample response to yours.

Sample Response

The debate reflects the enduring issue of the right to bear arms and the interpretation of the Second Amendment. Is there a connection between the right to bear arms, and the need for a well-regulated militia for the security of the state? In modern English, it could be read as, "Because we may need a militia from time to time, people must have the right to have weapons." The issue then becomes this: What connection is there between the need for a militia and the right of individuals to have weapons? This is indeed an enduring issue.

To me, the stronger argument in the commentary supports the interpretation that the government has no right to restrict ownership of firearms. The Second Amendment clearly states, "the right of the people to keep and bear Arms, shall not be infringed." The first part of the amendment, dealing with the militia is in my opinion simply a rationale from that time. While that rationale has faded, the right continues. Therefore, the issue of that interpretation continues to be relevant.

The commentary pushes the link between the right to bear arms and the possible need to organize civilians into a militia. That reflects a need from that time, and a reason for establishing that right. However, today we have a standing army, which eliminates the need for civilians to form a militia. That does not mean the right to bear arms is extinguished. Times have changed. The commentary itself agrees that recent argument from the Supreme Court say the militia is meant only as an example why individuals must have the right to bear arms.

Of course, the commentary is right to say that there are some practical restrictions we should consider. No one has the right to yell, "Fire" in a crowded theater, despite the right to free speech. By the same token, there are some restrictions that are simply reasonable. Some in fact exist, such as restrictions on automatic weapons, "cop killer" ammunition, and the like. We have restrictions on ownership by criminals and minors. Firearms should not be permitted in churches or schools, and the police should have the right to bar firearms from specific locations for safety reasons. These restrictions need a reasoned and thoughtful debate. Rules for firearm ownership can be implemented without infringing on Second Amendment rights.

The interpretation of the right to bear arms has changed over time, as has our society. But at the most basic level, the Constitution guarantees the right to bear arms. The interpretation of that right is certainly an enduring issue in American history.

Evaluation of Sample Response

After reading through the sample response once, reread it and answer the following questions about it.

- Is there a series of main points in this essay that clearly relate to the topic? (Underline the main points to check.)
- Does each paragraph have an introductory sentence or thought?
- Does each paragraph have a concluding sentence or thought?
- Do the sentences within each paragraph follow a logical sequence?
- Are the paragraphs organized in a natural flow from beginning to end? In other words, does each paragraph build on the previous one and lead to the next one?

- Have the ideas in the given topic and the first paragraph been developed throughout the essay?
- Are all the sentences grammatically correct?
- Are all the sentences properly structured?
- Are all the sentences correctly punctuated?
- Are all the words spelled correctly?

As far as this particular sample essay is concerned, a test-grader probably would have given it a high score because it has all the attributes of a good essay that we list earlier in this section. It isn't perfect, but no one's asking you to write a perfect essay. In the time you have available, only 25 minutes, you are expected to write a good first draft. Look over the list of characteristics that the evaluators are looking for, and try to determine whether your practice essay satisfies those requirements. Ask a friend to answer these same questions about your essay; then, rewrite your essay until you and your friend can answer yes to every question.

Remember: Your essay shouldn't be just a collection of grammatically correct sentences that flow from beginning to end. Rather, your essay needs to be interesting and even entertaining to read. After all, no one—not even a professional test-grader—wants to read a boring essay!